Clean Eating
For Every Season

Clean Eating
For Every Season

FRESH, SIMPLE EVERYDAY MEALS

ALICIA TYLER

Editorial Director, *Clean Eating* magazine

Globe
Pequot

Guilford, Connecticut

Tempeh
Taco Bowl
with Mango
Salsa
(See recipe, p. 283)

Globe
Pequot

An imprint of Rowman & Littlefield

Distributed by NATIONAL BOOK NETWORK

Copyright © 2018 *Clean Eating*/Active Interest Media

All rights reserved. No part of this book may be
reproduced in any form or by any electronic or
mechanical means, including information storage and
retrieval systems, without written permission from
the publisher, except by a reviewer who may quote
passages in a review.

British Library Cataloguing in Publication
Information Available

**Library of Congress Cataloging-in-
Publication Data Available**

ISBN 978-1-4930-3099-6 (paperback)
ISBN 978-1-4930-3100-9 (e-book)

Cover Photos:
Photographer: Ronald Tsang
Food Styling: Nancy Midwicki
Prop Styling: The Props

The paper used in this publication meets the
minimum requirements of American National Standard
for Information Sciences—Permanence of Paper for
Printed Library Materials, ANSI/NISO Z39.48-1992.

Printed in the United States

CONTENTS

Moroccan Chicken & Vegetable Soup
with Chickpea Croutons
(See recipe, p. 48)

ACKNOWLEDGMENTS

No book is the result of one person's work, especially in this case, where much of the content was the labor of love of a small village, pouring their hearts and souls into this brand every day.

First and foremost, immeasurable gratitude to *Clean Eating*'s editorial, design and digital players, Stacy Jarvis-Paine, Andrea Gourgy, Laura Schober, Alaina Greenberg, Angie Mattison and Mandy Major. For conceptualizing, strategizing, planning, scheduling, writing, designing, editing, tasting, analyzing and improving, day in and day out and then starting all over again at the top of each issue. Your passion, talent, positivity and ambition are palpable, and I am privileged to work with you every day. Not only are you publishing pros but also magicians as far as I'm concerned to consistently pull off what you do.

To the brilliant story contributors, recipe creators, recipe testers, photographers, food stylists, prop stylists, stylists' assistants, photo editors and artists' reps for bringing our vision to life and making it better than we'd dreamt up at the meeting table, issue after gorgeous issue.

Sincere thanks to our digital and marketing teams for all your clever work getting the message out about this book. To our awesome production director, Barbara Van Sickle, for keeping her whip within reach and keeping us up to speed on the erratic Boulder weather. Thanks to our GMs, past and present: Pat Fox, Kim Paulsen and Jonathan Dorn for always pushing us to expand and for your stalwart support; to our tenacious publishers, Joanna Shaw and Lisa Dodson, and their sales team for taking the stories we tell and spinning them into gold. To our all-seeing newsstand eye, Susan Rose, for keeping us competitive (and keeping it real). And to our diligent research department heads, Kristy Kaus and Lori Rodriguez, for digging deep and giving weight to every decision, big or small.

I'd be remiss if I didn't acknowledge the creative team's spouses, partners, families and friends for your understanding during those late nights at the office and for your patience around production deadlines. "Shipping again?!" Yes, Paul, again.

The biggest thanks of all is owed to our readers. The truth is, you guys did this. So, a whole-souled thank you for allowing us to spend our days doing what we love.

And last (but really first), the late Robert Kennedy. Bob, it all started with you. Likely the very first to utter the term "clean eating" decades ago, you were a visionary directed by your passion and instinct. Thank you for entrusting me with your vision and letting me run with it. I cherish every day I get to lead this brand, and I delighted in every moment spent working on this book.

Grilled Berry Cobbler

(See recipe, p. 230)

INTRODUCTION

We're Leaving Guilt Behind–and So Should You

One of our editors recently shared a quote with me that read, "If you're habitually using 'guilt-free' to mean 'good and nourishing,' maybe take a break from writing about food for a while to figure some stuff out."

This is the message we've been working on of late: Guilt and food are mutually exclusive and have no business hanging out together in the same cover line, headline or sentence. But it wasn't always that way. Do a quick internet search of *Clean Eating* and you'll find plenty of covers from our not-so-distant past that tout that very claim. It was a sign of the times.

Before the words "clean eating" became the double-edged sword that could either mean healthy meals made with pure ingredients or a restrictive deprivation diet when taken to extremes, everyone wanted to know what "cleaned-up" classics and desserts they could still enjoy but without the garbage ingredients of yesteryear. And we were the pioneers of the cleanup crusade, taking every imaginable meal our parents used to make with a pantry filled with nonperishables and loads of refined sugars, flours, cheap vegetable oil and food coloring and recreating them so that our readers could enjoy the tastes of home without the guilt associated with the growing mountain of research tied to the dangers of processed food. That was our intention behind "guilt-free" before it was made into a dirty term representing the self-abuse attached to unattainable perfection that's often a product of social media. But alas, as our psyches, food philosophies and societal norms change, the once-different meanings change too. Soon enough, eating clean, the pure and positive intention of eating real, nutrient-dense food, could mean either just that—or a dangerously restrictive diet that becomes a gateway to eating disorders, like orthorexia.

Well, I'm here to tell you with certainty that our food philosophy is the former. And if that means rethinking the language we use to describe the intrinsically healthy nature of the food we create and share, then I am completely on board.

One Size Doesn't–and Never Will–Fit All

Let's stop the food obsessing. Please resist the urge to fanatically weigh every morsel and log every bite; this can be a dangerous game. I say this—and by and large believe it applies to many of us—but, like anything else, there are always exceptions. Unless meticulously counting macros is something you are compelled or advised to do for medical reasons, because it's the only way you can reduce excess body weight that threatens your health or you struggle with portion control and balancing nutrients,

I implore you to embrace eating clean as it was always meant to be. It's not about obsessively counting calories and weighing food. By being overly mindful about what you're eating and how much, you risk missing out on the enjoyment of food and the bonding moments created by sharing a wonderful meal with those you love.

From the Macrobiotic Diet to Atkins and now Keto and Paleo, there's no denying that fad diets will cycle in and out of fashion during our lifetime and long after we all leave the planet, sweeping up converts by the hundreds of thousands. And I'll be the first to admit that there are elements of each of them that can occasionally serve your needs for a good ol' reboot in times of need. But as far as a long-term, sustainable lifestyle goes, it's my belief that you need (and your body deserves) that good old faithful way of eating that is balanced and healthy and that won't have you facedown in a tub of ice cream or bag of chips once your month-long "cleanse" is up. Everyone's lifelong, dependable return to healthy eating should be to eat clean, where at the core is the sensibility to eat real food mindfully, enjoying every morsel and stopping when you're full. Making the best choices the majority of the time and not depriving yourself of the occasional indulgence.

Food is one of life's most simple pleasures and one to share over moments with loved ones that you'll cherish forever. We never want to associate the pleasure of eating amazing food—which we are so fortunate to have—with a useless emotion like guilt. That is where the self-reproach creeps in and taints something so pure and beautiful, something meant to nourish our bodies, souls and minds.

I understand that everyone has varying degrees of nutrition knowledge and very different food pasts. Everyone's food journey started somewhere, whether you come from a home where from-scratch cooking was the norm or one where sugary boxed cereal was how you started your day. As we go through life, we have to reprogram how we think about food and fueling our bodies, about willpower, portion control and creating limitations around a healthy approach to eating. Most important, in my opinion, is to know where to draw that line that prevents us from slipping into obsessive territory. It is and always has been *Clean Eating*'s mission to help readers achieve that critical balance. And with today's stress-inducing fixation on food, it's needed more than ever, which is why it's the perfect time to release this book.

Don't Be a Slave to the Plans– Make Them Your Own

In our meal plans and at the bottom of our recipes, you'll see that we've included nutritional information and serving recommendations. Do with these what you will. Use them to scale up or down depending on your body's needs. Just promise me one thing: that you'll remember that the intention of this book is to help you *nourish* your body *enjoyably*. These guides are yours to follow as closely or loosely as you like—yours to adapt, customize and mix and match—but my hope is they ultimately steer you in a direction of stress-free balance, variety, consistency and eating along with the seasons. Instead of counting calories (and ever feeling an ounce of guilt), try instead to eat when you're hungry, stop when you're full and *love every bite*.

How Planning Leads to Success

"A goal without a plan is just a wish."
—Antoine de Saint-Exupéry

The best way to stay on track with your clean-eating lifestyle for thriving health? Proper planning. Lucky for you, we're pros at it so you don't have to be.

We've all had those weeks where we didn't get a chance to do a proper grocery shop over a busy weekend and then promised ourselves we'd go Monday, and then Monday runs late, so we pick up something prepared, and the rest of the week is just a hodgepodge of ordering in, picking up, skipping meals and scraping the bottom of the pantry and fridge for anything that can be cobbled together into a halfway decent meal.

This is no way to take care of a body that does so much for you every day, and it's certainly no way to keep your energy and brain fired up for all of those to-dos. You owe yourself more! Though I've been guilty of the "no shop" week and found myself scrounging more than once, there is no doubt that I'm happiest and most productive when I've set aside the time on a weekend—usually Sunday morning with a cup of coffee and my old-school notepad—to flip through the most recent issue of *Clean Eating,* select my meals and write out my grocery list for the week. Our readers tell us the same; it's therapeutic for them and ensures a stress-free week of deeply nourishing meals.

Once your meal plan or recipes are chosen for the week and you've had everyone in your household weigh in (psst, here's a tip: if they pick out a meal, they are much more likely to help you prepare it, enjoy it and finish every bite!), grab your reusable bags, head to the market and stock up. Once home, post the menu to the fridge so that everyone knows what's on tap for the week (and don't ask you 100 times).

Want to take your planning one step further? It doesn't have to stop as soon as you unload the car. You can save yourself some serious weekday time by washing and prechopping your fruits and veggies in advance and separating out exactly what you'll need for any upcoming recipes and snacks. Prepack all your clean snacks for the week in containers or reusable zip-top bags, portion out nuts, make some staples like quinoa or prepare a big batch of slow-cooker oats so that all week long you wake up to a wholesome breakfast made. There are so many ways you can utilize your weekend to get a jump start on the workweek. The sheer act of having all of this done will take one of life's big stressors right off the top, so you can focus on everything else that needs your attention like your family, work, the house. This stat is in no way scientific, but if I had to guess, I'd say that planning my meals ahead of time shaves an easy 25% of stress off my plate before the week even kicks off.

I can't say enough about making this time commitment for yourself and your family, even just a couple of hours on Sunday. If you can commit to this routine of meal planning and prepping for the week ahead, it will change your eating habits forever. So many of our longtime readers swear by it, which is why they've asked us time and time again to compile all of our best meal plans and recipes into one convenient resource to make their planning even more efficient—and we are so thrilled to deliver.

Chipotle
Cauliflower
Tacos
with Jalapeño
Cilantro Sauce
(See recipe, p. 137)

WHAT IS CLEAN EATING?

The soul of clean eating is consuming food the way nature delivered it, or as close to it as possible. It is not a diet; it's a lifestyle approach to food and its preparation. It's about eating real food for a healthy, happy life. Here are a few guidelines for living a clean-eating life.

Know thy enemies. Steer clear of trans fats, fried foods and foods high in sugar. Avoid preservatives, color additives and toxic binders, stabilizers, emulsifiers and fat replacers. In studies, trans fats, fried foods and sugar have all been linked to a greater risk of obesity, heart disease and cancer. Preservatives, emulsifiers and food dyes are also highly processed and have been found in animal studies to be potentially carcinogenic and/or disruptive to the balance of gut flora. Although the FDA maintains that these types of ingredients are added to food in amounts that are not harmful to humans, further study is needed, adding to the list of reasons why it's best to avoid them entirely.

Consume essential fatty acids (EFAs) every day. As the building blocks of healthy cell membranes, EFAs (such as omega-3s and omega-6s) are not made by the body and must be obtained through food. Studies show that EFAs may prevent atherosclerosis and cardiovascular disease. They also support cognitive health and may provide relief for symptoms of rheumatoid arthritis and menstrual pain. Good sources of essential fatty acids include fatty fish such as salmon, walnuts and flaxseeds.

Avoid processed and refined foods such as white flour, sugar, bread and pasta. Because key nutrients are lost during processing, refined foods lack fiber and important vitamins and minerals. You'll also want to avoid enriched grains, where food manufacturers fortify refined grains with vitamins and minerals to make up for the loss. Enjoy complex carbs such as whole grains instead. Studies have linked whole grains to a lower risk of obesity, diabetes, heart disease, stroke and certain types of cancers.

Eat five to six times per day: Aim for three meals and two to three small snacks. Include a protein, fresh fruit and vegetables, and a complex carbohydrate with each meal. This keeps your body energized while satisfying your appetite and controlling hunger so you won't feel the urge to overeat.

Drink at least 2 liters of water a day. Water is essential for keeping your body hydrated, for regulating body temperature and for keeping cells, tissues and organs functioning optimally. According to the American Heart Association, proper hydration allows the heart to more easily pump blood through the blood vessels to the muscles, helping them function better.

Limit your alcohol intake to one glass of antioxidant-rich red wine a day. Research has found that red wine contains the free radical–fighting polyphenol resveratrol, which may prevent heart disease by lowering inflammation, protecting blood vessels and preventing blood clots.

Get label savvy. Clean foods contain short ingredient lists. Any product with a long ingredient list is typically factory-made and not considered clean.

Learn about portion sizes and work toward eating within them. If your goal is to maintain the weight you're currently at, find out how many carbs, fats and proteins your body needs for your current height, weight and activity level and aim to loosely eat within those perimeters each day, without them taking over the focus of mealtime.

Reduce your carbon footprint. Eat produce that is seasonal and local. It is less taxing on your wallet and the environment, it tastes better and you'll never get bored if you eat with the seasons.

Shop with a conscience. Consume humanely raised, local meats and ocean-friendly seafood. Visit **seachoice.org** for a printable pamphlet.

Practice mindful eating. Never rush through a meal. Food tastes best when savored. Enjoy every bite.

Take it to go. Pack a cooler for work or outings so you always have clean eats on the go and aren't tempted to eat out when hunger strikes.

Apple Pie
Overnight Oats
(See recipe, p. 236)

EATING SEASONALLY & LOCAL

Why Eat Seasonally?

By now, you understand the health, community, earth and cost benefits of shopping and eating locally and in season. But it can also be easy to forget when you're in a hurry, craving a recipe that's not exactly in season or you have no choice but to swing by the monster superstore instead of your local farmers' market that closed an hour ago. We get it. But just to keep things honest and to keep us all driven toward that all-important, common goal, let's run through six undeniable reasons to continue to eat seasonally and buy local as often and as much as possible, you know, without completely stressing yourself out.

If you live in one of the colder regions of North America like our creative team based in Toronto, Canada, a wide variety of fresh, local food isn't always as accessible as it is May through October.

That's why summer is such a magical food season and one we never take for granted. But whether you're on the sunny West Coast or down South where you have access to producer markets throughout the year or you're in the Northeast relying on indoor markets (which are booming in Maryland, Massachusetts, Michigan, New York and Pennsylvania, by the way!), there are so many compelling reasons to eat this way as often as possible and all year long. Here's why:

1. It's Better for the Planet.

Buying your meat, dairy, eggs and produce from local farmers means it didn't have to travel great distances before arriving at your table, reducing fuel, energy and the time it spent in trucks, on planes and in warehouses before finally reaching the supermarket. Going local is a solid first step in reducing your carbon footprint—a very, very good thing. Plus, local farms preserve outdoor space and fertile soil, ideal for communities.

2. It's Cheaper.

It's the concept of supply and demand: The more of a particular food growing, the faster it needs to unload before it spoils, and therefore the cheaper it is! If you're buying strawberries in the dead of winter, you're going to pay a premium for shipping them here from other countries and they won't taste like much. Shopping in season will slash your grocery bill and enrich your eating experience. Which leads me to my next point...

3. It Tastes Better!

Food always tastes best when it's picked at its peak and sold within days. Often, food traveling long and far is picked prematurely and then refrigerated to prevent spoiling. Fruit and vegetables that are picked before they ripen and chilled for transport never reach their potential for amazing, flavor-explosion juiciness.

Open-Faced Veggie Melts
with Smoked Mozzarella
(See recipe, p. 186)

4. You'll Never Get Bored.

Eating with the seasons is how nature intended us to nourish ourselves. It's no accident that root veggies and potatoes are seasonal in the winter months when our bodies need warmth and substance, and lighter veggies like tomatoes, peppers, cucumbers and watermelon are in abundance in summer to enjoy raw and keep us cool. The best perk about eating this way is that every season brings a new crop of clean eats, so you never tire of or overdo certain foods.

5. It's More Nutritious.

Remember that harvested-early point I made earlier? Not only does it affect flavor, but it also results in a less nutritious fruit or vegetable because the nutrients haven't had a chance to fully develop through the ripening process. And far-traveling food is often sprayed with preservatives so it lasts the trek.

6. It's Great for Your Community.

When you buy from local farmers, you eliminate the middleman, which means neighboring farm families keep more in their pocket, leading to a thriving community and local farms in your area for years to come. It's also relationship building—not only good for making friends but for learning about seasonality, nature, farming and agriculture!

10 (VERY GOOD) REASONS TO EAT CLEAN

We now know the who (you), what (eat clean), where (everywhere!), how (see page xiii), but what about the why? Most of us know we should be eating better for health reasons and can list off a few immediate concerns (the usual suspects: heart health, cancer prevention), but sometimes we don't take all the necessary steps to fully get there or truly realize all the areas of life that are impacted by a clean diet, big or small. Here are 10 science-backed reasons to wholly commit to a delicious life of eating clean that also serve as an encouraging reminder you can post on your fridge when you find yourself halfway through a meal plan on a stressful day and tempted by the pizza delivery flyer that was left in your mailbox.

1. You'll become more mindful.

Picture trying to eat a processed, fast-food burger in your car. Now picture spearing a forkful of salad. Which one takes longer and really makes you slow down? You got it— the salad. Eating clean also means eating with purpose and savoring food. That means a better relationship with everything from radishes and radicchio to red velvet cupcakes (which you'll no longer crave).

2. You'll be smarter.

Eating a healthy diet rich in fruits, vegetables, fish and nuts keeps your mind sharper and your memory better by a whopping 24%, proved a study published in 2015 in *Neurology*. Your brain also functions better with nutrients such as omega-3 fatty acids, as shown in *Nature Reviews Neuroscience*, while it sputters and slows down when it gets hit with sugar, alcohol, fast food and the wrong kinds of fats. If that's all too much to think about, remember one point from the report: A balanced diet means better brain health.

3. You'll save money.

Kiss sick days goodbye when you get nutrients from real food. Plus, shopping locally and in season makes sense—and cents. Planning clean meals for the week is cost-effective if you make a list and stick to it, as there's no chance of overspending at the store. And by skipping pricey restaurants and unhealthy takeout orders, you're doing your wallet and not just your waistline a favor. Want to really stretch your clean-eating dollars? Take leftovers for lunch.

4. You'll live longer.

Picture the fountain of youth made out of whole grains, fruits and vegetables. A recent *JAMA Internal Medicine* report found that each additional 28-gram serving of whole grains per day was associated with a 5% lower risk of dying from any cause. And in a study published in the *American Journal of Epidemiology*, European researchers found that increasing your produce intake to more than 569 grams per day reduces your risk of mortality by 10%. Choose raw veggies whenever you can; in the same study, they were associated with a drop in mortality of 16%.

5. You'll have better relationships.

Preparing clean meals takes time, just the kind of time that allows for easy, relaxed conversations with family and friends. If they're too busy with screen time to share stove-top time, point them to the Johns Hopkins Bloomberg School of Public Health 2014 study, published in *Public Health Nutrition*, showing that good health comes from home cooking. People who cook dinner six to seven times a week consume 137 fewer calories along with 16 fewer grams of sugar per day than those who cook once a week or less.

6. You'll have more energy.

Perfectly portioned and conveniently portable, fresh fruit is just one of many clean foods that provide an instant dose of energy. High-fiber fruits like apples take longer to digest and can instantly stave off that afternoon slump while providing critical vitamins. Other pick-me-ups include quinoa, almonds, eggs, kale, citrus fruits and a good old-fashioned glass of water.

7. You'll be better in bed.

Mamma mia! Women in Italy and other regions of the Mediterranean enjoy a healthier sex life than those in the United States, thanks to the components of their diet—yep, vegetables, fruits, nuts, whole grains and olive oil. That's what researchers found in a comprehensive study published in the *International Journal of Impotence Research*.

8. You'll help the planet survive.

There's an oft-quoted statistic that food travels approximately 1,500 miles from farmer to consumer in the United States. By eating local and seasonal foods, you can help reduce your carbon footprint. Want to make an even greater impact? Try eating vegetarian a few times a week. While you may not want to completely give up meat, fish and poultry, leaning toward a lacto-ovo vegetarian diet (which includes eggs and dairy) can help protect the earth's resources. As the *American Journal of Clinical Nutrition* reported in 2003, "the lacto-ovo vegetarian diet is more sustainable than the average American meat-based diet." Eating clean helps the planet stay green.

9. You'll be stronger.

The lean protein that comprises part of the clean-eating philosophy builds lean muscle mass and boosts metabolism, found a study presented at the Obesity Society's annual meeting in 2014. Some mighty choices for your muscles (in addition to animal-based products like chicken, fish and lean beef) include quinoa, chickpeas, nuts, spinach and seeds.

10. You'll be happier.

Food and mood go hand in hand. And the better the food, the better your mood. If you need to brighten your day, go for berries, bananas, coffee, lean proteins, chocolate, turmeric and omega-3 fatty acids, all proven to boost your mental state.

**Honeydew &
Blackberry Bowl**
with Basil & Lime Drizzle
(See recipe, p. 161)

HOW TO USE THIS BOOK

It's simple, really.

Easy-to-follow *Clean Eating* meal plans take the guesswork out of meal prep and keep your clean-eating lifestyle on track. The perfect plan is three meals and several small, clean snacks a day comprised of fresh, seasonal fare that ensure that energy levels are high and the stress of what to eat next is low. *Clean Eating* meal plans average 1,400 to 1,600 calories a day, but they are modifiable if you require a little more or a little less. Pick the one that's best for you. Some of our meal plans cater to common dietary restrictions such as gluten-free, weight loss, Paleo and vegetarian—so no matter how you prefer to eat, we've got you covered. And if you choose another plan and want to modify it yourself, we have a substitution guide at the back of the book that will help you do just that. More on that later.

We've created the detailed plans, built your shopping lists and calculated all the nutritionals so you can hit the ground running. Enjoy 14 weeks of easy, breezy clean eating with our no-fuss, no-fail plans that are packed with recipes, mini meals and snacks that are every bit delicious. Don't worry, we're not suggesting you commit to 14 consecutive weeks; take it one week at a time. Unless, of course, you get hooked on the ease of the plans and never want to stop, which is entirely possible.

Depending on where you are in your clean-eating journey and how regimented you'd like to be, you can use this book as your season-by-season weekly meal planner or a little more casually as you alternate between off-the-cuff recipes and a desire to follow a more organized plan. Perhaps a detailed meal plan better suits you leading up to a big event when you want to feel your best or when you're feeling low-energy, stressed or fuzzy-headed and need a powerful clean-eating reboot to get you back on your game. Even if you're not following the plans in this book, the wealth of recipes will serve as daily meal inspiration through the seasons, whether you are looking for breakfast, lunch, dinner or snacks.

Where should I start?

I encourage you to turn to the meal plans that start on page 298 and begin with the season you are currently in. Comb each carefully and settle on a plan that contains meal and snack suggestions that appeal to you the most. The best way to start on a plan if you've never done one before is to be sure you're going to thoroughly enjoy every meal, and then later, once you become a seasoned pro, you can customize the plans and substitute things that are not quite to your liking. If you've never followed a structured meal plan in the past, this may seem intimidating at first glance, but I'm here to tell you that these beloved meal plans have earned cult status among our readers and have been a cornerstone of the magazine since we launched the publication a decade ago. When we've published the occasional issue without a meal plan, the backlash we got from devoted, regular readers was overwhelming. (But it's nice to know they are paying attention!) Our meal plan devotees are serious about their plans.

Are they hard to follow?

In a word, no. But they are detailed and perhaps look a little complex at first. Just remember that, at a glance, you're looking at *everything* you're going to be eating for the next seven to 14 days. Imagine you logged a food diary now for the next week—chances are, you'd be surprised at how much you ingest in seven days, healthy or otherwise. The truth is, the plans are detailed but are actually very simple once you start and take it day by day. The feedback we consistently hear from readers is that these plans make life exponentially easier by taking 100% of the guesswork out of meal planning—a stress point for most people. And once the weekly shop is done using the handy lists we provide—another significant time savings—everything is in place, so all you have to do is prep your meals, feel great about eating healthy, satisfying food and watch your energy soar, stress levels sink... and maybe your pants loosen up a little.

Can I customize the plans to better suit my needs?

Absolutely. If you're following a restrictive diet or have a food allergy, alter the plans to suit your needs right away. If you're new to clean eating and not quite sure how you'd like to change the plan, we recommend waiting until after you've tried a plan or two and are a little more familiar to start nip-tucking the plans and shopping lists. Once comfortable, go ahead and have fun customizing the plans to suit your particulars. If you're finding that you're still hungry and getting too little, or unable to finish as it's too much, then simply omit a snack, slash a serving size in half or double it up. Just be sure to adjust your shopping list to ensure you're not buying too much or too little.

Are you cutting back on grains these days? You can reduce or remove grains entirely and sub in cauliflower rice or more vegetables, for example. Off dairy? Replace dairy cheese with nut cheese. Not doing the meat thing? There's often an equally delicious substitute you can pop in to replace every ounce of animal protein called for. For the most common substitutions and ideas for what you can replace them with, flip to page 296. We've got you covered.

We completely understand that today's dietary needs vary and are more radically different from one person to the next than ever before, so we've been working hard to adjust to the ever-changing landscape of healthy eating to be as inclusive as we can and offer solutions to all readers looking to eat clean but on your terms.

ORGANIZE A CLEAN-EATING KITCHEN & PANTRY

5 STEPS TO ORGANIZING YOUR KITCHEN FOR SUCCESS

Here's a comprehensive guide to decluttering and organizing your space for the ultimate clean kitchen, fridge and pantry. When starting or continuing on a clean-eating path and incorporating healthful new recipes and meal plans into your routine, it's highly recommended to regularly take stock of what's in your fridge and kitchen cupboards and to clean out any insidious treats and any "off plan" items that may have mysteriously found their way into your home over time. Clearing out the junk and bringing all the wholesome stuff to the forefront—in addition to clearing clutter for an organized, serene kitchen—will all contribute greatly to your clean-eating success.

STEP 1: Set your goals, then set up your kitchen.

The state of organization in your pantry—as well as the rest of your kitchen—has a direct impact on how well you stick to your healthy eating goals. Some experts, such as organizational design expert Peter Walsh, go so far as to argue that the clutter in your kitchen goes hand in hand with excess weight.

In his book, *Lose the Clutter, Lose the Weight* (Rodale, 2015), Walsh contends that a cluttered environment might be a factor in making poor food choices. He points to a 2013 study where researchers asked students to answer a questionnaire in either an orderly room or a messy room. When the students were leaving the room, they were given a choice of a snack—either an apple or a candy bar. Interestingly enough, those leaving the clean room were likely to opt for the apple while those leaving the messy room more often chose the candy bar.

Of course, Walsh doesn't argue that clutter causes weight gain directly, but he does believe there is a relationship. According to him, both are a type of imbalance—if you're overweight, you're taking in too many calories; if you have a cluttered home, you're taking too much stuff into your home.

But once you've set your mind to correcting that imbalance and decluttering your home, where do you start? Jumping right into organizing can be difficult if you haven't set goals for yourself. Professional organizer and best-selling author of *Organizing from the Inside Out* (Holt/Owl Books, 2004) Julie Morgenstern suggests asking how you can best set up your pantry or fridge to support your clean-eating values, habits and routines. For example, if you want to juice more often, you might consider setting up an area on your countertop as a juicing station or keeping a spot in your fridge where you store your juicing ingredients. This is why mapping out your goals should always be the first step in organizing your kitchen.

In this section, we're sharing some of our favorite tips we've learned over the years from top experts in the field for reorganizing your fridge, pantry and countertops. But remember, just like keeping up with healthy eating and exercising, organizing isn't something you do only once a year. The key to not letting your kitchen slip back into disarray is regularly making time to maintain order and to keep up the system you've set up for you and your family.

Once you've determined your clean-eating goals, reorganizing an area of your kitchen like your pantry or fridge becomes a lot easier. Morgenstern suggests a five-step process, which she refers to as SPACE. The SPACE system helps to give context when you are sorting through your belongings to see what fits—or doesn't fit—within the goals you've set for yourself. Apply the SPACE system to every section of your kitchen and home that needs attention.

SORT

Pull items out and group similar items; take inventory of what you have.

PURGE

Get rid of anything that doesn't fit within your current goals; donate anything that hasn't expired and toss the rest.

ASSIGN A HOME

Put things you use often in easier-to-reach areas. Flip to page xxviii for more information on mapping out your space.

CONTAIN

Once you know where things will go, you can purchase the appropriate-sized containers for the space where needed.

EQUALIZE

After you're all set up, you need to maintain your system; clean as you go to keep everything organized and tidy. But instead of thinking of kitchen maintenance as ordinary cleaning, Morgenstern suggests approaching it as "setting things up for their next use," which feels more intentional.

STEP 2: Zone in on Your Pantry.

How do you decide where everything should go in your pantry? Morgenstern suggests thinking of your pantry in terms of zones, or areas, where different types of foods live. A typical clean pantry could be organized into broad categories such as the ones below.

These zones are flexible, depending on your needs. If you're a frequent baker, then baking staples can be given their own zone. Store spices, oils and vinegars close enough to your cooking station for easy access, but remember that they should be kept in a cool, dark area for ultimate freshness. And keep things that are used more often, like snacks, for example, in easier-to-reach areas.

OILS & VINEGARS

BEANS & LENTILS
....

SNACKS
....

SPICES
....

SAUCES & BROTHS
....

OILS & VINEGARS
....

PASTAS & GRAINS
....

SNACKS

SPICES

BEANS & LENTILS

PASTA & GRAINS

SAUCES & BROTHS

DO'S AND DON'TS FOR AN ORDERLY KITCHEN

DO have an area near your front door where your keys, purse, mail and other items live. That way, those things don't end up making their way into your kitchen or getting lost.

DON'T transfer all pantry items to containers. Most of the time this is wasted effort. Instead, use containers selectively—they're mostly necessary for items you pick up in the bulk department. And choosing rectangular and square containers over rounded jars allows you to use your space most efficiently.

DO a reckoning of your food-storage containers at least once a year. Match up each container with the lid it belongs to, and then donate, recycle or repurpose any odds and ends that remain.

DON'T label everything in your pantry unless you have multiple items in containers that all look the same, such as flours. It is a good idea to label your shelves, however, to keep track of where everything belongs in the pantry.

DO go digital to save space in your kitchen. Organize your recipes on your tablet so you can refer to them while you cook—that way you don't have to keep all your cookbooks in the kitchen. Alternatively, scan and print your favorite recipes from your cookbooks and keep them in a binder.

Be your own sous chef and prep ingredient bins for weeknight meals!

Air vents

STEP 3: Organize Your Fridge Like a Pro.

When deciding what to place where in the fridge, there are two main issues to consider: functionality and food safety. Follow these expert tips to organize your fridge like a pro.

1. Put more temperature-stable items, such as dressings, juices and condiments, in door compartments. The temperature in this zone fluctuates every time you open and shut the door, so temperature-sensitive ingredients like eggs shouldn't be stored here. Make sure to store butter in the butter compartment, as the door of this compartment is designed to protect oils and fats from picking up other aromas within the fridge.

2. Keep your leftovers, snacks and other ready-to-eat foods on the upper shelves. Because you may not cook these items before eating, you don't want to keep them on a lower shelf and risk having something else leak onto them.

3. Have a look inside your fridge and locate the air vent, usually on the back wall of the fridge. This is the coldest spot in your fridge, so keep your dairy and fish here.

4. Raw proteins (chicken, beef, eggs) should be kept on the lowest shelf to avoid leakage onto other foods. Most fridges will have this shelf sealed so that there is limited risk of leakage into the crisper. If your shelf doesn't have a seal, make sure to put your proteins in a bowl or container.

5. Keep your vegetables in the crisper either out of bags or loosely covered, as produce kept tightly in bags will spoil faster. If you have two crispers that are stacked, keep the produce that will be cooked in the upper crisper and the produce that will be eaten raw in the lower crisper.

TEMPERATURE CHECK

The temperature of your fridge should always be at or below 40°F. If your fridge doesn't have a temperature display, an inexpensive fridge thermometer can help make sure the temperature is always in the right range. And what if frost is building up in your fridge? While humid weather can sometimes contribute to this, frost buildup usually means someone is leaving the door open too long or one of the door gaskets is not properly sealing when it's closed.

THE BENEFITS OF BINS

Don't have a lot of time to cook during the week? Morgenstern urges you to "be your own sous chef" by assembling and prepping ingredients for meals on the weekend and placing the prepared ingredients for each meal into individual bins labeled for the day of the week they'll be used. When you're ready to cook, simply pull the appropriate bin out of the fridge and you have all your ingredients ready to go. Grouping similar items like cheeses, snacks or leftovers in bins in the fridge helps add order, structure and visibility to things that don't stand up on their own.

SNACK WELL

Always keep pre-portioned snacks handy so that you can just grab and go, recommends Walsh. That way when you or your children open the fridge, you have the appropriate healthy snack waiting.

TO CHILL OR NOT TO CHILL

Unsure of what fruits and vegetables to refrigerate and what to leave out on your countertop? When in doubt, look to how things are stored in the supermarket. The food industry spends a lot of time and money figuring out the best ways to store produce for lasting freshness, so that's usually a very good indicator of how they should be stored at home. And even though it's safe to keep certain items like tomatoes, onions and potatoes on your countertop, remember that once they're cut up, they have to go into the fridge for food safety reasons.

DO: Salad greens such as spinach, arugula and kale, cucumbers, bell peppers, asparagus, carrots, eggplant, oranges, broccoli and cauliflower

DON'T: Tomatoes, onions, potatoes, apples, pears and tropical fruits such as avocados, bananas, kiwis and papayas

Only keep items on the countertop that you use often, such as a blender if you prepare daily smoothies.

STEP 4: Consider the Magic Triangle.

The magic triangle is the area in your kitchen where all the action happens. Depending on the layout of your space, the triangle can be formed by the cooktop, refrigerator and oven.

   You spend most of your time in the kitchen within that work triangle, and for this reason, Walsh recommends only keeping items you use frequently within or on the edges of the triangle. Think of it as the most valuable real estate in your kitchen. If you are an avid baker and use a whisk almost daily, then by all means, keep it in a container or a drawer inside the magic triangle—if not, it can be demoted to a less-central place.

   Walsh firmly believes in keeping as much off the countertop as possible—in his own home, he even keeps his knife block in a drawer. "If the countertop is clear," he explains, "it says, this room is ready for action; it welcomes you. It says this space is ready for you to get started immediately."

STEP 5: Your Kitchen Is Impeccable–Now Keep It Up.

You can spend days getting your kitchen in perfect order, but without a commitment to regularly uphold the new system, it'll revert to an unruly mess in no time. Try posting chores in a prominent place in your kitchen or rotating them between different family members to make sure everyone participates in maintaining your clean kitchen.

FRIDGE: Edit the contents of your fridge weekly to use up any items before they go off. Tie this habit to garbage-collection day so that any smelly foods that need to be tossed will be taken away immediately. We recommend disinfecting refrigerator shelves every two months and spot-cleaning spills as they happen.

PANTRY: Edit the contents of your pantry every season, and disinfect the pantry shelves twice per year, cleaning up any spills as they occur.

OVEN: You don't need to use toxic cleaners to keep your oven spotless. Simply sprinkle baking soda over the bottom of the oven until it's coated then drizzle hot water over top. Wearing rubber gloves, swirl the water and baking soda around to combine. Let it sit overnight then scrub with an abrasive sponge. *CE* recommends cleaning your oven twice a year, or as needed, and spot-clean spills as soon as the oven is cool.

DISHWASHER: Clean your dishwasher about once a month. Use a soapy, hard-bristled toothbrush to brush some of the harder-to-reach nooks and crannies. Then fill a dishwasher-safe cup with white vinegar, put it upright on the top shelf and run the cycle with hot water to kill off any mold or bacteria.

GARBAGE BINS: Wash trash bins once per month and compost bins with leaky food waste weekly. Keep them smelling fresh by sprinkling baking soda at the bottom.

THE SUNDAY RITUAL: If you find yourself coming home from work with no idea what's going on the dinner table, the meal-planning routines found in this book are just the remedy. Now that you've found this book, planning your meals ahead of time will be a breeze. Sit down with your family for 10 minutes on Sunday to select your meals or plans for the week, schedule each meal in then write your shopping list. The grocery lists for the meal plans are available to download online at **cleaneating.com/booklists**. The Sunday ritual will become the single most critical change you can make to getting your eating on track. Luckily, everything you need is already in your hands. Now it's time to flip the page and get started. Happy meal planning!

Winter Recipes

Cranberry-Glazed Pork Loin Roast

with Cranberry Shallot Compote

(See recipe, p. 47)

No-Cook Almond Cherry Bars

Makes **8 Bars.**
Hands-On Time: **15 Minutes.**
Total Time: **15 Minutes.**

INGREDIENTS

1 cup	pitted and chopped Medjool dates
½ cup	natural unsalted almond butter
½ cup	unsalted pumpkin seeds
½ cup	unsalted raw almonds
1 cup	unsweetened dried tart cherries (or naturally sweetened cranberries)
1 tsp	ground cinnamon
1 tsp	sesame seeds, toasted

INSTRUCTIONS

Lightly mist a 9 x 5-inch loaf pan with cooking spray, then line with parchment paper.

To a food processor, add dates, almond butter, pumpkin seeds, almonds, cherries and cinnamon; pulse until about three-quarters combined, leaving some chunks intact.

Press mixture evenly into loaf pan. Sprinkle with sesame seeds.

Refrigerate for at least 1 hour, ideally overnight. Cut into 8 equal-sized bars. (**NOTE:** You will have leftover bars; freeze remaining for future use.)

Nutrition Information Per serving (1 bar): Calories: 287, Total Fat: 15 g, Sat. Fat: 1 g, Monounsaturated Fat: 9 g, Polyunsaturated Fat: 3.5 g, Carbs: 36 g, Fiber: 8 g, Sugars: 22 g, Protein: 6 g, Sodium: 0 mg, Cholesterol: 0 mg

Lemon, Coconut & Cayenne Mousse

Try garnishing with toasted coconut, lemon zest or a drizzle of maple syrup.

Serves **8.**
Hands-On Time: **20 Minutes.**
Total Time: **20 Minutes.***
*Plus 4 Hours Chilling Time.

INGREDIENTS

3	medium eggs
1½ tbsp	lemon zest + ½ cup fresh lemon juice, divided
½ cup	pure maple syrup
¼ cup	coconut oil
2 13.5-oz	BPA-free cans coconut milk, refrigerated overnight
¼ tsp	ground cayenne pepper

INSTRUCTIONS

In a medium saucepan, whisk eggs. Add lemon zest and maple syrup; set on medium heat and whisk constantly until mixture turns pale yellow and creamy, about 5 minutes. To saucepan, alternate adding coconut oil and lemon juice a little at a time. (**NOTE:** *It should take you about 3 rounds*.) Whisk constantly until mixture is creamy, color is even and bubbles just begin to form. Remove from heat and pour through a fine mesh sieve into a jar or bowl, pressing to make sure as much of the mixture as possible goes through. Cover and refrigerate for at least 4 hours, or overnight.

Just before serving, remove cans from refrigerator and open from bottom (coconut milk will have separated into solidified cream and water). Pour out water and reserve for another use; scoop solidified, white cream into a chilled metal bowl. Add cayenne and beat with an electric hand mixer on medium-high for 30 seconds, until creamy. Gently fold in chilled lemon mixture.

Nutrition Information Per serving (¼ cup): Calories: 287, Total Fat: 24 g, Sat. Fat: 20 g, Monounsaturated Fat: 2 g, Polyunsaturated Fat: 1 g, Carbs: 15 g, Fiber: 0 g, Sugars: 13 g, Protein: 4 g, Sodium: 42 mg, Cholesterol: 70 mg

Sweet Cherry Almond Flaxseed Smoothie

Serves **2.**
Hands-On Time: **5 Minutes.**
Total Time: **5 Minutes.**

INGREDIENTS

2 cups	frozen unsweetened pitted cherries
½ cup	fresh orange juice
½ cup	ground almonds
2 tbsp	flaxseed meal
½ tsp	pure almond extract
	chopped almonds, optional

INSTRUCTIONS

Combine all ingredients except chopped almonds in a blender. Blend until smooth. Divide between 2 glasses and sprinkle with chopped almonds (if using).

Nutrition Information
Per serving (½ of recipe): Calories: 296, Total Fat: 15 g, Sat. Fat: 1 g, Monounsaturated Fat: 8 g, Polyunsaturated Fat: 5 g, Carbs: 36 g, Fiber: 8 g, Sugars: 24 g, Protein: 8 g, Sodium: 3 mg, Cholesterol: 0 mg

NOTE: This recipe yields 2 servings that are used on two different days in the Meal Plan. You can store 1 serving covered in the refrigerator overnight, or you can blend half the recipe at a time for maximum freshness.

Earl Grey French Toast
with Orange Maple Syrup

INGREDIENTS

¾ cup	whole milk
4	unbleached Earl Grey tea bags, divided
2	eggs
4 tbsp	pure maple syrup, divided + additional for serving
20	¼-inch-thick slices whole-wheat baguette (4 to 5 oz) (*TIP: Use yesterday's bread*.)
1 cup	fresh orange juice + additional orange slices for garnish
5 tsp	organic unsalted butter, divided
¼ cup	chopped unsalted pecans, for garnish, optional

Serves **4.**
Hands-On Time: **20 Minutes.**
Total Time: **1 Hour.**

INSTRUCTIONS

In a small saucepan, bring milk to a boil. Remove from heat. Steep 2 tea bags in hot milk for 10 minutes. Squeeze liquid from tea bags. Let cool slightly and rinse out saucepan.

Whisk eggs and 1 tbsp maple syrup in a 13 x 9-inch baking dish. Slowly whisk in milk-tea mixture. In baking dish, add bread slices and soak for 3 to 5 minutes per side.

To saucepan, add orange juice and remaining 3 tbsp maple syrup; bring to a boil. Add remaining 2 tea bags and steep over medium for 10 minutes. Remove tea bags and simmer 3 to 5 more minutes, still on medium, until mixture is thickened and syrupy. Remove saucepan from heat and swirl in 4 tsp butter. Keep warm in pot.

Heat a large nonstick skillet or griddle pan over medium-low. Brush with remaining 1 tsp butter. Transfer bread slices from baking dish to skillet, allowing excess egg mixture to drip back into baking dish. Cook slices 2 to 4 minutes per side until golden to deep brown. (**NOTE:** *Leave ½ inch between slices in skillet; you may need to work in 2 to 3 batches, depending on size of skillet.*)

To serve, arrange 5 slices of French toast on each plate. Drizzle each plate with additional maple syrup. Garnish with orange slices and pecans (if using).

Nutrition Information Per serving (5 pieces toast and 2 tbsp syrup): Calories: 267, Total Fat: 9 g, Sat. Fat: 5 g, Monounsaturated Fat: 3 g, Polyunsaturated Fat: 1 g, Carbs: 39 g, Fiber: 2 g, Sugars: 21 g, Protein: 8 g, Sodium: 239 mg, Cholesterol: 110 mg

Brazil Nut Bread
with Honey Butter

INGREDIENTS

	organic unsalted butter, for greasing
6 tbsp	white whole-wheat flour + additional for dusting
1 tbsp	orange zest
2 tsp	unsweetened cocoa powder
½ tsp	each ground cinnamon and baking powder
⅛ tsp	kosher salt or sea salt
3 large	eggs
1 cup	finely chopped pitted Medjool dates
1 cup	raw unsalted Brazil nuts, roughly chopped
2 tbsp	whole milk

Honey Butter

½ stick	organic unsalted butter (¼ cup), softened
2 tbsp	raw honey (preferably orange blossom)

Serves **10.**
Hands-On Time: **25 Minutes.**
Total Time: **1 Hour.**

INSTRUCTIONS

Preheat oven to 325ºF. Butter a 9-inch cake pan or pie plate, then dust with flour (tap out excess). Or butter then line bottom with a circle of parchment paper.

In a medium bowl, combine flour, zest, cocoa, cinnamon, baking powder and salt.

Add eggs, dates, nuts and milk and mix well. (**TIP:** *It'll be thick and chunky, so you'll need to use some elbow grease.*) Pour into pan, leveling off with the back of a spoon. Place pan on a baking sheet and bake for 40 to 45 minutes, until top is light to golden brown and center springs back when pressed.

Meanwhile, prepare butter: In a small bowl, combine butter and honey. Serve with bread. Bread can be served warm or at room temperature.

Nutrition Information Per serving (¹⁄₁₀ of bread and butter): Calories: 227, Total Fat: 16 g, Sat. Fat: 6 g, Monounsaturated Fat: 5 g, Polyunsaturated Fat: 4 g, Carbs: 20 g, Fiber: 3 g, Sugars: 14 g, Protein: 5 g, Sodium: 76 mg, Cholesterol: 69 mg

Turkey & Black Bean Tacos
with Green Herb Salsa

Don't get too fussy with this salsa–think of it as a Mexican-style pesto you can switch up according to your taste preference. Use less jalapeño for a milder salsa, or use parsley or basil if you don't like cilantro. For a lower-carb version of the recipe, swap out the tortillas for lettuce and serve as a hearty salad. Add any toppings you like such as shredded cheese, sour cream or sliced radish or avocado.

INGREDIENTS

4½ tsp	olive oil, divided
1	yellow onion, thinly sliced
1	red bell pepper, thinly sliced
1½ tsp	ground cumin
1 tsp	each ground coriander, garlic powder and paprika
½ tsp	sea salt
1 lb	boneless, skinless turkey breast, cut into thin strips
1½ cups	cooked black or pinto beans
8	6-inch soft corn tortillas, warmed

Salsa

1 small	jalapeño chile pepper, seeded and roughly chopped
1½ cups	loosely packed fresh cilantro
¼ cup	sliced green onions
3 tbsp	fresh oregano
1 small	clove garlic
Pinch	sea salt
4 tsp	fresh lime juice
4 tsp	olive oil

Serves **4**.
Hands-On Time: **45 Minutes.**
Total Time: **45 Minutes.**

INSTRUCTIONS

Prepare salsa: On a cutting board, mound jalapeño, cilantro, green onions, oregano, garlic and pinch salt; finely chop mixture. (Alternatively, pulse in a food processor until finely chopped.) Transfer to a small bowl; stir in lime juice and 4 tsp oil. Set aside.

In a large nonstick skillet on medium-high, heat 1 tbsp oil. Add yellow onion and bell pepper and sauté, stirring frequently, until tender and golden, about 5 minutes. Transfer to a plate; set aside.

In a large bowl, stir together cumin, coriander, garlic powder, paprika and ½ tsp salt. Add turkey and toss to coat. In same skillet on medium-high, heat remaining 1½ tsp oil. Add turkey and sauté until no longer pink inside, about 4 minutes. Stir in onion mixture and beans; heat through.

Divide turkey-bean mixture among tortillas. Top with salsa, dividing evenly.

Nutrition Information Per serving (2 tacos): Calories: 456, Total Fat: 14 g, Sat. Fat: 2 g, Monounsaturated Fat: 9 g, Polyunsaturated Fat: 2 g, Carbs: 46 g, Fiber: 11 g, Sugars: 4 g, Protein: 37 g, Sodium: 595 mg, Cholesterol: 65 mg

BLACK BEANS FOR THE WIN: Fiber-rich black beans may aid in lowering your risk of certain types of cancer, cardiovascular disease and type 2 diabetes, according to studies. The seed coat of black beans contains a class of flavonoids called anthocyanins, which are phytonutrient pigments that act as antioxidants in the body to help prevent chronic diseases.

Cauliflower & Cardamom Soup
with Spiced Chickpeas

Few things can instantly warm you up on a cold day like a comforting bowl of soup. Enlivened with turmeric, cardamom and saffron, this soup can be put together with only 15 minutes of hands-on work.

INGREDIENTS

2 tbsp	olive oil
1 cup	chopped sweet onion
1½ tsp	each ground turmeric and cardamom
Pinch	each saffron and red pepper flakes
3	cloves garlic, chopped
1	head cauliflower (about 1½ lbs), roughly chopped
1 tbsp	Dijon mustard
3 cups	low-sodium vegetable broth
1 tbsp	fresh lemon juice
	sea salt and ground black pepper, to taste

Spiced Chickpeas

½ cup	cooked chickpeas
½ tsp	each ground coriander, turmeric and fennel
Pinch	red pepper flakes
1 tsp	peeled and grated ginger
1 tbsp	olive oil
1 tbsp	fresh lemon juice
1 tbsp	chopped fresh cilantro
	sea salt and ground black pepper, to taste

Serves **6.**
Hands-On Time: **15 Minutes.**
Total Time: **3 Hours, 15 Minutes.**

INSTRUCTIONS

Prepare spiced chickpeas: In a bowl, add all chickpea ingredients and toss to combine. Serve at room temperature or refrigerate, tightly sealed, for up to 3 days. Allow chickpeas to return to room temperature before serving.

In a skillet on medium, heat oil. Add onion and cook until softened, about 2 minutes. Add turmeric, cardamom, saffron and pepper flakes and stir for 1 minute. Transfer to slow cooker; add garlic, cauliflower, Dijon, broth and 2 cups water. Stir well, cover with lid and cook on low heat for 3 hours.

Purée soup using an immersion blender (or using an upright blender). Transfer to a large bowl or pot; add lemon juice and season with salt and black pepper. Ladle soup into bowls and garnish with about 3 tbsp spiced chickpeas per bowl. Soup can be tightly sealed and frozen for up to 1 month.

Nutrition Information Per serving (1 cup soup and 3 tbsp chickpeas): Calories: 160, Total Fat: 8 g, Sat. Fat: 1.5 g, Carbs: 17 g, Fiber: 4 g, Sugars: 6 g, Protein: 6 g, Sodium: 210 mg, Cholesterol: 0 mg

POWERFUL PULSES: Chickpeas offer impressive amounts of vegetable-based protein, folate and vitamin B6, a water-soluble nutrient that is not stored in the body and must be consistently replenished each day for good health. The vitamin is vital in the processing of carbohydrates and the breakdown of glycogen, the body's main source of stored energy.

Egg Drop Soup
with Shiitake Mushrooms & Shrimp

With a light sesame flavor and a surprising crunch, this soup is a staff favorite. Try topping with a drizzle of additional sriracha and sesame oil, or if you prefer to go sweet, try a drizzle of honey.

INGREDIENTS

3 tbsp	avocado or peanut oil
2	cloves garlic, minced
2 tsp	peeled and minced fresh ginger
4	green onions, thinly sliced + additional for garnish
7 oz	shiitake mushrooms, thinly sliced
6 cups	low-sodium vegetable or chicken broth
2 cups	thinly sliced green cabbage
¼ cup	reduced-sodium soy sauce or tamari
¼ cup	rice vinegar
1 tbsp	toasted sesame oil
1 tsp	raw honey, or to taste
1 tsp	sriracha sauce, or to taste
	ground black pepper, to taste
1 lb	medium shrimp, peeled and deveined (***NOTE:*** *Medium shrimp are ideal, but if you can only find large shrimp, they can be halved.*)
2 large	eggs, beaten

Serves **6.**
Hands-On Time: **30 Minutes.**
Total Time: **30 Minutes.**

INSTRUCTIONS

In a medium pot on medium, heat avocado oil. Add garlic, ginger and onions and sauté until fragrant, 1 minute. Add mushrooms; sauté until softened, about 3 minutes.

Add broth, cabbage, soy sauce, vinegar, sesame oil, honey, sriracha and pepper. Bring to a boil and simmer for 2 minutes. Add shrimp and simmer until cooked through, about 3 minutes.

Whisk soup and pour in eggs, whisking constantly. Divide soup among bowls and garnish with additional onions.

Nutrition Information Per serving (⅙ of soup): Calories: 216, Total Fat: 11.5 g, Sat. Fat: 2 g, Monounsaturated Fat: 7 g, Polyunsaturated Fat: 2 g, Carbs: 11 g, Fiber: 3 g, Sugars: 6 g, Protein: 18 g, Sodium: 652 mg, Cholesterol: 168 mg

Cauliflower "Risotto"
with Mushrooms & Truffle Oil

INGREDIENTS

1 large	head cauliflower, chopped into florets (leaves and thick core discarded)
1 15-oz	BPA-free can unsalted cannellini beans, drained and rinsed
1 cup	low-sodium chicken or vegetable broth
	olive oil cooking spray
8 oz	cremini mushrooms, sliced
1	yellow onion, chopped
3	cloves garlic, minced
¼ tsp	sea salt
¼ tsp	ground black pepper
2 tbsp	fresh lemon juice
1½ oz	grated Pecorino Romano cheese, divided (about ⅓ cup)
⅓ cup	chopped fresh flat-leaf parsley leaves
4 tsp	truffle oil

Serves **4.**
Hands-On Time: **25 Minutes.**
Total Time: **35 Minutes.**

INSTRUCTIONS

To a large food processor, add one-third of cauliflower and process for about 15 seconds, until pieces are about the size of grains of rice. Transfer to a large bowl and repeat with remaining cauliflower to yield 6 cups of cauliflower "rice." (**NOTE:** It is important to work in batches in order to get even-sized pieces.)

To a blender, add beans and broth and process until smooth, about 1 minute.

Mist a large saucepan with cooking spray and heat on medium-low. Add mushrooms and onion and cook for 5 to 7 minutes, stirring often, until soft, lightly browned and most of liquid has evaporated. Add garlic, salt and pepper and cook for 1 minute more. Add lemon juice, increase heat to medium-high, and cook, stirring, until liquid has evaporated, about 1 minute.

Pour bean-broth purée into saucepan and bring to a simmer. Add 6 cups cauliflower "rice" and stir well. Reduce heat to medium, cover and cook for 8 to 10 minutes, stirring occasionally, until cauliflower is tender.

Uncover and reduce heat to low. Stir in ¾ oz cheese. Turn off heat and stir in parsley. Divide among bowls. Drizzle truffle oil over each serving and sprinkle with remaining ¾ oz cheese, dividing evenly.

Nutrition Information Per serving (1⅓ cups): Calories: 260, Total Fat: 10 g, Sat. Fat: 3 g, Monounsaturated Fat: 2 g, Polyunsaturated Fat: 3 g, Carbs: 32 g, Fiber: 9 g, Sugars: 7 g, Protein: 16 g, Sodium: 382 mg, Cholesterol: 11 mg

Mexican Spice Chile Soup

Cooking with chiles is a skill that Mexican cooks have honed into an art form over centuries. This bowl with soul contains beans and corn, two staples of south-of-the-border recipes, but also keeps things light and fresh with cubed avocado and thinly sliced radishes.

INGREDIENTS

2 lb	boneless, skinless chicken thighs, trimmed and cubed
1 tsp	dried oregano
1¼ tsp	sea salt, divided + additional to taste
	ground black pepper, to taste
2	dried ancho chiles, stems and seeds removed
3	dried guajillo chiles, stems and seeds removed
½	yellow onion, chopped
3	cloves garlic, chopped
¼ tsp	ground cumin
⅛ tsp	ground cloves
2 tbsp	extra-virgin olive oil
4–6 cups	low-sodium chicken broth
1¾ cups	cooked pinto beans
1¾ cups	frozen and thawed corn

Optional garnishes:
cubed avocado, sliced radishes, lime wedges and cilantro

Serves **6.**
Hands-On Time: **30 Minutes.**
Total Time: **50 Minutes.**

INSTRUCTIONS

Season chicken with oregano, ¾ tsp salt and black pepper. Set aside.

In a saucepan, place dried chiles and cover with water (at least 1 cup). Bring to a boil, reduce to a simmer and cook for about 10 minutes, or until very soft.

To a blender, transfer chiles with ¾ cup liquid from saucepan and add onion, garlic, cumin, cloves and ½ tsp salt; purée until smooth.

In a large saucepan on medium, heat oil. Pour purée into pan and reduce to medium-low. Cook, uncovered, stirring frequently, until thickened, about 10 minutes. Add broth, beans, corn and chicken. Cover and simmer until chicken is tender and cooked through, about 10 minutes. Season with additional salt, as needed. Serve with suggested garnishes (if using).

Nutrition Information Per serving (⅙ of soup): Calories: 369, Total Fat: 13.5 g, Sat. Fat: 3 g, Monounsaturated Fat: 7 g, Polyunsaturated Fat: 3 g, Carbs: 24 g, Fiber: 4 g, Sugars: 1 g, Protein: 37 g, Sodium: 811 mg, Cholesterol: 142 mg

Walnut-Crusted Shrimp
with Roasted Red Pepper Dip

INGREDIENTS

½ cup	whole-wheat panko bread crumbs
⅓ cup	raw unsalted walnuts
1 tbsp	packed fresh rosemary leaves
¼ tsp	fresh ground black pepper
¼ tsp	sea salt
¼ cup	arrowroot starch
1 large	egg, beaten
1 lb	fresh or frozen and thawed peeled and deveined shrimp (16 to 20 per lb), with or without tails

Dip

1 large	red bell pepper
1 large	clove garlic
2 tbsp	plain yogurt
1½ tbsp	unsweetened raisins
1 tbsp	balsamic vinegar
1 tsp	dried basil
¼ tsp	red pepper flakes
¼ tsp	sea salt

Serves **4.**
Hands-On Time: **30 Minutes.**
Total Time: **45 Minutes.**

INSTRUCTIONS

Roast bell pepper: Over a grill on medium-high or a medium gas flame, roast bell pepper for about 10 minutes, turning every few minutes until all sides are charred and pepper is soft. Transfer to a heat-proof bowl, cover with plastic wrap and set aside to cool. When bell pepper is cool enough to handle, rub charred skins off and remove seeds. Coarsely chop.

Prepare dip: To a small food processor, add bell pepper along with remaining dip ingredients. Process for 15 to 30 seconds to form a chunky sauce. Set aside until ready to serve.

Preheat oven to 400°F. Place a wire rack on top of a baking sheet and mist with cooking spray.

In a small food processor, combine panko, walnuts, rosemary, black pepper and ¼ tsp salt. Pulse until walnuts are finely ground. Pour mixture into a medium, rimmed baking dish. Onto a large plate, pour arrowroot. In a small bowl, add egg.

Working a few shrimp at a time, dredge shrimp in arrowroot and shake off excess, then dip in egg and then in walnut mixture, turning to coat. Place on wire rack and repeat with remaining shrimp. Mist shrimp with cooking spray. Bake for 8 to 10 minutes, until shrimp are just beginning to turn opaque. Turn shrimp and switch to broiler setting on high; cook for 2 to 3 minutes more, until tops are lightly browned and shrimp are opaque throughout. Serve with dip.

Nutrition Information Per serving (4 to 5 shrimp and 2 tbsp sauce): Calories: 278, Total Fat: 8 g, Sat. Fat: 1 g, Monounsaturated Fat: 2 g, Polyunsaturated Fat: 5 g, Carbs: 25 g, Fiber: 2.5 g, Sugars: 8 g, Protein: 28 g, Sodium: 412 mg, Cholesterol: 230 mg

No-Cook Zoodles
with Wakame Pesto

Wakame seaweed's emerald green color and tender texture make it an unexpectedly stellar stand-in for basil in this nutrient-dense twist on pesto pasta. You'll need a spiralizer to cut the noodles into long pasta-like strands, but if you don't have one, you can use a julienne peeler.

INGREDIENTS

2 large	zucchini (about 1½ lb total), trimmed
½ tsp + ⅛ tsp	sea salt, divided
¼ cup	dried wakame seaweed
3 tbsp	chopped roasted unsalted cashews, divided
2 tbsp	nutritional yeast
3 tbsp	fresh lemon juice
1	clove garlic, roughly chopped
¼ cup	extra-virgin olive oil
1 cup	chopped vine-ripened or cherry tomatoes
½ tsp	ground black pepper

Serves **4.**
Hands-On Time: **25 Minutes.**
Total Time: **40 Minutes.**

INSTRUCTIONS

Working 1 piece at a time, secure zucchini into a spiralizer and turn crank to create long ribbons. In a bowl, toss noodles with 1/8 tsp salt and transfer to a colander for 15 to 20 minutes to drain excess liquid.

Meanwhile, in a small bowl, add wakame and enough cold water to cover. Soak for 5 minutes, or according to package directions. Reserving 2 tbsp soaking liquid, drain wakame.

In a food processor or blender, pulse wakame, reserved soaking liquid, 2 tbsp cashews, yeast, lemon juice, garlic and remaining ½ tsp salt, stopping to scrape down side of bowl, until cashews are finely chopped. With motor running, slowly drizzle in oil and blend until smooth. Set aside.

Arrange noodles on a large tray lined with a clean, dry towel. Cover with a second towel and gently pat to absorb any excess water. In a large bowl, gently toss together zucchini, wakame mixture, tomato and pepper. Sprinkle with remaining 1 tbsp cashews.

Nutrition Information Per serving (¼ of recipe): Calories: 219, Total Fat: 18 g, Sat. Fat: 3 g, Monounsaturated Fat: 13 g, Polyunsaturated Fat: 2 g, Carbs: 12 g, Fiber: 3 g, Sugars: 5 g, Protein: 5.5 g, Sodium: 418 mg, Cholesterol: 0 mg

FREE RADICAL FIGHTERS: As a lower-carb substitute for whole-wheat noodles, zucchini contains several sources of free radical-fighting antioxidants including beta-carotene and vitamin C, both of which are essential for optimal functioning of the immune system.

Thai Kabocha Squash Soup

Kabocha, also called Japanese pumpkin, has a delectably sweet, creamy flesh. Slow-roasting this squash really brings out maximum flavor. If kabocha is not available in your area, feel free to substitute an equal weight of acorn squash. Although acorn squash won't be as sweet, you can add a few drops of maple syrup to the mix to make up for it. Do add in all the toppings, though, which provide great flavor and texture to the soup.

INGREDIENTS

1 3-lb	kabocha squash, quartered and seeds removed (***TIP:*** *Alternatively, replace with an equal weight of acorn squash. If using extra-small acorn, halve them instead of quartering.*)
1-inch piece	ginger, peeled and thinly sliced
1	yellow onion, peeled and sliced
4 cups	low-sodium vegetable or chicken broth, divided
¾ cup	coconut milk + additional for finishing
2 tbsp	red curry paste
1 tsp	sea salt
2	limes, cut into thirds
	handful fresh mint leaves (sliced, if desired)
2	red chiles, sliced, optional

Serves **6.**
Hands-On Time: **25 Minutes.**
Total Time: **2 Hours.**

INSTRUCTIONS

Preheat oven to 350°F. In a large roasting pan, place squash cut side up. Divide ginger slices evenly among squash cavities. Arrange onion around squash. Pour 2 cups broth in the pan and cover tightly with foil. Bake for 1 hour, 30 minutes, until squash is very tender.

Set vegetables aside until cool enough to handle. Scoop squash flesh from skins and transfer to a large pot; discard skins. To pot, add onions and, if desired, ginger (adding the ginger slices will add a stronger ginger flavor to your soup) and cooking liquid from pan.

Add remaining 2 cups broth, milk, curry paste and salt. Stir and bring to a boil; reduce heat and simmer for 10 minutes. With an immersion blender or upright blender, purée until smooth. (***TIP:*** *If using an upright blender, remove plastic stopper in lid and cover with a towel for steam to escape*.) Divide among bowls; top each with an additional drizzle of milk, lime juice, mint and chiles (if using).

Nutrition Information Per serving (⅙ OF SOUP): Calories: 184, Total Fat: 8 g, Sat. Fat: 7 g, Monounsaturated Fat: 1 g, Polyunsaturated Fat: 0 g, Carbs: 24 g, Fiber: 4 g, Sugars: 9 g, Protein: 7 g, Sodium: 512 mg, Cholesterol: 0 mg

Persian-Style Chicken Stew
with Walnuts & Pomegranate Molasses

INGREDIENTS

8 oz	pomegranate juice
1 tbsp	raw honey
1 tsp	fresh lemon juice
½ tsp + ⅛ tsp	sea salt, divided
¾ cup	unsalted raw walnut pieces (3 oz)
2 tbsp	extra-virgin olive oil
1¼ lb	boneless, skinless chicken breasts, cut into 2-inch cubes
2 tbsp	white whole-wheat flour
Pinch	ground black pepper
1	yellow onion, chopped
3	cloves garlic, minced
1 tsp	ground turmeric
½ tsp	each ground cinnamon and nutmeg
2 cups	low-sodium chicken broth
⅓ cup	chopped fresh flat-leaf parsley
½ cup	pomegranate seeds

Makes **5 cups.**
Hands-On Time: **30 Minutes.**
Total Time: **1 Hour, 15 Minutes.**

INSTRUCTIONS

Prepare pomegranate molasses: In a small saucepan, bring pomegranate juice, honey, lemon juice and pinch salt to a boil. Reduce heat to a simmer, stirring occasionally, until reduced to ⅓ cup, about 40 minutes. Set aside.

Meanwhile, in a small skillet on medium, toast walnuts until starting to brown. Grind in a food processor to small crumbs. Set aside.

In a Dutch oven on medium, heat oil. Toss chicken with flour and pinch each salt and pepper. Cook chicken in batches until lightly browned, 3 to 4 minutes each side. Transfer to a plate.

To same pan, add onions and sauté until soft and light golden, about 8 to 10 minutes. (**NOTE:** *Add a splash of oil or water to pan if it becomes dry*.) Add garlic, turmeric, cinnamon, nutmeg and remaining ½ tsp salt and cook for 30 seconds, until fragrant.

Add broth, pomegranate molasses and walnuts. Bring to a boil. Reduce heat and simmer, adding chicken and any juices back into stew, for 15 minutes, until chicken is cooked through and flavors are blended.

Sprinkle portions with parsley and pomegranate seeds. (**NOTE:** *Three servings are used in Meal Plan; freeze remaining for future use.*)

Nutrition Information Per serving (1¼ cups): Calories: 466, Total Fat: 26 g, Sat. Fat: 3 g, Monounsaturated Fat: 8.5 g, Polyunsaturated Fat: 12 g, Carbs: 22 g, Fiber: 3 g, Sugars: 11 g, Protein: 35 g, Sodium: 495 mg, Cholesterol: 91 mg

Orange-Scented Asparagus & Beef Stir-Fry

INGREDIENTS

2	oranges
2 tbsp	coconut oil, divided
1 lb	boneless beef sirloin, cut into bite-size strips
1 lb	asparagus, fresh or frozen and thawed, trimmed and cut into 2-inch pieces
1 8-oz	package sliced shiitake mushrooms
1	sweet onion, sliced
2 tsp	grated or minced fresh ginger
2	cloves garlic, minced
2 tsp	arrowroot starch
½ cup	sliced unsalted almonds, toasted

Serves **4.**
Hands-On Time: **20 Minutes.**
Total Time: **30 Minutes.**

INSTRUCTIONS

Remove 1 tsp zest and squeeze 2/3 cup juice from oranges; set aside. In a wok or extra-large skillet, heat 1 tbsp oil on high. Add beef; cook and stir 3 to 4 minutes or until desired doneness. Remove beef from wok.

Add remaining 1 tbsp oil to wok. Add asparagus, mushrooms and onion and cook, stirring, 5 minutes or until crisp-tender. Add ginger and garlic; cook, stirring, 1 minute more.

In a small bowl, stir together orange zest, juice and arrowroot until smooth. Return beef to wok; reduce heat to medium. Stir orange mixture into wok and cook for 2 minutes or until sauce is slightly thickened. Sprinkle with almonds.

Nutrition Information Per serving (¼ of stir-fry): Calories: 438, Total Fat: 27.5 g, Sat. Fat: 12 g, Monounsaturated Fat: 10 g, Polyunsaturated Fat: 2 g, Carbs: 21 g, Fiber: 5 g, Sugars: 10 g, Protein: 29 g, Sodium: 80 mg, Cholesterol: 85 mg

NOTE: If following our Meal Plan, refrigerate leftovers.

Quinoa-Stuffed Acorn Squash
with Walnuts & Cranberries

INGREDIENTS

2 medium to large	acorn squashes, halved and seeded
¼ cup	olive oil, divided
2 pinches	each sea salt and ground black pepper, divided
½ cup	quinoa, rinsed
1	yellow onion, diced
2 tbsp	apple cider vinegar
2 tbsp	raw honey
4 tsp	fresh lime juice
1 tbsp	Dijon mustard
½ tsp	ground cayenne pepper, optional
2 cups	spinach, finely chopped
½ cup	naturally sweetened dried cranberries, chopped
½ cup	raw unsalted walnuts, chopped

Serves **4.**
Hands-On Time: **30 Minutes.**
Total Time: **1 Hour, 20 Minutes.**

INSTRUCTIONS

Preheat oven to 350°F. Cut a little bit off the end of each squash half, if needed, to help it stand cut side up. Lightly coat squash with 1 tbsp oil, sprinkle with pinch each salt and pepper and place cut side down on a large baking sheet. Bake for 40 minutes.

Meanwhile, cook quinoa: In a small saucepan, bring quinoa and ¾ cup water to a boil. Reduce heat to low, cover and simmer for 10 minutes. Remove from heat; fluff with a fork.

Meanwhile, in a small skillet on medium, heat 1 tbsp oil. Add onion and cook until softened and starting to turn golden, 4 to 6 minutes.

In a large bowl, whisk together remaining 2 tbsp oil, vinegar, honey, lime juice, mustard, cayenne pepper (if using), and remaining pinch each salt and pepper. Add quinoa, onion, spinach, cranberries and walnuts; toss to coat.

Spoon one-quarter of quinoa mixture into each squash cavity, pressing to fit.

Arrange squash halves on baking sheet and bake for 15 minutes at 350°F or until squash is soft and filling is hot.

Nutrition Information Per serving (1 stuffed acorn half): Calories: 475, Total Fat: 23 g, Sat. Fat: 3 g, Monounsaturated Fat: 11 g, Polyunsaturated Fat: 8 g, Carbs: 65 g, Fiber: 8 g, Sugars: 20 g, Protein: 8 g, Sodium: 124 mg, Cholesterol: 0 mg

Chicken Adobo
with Orange & Wilted Spinach

INGREDIENTS

1 14.5-oz	can unsalted diced tomatoes, drained
1 cup	apple cider vinegar
3	cloves garlic, minced
1 tsp	paprika
¼ tsp	red pepper flakes
2	bay leaves
8	skinless, boneless chicken thighs
3 tbsp	extra-virgin olive oil, divided
¼ cup	coarsely chopped yellow onion
10 oz	baby spinach
1 large	orange, peeled and sectioned

Serves **4.**
Hands-On Time: **20 Minutes.**
Total Time: **30 Minutes.**

INSTRUCTIONS

Prepare sauce: In a large skillet, stir together tomatoes, vinegar, garlic, paprika, pepper flakes and bay leaves. Add chicken, covering with sauce; bring to a boil. Reduce heat, cover and simmer 8 minutes. Remove chicken and pat dry with paper towels; set aside. Increase heat to medium-high; cook 10 minutes or until the sauce is slightly reduced.

Meanwhile, in another large skillet, heat 2 tbsp oil on medium. Carefully add chicken and onion. Cook until an instant-read thermometer inserted into chicken reads 165°F, turning chicken once and stirring onion as needed to avoid burning. Remove chicken and onion; cover to keep warm. Add remaining 1 tbsp oil to same skillet. Add spinach; cook just until wilted. Stir in orange sections.

Remove bay leaves from sauce and discard. Divide spinach among plates; add chicken and onion. Spoon sauce over chicken.

Nutrition Information Per serving (2 thighs with spinach and sauce): Calories: 338, Total Fat: 16 g, Sat. Fat: 3 g, Monounsaturated Fat: 10 g, Polyunsaturated Fat: 2 g, Carbs: 14 g, Fiber: 4 g, Sugars: 7 g, Protein: 30 g, Sodium: 198 mg, Cholesterol: 130 mg

Mexican Chicken Stuffed Peppers

INGREDIENTS

2 tbsp	extra-virgin olive oil
½ cup	chopped yellow onion
4	cloves garlic, minced
1	jalapeño or Serrano chile pepper, seeded and chopped
2 lb	ground chicken or turkey
1 14.5-oz	can unsalted fire-roasted diced tomatoes, with juices
½ cup	chopped fresh cilantro, divided
4	red, yellow and/or orange bell peppers
	lime wedges

Seasoning

1 tbsp	cumin seeds
4 tsp	paprika
1 tbsp	granulated garlic
1 tsp	dried oregano
½–1 tsp	ground cayenne pepper, optional
½ tsp	ground cinnamon
¼ tsp	ground saffron

Serves **4.**
Hands-On Time: **30 Minutes.**
Total Time: **40 Minutes.**

INSTRUCTIONS

Prepare seasoning: In a small dry skillet on medium-low, toast cumin seeds for 1 to 2 minutes, until fragrant, shaking skillet occasionally. Remove from heat; cool 2 minutes. Transfer seeds to a spice grinder; grind to a powder. Transfer cumin to a small bowl and stir in remaining seasoning ingredients.

In a large skillet on medium, heat oil. Add onion, garlic, and chile; cook, stirring, 2 minutes. Add chicken; cook until no longer pink. Sprinkle with 2 tbsp seasoning mixture (reserve remaining mixture for use in Meal Plan); stir well. Stir in tomatoes and bring to a boil. Reduce heat; then simmer, uncovered, 5 to 7 minutes or until most of the liquid has evaporated. Stir in ¼ cup cilantro.

Meanwhile, cut bell peppers in half vertically (from stems to bottoms). Remove and discard stems, seeds and membranes. In a large pot, blanch peppers in boiling water, 2 to 3 minutes or just until tender; drain. Fill peppers with chicken mixture.

For each serving, arrange 2 pepper halves on a plate. Sprinkle with remaining ¼ cup cilantro and serve with lime wedges.

Nutrition Information Per serving (2 stuffed pepper halves): Calories: 474, Total Fat: 26 g, Sat. Fat: 6 g, Monounsaturated Fat: 14 g, Polyunsaturated Fat: 4 g, Carbs: 18 g, Fiber: 4 g, Sugars: 7 g, Protein: 42.5 g, Sodium: 157 mg, Cholesterol: 195 mg

NOTE: Refrigerate 1 serving and freeze 2 servings; thaw and reheat when called for. Save extra spice mixture in an airtight container for use in the Meal Plan.

Braised Beef
with Caramelized Onions & Greens Chiffonade

Turnips stand in as a less-starchy substitute for potatoes in this classic dish, while caramelized onions add a rich depth of flavor with the help of a little healthy fat. And don't be afraid to tweak the dish to your liking: If you'd prefer a more stew-like meal, add more broth. In search of a flavorful gravy? Simply reduce the cooking liquid and serve over top!

INGREDIENTS

1 lb	lean beef stew meat
¼ tsp	sea salt + additional, to taste
½ tsp	ground black pepper + additional, to taste
1 tbsp	olive oil
1	yellow onion, thinly sliced
3½ cups	low-sodium beef broth, divided
4	carrots, peeled and halved (if small) or sliced ½ inch thick on the diagonal
1 large	turnip, cubed
5	cloves garlic, chopped
1 large	rosemary sprig
1 small	bunch turnip greens (**TIP:** If you have a hard time finding turnip greens, substitute chard.
	chopped fresh flat-leaf parsley for garnish

Serves **4.**
Hands-On Time: **30 Minutes.**
Total Time: **2 Hours, 30 Minutes.**

INSTRUCTIONS

Pat beef dry with paper towel and season with salt and pepper. In a large Dutch oven or heavy pot, heat oil on medium-high. Working in batches, sear beef in pot, browning well on all sides, for about 8 minutes. (**NOTE:** *By working in batches, you'll avoid overcrowding.*) Transfer to a plate and cover to keep warm.

Reduce heat to low, add onion to pot and cook for 15 to 20 minutes, until caramelized and golden, stirring occasionally. Stir in ½ cup broth and increase heat to bring to a boil, scraping browned bits from bottom of pot with a wooden spoon.

Stir in carrots, turnip, garlic, rosemary, beef and remaining 3 cups broth. Return to a boil; reduce heat to low and simmer, partially covered, for 2 hours, until beef is very tender.

About 5 minutes before beef is done, prepare greens chiffonade: Wash greens well and remove and discard stems. Stack greens and thinly slice crosswise into strips, about ¼ inch thick.

Remove rosemary and discard. Stir in greens and season with additional salt and pepper. Garnish with parsley.

Nutrition Information Per serving (3 oz beef and 2 cups vegetable-broth mixture): Calories: 310, Total Fat: 12 g, Sat. Fat: 3.5 g, Monounsaturated Fat: 6 g, Polyunsaturated Fat: 1 g, Carbs: 19 g, Fiber: 5 g, Sugars: 8 g, Protein: 32 g, Sodium: 370 mg, Cholesterol: 65 mg

A CANCER-FIGHTING FOOD: Turnips and turnip greens contain isothiocyanates, phytochemicals found in cruciferous veggies (others include broccoli, cauliflower, kale and radish) that are responsible for the flavor of these familial foods and have also been found to have cancer risk-reducing effects.

Skillet Chicken
with Tomatoes, Fennel & Fresh Thyme

If your family's main complaint about boneless, skinless chicken breast is that it's dry, then braising may be your answer! The slow-and-low technique keeps meat moist.

INGREDIENTS

4 4-oz	boneless, skinless chicken breasts
Pinch	sea salt
½ tsp	ground black pepper
1 tbsp	olive oil
1	yellow onion, diced
4 large	cloves garlic, minced
¼ tsp	red pepper flakes + additional to taste
1 large	fennel root, cored and thinly sliced
2 cups	sliced cremini mushrooms
1¾ cups	boxed or jarred unsalted crushed tomatoes
2 tsp	dried oregano
2 large	sprigs fresh thyme
¼ cup	pitted and chopped Kalamata olives, optional
	fresh oregano leaves and chopped fresh flat-leaf parsley for garnish, optional

Serves **4.**
Hands-On Time: **10 Minutes.**
Total Time: **25 Minutes.**

INSTRUCTIONS

Pat chicken dry with paper towel and season with salt and black pepper. In a large braiser or heavy skillet, heat oil on medium-high. Add chicken and sear for 2 minutes per side, until lightly browned. Transfer to a plate and keep warm.

Reduce heat to medium, add onion and cook, stirring, until softened, about 3 minutes. Add garlic and pepper flakes and cook for 1 minute, stirring. Stir in fennel, mushrooms, tomatoes, oregano and thyme. Return chicken to braiser, spooning vegetables and sauce over top. Cover and simmer for 12 to 15 minutes, until chicken's juices run clear and no pink remains. Remove and discard thyme.

Divide mixture among plates, dividing evenly. If using, top with olives, oregano and parsley.

Nutrition Information Per serving (1 chicken breast and 1¼ cups vegetable sauce): Calories: 260, Total Fat: 9 g, Sat. Fat: 1.5 g, Monounsaturated Fat: 5 g, Polyunsaturated Fat: 1 g, Carbs: 20 g, Fiber: 5 g, Sugars: 3 g, Protein: 27 g, Sodium: 380 mg, Cholesterol: 65 mg

KEEP IT COVERED: Make sure ingredients are partially—one-quarter to one-third—submerged in cooking liquid, and use a tight-fitting lid to concentrate flavors and keep liquid from cooking off.

Chicken Pot Pie
with Chive Biscuits

Rich and satisfying classic chicken pot pie filling is topped with quick homemade biscuits in this family favorite.

INGREDIENTS

4	6-oz boneless, skinless chicken breasts
1 tsp	ground black pepper
½ tsp	each sea salt and dried thyme
4 small	redskin potatoes, scrubbed and finely chopped
2	carrots, peeled and diced
2	stalks celery, thinly sliced
2 tbsp	organic unsalted butter
2	leeks, halved lengthwise and thinly sliced (white and light green parts only) (**TIP:** *To clean leeks, slice lengthwise and rinse the dirt out under warm running water, separating the segments to allow the water through.*)
2 tbsp	white whole-wheat flour
1 cup	low-sodium chicken broth
1 cup	frozen peas, thawed
½ cup	whole milk
1 tbsp	potato starch
1 tsp	fresh thyme leaves

Biscuits

1½ cups	white whole-wheat flour + additional for dusting
2 tsp	baking powder
¼ tsp	sea salt
¼ cup	organic unsalted butter, well chilled
½ cup	whole milk
2 tbsp	chopped fresh chives

Serves **8.**
Hands-On Time: **35 Minutes.**
Total Time: **4 Hours, 35 Minutes.**

INSTRUCTIONS

To a 5-qt slow cooker, add chicken and season with pepper, ½ tsp salt and dried thyme. Add potatoes, carrots and celery.

Prepare sauce: In a large saucepan on medium-high, melt 2 tbsp butter. Add leeks and cook, stirring constantly until slightly softened, about 1 minute. Add 2 tbsp flour and cook, stirring constantly until golden, about 1 minute. Whisk in broth and cook, stirring constantly until slightly thickened, about 1 minute more. Add sauce to slow cooker, stirring to evenly distribute. Cover and cook on low for 3½ to 4½ hours, or until potatoes are tender and chicken is no longer pink inside. (**NOTE:** *Check chicken and potatoes after 3½ hours; if chicken is still pink inside, cook for 1 more hour.*)

Remove chicken and transfer to a cutting board; shred using 2 forks. Return chicken to slow cooker and add peas. In a small bowl, whisk together ½ cup milk and potato starch until no lumps remain. Add to slow cooker and stir to distribute evenly. Replace lid and continue cooking for an additional 30 minutes.

Just after adding milk mixture to slow cooker, prepare biscuits: Preheat oven to 400°F. Line a baking sheet with parchment paper. In a food processor, pulse 1½ cups flour, baking powder and ¼ tsp salt until well combined. Add ¼ cup chilled butter and pulse until a fine crumb is formed, about 10 pulses. Through the feed tube of processor, stream in ½ cup milk and process until a ball of dough forms. Turn dough out onto a lightly floured surface and knead until no longer sticky; knead in chives. Press dough into an oval shape about the same size as the surface of your slow-cooker lid, about ¼-inch thick. Cut dough into 8 equal parts and place on prepared baking sheet. Bake until golden, 15 to 18 minutes. Top each serving of chicken mixture with 1 biscuit. Garnish with fresh thyme.

Nutrition Information Per serving (1 cup chicken mixture and 1 biscuit): Calories: 387, Total Fat: 13 g, Sat. Fat: 7 g, Monounsaturated Fat: 3 g, Polyunsaturated Fat: 1 g, Carbs: 40 g, Fiber: 6 g, Sugars: 5 g, Protein: 27 g, Sodium: 434 mg, Cholesterol: 88 mg

Cheesy Italian Eggplant Casserole

A quick and easy take on eggplant Parmigiana, our version skips breading and frying the eggplant while still oozing with saucy, cheesy goodness. Try serving alongside simple tossed and steamed veggies topped with shaved Parmesan for a complete meal.

INGREDIENTS

1 oz	Parmesan cheese, grated
1 cup	reduced-fat or whole-milk ricotta cheese
1 cup	reduced-fat or whole-milk cottage cheese
3	cloves garlic, peeled
1	egg
½ cup	packed fresh basil leaves + additional basil leaves for garnish
¼ tsp	ground black pepper
3 cups	all-natural jarred marinara sauce
1 large	eggplant, trimmed and sliced into ¼-inch rounds

Serves **6.**
Hands-On Time: **20 Minutes.**
Total Time: **6 Hours, 20 Minutes.**

INSTRUCTIONS

In a food processor, process cheeses, garlic, egg, ½ cup basil and pepper until combined and smooth.

Mist a 5- to 6-qt slow cooker with cooking spray. Spread a thin layer of marinara (about ⅓ cup) over bottom of slow cooker. Arrange one-third of eggplant slices over sauce, overlapping edges. Spread half of cheese mixture over eggplant and then spoon one-third of remaining marinara evenly over top. Repeat with another one-third of eggplant, half of cheese mixture and one-third of sauce, and finish with remaining one-third of eggplant and sauce.

Cover and cook on low for 6 to 8 hours. (**TIP:** If casserole is still watery, cook on high, uncovered, for an additional 10 minutes.) Garnish with additional basil.

Nutrition Information Per serving (⅙ of casserole): Calories: 165, Total Fat: 6 g, Sat. Fat: 2.5 g, Monounsaturated Fat: 1 g, Polyunsaturated Fat: 0.5 g, Carbs: 16 g, Fiber: 4 g, Sugars: 10 g, Protein: 14 g, Sodium: 451 mg, Cholesterol: 53 mg

KEEP THE SKIN ON: Eggplant's skin contains a powerful compound called nasunin that works as an antioxidant, protecting both your heart and brain from free-radical damage.

Tuscan Turkey & White Bean Chili

This satisfying chili boasts classic flavors such as thyme, oregano and basil. Grilled corn lends the dish a modern flair, but frozen corn kernels work just as well if you want to save time.

INGREDIENTS

1 tbsp	olive oil
1½ lb	ground turkey breast
4	cloves garlic, coarsely chopped
1	yellow onion, coarsely chopped
12 mini	redskin potatoes, scrubbed and halved
5	sprigs fresh thyme
1	red bell pepper, coarsely chopped
2 cups	low-sodium chicken or vegetable broth
1¼ cups	dried navy beans, soaked in water for 24 hours (**TIP:** *If you don't have time to soak beans for 24 hours, boil them for 1 hour, until al dente, then drain and set aside.*)
1 cup	tomato purée (passata)
1½ tsp	Italian seasoning
¼ tsp	each dried oregano, red pepper flakes and ground black pepper
3	ears corn or 2 cups frozen and thawed corn kernels
¼ cup	thinly sliced fresh basil leaves
3 tbsp	freshly grated Parmesan cheese, optional

Serves **6.**
Hands-On Time: **50 Minutes.**
Total Time: **3 Hours, 50 Minutes.***
*Plus soaking time.

INSTRUCTIONS

In a large skillet on medium, heat oil. Add turkey and cook, stirring frequently, until beginning to brown, about 10 minutes. Add garlic and onion, stir and cook for 5 minutes, until softened.

Transfer mixture to a 4- to 6-qt slow cooker. Add potatoes, thyme, bell pepper, broth, beans, tomato purée, Italian seasoning, oregano, pepper flakes and black pepper; stir. Cover and cook on high for about 3 hours, until potatoes are tender.

Meanwhile, if using corn cobs, heat indoor grill or grill pan on medium and lightly char corn all over, about 10 minutes. When cool enough to handle, shave kernels from cob. Set aside. Just before serving, stir corn into stew and remove and discard thyme sprigs. Garnish with basil and cheese (if using).

Nutrition Information Per serving (1½ cups): Calories: 420, Total Fat: 5 g, Sat. Fat: 1 g, Monounsaturated Fat: 2 g, Polyunsaturated Fat: 1 g, Carbs: 53 g, Fiber: 14 g, Sugars: 7 g, Protein: 41 g, Sodium: 110 mg, Cholesterol: 55 mg

FIGHT FREE RADICALS: This dish is packed with more than 60% of your daily value (DV) of vitamin C per serving. The water-soluble vitamin also functions as an antioxidant, helping protect the body's cells from free radical damage.

Mexican-Style Chicken Soup

Just 15 minutes of Hands-On Time is all it takes to prep this subtly spicy and exotic south-of-the border soup.

INGREDIENTS

10 oz	grape tomatoes, halved
1	each green and red bell pepper, chopped
1 cup	diced yellow onion
1	zucchini or yellow summer squash, thinly sliced
2	cloves garlic, minced
1 lb	boneless, skinless chicken breasts (2 8-oz breasts)
1 tbsp	chile powder
2 tsp	ground cumin
1 tsp	dried oregano
½ cup	chopped fresh cilantro + additional for garnish
1½ tbsp	fresh lime juice + additional lime wedges for garnish, optional
2 tbsp	extra-virgin olive oil
½ tsp	sea salt
2 cups	cooked brown rice
½ cup	sour cream, optional

Serves **4.**
Hands-On Time: **15 Minutes.**
Total Time: **3 Hours, 15 Minutes.**

INSTRUCTIONS

Mist a 3- to 3½-qt slow cooker with cooking spray. Add tomatoes, bell peppers, onion, squash, garlic and ¼ cup water; stir gently. Arrange chicken on top and mist with cooking spray.

In a small bowl, combine chile powder, cumin and oregano. Sprinkle evenly over top of contents of slow cooker. Cover and cook until chicken is no longer pink in center, 3 hours on high or 6 hours on low.

Turn off slow cooker. Remove chicken and transfer to a cutting board. Stir cilantro, lime juice, oil and salt into tomato-pepper mixture. Pull chicken apart into large pieces, or shred coarsely with 2 forks. Return chicken to slow cooker, gently stir and let mixture sit, uncovered, for 15 minutes, until thickened slightly. Divide rice among shallow soup bowls and spoon tomato-chicken mixture over top, dividing evenly. If desired, top with additional cilantro. If using, serve with sour cream and lime wedges.

Nutrition Information Per serving (1¼ cups tomato-chicken mixture and ½ cup rice): Calories: 366, Total Fat: 10.5 g, Sat. Fat: 2 g, Monounsaturated Fat: 6 g, Polyunsaturated Fat: 2 g, Carbs: 36.5 g, Fiber: 6 g, Sugars: 7 g, Protein: 32 g, Sodium: 354 mg, Cholesterol: 66 mg

Slow-Cooker Beef & Black Bean Chili
with Corn Bread

There's no need to soak the beans overnight for this easy slow-cooker version of an all-American favorite. The corn bread recipe makes more than you'll need, but here's a tip: Heat up the leftovers and drizzle with honey for a superfast breakfast the next day.

INGREDIENTS

1 lb	extra-lean ground beef
2 tsp	olive oil
1	yellow onion, chopped
1 large	red bell pepper, chopped
3 tbsp	unsalted tomato paste
1 tbsp	chile powder
2 tsp	cumin seeds
1 tsp	dried oregano
3 cups	low-sodium beef broth, divided
1 cup	dried black beans, rinsed
2 tbsp	unsweetened cocoa powder
¾ tsp	sea salt

Corn Bread

1 cup	whole-grain yellow cornmeal, divided
2 tbsp	organic unsalted butter
¾ cup	whole-milk plain yogurt
1 large	egg
2 tsp	organic evaporated cane juice
1 tsp	baking powder
½ tsp	sea salt
¼ tsp	baking soda

Serves **4.**
Hands-On Time: **30 Minutes.**
Total Time: **8 Hours, 30 Minutes.**

INSTRUCTIONS

Heat a large nonstick skillet on medium. Add beef and cook, breaking up with a spoon, until browned, about 8 minutes. Drain and transfer to a 3-qt. slow cooker.

In same skillet on medium-high, heat oil. Add onion and bell pepper and sauté, stirring often, until tender, about 5 minutes. Stir in tomato paste, chile powder, cumin and oregano and cook, stirring constantly, until fragrant, about 30 seconds. Add 1 cup broth and bring to a boil, scraping up browned bits from bottom of pan.

Scrape onion mixture into slow cooker. Add remaining 2 cups broth, beans, cocoa powder and ¾ tsp salt and stir to combine. Cover and cook on low until beans are tender, 8 to 9 hours.

Prepare corn bread: Preheat oven to 425°F. Mist an 8-inch pie plate with cooking spray. In a large bowl, add ½ cup cornmeal, butter and ⅓ cup boiling water and stir until butter melts. Add yogurt and egg and stir to combine.

In a separate bowl, whisk together remaining ½ cup cornmeal, cane juice, baking powder, ½ tsp salt and baking soda. Add to yogurt mixture and stir to combine. Scrape into prepared pie plate and bake on a rimmed baking sheet until a toothpick inserted in center comes out clean, about 18 minutes. Let cool for 2 minutes. Cut into 8 wedges. Serve with chili.

Nutrition Information Per serving (¼ of chili and ⅛ of corn bread): Calories: 525, Total Fat: 18 g, Sat. Fat: 7 g, Monounsaturated Fat: 7 g, Polyunsaturated Fat: 2 g, Carbs: 54 g, Fiber: 15 g, Sugars: 8 g, Protein: 41 g, Sodium: 852 mg, Cholesterol: 113 mg

Seared Scallops
with Caponata & Roasted Cauliflower Purée

INGREDIENTS

	olive oil cooking spray
1	head cauliflower (2¼ to 2½ lb), cut into florets
½ tsp	sea salt, divided
2	large cloves garlic, unpeeled
1 tbsp	organic unsalted butter, room temperature
⅔ cup	whole milk
3 tbsp	raw unsalted pine nuts
½	red onion, chopped
12 oz	grape tomatoes, halved
¾ tsp	fresh ground black pepper, divided
¼ tsp	red pepper flakes, optional
¼ cup	unsweetened raisins
2 tbsp	red wine vinegar
4 tsp	drained and rinsed jarred capers (not salt-packed), roughly chopped
5 tbsp	chopped fresh flat-leaf parsley leaves, divided
1 lb	sea scallops, muscle removed and rinsed
4 tsp	olive oil

Serves **4.**
Hands-On Time: **40 Minutes.**
Total Time: **1 Hour.**

INSTRUCTIONS

Preheat oven to 425°F. Line a large rimmed baking sheet with foil and mist with cooking spray. Spread cauliflower on sheet and mist again. Sprinkle with ¼ tsp plus ⅛ tsp salt. Roast for 20 minutes, then toss with a spatula. To baking sheet, add garlic and continue roasting until cauliflower is browned and very tender, 15 to 20 minutes more. To a food processor, add cauliflower and butter. Remove skin from garlic and add to processor with cauliflower. Turn processor on high and slowly pour milk through the feed tube. Purée until smooth, scraping down bowl as needed.

Meanwhile, prepare caponata: Heat a large nonstick skillet on medium. Add nuts and toast, stirring frequently, until golden brown, 3 to 4 minutes, watching closely to prevent burning. Transfer to a small bowl and set aside. Mist same skillet with cooking spray and heat on medium. Add onion and cook, stirring frequently, until lightly browned and translucent, 4 to 5 minutes. Add tomatoes, remaining ⅛ tsp salt, ¼ tsp black pepper and pepper flakes (if using) and cook, stirring frequently, until tomatoes just begin to soften, 3 to 4 minutes. Reduce heat to low and add raisins, vinegar and capers. Stir until combined and heated through, 1 to 2 minutes. Remove from heat and stir in 3 tbsp parsley and nuts.

Pat scallops dry with a paper towel and sprinkle with remaining ½ tsp black pepper. Heat a large heavy skillet (such as cast iron or stainless steel) on medium-high. Working in two batches to prevent overcrowding, heat half of oil and add half of scallops. Cook until bottom sides are deep golden brown, about 3 minutes. Turn and cook until opposite sides are browned and scallops spring back slightly when pressed in center, about 2 minutes more. Transfer to a plate and cover to keep warm. Repeat with remaining half of oil and scallops.

If cauliflower and caponata have cooled down, reheat on low while scallops are cooking (transfer cauliflower to a medium saucepan). Divide cauliflower, scallops and caponata evenly among plates and sprinkle with remaining 2 tbsp parsley.

Nutrition Information Per serving (⅓ cup cauliflower purée, 3 scallops, ½ cup caponata): Calories: 297, Total Fat: 12 g, Sat. Fat: 4 g, Monounsaturated Fat: 4 g, Polyunsaturated Fat: 3 g, Carbs: 29 g, Fiber: 5 g, Sugars: 17 g, Protein: 20 g, Sodium: 646 mg, Cholesterol: 39 mg

Five-Spice Meatballs
with Rice Noodles
& Honey Lime Sauce

Baking these spiced meatballs on a rack allows the fat to drip away, which keeps them from sitting in their own juices and becoming greasy. For easy cleanup, line the baking sheet with foil to catch the drippings. Be gentle when mixing and shaping the meatballs–packing them tightly makes them too dense and tough.

INGREDIENTS

1 lb	lean ground pork, chicken or turkey
1 tbsp	peeled and grated ginger
2	cloves garlic, finely chopped
1½ tsp	Chinese five-spice powder
½ tsp	ground black pepper
¼ tsp	sea salt
3 tbsp	fresh lime juice
2 tbsp + 1 tsp	raw honey
2 tbsp	reduced-sodium tamari
4 tsp	toasted sesame oil
8 oz	brown rice pad Thai noodles
2 cups	matchstick-cut carrots
5	green onions, thinly sliced
½ cup	packed fresh cilantro, roughly chopped or whole leaves
4 tsp	black sesame seeds

Serves **4.**
Hands-On Time: **30 Minutes.**
Total Time: **50 Minutes.**

INSTRUCTIONS

Preheat oven to 350°F. Arrange an ovenproof rack on a foil-lined rimmed baking sheet; mist with cooking spray.

In a large bowl, stir together pork, ginger, garlic, five-spice powder, pepper and salt until combined. Shape into balls 2 tbsp in size, making about 20 meatballs. Arrange 1 inch apart on prepared rack. Bake, rotating baking sheet halfway through, until no longer pink inside and an instant-read thermometer reads 160°F when inserted in center, 30 to 34 minutes. (**NOTE:** *If using ground turkey or chicken, cook meatballs to an internal temperature of 165°F.*)

Meanwhile, in a small bowl, whisk together lime juice, honey, tamari and oil until combined. Set aside.

Bring a large pot of water to a boil. Add noodles and cook, stirring occasionally, for 3 minutes. Stir in carrots and cook until tender-crisp and noodles are al dente, about 2 minutes. Drain and rinse under cold water. Return to pot and heat on medium-low. Add onions and lime juice mixture and cook, stirring, until heated through, 1 to 2 minutes.

Divide noodle mixture and meatballs among bowls. Sprinkle with cilantro and seeds, dividing evenly.

Nutrition Information Per serving (1¼ cups noodle mixture and 5 meatballs): Calories: 505, Total Fat: 13 g, Sat. Fat: 3 g, Monounsaturated Fat: 5 g, Polyunsaturated Fat: 3.5 g, Carbs: 67 g, Fiber: 7 g, Sugars: 15 g, Protein: 34 g, Sodium: 605 mg, Cholesterol: 72 mg

Herb-Stuffed Turkey Breast
with Apple Cider Pan Sauce

The stuffing in this rolled-up turkey breast is a lot like traditional stuffing, but instead of being in the cavity of the bird, it's in a ribbon throughout the meat. So each no-carving-necessary slice has a spiral of bready, herb-laced goodness.

INGREDIENTS

1 tbsp	each chopped fresh marjoram, thyme and sage
1½ tsp	chopped fresh rosemary
3 1-oz	slices all-natural bacon, (no added nitrates or nitrites), cut crosswise into ¼-inch strips
1 large	yellow onion, cut into ½-inch dice
2 cups	diced whole-wheat bread (½-inch dice)
½ cup	grated Parmesan cheese
1 tsp	ground black pepper, divided + additional to taste
¾ tsp	sea salt, divided + additional to taste
2 2-lb	boneless turkey breasts (2 halves, separated), skin removed
1 cup	low-sodium chicken broth
1 cup	100% apple cider or unsweetened apple juice, divided
2 tbsp	arrowroot powder dissolved in 2 tbsp cold water

Serves **10.**
Hands-On Time: **1 Hour.**
Total Time: **3 Hours.**

INSTRUCTIONS

In a small bowl, combine marjoram, thyme, sage and rosemary. Set aside.

In a medium skillet on medium, add bacon and onion and cook, stirring occasionally, for 8 to 10 minutes, until onion is translucent and very soft. To a large bowl, transfer bacon-onion mixture along with cooking juices; add bread, cheese, ½ tsp pepper, ½ tsp salt and all but 1 tbsp herb mixture. Set bread mixture and remaining herb mixture aside.

Preheat oven to 400°F. Arrange 1 turkey breast on a work surface. Using a long, thin knife, cut almost entirely in half parallel to work surface, leaving one side attached. Repeat with remaining breast. Open both breasts like a book and arrange side by side, skinned side down, with long edges overlapping by about 2 inches. Cover with plastic wrap and pound ¾ inch thick. Arrange bread mixture on turkey, leaving a ½-inch border. Starting at one short side, roll into a log. Use kitchen string to tie at 1½- to 2-inch intervals. Sprinkle with remaining 1 tbsp herb mixture, ½ tsp pepper and ¼ tsp salt.

Arrange turkey, seam side down, in a roasting pan. To roasting pan, add broth and ½ cup apple cider. Transfer to oven and immediately reduce heat to 375°F. Roast for 30 minutes.

Baste turkey with pan juices. Continue roasting and basting every 20 to 30 minutes, until an internal thermometer inserted into the centermost part of roll reads 165°F, 1¾ to 2¼ hours total cooking time. (**NOTE:** *If pan gets dry, add broth or water to maintain ¼ inch liquid. If turkey gets too browned, loosely cover with foil.*) Transfer turkey to a cutting board and let rest, loosely covered with foil, for 15 minutes.

Meanwhile, place roasting pan on stove top, straddled over 2 burners if necessary, and add remaining ½ cup apple cider. Bring to a boil on medium, scraping up any browned bits in the pan. Whisk in arrowroot-water mixture and cook until sauce is thickened and smooth, 30 to 60 seconds. Season with additional salt and pepper.

Slice turkey crosswise. Serve pan sauce on the side.

Nutrition Information Per serving (6 oz meat and stuffing and 3 tbsp pan sauce): Calories: 308, Total Fat: 8 g, Sat. Fat: 2.5 g,
Monounsaturated Fat: 2.5 g, Polyunsaturated Fat: 1 g, Carbs: 11 g, Fiber: 1 g, Sugars: 4 g, Protein: 46.5 g, Sodium: 514 mg, Cholesterol: 111 mg

Cranberry-Glazed Pork Loin Roast
with Cranberry Shallot Compote

You can't get more simply delicious than a pork loin. Here, the moist, tender meat is brushed with a tart-sweet glaze and served with a fruity compote that cooks right in the roasting pan.

INGREDIENTS

1 4-lb	boneless pork loin, trimmed
1 tsp	sea salt + additional to taste
1 tsp	ground black pepper
1 lb	shallots (16 to 18), peeled and quartered lengthwise
1½ cups	fresh or frozen cranberries
½ cup	low-sodium chicken broth
1 cup	unsweetened cranberry juice, divided
6 tbsp	organic evaporated cane juice (aka organic cane sugar)
5	each whole black peppercorns, allspice berries and cloves
1	cinnamon stick

Serves **10.**
Hands-On Time: **35 Minutes.**
Total Time: **2 Hours.**

INSTRUCTIONS

Preheat oven to 450°F. Sprinkle pork all over with salt and pepper. Arrange pork, fat side up, in a roasting pan. Arrange shallots and cranberries in pan around pork. Pour broth and ½ cup cranberry juice over shallots and cranberries. Transfer to oven, immediately reduce heat to 350°F; roast for 15 minutes.

Meanwhile, prepare glaze: In a small saucepan on medium-high, combine cane juice, peppercorns, allspice, cloves, cinnamon and remaining ½ cup cranberry juice. Bring to a boil, stirring to dissolve cane juice, and cook until mixture is reduced to ¼ cup, about 8 minutes. Strain mixture (discard whole spices); set aside.

Brush pork with cranberry glaze and continue roasting for 20 minutes. Baste with pan juices and continue roasting and basting every 20 to 30 minutes, until an internal thermometer inserted into the centermost part of roast reads 145°F, about 1½ hours total cooking time. (**NOTE:** *If pan gets dry, add more broth or water to maintain about ¼ inch liquid. If pork gets too browned, loosely cover with foil.*) Transfer pork to a cutting board and let rest, loosely covered with foil, for 15 minutes.

Meanwhile, using a slotted spoon, transfer cranberry-shallot mixture to a serving bowl and season with additional salt.

Slice pork crosswise and arrange on a serving platter. Serve cranberry-shallot compote on the side.

Nutrition Information Per serving (5½ oz meat with cranberry-shallot compote):
Calories: 460, Total Fat: 26 g, Sat. Fat: 9 g, Monounsaturated Fat: 11 g, Polyunsaturated Fat: 3 g, Carbs: 19 g, Fiber: 2 g, Sugars: 14 g, Protein: 37.5 g, Sodium: 302 mg, Cholesterol: 109 mg

Moroccan Chicken & Vegetable Soup

with Chickpea Croutons

Seasoned roasted chickpeas adorn this soup that's brimming with hearty vegetables and warming spices.

INGREDIENTS

Chickpea Croutons

1½ cups	cooked chickpeas or 1 15-oz BPA-free can, drained and rinsed, patted dry
1½ tbsp	coconut oil
Pinch	sea salt
¼ tsp	ground cumin
⅛ tsp	ground cinnamon
Pinch	ground ginger

Soup

2 tbsp	coconut oil
2	stalks celery, diced
1	carrot, diced
1	yellow onion, diced
1¼ tsp	ground turmeric
¾ tsp	each ground ginger and cinnamon
½ tsp	ground cumin
Pinch	ground black pepper
1 18-oz	jar unsalted diced tomatoes (with juices)
1 tsp	sea salt + additional to taste
2	sweet potatoes, peeled and diced (about 1 lb)
6 cups	low-sodium chicken or vegetable broth, or as needed
2 cups	diced or shredded cooked chicken
¼ cup	each chopped fresh cilantro and flat-leaf parsley
3 cups	lightly packed fresh spinach leaves
1	lemon, cut into wedges

Serves **4 to 6.**
Hands-On Time: **40 Minutes.**
Total Time: **1 Hour, 40 Minutes.**

INSTRUCTIONS

Prepare chickpeas: Preheat oven to 400°F. Place chickpeas on a parchment-lined baking sheet; remove any loose skins. Roast for 20 minutes. Add 1½ tbsp oil and pinch salt; toss. Return to oven; roast for 15 to 20 minutes more, until golden brown. (If a few pop, that's OK!)

Turn oven off. Toss chickpeas with ¼ tsp cumin, ⅛ tsp cinnamon and pinch ginger. Return to oven with door closed and heat off for 1 hour, or until crunchy. Set aside to cool.

Meanwhile, prepare soup: In a medium stockpot on medium, heat 2 tbsp oil. Add celery, carrots and onion. Cook until tender, about 6 minutes. Add turmeric, ¾ tsp each ginger and cinnamon, ½ tsp cumin and black pepper and cook 1 minute, stirring. Add tomatoes and 1 tsp salt. Cook until fragrant, about 2 minutes.

Add potatoes and broth and bring to a boil. Reduce heat to low and simmer, covered for 20 to 25 minutes, until potato is tender.

Add chicken, cilantro and parsley and heat through, 2 to 3 minutes. Add additional broth to thin out as desired; season with additional salt as needed. Stir in spinach. Top servings with chickpeas and serve with lemon wedges.

Nutrition Information Per serving (⅙ of soup) Calories: 342, Total Fat: 12 g, Sat. Fat: 8 g, Monounsaturated Fat: 2 g, Polyunsaturated Fat: 1 g, Carbs: 34 g, Fiber: 7 g, Sugars: 10 g, Protein: 25 g, Sodium: 507 mg, Cholesterol: 40 mg

BRAINY SPICE: This soup is rich in turmeric, known for its anti-inflammatory benefits. Turmeric contains a component known as curcumin, which has shown exceptional promise in improving cognition and memory. Although more research is needed, curcumin has shown promise in breaking down beta-amyloid plaques, an indication of Alzheimer's disease, in the brain.

Spicy Chipotle Butternut Squash Soup

The smokiness of dried chipotle chiles provides the perfect counterpoint to sweet butternut squash in this easy, 8-ingredient soup. If you want to go milder, use only one chile; if you like the heat, go for all three.

INGREDIENTS

1–3	dried chipotle chiles
1 4-lb	butternut squash (or 2 2-lb squashes), halved lengthwise and seeded
3 tbsp	organic unsalted butter
1 tbsp	pure maple syrup
2 small	carrots, halved crosswise
1 small	yellow onion, thinly sliced
6–7 cups	low-sodium vegetable or chicken broth, divided
1½ tsp	sea salt + additional to taste

Optional garnishes:

toasted unsalted pumpkin seeds, cilantro, Greek yogurt

Serves **6.**
Hands-On Time: **30 Minutes.**
Total Time: **2 Hours, 40 Minutes.**

INSTRUCTIONS

In a small bowl, soak chiles in warm water for 2 to 6 hours; drain.

Meanwhile, preheat oven to 350°F. In a roasting pan, place squash halves cut side up. Divide butter and maple syrup evenly between squash cavities. Arrange carrot and onion around squash. Pour 1 cup broth in pan and cover tightly with foil. Bake for 2 hours. Set aside until cool enough to handle.

Scoop squash flesh from skins and transfer to a stockpot. Add carrots, onions, cooking liquid from pan, drained chiles, 5 cups broth and salt. Stir well and bring to a boil. Reduce heat to a simmer, uncovered, for 10 minutes.

Using an immersion blender, purée soup until smooth. Add 1 cup additional broth if you prefer a thinner soup. Add additional salt as needed. Serve with optional garnishes (if using).

Nutrition Information Per serving (⅙ of soup): Calories: 229, Total Fat: 8 g, Sat. Fat: 4 g, Monounsaturated Fat: 2 g, Polyunsaturated Fat: 1 g, Carbs: 38 g, Fiber: 6 g, Sugars: 9.5 g, Protein: 8 g, Sodium: 582 mg, Cholesterol: 15 mg

A SOUP FOR SORE EYES: Winter squash like butternut are a top source of lutein and zeaxanthin, carotenoids that help protect against damage to the macula, a part of the retina. Regular intake of foods rich in these carotenoids may help protect against cataracts and age-related macular degeneration.

Seared Coriander Scallops
with Nori Brown Butter & Asparagus

Ground nori melts seamlessly into this elegant brown butter pan sauce, adding its signature earthy-salty flavor. The keys to browning butter without burning it are watching the pan carefully and swirling it often. The butter will melt and then start to foam, at which point you'll notice the color change from yellow to golden brown. Take it off the heat as soon as it starts to smell nutty.

INGREDIENTS

2	sheets toasted nori seaweed, broken into small pieces
1 tsp	sesame seeds, toasted
16 large	sea scallops (about 1½ lb total), muscle removed (**NOTE:** *For the most sustainable option, choose farmed sea scallops.*)
1 tsp	ground coriander
½ tsp	sea salt
¼ tsp	ground black pepper
5 tbsp	organic unsalted butter
4½ tsp	fresh lemon juice
1½ lb	asparagus, trimmed

Serves **4.**
Hands-On Time: **25 Minutes.**
Total Time: **25 Minutes.**

INSTRUCTIONS

In a spice grinder or small food processor, pulse nori into powder, leaving some ¼-inch pieces intact. Transfer half of the nori powder to a small bowl; stir in sesame seeds and set aside for garnish. Reserve remaining nori powder for butter mixture.

Pat scallops dry with paper towel; sprinkle with coriander, salt and pepper. Mist a large cast iron or heavy-bottomed skillet with cooking spray; heat on medium-high. Working in batches, add scallops and cook, turning once, until golden brown but still slightly translucent in centers, about 4 minutes for ½- to ¾-inch-thick scallops or 6 minutes for 1-inch-thick scallops. Transfer to a large plate; cover with foil to keep warm.

Turn off heat to skillet, leaving skillet on burner. Add butter; stir or swirl pan until melted, light brown and nutty, about 1 minute. (**TIP:** *If butter doesn't begin to brown, heat skillet on medium-low and cook until light brown and nutty.*) Stir in lemon juice and plain nori powder (without seeds). Scrape into a separate small bowl; set aside.

Meanwhile, in a steamer basket set over a saucepan of boiling water, steam asparagus until tender-crisp, 3 to 4 minutes. Divide among plates. Top with scallops, butter mixture and sesame seed mixture, dividing evenly.

Nutrition Information Per serving (¼ of recipe): Calories: 280, Total Fat: 16 g, Sat. Fat: 9 g, Monounsaturated Fat: 5 g, Polyunsaturated Fat: 1 g, Carbs: 10 g, Fiber: 2 g, Sugars: 1 g, Protein: 23 g, Sodium: 553 mg, Cholesterol: 79 mg

Pear & Almond Crumble

The humble crumble gets dressed up for the holidays with almonds and almond extract in the topping and a touch of cardamom in the whipped cream. Look for pears that are ripe but not overly so—they should be tender at the stem, but not mushy.

INGREDIENTS

3 lb	pears (6 to 8), cored and thinly sliced
1 tbsp	fresh lemon juice
6 tbsp + ½ tsp	organic evaporated cane juice (aka organic cane sugar), divided
1½ tbsp	arrowroot powder
¾ cup	whole-wheat pastry flour
¾ tsp	baking powder
½ tsp	sea salt
¼ cup	(½ stick) organic unsalted butter, chilled, cut into 6 or 8 pieces
6 tbsp	sliced unsalted almonds
⅛ tsp	pure almond extract
½ cup	heavy whipping cream (36% or more)
½ tsp	ground cardamom

Serves **10.**
Hands-On Time: **40 Minutes.**
Total Time: **1 Hour, 20 Minutes.**

INSTRUCTIONS

Preheat oven to 375°F. In a large bowl, combine pears, lemon juice and 2 tbsp cane juice. Sprinkle arrowroot over mixture and toss until evenly distributed. Transfer mixture to a 2-qt baking dish, smoothing it into an even layer. Set aside.

In another large bowl, whisk together flour, baking powder, salt and ¼ cup cane juice. Use a pastry cutter, a fork or your fingertips to work butter into flour mixture, forming heavy crumbs. Stir in almonds and almond extract. Scatter topping evenly over fruit and bake until fruit juices are bubbling and topping is browned, 40 to 45 minutes. Set aside to cool slightly.

Meanwhile, in the bowl of a stand mixer using the whisk attachment or in a large mixing bowl using a handheld electric mixer, whip cream to very soft peaks. Add cardamom and remaining ½ tsp cane juice and whip to soft peaks.

Serve crumble warm or at room temperature topped with whipped cream.

Nutrition Information Per serving (⅔ cup crumble and 1½ tbsp whipped cream): Calories: 246, Total Fat: 11 g, Sat. Fat: 6 g, Monounsaturated Fat: 4 g, Polyunsaturated Fat: 1 g, Carbs: 37 g, Fiber: 5 g, Sugars: 20 g, Protein: 2.5 g, Sodium: 129 mg, Cholesterol: 26 mg

PB & Oatmeal Cookies

These chewy, spiced cookies with creamy peanut butter, oats and dried fruit make the perfect breakfast, snack or light dessert.

INGREDIENTS

1 cup	natural creamy peanut butter
⅔ cup	coconut sugar
1 large	egg, lightly beaten
1 tsp	pure vanilla extract
½ cup	large flake oats (**NOTE:** Look for certified gluten-free oats if you're aiming to keep this recipe gluten-free.)
¼ cup	chopped unsweetened dried apples (**TIP:** *Use kitchen shears to cut apples.*)
¼ cup	unsweetened sultana raisins
1 tsp	ground cinnamon
½ tsp	ground allspice

Nutrition Information Per serving (1 cookie): Calories: 108, Total Fat: 5 g, Sat. Fat: 1 g, Monounsaturated Fat: 3 g, Polyunsaturated Fat: 1 g, Carbs: 12 g, Fiber: 1 g, Sugars: 8 g, Protein: 3 g, Sodium: 38 mg, Cholesterol: 7 mg

Makes **26 Cookies.**
Hands-On Time: **15 Minutes.**
Total Time: **25 Minutes.***
**Plus Cooling Time.*

INSTRUCTIONS

Preheat oven to 350°F. Line a large baking sheet with parchment paper.

In a large bowl, mix together peanut butter, coconut sugar, egg and vanilla until well blended.

Add oats and stir until well combined. Add apples, raisins, cinnamon and allspice; stir to combine.

Form a 1¼-inch ball and place on prepared sheet, gently flattening with your finger. Repeat with remaining dough, forming 26 balls and spacing them 1 inch apart on sheet.

Bake for 9 to 11 minutes, until just starting to brown. Remove from oven and let cool on sheet for 10 minutes. Transfer cookies to a wire rack and cool completely.

Salted Caramel Pudding

with Whipped Cream
& Chocolate Topping

Rich, velvety and with just the right amount of salt to offset its sweetness, this 25-minute dessert is a surefire win for any occasion.

INGREDIENTS

2¾ cups	whole milk, divided
2 extra-large	egg yolks
3 tbsp	tapioca starch
3 tbsp	organic unsalted butter
⅔ cup	coconut sugar
½ tsp	sea salt
1 tsp	pure vanilla extract

Garnish, optional

⅓ cup	whipping cream (35%)
2 tsp	coconut sugar
½ oz	dark chocolate (75 to 85%), finely grated

Serves **8.**
Hands-On Time: **25 Minutes.**
Total Time: **25 Minutes.**
Plus chilling time.

INSTRUCTIONS

In a medium saucepan on medium, heat 2¼ cups milk just until a small amount of steam starts to rise from the surface and small bubbles appear around the edge of the pan, 2 to 3 minutes. Do not boil.

Meanwhile, in a medium heat-proof bowl, whisk together remaining ½ cup milk, egg yolks and tapioca until well combined. While whisking constantly, slowly pour heated milk into egg mixture.

In a large saucepan on medium, melt butter. Add ⅔ cup coconut sugar and salt, stirring with a wooden spoon until sugar dissolves and mixture comes together and slides around the bottom of the pan, 30 seconds. Slowly add milk mixture while stirring constantly to combine thoroughly. Continue cooking, stirring constantly, until mixture comes to a boil, 4 to 5 minutes. Boil for 30 seconds, stirring constantly. Remove from heat and stir in vanilla. Divide among 8 ramekins or serving dishes. Cover with plastic wrap and transfer to refrigerator until set, at least 1 hour. (**TIP:** *To make these portable, pour into small Mason jars*.)

Prepare garnish (if desired): To a medium bowl, add cream and 2 tsp coconut sugar. Using a handheld electric mixer on high, beat cream until stiff peaks form. Divide whipped cream among servings and top with chocolate shavings.

Nutrition Information Per serving (3 oz pudding and 1 tbsp whipped topping): Calories: 238, Total Fat: 13 g, Sat. Fat: 7.5 g, Monounsaturated Fat: 4 g, Polyunsaturated Fat: 1 g, Carbs: 29 g, Fiber: 0 g, Sugars: 26 g, Protein: 4 g, Sodium: 171 mg, Cholesterol: 89 mg

Red Velvet Cake
with Beets & Cream Cheese Glaze

INGREDIENTS

½ cup	safflower oil + 1 tsp for greasing pan, divided
1 large	beet, peeled and chopped (3-inch diameter)
¼ cup	white vinegar
2¼ cups	light spelt flour
¼ cup	unsweetened cocoa powder
2 tsp	baking powder
1 tsp	baking soda
1 tsp	sea salt
2 large	eggs
1¼ cups	maple flakes
1 tsp	pure vanilla extract
¾ cup	whole buttermilk
¼ cup	Balkan-style plain yogurt
¼ cup	fresh orange juice
1 tbsp	apple cider vinegar
1 tsp	instant espresso powder

Glaze

2 oz	cream cheese, room temperature
2 tbsp	organic unsalted butter, room temperature
½ tsp	pure vanilla extract
2 tbsp	pure maple syrup
1½ tbsp	whole buttermilk

Makes **16 slices.**
Hands-On Time: **25 Minutes.**
Total Time: **1 Hour, 25 Minutes.***
Plus Cooling Time.

INSTRUCTIONS

Preheat oven to 350°F. Brush a 10-inch Bundt pan with 1 tsp oil.

To a small pot, add beets and white vinegar; add enough water to just cover. Bring to a simmer on medium-high and simmer until beets are tender, about 20 minutes. Drain, reserving ⅓ cup cooking water. Transfer beets and reserved cooking water into a food processor and process until very smooth, about 4 to 5 minutes.

In a large bowl, whisk together flour, cocoa powder, baking powder, baking soda and salt. (**TIP:** *Stirring with a whisk aerates the dry ingredients and breaks up any lumps. It's a quick and easy alternative to sifting.*)

In a stand mixer fitted with paddle attachment, add eggs, maple flakes, remaining ½ cup oil and 1 tsp vanilla. Beat on high until mixture is pale yellow in color. Add beet purée, ¾ cup buttermilk, yogurt, orange juice, cider vinegar and espresso powder and mix on low until combined, about 30 seconds. With mixer running on low, slowly add flour mixture, stopping to scrape down sides of bowl with a spatula if necessary. Increase speed to medium and beat for 2 minutes. Pour batter into prepared pan and bake until a toothpick comes out clean when inserted, about 40 to 50 minutes. Remove cake from oven and cool for 5 minutes in pan. Invert cake onto wire rack and allow to cool completely, about 45 minutes to 1 hour.

Meanwhile, in a medium bowl with a hand mixer set on medium, beat cream cheese, butter and ½ tsp vanilla until smooth. Add maple syrup and 1½ tbsp buttermilk and beat on low until combined. Mixture should be slightly runny. Spoon glaze over cooled cake and chill until ready to serve.

Nutrition Information Per serving (1 slice): Calories: 209, Total Fat: 11.5 g, Sat. Fat: 3 g, Monounsaturated Fat: 3 g, Polyunsaturated Fat: 5 g, Carbs: 24 g, Fiber: 2 g, Sugars: 11.5 g, Protein: 4 g, Sodium: 310 mg, Cholesterol: 33 mg

Superfood Chocolate Bar

INGREDIENTS

1 1-inch piece ginger, peeled, thinly sliced and then slivered

1 tbsp roughly chopped orange zest (**TIP:** *Use a peeler or zester to remove only the outer peel, then chop the zest.*)

1 tbsp raw honey

½ cup (3 oz) roughly chopped cocoa butter (**NOTE:** *It usually comes in large nuggets that should be chopped before measuring.*)

½ cup raw unsweetened cacao powder

3 tbsp coconut sugar

2 tbsp goji berries, roughly chopped

EQUIPMENT:

3 2-oz chocolate bar molds (**TIP:** *Molds are fairly inexpensive and can be purchased at specialty baking shops or online retailers.*)

Makes **3 2-oz Bars.**
Hands-On Time: **25 Minutes.**
Total Time: **25 Minutes.***
*Plus Chilling Time.

INSTRUCTIONS

Line a baking sheet with parchment paper. In a small saucepan, combine ginger, orange zest and 1 cup water. Bring to a boil, reduce heat to medium-low and simmer for 5 minutes. Drain, reserving ¼ cup of cooking liquid, ginger and zest in pot. Add honey, stirring to combine. Set over medium heat and cook until most of liquid has evaporated and mixture is sticky, 5 to 7 minutes. Spread mixture onto prepared sheet and cool to room temperature.

Meanwhile, fill a medium saucepan with 2 inches water and bring to a boil; turn heat off. To a heat-proof bowl, add cocoa butter, cacao powder and coconut sugar, and place bowl over pot, making sure bowl does not touch water, stirring occasionally until completely smooth, 5 to 7 minutes. Remove bowl and let chocolate cool slightly. (**NOTE:** *You are looking to cool mixture to 90°F on a candy thermometer. If you do not have a candy thermometer, you can test it by putting a tiny amount of the chocolate on your lip; if you can't feel a temperature difference, then it's perfect.*)

Stir in ginger mixture and goji berries. Pour into molds. Refrigerate until firm, about 1 hour. Turn mold upside down to release bars. Store in the refrigerator wrapped in parchment for up to 1 week.

Nutrition Information Per serving (⅓ of a bar): Calories: 268, Total Fat: 13 g, Sat. Fat: 3 g, Monounsaturated Fat: 8 g, Polyunsaturated Fat: 2 g, Carbs: 18 g, Fiber: 9 g, Sugars: 7 g, Protein: 23 g, Sodium: 452 mg, Cholesterol: 51 mg

Chestnut-Crusted Cheesecake
with Cranberry Sauce

Velvety cheesecake gets a festive makeover with a fragrant chestnut crust and a maple cranberry sauce drizzled over top.

INGREDIENTS

Crust

1 cup	vacuum-packed peeled roasted unsalted chestnuts (about 5 oz) (**NOTE:** *This recipe works best with vacuum-packed chestnuts that you can find at grocery stores.*)
3 tbsp	almond meal
2 tbsp	maple flakes

Filling

3 large	eggs
1 8-oz	package full-fat cream cheese, room temperature
1½ cups	whole-milk ricotta cheese
1 cup	plain whole-milk Greek yogurt
¾ cup	maple flakes
2 tsp	finely grated orange zest + ¼ cup fresh orange juice
1 tsp	each pure almond extract and pure vanilla extract

Topping

2 cups	fresh or frozen cranberries
½ cup	maple flakes

Serves **12.**
Hands-On Time: **20 Minutes.**
Total Time: **1 Hour, 15 Minutes.**
Plus Cooling Time.

INSTRUCTIONS

Preheat oven to 375°F. Prepare crust: Mist a 9-inch springform pan with cooking spray. In a food processor, pulse chestnuts until coarsely chopped. Add almond meal and 2 tbsp maple flakes and pulse to a crumb consistency. Press mixture into the bottom of prepared pan. Bake until golden brown, 8 to 10 minutes. Set aside to cool slightly. Reduce oven temperature to 325°F.

Prepare filling: Wipe out bowl of food processor and add all filling ingredients; process until smooth. Pour filling over crust and place pan on a baking sheet. Bake until filling is set, 45 minutes to 1 hour. (**TIP:** *To help prevent cracking, turn off oven and let cheesecake come to room temperature with oven door ajar, about 1 hour longer.*)

Meanwhile, prepare topping: In a small saucepan on medium-high, bring cranberries, ½ cup water and ½ cup maple flakes to a boil. Reduce heat to medium-low and cook, stirring occasionally, until cranberries burst open and sauce has thickened slightly, about 3 minutes. Remove from heat and cool to room temperature. Drizzle sauce over entire cheesecake, or slice and drizzle over individual servings.

Nutrition Information Per serving (½₂ of cake and 1½ tbsp sauce): Calories: 268, Total Fat: 13 g, Sat. Fat: 3 g, Monounsaturated Fat: 8 g, Polyunsaturated Fat: 2 g, Carbs: 18 g, Fiber: 9 g, Sugars: 7 g, Protein: 23 g, Sodium: 452 mg, Cholesterol: 51 mg

Sticky Date Cake
with Caramel Sauce

This light and fluffy cake has a creamy caramel sauce that soaks into it for extra sweetness and stickiness.

INGREDIENTS

¾ cup	coarsely chopped pitted dates (about 15 dates)
¼ cup	unsweetened sultana raisins
2 large	eggs
¾ cup	coconut sugar, divided
½ cup	sunflower oil
1 tsp	pure vanilla extract
½ cup	plain whole-milk yogurt
1½ cups	whole-wheat pastry flour
2 tsp	ground cinnamon
1½ tsp	baking soda
1 tsp	ground ginger
½ tsp	each sea salt and ground nutmeg
½ cup	grated apple (such as Gala)
⅓ cup	whipping cream (35%)

Serves **12**.
Hands-On Time: **25 Minutes.**
Total Time: **1 Hour, 20 Minutes.***
Plus Cooling Time.

INSTRUCTIONS

Preheat oven to 350°F. To a heat-proof bowl, add dates and raisins and cover with 1 cup boiling water. Set aside for 5 minutes. Mist a 9½-inch Bundt pan generously with cooking spray. (You can also use an 8-inch round baking pan misted with cooking spray and a circle of parchment to line the bottom.)

In a food processor, process eggs, ½ cup sugar, oil and vanilla until doubled in volume, about 1 minute. Add yogurt and date mixture (including water) and pulse 1 to 2 times to combine.

In a large mixing bowl, combine flour, cinnamon, baking soda, ginger, salt and nutmeg. Add mixture from food processor and stir with a wooden spoon until incorporated, 30 seconds. Stir in apple. Pour into prepared pan and bake for 35 to 40 minutes, or until a toothpick inserted in center comes out clean and sides of cake are starting to pull away from edges of pan. Cool on a wire rack for 10 to 15 minutes, then place a serving platter over pan, and with gloved hands, flip platter and pan over to release cake onto platter. Cool completely on platter.

Prepare sauce: In a small saucepan, combine remaining ¼ cup sugar and 3 tbsp water. Bring to a boil on medium-high; let boil 1 minute without stirring. Reduce heat to medium-low and add cream. Return to boil and then simmer until sauce thickly coats the back of a spoon, 1½ to 2 minutes. Remove from heat and let stand 5 minutes. Pour sauce over cooled cake.

Nutrition Information Per serving (1⁄12 of cake): Calories: 254, Total Fat: 13 g, Sat. Fat: 3 g, Monounsaturated Fat: 3 g, Polyunsaturated Fat: 6 g, Carbs: 35 g, Fiber: 3 g, Sugars: 24 g, Protein: 3 g, Sodium: 263 mg, Cholesterol: 40 mg

Salted Chocolate Almond Butter Cups

INGREDIENTS

12 oz	high-quality semisweet or dark chocolate, finely chopped (**NOTE:** Semisweet chocolate will provide a mellower flavor and dark will be a bit more bitter. Choose your favorite.)
½ cup	natural smooth almond butter
2 tbsp	coconut oil, melted
¼ cup	yacon syrup
¼ tsp	fine sea salt
	Flaked sea salt, for garnish

Serves **12.**
Hands-On Time: **30 Minutes.**
Total Time: **40 Minutes.***
Plus Refrigeration Time.

INSTRUCTIONS

Line a 12-cup muffin tray with paper muffin liners.

To a small saucepan, add chocolate and heat over low to melt, stirring constantly. (**NOTE:** *Chocolate burns easily, so keep a very close eye on the pot, and do not turn up heat beyond low.*) Once chocolate is mostly melted, remove from heat and continue stirring to melt remaining chunks. Spoon 1½ tsp chocolate into a muffin liner and rotate it around to coat the bottom and about ½ inch up the sides. Use a pastry brush to paint the sides more evenly, if needed. Tuck the chocolate-filled liner back into the tray. Repeat with remaining muffin liners. Place tray in the refrigerator for at least 15 minutes or until chocolate is hard to the touch.

Meanwhile, prepare filling: In a small bowl, combine almond butter, coconut oil, yacon syrup and fine salt, mixing until smooth.

Divide filling mixture among hardened chocolate shells and use your fingers to flatten and spread the filling as needed. One at a time, top each shell with 1 tsp of remaining melted chocolate and use the back of a spoon to spread into a flat layer, filling in any gaps or holes with chocolate. Once all cups are filled, sprinkle their tops lightly with flaked sea salt and place in refrigerator for at least 30 minutes more, until chocolate and filling are solidified.

Remove cups from their liners before serving. Cups will keep for several weeks in an airtight container in the fridge.

Nutrition Information Per serving (1 cup): Calories: 238, Total Fat: 18 g, Sat. Fat: 8 g, Monounsaturated Fat: 7 g, Polyunsaturated Fat: 2 g, Carbs: 21 g, Fiber: 4 g, Sugars: 13.5 g, Protein: 3 g, Sodium: 242 mg, Cholesterol: 0 mg

Spring Recipes

Mexican Cobb Salad
(See recipe, p. 140)

Mini Blueberry Muffins

Makes **16 Muffins.**
Hands-On Time: **10 Minutes.**
Total Time: **25 Minutes.**

INGREDIENTS

1 cup	almond flour
¼ tsp	baking soda
2	large eggs
2 tbsp	raw honey
½ tsp	pure vanilla extract
½ tsp	apple cider vinegar
¾ tsp	ground cinnamon
Pinch	sea salt
½ cup	frozen wild blueberries (**NOTE:** Do not thaw.)

INSTRUCTIONS

Preheat oven to 350°F. Mist a mini muffin tin with cooking spray or line with paper cups.

In a large mixing bowl, whisk flour and baking soda. In another medium bowl, whisk together eggs, honey, vanilla, vinegar, cinnamon and salt; pour into flour mixture and mix until combined. Fold in blueberries.

Place about 1 tbsp batter in each of 16 muffin cups. Bake for 15 minutes, or until lightly golden.

Nutrition Information Per serving (4 mini muffins):
Calories: 246, Total Fat: 17 g, Sat. Fat: 2 g, Monounsaturated Fat: 10 g, Polyunsaturated Fat: 4 g, Carbs: 18 g, Fiber: 5 g, Sugars: 11 g, Protein: 9 g, Sodium: 145 mg, Cholesterol: 93 mg

Sweet Potato Hash
with Sunny-Side Up Eggs

Makes **2 Servings.**
Hands-On Time: **20 Minutes.**
Total Time: **30 Minutes.**

INGREDIENTS

2 1-oz	slices all-natural turkey bacon (no added nitrites or nitrates), chopped
⅓ cup	chopped yellow onion
1	sweet potato, peeled and shredded (about 2 cups shredded)
Pinch	sea salt
Pinch	ground black pepper + additional, to taste
¼ cup	chopped fresh cilantro
2	large eggs

INSTRUCTIONS

Mist a large nonstick skillet with cooking spray and heat on medium-high. To skillet, add bacon and onion and sauté for 4 minutes, until onion is translucent. Add potato, salt and pepper and sauté, about 7 to 8 minutes, until potato is cooked through. Stir in cilantro; divide between 2 plates.

Reduce heat to medium and mist same skillet with cooking spray. Crack eggs onto separate sides of skillet and cook until set (or flip over for over easy eggs). Place 1 egg over each serving of hash. Sprinkle egg with additional pepper, to taste.

Nutrition Information Per serving (⅔ cup hash and 1 egg):
Calories: 188, Total Fat: 7 g, Sat. Fat: 2 g, Monounsaturated Fat: 3 g, Polyunsaturated Fat: 2 g, Carbs: 17 g, Fiber: 3 g, Sugars: 6 g, Protein: 14 g, Sodium: 359 mg, Cholesterol: 211 mg

Purple Potato Egg Salad

Serves **2.**
Hands-On Time: **15 Minutes.**
Total Time: **30 Minutes.**

INGREDIENTS

2 small	purple potatoes, chopped in ¾-inch pieces
2 large	eggs
2 1-oz	slices all-natural turkey bacon (no added nitrites or nitrates)
1	green onion, thinly sliced
2 tbsp	apple cider vinegar
2 tbsp	Dijon mustard
1 tsp	olive oil
⅛ tsp	cracked black pepper

INSTRUCTIONS

To a saucepan, add potatoes and cover with cold water. Bring to a boil, reduce to a simmer and cook until fork-tender, about 6 to 7 minutes. Drain and place in a large bowl.

To another saucepan, add eggs and cover with cold water. Set on medium-high and bring to a boil. Set timer for 10 minutes; drain and let sit 1 minute. Refresh under cold water and peel. Chop eggs and add to bowl with potatoes.

To a small skillet on medium, add bacon and cook about 2 to 3 minutes per side, or until desired doneness. Remove and chop. Add to bowl with potato-egg mixture. Add onions.

In a small bowl, whisk together vinegar and mustard. Whisk in oil. Add pepper and whisk again. Pour over potato-egg mixture and fold to coat.

Nutrition Information Per serving (½ of recipe): Calories: 243, Total Fat: 8 g, Sat. Fat: 2 g, Monounsaturated Fat: 4 g, Polyunsaturated Fat: 1 g, Carbs: 27 g, Fiber: 2 g, Sugars: 1 g, Protein: 12 g, Sodium: 552 mg, Cholesterol: 197 mg

PACK IT WITH PROTEIN: This potato salad packs an impressive 12 grams of protein per serving.

Cinnamon Maca Bliss Bars

Makes **12 Bars.**
Hands-On Time: **15 Minutes.**
Total Time: **30 Minutes.**

INGREDIENTS

2 cups	raw unsalted almonds
2 cups	pitted Medjool dates
2 tbsp	pure maple syrup
2 tbsp	maca powder
2 tbsp	coconut oil (**TIP:** *If you have some on hand, butter-flavored coconut oil makes these bars extra-luscious.*)
2 tsp	ground cinnamon
½ tsp	pure vanilla extract
½ tsp	sea salt

INSTRUCTIONS

To a food processor, add all ingredients and blend until nuts are finely chopped and you have a well-combined mass.

In a 6 x 9 baking dish or container, press mixture until flat. Refrigerate for 30 minutes, then cut into 12 bars. Keep refrigerated for up to 5 days or freeze up to 3 months.

Nutrition Information Per serving (1 bar): Calories: 247, Total Fat: 14 g, Sat. Fat: 3 g, Monounsaturated Fat: 8 g, Polyunsaturated Fat: 3 g, Carbs: 29 g, Fiber: 5 g, Sugars: 21 g, Protein: 6 g, Sodium: 81 mg, Cholesterol: 0 mg

Savory Buckwheat Crepes
with Mushrooms, Corn & Fontina Cheese

These simple-to-make buckwheat crepes are stuffed to the brim with vegetables and cheese then baked in a luscious creamy yogurt sauce.

INGREDIENTS

½ cup	whole-wheat pastry flour
¼ cup	buckwheat flour
1¼ tsp	sea salt, divided
2 cups	whole milk
2 tbsp	organic unsalted butter, melted and cooled slightly
1½ lb	white mushrooms, stemmed and thinly sliced
½ tsp	dried thyme
1 tsp	ground black pepper, divided
5	scallions, white and light green parts, sliced (about ⅓ cup)
2½ cups	fresh or frozen corn kernels (if fresh, from 3 to 4 cobs)
1 tsp	smoked paprika + additional for garnish
4 oz	Fontina cheese, grated (1 packed cup)
2	large eggs, yolks and whites separated, divided
2 cups	whole-milk Greek yogurt
2½ tbsp	chopped fresh chives, divided
1 tsp	fresh thyme leaves

Serves **10.**
Hands-On Time: **1 Hour, 10 Minutes.**
Total Time: **1 Hour, 35 Minutes.**

INSTRUCTIONS

Prepare crepe batter: In a large bowl, whisk together flours and ¾ tsp salt. Slowly pour in milk and ¾ cup water, whisking constantly. Add butter and whisk until dry ingredients are moistened. Set aside.

Mist a large skillet with cooking spray and heat on medium-high. Add mushrooms, dried thyme, ¼ tsp salt and ½ tsp pepper and cook, stirring frequently, until liquid evaporates, 6 to 8 minutes. Reduce heat to medium and continue cooking, stirring frequently, until lightly browned and tender, 6 to 8 minutes more. (**TIP:** *Do this in 2 batches if your skillet won't hold all the mushrooms comfortably.*) Transfer to a medium bowl. Mist same skillet with additional cooking spray and heat on medium-high. Add scallions, corn, 1 tsp paprika, ⅛ tsp salt and remaining ½ tsp pepper and cook, stirring frequently until crisp-tender, about 6 minutes. (**NOTE:** *If using frozen corn, cook just until the water evaporates and corn is heated through*.) Add to bowl with mushrooms and set aside.

Cut 12 pieces of parchment paper, each about 8 x 10 inches. Mist an 8-inch nonstick skillet with cooking spray and heat on medium-high. Add a scant ⅓ cup crepe batter. Immediately swirl skillet until batter coats bottom in an even layer. Cook until a few bubbles form and crepe easily releases from skillet when you slide a thin spatula underneath it, about 1 minute. Lift crepe using spatula and quickly flip. The top of the crepe should be a deep golden brown. Continue cooking until bottom is golden, about 30 seconds. Gently slide onto a piece of parchment paper. Repeat, making a total of 10 crepes, misting skillet with cooking spray each time and placing a piece of parchment between each crepe. (**TIP:** *This recipe makes enough batter for about 12 crepes, so you can do some practice rounds to get the hang of it. The key is to have the skillet hot enough so that the first side of the crepe sets and can be easily flipped without tearing. If your crepe tears, the skillet may not be hot enough.*)

Mist a 9 x 13-inch baking dish with cooking spray. Place a generous ¼ cup mushroom mixture and about 1½ tbsp cheese down the center of a crepe and gently fold the sides over the filling. Place in baking dish. Repeat with remaining crepes, lining up 8 crepes in the baking dish and placing the last 2 crepes perpendicular to the first 8, along the length of the dish. (**MAKE AHEAD:** *This can be done 1 day ahead. Cover with foil and refrigerate. Before baking, allow 1 to 2 hours to come to room temperature.*)

In a large bowl, stir together egg yolks, yogurt and remaining ⅛ tsp salt. In a medium bowl, beat egg whites with an electric mixer on medium-high speed until they hold soft peaks. Fold in about one-third of whites to yogurt mixture until combined. Add remaining whites, 2 tbsp chives and fresh thyme and fold until combined. (**MAKE AHEAD:** *This can be done 1 day ahead. Cover and refrigerate. Before baking, allow 1 hour to come to room temperature.*)

Preheat oven to 400°F. Spread yogurt mixture over crepes, covering completely. Bake until yogurt feels slightly firm to the touch and has a fluffy texture, 20 to 25 minutes. Rest for 5 to 10 minutes. Sprinkle with remaining ½ tbsp chives and additional paprika before serving.

Nutrition Information Per serving (1 crepe): Calories: 299, Total Fat: 15 g, Sat. Fat: 9 g, Monounsaturated Fat: 4 g, Polyunsaturated Fat: 1 g, Carbs: 29 g, Fiber: 4 g, Sugars: 8 g, Protein: 15 g, Sodium: 391 mg, Cholesterol: 69 mg

GLUTEN-FREE FLOUR: Contrary to popular belief, buckwheat is not a cereal grain but a fruit seed. It's both wheat- and gluten-free, making it a wonderful alternative to refined white flour. Buckwheat flour is rich in zinc, copper, potassium and protein while it's also a good source of soluble fiber, which helps lower cholesterol and aids in controlling blood sugar.

Asparagus Goat Cheese Tart
with Whole-Grain Crust

Three flours–spelt, oat and whole-wheat pastry flour–
combine to create a delicious, whole-grain crust for
this fresh spring tart.

INGREDIENTS

8 tbsp	cold organic unsalted butter, divided
¾ cup	whole-wheat pastry flour
½ cup	whole-grain spelt flour
½ cup	oat flour
¾ + ⅛ tsp	sea salt, divided
¾ lb	thin asparagus (**NOTE:** Trim asparagus tips to 5 inches and discard stalks or save for another use.)
⅛ tsp	ground black pepper
6 oz	goat cheese
1 cup	whole-milk ricotta cheese
2 large	eggs
	zest of 1 lemon
1 tsp	fresh thyme leaves

Serves **8.**
Hands-On Time: **25 Minutes.**
Total Time: **1 Hour, 20 Minutes.**

INSTRUCTIONS

Preheat oven to 350°F. Lightly grease a 9-inch fluted tart pan with removable bottom with ½ tbsp butter (keep remaining butter in refrigerator until ready to use). To a food processor, add flours and ½ tsp salt. Pulse until combined. Cut remaining 7½ tbsp butter into cubes and add to flour mixture. Process until mixture is coarse and sandy with small pieces of butter visible, about 3 5-second pulses. With processor running, pour in ¼ cup cold water and process just until combined, 5 to 10 seconds. (**NOTE:** Dough will stick together if pressed between your fingers but will not form a ball.)

Transfer dough to prepared tart pan, distributing clumps of dough evenly in pan. With floured hands, press dough into pan, working it to edges and up sides. Prick all over with a fork. Cover with foil and add about 1½ cups dried beans, uncooked rice or pie weights over top. Bake in center of oven for 15 minutes. Remove foil and weights and continue baking until barely beginning to brown, 10 minutes more. Transfer to a wire rack. (**MAKE AHEAD:** Crust can be made up to 1 day ahead. Cool completely, wrap in 2 layers of plastic wrap, keeping crust in pan, and refrigerate. Before proceeding, bring to room temperature, about 1 hour.)

Preheat broiler to high and arrange a rack 6 to 8 inches from heat source. Line a large rimmed baking sheet with foil, mist with cooking spray and add asparagus in a single layer. Mist with cooking spray and sprinkle with ⅛ tsp salt and pepper. Broil for 5 to 6 minutes, tossing halfway, until lightly browned and crisp-tender. (**MAKE AHEAD:** This can be done up to 1 day ahead. Refrigerate in an airtight container then bring to room temperature, about 30 minutes.)

Preheat oven to 375°F. Clean processor bowl and blade. To food processor, add cheeses and remaining ¼ tsp salt and process until combined, about 8 seconds. Add eggs and process until combined, scraping down bowl as needed, about 8 seconds. (**MAKE AHEAD:** *This can be made up to 1 day ahead. Cover and refrigerate. Before proceeding, bring to room temperature, about 1 hour.*) Pour into tart shell. Arrange asparagus over top. Bake in center of oven until set in center, 22 to 25 minutes. Cool on a rack for 10 minutes. Garnish with lemon zest and thyme. Serve warm or at room temperature.

Nutrition Information Per serving (⅛ of tart):
Calories: 326, Total Fat: 22 g, Sat. Fat: 13.5 g, Monounsaturated Fat: 6 g, Polyunsaturated Fat: 1 g, Carbs: 20 g, Fiber: 3 g, Sugars: 1 g, Protein: 12.5 g, Sodium: 341 mg, Cholesterol: 103 mg

AMAZING ASPARAGUS: Asparagus is an excellent source of both vitamin K and folate. Known as the "clotting vitamin," vitamin K is key in helping your blood clot, while folate is essential for heart health and red blood cell production, the latter of which is important in preventing anemia.

Cinnamon Raisin Banana French Toast Casserole
with Oat Crumble

Whole-wheat cinnamon raisin bread is layered with bananas and covered with an egg and milk mixture before baking. An oat crumble topping adds a touch of sweetness and texture.

INGREDIENTS

½ cup	old-fashioned rolled oats
¼ cup	white whole-wheat flour
5 tbsp	maple sugar, divided
¼ tsp	sea salt
3 tbsp	organic unsalted butter, melted
14	slices whole-wheat cinnamon raisin swirl bread
3	small bananas, sliced
6	large eggs
3¾ cups	whole milk
2 tsp	pure vanilla extract
1 tsp	ground cinnamon

Serves **12.**
Hands-On Time: **10 Minutes.**
Total Time: **60 Minutes.***
Plus Overnight Resting Time.

INSTRUCTIONS

Prepare oat crumble: In a medium bowl, stir together oats, flour, 3 tbsp maple sugar and salt until combined. Add butter and stir until moistened. Set aside.

Mist a 9 x 13-inch baking dish with cooking spray. Arrange 7 slices bread in a single layer (2 rows of 3½ slices each). Top with banana slices in a single layer, then top with remaining 7 slices bread in a single layer. In a large bowl, whisk eggs. As you whisk, slowly pour in milk until combined. Whisk in vanilla, cinnamon and remaining 2 tbsp maple sugar. Pour mixture over bread, then sprinkle evenly with oat crumble. Cover with foil and refrigerate overnight.

Preheat oven to 350°F. Bring casserole to room temperature, up to 2 hours. Remove foil and bake until bread is puffed up and egg mixture is set (a bit of liquid in center is fine as it will firm up as it cools), about 40 minutes. (**NOTE:** *If you skipped bringing casserole to room temperature, bake another 10 to 15 minutes*.) Cool on a rack for 10 minutes before serving.

Nutrition Information Per serving (1⁄12 of casserole): Calories: 261, Total Fat: 10 g, Sat. Fat: 4 g, Monounsaturated Fat: 3 g, Polyunsaturated Fat: 2 g, Carbs: 33 g, Fiber: 4 g, Sugars: 15 g, Protein: 10 g, Sodium: 232 mg, Cholesterol: 108 mg

SWEET BENEFIT: Not only do the bananas in this muffin recipe impart sweetness, but they also bestow a wealth of good-for-you nutrients. Bananas are an important source of energizing vitamin B6 (also known as pyridoxine) as well as potassium, a mineral that helps the body's nerves, cells and muscles function normally.

Banana Walnut Crumble Muffins

with Chocolate Chips

This classic muffin is a total crowd-pleaser, packed with sweet banana, crunchy walnuts and fragrant cinnamon. We opted for mini chocolate chips for chocolaty flavor in every single bite.

INGREDIENTS

1 cup	white whole-wheat flour
1 cup	oat bran
1½ tsp	baking powder
1 tsp	baking soda
1 tsp	ground cinnamon
¼ tsp	sea salt
½ cup	mini chocolate chips
1 large	egg
3	very ripe bananas, mashed (about 1¼ cups)
½ cup	whole milk
¼ cup	pure maple syrup
3 tbsp	safflower oil

Crumb Topping

¼ cup	finely chopped unsalted walnuts (about 1 oz)
3 tbsp	white whole-wheat flour
2 tbsp	maple sugar
½ tsp	ground cinnamon
¼ tsp	sea salt
2 tbsp	organic unsalted butter, melted

Makes **12 Muffins.**
Hands-On Time: **25 Minutes.**
Total Time: **50 Minutes.**

INSTRUCTIONS

Line a 12-count muffin tin with paper liners and preheat oven to 350°F. Prepare crumb topping: To a small bowl, add all crumb topping ingredients except butter and stir with a fork until combined. Add butter and stir until dry ingredients are moistened; set aside. (***MAKE AHEAD:*** *This can be done 1 day ahead. Cover and refrigerate. Before proceeding with recipe, allow to come to room temperature, 1 to 2 hours. The topping will have firmed up, so use a spoon to crumble it again.*)

Prepare muffins: In a large bowl, whisk together 1 cup flour, oat bran, baking powder, baking soda, 1 tsp cinnamon and ¼ tsp salt. Add chocolate chips and whisk to combine. (***MAKE AHEAD:*** *This can be done 1 day ahead. Cover and store at room temperature.*) In another large bowl, lightly whisk egg, then add bananas and whisk until combined. Add milk, maple syrup and oil and whisk until combined. (***MAKE AHEAD:*** *This can be done 1 day ahead. Cover and refrigerate. Allow to come to room temperature and whisk again before proceeding with recipe, about 1 hour.*)

Add banana mixture to flour mixture and stir until dry ingredients are moistened. Add to muffin tin, filling each cup almost to the top. Sprinkle crumb topping over muffins (about 1 tbsp per muffin) and press down slightly on topping so it adheres. Bake until a toothpick inserted into center of a muffin comes out with a few moist crumbs, 18 to 20 minutes. Cool in pan for 5 minutes, then transfer to a rack. Serve warm. (***MAKE AHEAD:*** *Muffins can be baked up to 1 month ahead. Cool completely and freeze in zip-top freezer bags or airtight containers. Defrost at room temperature for 1 hour. Place muffins on a large rimmed baking sheet and loosely tent with foil. Heat in a 250°F oven for 7 to 8 minutes.*)

Nutrition Information Per serving (1 muffin): Calories: 226, Total Fat: 11 g, Sat. Fat: 3 g, Monounsaturated Fat: 2 g, Polyunsaturated Fat: 4 g, Carbs: 33 g, Fiber: 4 g, Sugars: 17 g, Protein: 5 g, Sodium: 267 mg, Cholesterol: 22 mg

Curried Chicken Salad
with Mango & Cashews

Serve this sweet and fragrant salad in whole-wheat pita pockets or in lettuce wraps. To keep the cashews crunchy, toss all the ingredients together and add the nuts just before serving.

Serves **4.**
Hands-On Time: **20 Minutes.**
Total Time: **20 Minutes.**

INGREDIENTS

⅓ cup	olive oil mayonnaise
	juice of ½ lime
2 tbsp	unsweetened apricot preserves
2 tsp	curry powder
	sea salt and ground cayenne pepper, to taste
2 cups	cubed, cooked chicken
1	mango, pitted, peeled and diced
½ cup	diced celery
¼ cup	sliced green onions
1 tbsp	chopped fresh cilantro
½ cup	chopped unsalted cashews

INSTRUCTIONS

In a large bowl, combine mayonnaise, lime juice, preserves and curry powder. Season mixture with salt and cayenne.

To mixture, add chicken, mango, celery, onions and cilantro; toss to combine. Stir in cashews just before serving.

Nutrition Information Per serving (¼ of recipe): Calories: 411, Total Fat: 28 g, Sat. Fat: 5 g, Monounsaturated Fat: 11 g, Polyunsaturated Fat: 10 g, Carbs: 22 g, Fiber: 4 g, Sugars: 13 g, Protein: 21 g, Sodium: 226 mg, Cholesterol: 59 mg

Nori-Wrapped Salmon Hand Rolls
with Wasabi Aioli

Serves **2.**
Hands-On Time: **25 Minutes.**
Total Time: **25 Minutes.**

INGREDIENTS

2 sheets	nori, each sheet cut in half
4 oz	wild Alaskan smoked salmon
½	English or hothouse cucumber, seeded and cut into matchsticks
½	avocado, thinly sliced
2 tbsp	chopped fresh cilantro

Aioli

1	large egg yolk
1 tsp	Dijon mustard
1 tsp	wasabi paste
1 tbsp	olive oil
1 tsp	fresh lemon juice

INSTRUCTIONS

Prepare aioli: In a large bowl, whisk together egg yolk, Dijon and wasabi. Slowly drizzle in oil while whisking vigorously until mixture thickens. Mix in lemon juice. Set aside.

Lay nori on a flat surface. Lay 1 oz salmon along one side of each sheet, toward one of the corners. Divide cucumber, avocado and cilantro among nori, layering over salmon. Starting from the corner with filling, roll into a cone shape. (You may need a few drops of water to seal.) Serve with aioli.

Nutrition Information Per serving (2 rolls and 1½ tbsp aioli): Calories: 248, Total Fat: 19 g, Sat. Fat: 4 g, Monounsaturated Fat: 11.5 g, Polyunsaturated Fat: 2.5 g, Carbs: 5 g, Fiber: 1 g, Sugars: 1 g, Protein: 14 g, Sodium: 551 mg, Cholesterol: 105 mg

Spinach & Potato Puffs

INGREDIENTS

4	eggs, separated
1 large	white potato, peeled and diced
1 10-oz	pkg frozen chopped spinach, thawed
2 tbsp	olive oil
½	yellow onion, diced
1	clove garlic, minced
3 tbsp	white whole-wheat flour
1 cup	whole milk
¼ tsp	each ground nutmeg and black pepper
1½ cups	shredded cheddar cheese

Serves **4.**
Hands-On Time: **15 Minutes.**
Total Time: **45 Minutes.**

INSTRUCTIONS

Add egg whites to a mixing bowl and place in refrigerator to keep cold. In a separate bowl, beat egg yolks and set aside at room temperature. Ensure that oven rack is in middle position and preheat oven to 375°F.

Fill a small saucepan with water and bring to a boil on medium-high. Add potato, return to a boil and cook for 10 minutes. Drain potato and add back to dry pot. Heat on medium-high for about 2 minutes, until dry. Set aside.

Squeeze as much liquid from spinach as possible and set aside. In a large saucepan, heat oil on medium-high. Add onion and garlic and sauté until soft, about 1 to 2 minutes. Add flour and cook for an additional 1 to 2 minutes.

Whisk milk slowly into onion mixture until smooth and mixture thickens, about 1 to 2 minutes. Add nutmeg and pepper. Gradually add cheese, mixing until incorporated. Remove mixture from heat. Temper egg yolks by adding about ½ cup hot cheese sauce to yolks, beating constantly. Then whisk egg yolk–cheese mixture back into cheese sauce, beating constantly until incorporated and smooth, about 1 minute.

In the bowl of a large food processor, add potato, spinach and cheese sauce; purée for 30 seconds to 1 minute, until smooth.

Remove egg whites from refrigerator. Beat with an electric mixer on high speed until stiff peaks form, about 3 minutes.

Using a spatula, gently fold egg whites into spinach mixture. Mist 8 6-oz ramekins with cooking spray. Fill each ramekin with spinach mixture, until about ½ inch from the top. Place ramekins directly on middle oven rack and bake for 25 to 30 minutes, until well browned. (Soufflés will rise.)

Nutrition Information Per serving (1 puff): Calories: 177, Total Fat: 8 g, Sat. Fat: 2 g, Monounsaturated Fat: 4 g, Polyunsaturated Fat: 1 g, Carbs: 14 g, Fiber: 2 g, Sugars: 3 g, Protein: 12 g, Sodium: 238 mg, Cholesterol: 112 mg

Shredded Papaya Salad

All over Thailand, you'll see cooks in makeshift sidewalk food carts working huge mortars and pestles, pounding together the ingredients for this spicy, refreshing salad. If you don't have a mortar and pestle, chop and smash the chiles and garlic with the side of a chef's knife before mixing them with the remaining dressing ingredients. Traditionally, the papaya is cut into julienne threads with a large, sharp knife, but you can also use a julienne peeler.

INGREDIENTS

¼ cup	sliced green beans (½-inch lengths)
½–1	red Thai chile pepper, stemmed
1 tbsp	date sugar
2 large	cloves garlic, peeled
2 tbsp	fresh lime juice
1 tbsp	fish sauce
4 cups	julienne, shredded or grated green papaya or green mango
1 cup	cherry tomatoes, halved
2 tbsp	unsalted roasted peanuts, chopped
2 tbsp	chopped fresh cilantro

Serves **4.**
Hands-On Time: **30 Minutes.**
Total Time: **30 Minutes.**

INSTRUCTIONS

Into a medium heat-proof bowl, pour 2 cups boiling water over beans. let sit for 30 seconds; drain and refresh with cold water. Drain and set aside.

Place chile pepper, sugar and garlic in a large mortar and pestle and pound until the mixture is a fine paste, or smash it with the side of a chef's knife. Add lime juice and fish sauce and stir to dissolve sugar. Pour into a small bowl.

Add 1 cup papaya to the mortar and pound with the pestle until the fruit is a little bruised and limp, about 20 seconds. Transfer papaya to a large bowl and toss with the dressing and remaining ingredients. If you don't have a mortar and pestle, vigorously mix the papaya and dressing together with your hands, squeezing gently to bruise the fruit slightly. (**MAKE AHEAD:** *This salad can be made up to 2 hours in advance and refrigerated until ready to serve.*)

Nutrition Information Per serving (1½ cups): Calories: 88, Total Fat: 2.5 g, Sat. Fat: 0.5 g, Carbs: 15.5 g, Fiber: 2 g, Sugars: 9 g, Protein: 4 g, Sodium: 312 mg, Cholesterol: 0 mg

PAPAYA POWER: This soft tropical fruit is an excellent source of carotenoids, flavonoids and vitamin C, all potent antioxidants that protect the arteries and help prevent heart disease. Papaya also contains papain, an enzyme that aids in the digestion of proteins and helps your body recover from inflammation and injuries.

Chicken Sausage Penne
with Dandelion Greens

Dandelion greens pack a tasty, bitter punch that is best paired with other bold ingredients that can stand up to its flavor, such as the sharp Parmesan and flavorful sausage in this quick pasta. The leaves mellow as they cook, so hold back some fresh ones to toss in at the end of cooking for an extra kick. Serve with lemon wedges and red pepper flakes.

INGREDIENTS

8 oz	whole-grain penne
2 tsp	olive oil
8 oz	all-natural mild Italian chicken sausage, no added nitrites or nitrates, casings removed
5 cups	dandelion greens, chopped, divided
1 large	clove garlic, thinly sliced
¼ tsp	ground black pepper
Pinch	sea salt
3 tbsp	heavy whipping cream (35%)
5 tbsp	grated Parmesan cheese

Serves **4.**
Hands-On Time: **20 Minutes.**
Total Time: **20 Minutes.**

INSTRUCTIONS

Cook pasta al dente according to package directions. Reserve ½ cup cooking liquid before draining.

Meanwhile, in a large sauté pan, heat oil on medium. Add sausage and cook, breaking up meat with a wooden spoon, until no longer pink, about 3 minutes. Add 4 cups dandelion greens, garlic, pepper and salt and sauté, stirring often, until greens are wilted, about 2 minutes.

Reduce heat to low and stir in cream, scraping up browned bits from bottom of pan with a wooden spoon. Add pasta, reserved cooking liquid, cheese and remaining 1 cup dandelion greens and stir to combine.

Nutrition Information Per serving (1⅓ cups): Calories: 396, Total Fat: 13.5 g, Sat. Fat: 5.5 g, Monounsaturated Fat: 5 g, Polyunsaturated Fat: 2 g, Carbs: 50 g, Fiber: 7.5 g, Sugars: 2 g, Protein: 22 g, Sodium: 537 mg, Cholesterol: 68 mg

White Bean Falafel

with Pickled Vegetables & Yogurt Sauce

Navy beans stand in for chickpeas in this twist on falafel. Sweet and sour pickled radish, garlic yogurt sauce and pita triangles round out the meal.

INGREDIENTS

½ cup	apple cider vinegar
1 tsp	organic evaporated cane juice (aka organic cane sugar)
1 tsp	sea salt, divided
1 cup	thinly sliced red onion
1 cup	thinly sliced radish
½ cup	Balkan-style yogurt
1 tsp	lemon zest + 3 tbsp fresh lemon juice, divided
3	cloves garlic, minced, divided
3 small	whole-grain pitas, halved and split open
4 cups	BPA-free canned navy beans, drained and rinsed
1 large	egg
1	green onion, thinly sliced
¼ cup	white whole-wheat flour
¼ cup	whole-wheat panko bread crumbs
3 tbsp	chopped fresh rosemary leaves
¼ tsp	ground black pepper
3 tbsp	olive oil, divided
3 cups	loosely packed fresh flat-leaf parsley leaves
½ cup	roughly chopped grape tomatoes

Serves **6.**
Hands-On Time: **30 Minutes.**
Total Time: **30 Minutes.**

INSTRUCTIONS

In a small pot, bring vinegar, cane juice and ½ tsp salt to a boil, stirring until cane juice is dissolved. Add red onion and radish. Remove from heat and cool to room temperature. Drain and set aside.

Meanwhile, prepare yogurt sauce: In a small bowl, mix together yogurt, 1 tbsp lemon juice and 1 minced clove garlic. Set aside.

Toast pita and cut into triangles. In a large bowl, mash beans with a potato masher; mixture should be slightly lumpy. Add egg, green onion, flour, bread crumbs, rosemary, pepper, 1 tsp lemon zest, 1 tbsp lemon juice, remaining 2 minced cloves garlic and ½ tsp salt; mix until well combined. Form 12 golf ball–sized balls and place them on a large rimmed parchment-lined baking sheet. Gently flatten into patties.

In a large skillet on medium-high, heat 1 tbsp oil. Working in 2 batches to prevent overcrowding, add patties and cook for about 4 minutes, turning once, until crisp and golden. Add another 1 tbsp oil between batches. Transfer to a paper towel–lined plate and cover to keep warm.

Meanwhile, in a medium bowl, combine parsley, tomatoes, remaining 1 tbsp lemon juice and 1 tbsp oil, tossing to coat.

Place 2 patties on each plate. Divide pickled vegetables, yogurt sauce, salad and pita among plates.

Nutrition Information Per serving (2 falafels and ⅙ of trimmings): Calories: 312, Total Fat: 8 g, Sat. Fat: 2 g, Monounsaturated Fat: 4 g, Polyunsaturated Fat: 1 g, Carbs: 47.5 g, Fiber: 13 g, Sugars: 3 g, Protein: 15 g, Sodium: 148 mg, Cholesterol: 34 mg

Sheet Pan Pizza
with Fingerlings & Gorgonzola

Small, knobby fingerling potatoes have a thin, delicate skin, so there's no need to peel them. If you can't find fingerlings, substitute with baby potatoes instead. Be sure to remove the dough from the fridge about 30 minutes ahead; this makes it much easier to handle. Don't worry if it seems like there's a lot of radicchio; it shrivels as the pizza bakes.

INGREDIENTS

	whole-wheat flour, for dusting
1 lb	whole-grain pizza dough, room temperature (**TIP:** *You can use an all-natural purchased crust or make your own with our Whole-Wheat Pizza Dough recipe at **cleaneating.com**.*)
7 oz	fingerling potatoes, cut into ⅛-inch-thick slices
¼	red onion, thinly sliced
2 tbsp	chopped raw unsalted walnuts
2	cloves garlic, thinly sliced
1 tbsp	chopped fresh rosemary
½ tsp	ground black pepper
¼ tsp	sea salt
¾ cup	crumbled Gorgonzola cheese
1	head radicchio, cored and shredded (about 4 cups)
⅓ cup	grated mozzarella cheese
1 tbsp	extra-virgin olive oil

Serves **4.**
Hands-On Time: **20 Minutes.**
Total Time: **35 Minutes.**

INSTRUCTIONS

Preheat oven to 450°F. Mist an 18 x 13-inch heavy rimmed baking sheet with cooking spray. Dust a clean work surface with flour; roll out dough to an 18 x 13-inch rectangle. Transfer dough to sheet and let rest for 5 minutes. If necessary, stretch dough toward corners and edges of sheet to make even thickness throughout.

Arrange potatoes and onion in even layers over dough. Sprinkle with walnuts, garlic, rosemary, pepper and salt. Top with Gorgonzola and radicchio. Sprinkle with mozzarella and drizzle with oil.

Bake until bottom of crust is deep golden brown, radicchio is wilted and mozzarella is bubbly, 15 to 20 minutes.

Nutrition Information Per serving (¼ of pizza): Calories: 424, Total Fat: 22 g, Sat. Fat: 8 g, Monounsaturated Fat: 10 g, Polyunsaturated Fat: 3.5 g, Carbs: 45 g, Fiber: 7 g, Sugars: 3.5 g, Protein: 16 g, Sodium: 722 mg, Cholesterol: 26 mg

Summer Roll-Inspired Noodle Bowl

Don't let this noodle bowl fool you. Although it's full of crunchy and colorful vegetables, it's really about the herbs, with refreshing basil and mint in every bite.

INGREDIENTS

1 lb	pad Thai–style brown rice noodles
¼ cup	fresh lime juice
2 tbsp	safflower or grape seed oil
1 tbsp	fish sauce
1 tbsp	raw honey
½ tsp	red pepper flakes
¼ cup	chiffonade fresh basil leaves, ideally Thai basil, divided (**TIP:** *To chiffonade your herbs, pile several leaves on top of one another, roll tightly lengthwise into a cylinder and then cut thinly widthwise, creating fine ribbons.*)
¼ cup	chiffonade fresh mint leaves, divided
4	scallions, thinly sliced, divided
1	carrot, cut into matchsticks or shredded
½	cucumber, peeled and cut into matchsticks
½	red bell pepper, cut into matchsticks
1 cup	bean sprouts
1 cup	shredded cooked chicken breast
¼ cup	unsalted dry-roasted peanuts

Serves **4.**
Hands-On Time: **30 Minutes.**
Total Time: **40 Minutes.**

INSTRUCTIONS

Cook noodles according to package directions.

Meanwhile, prepare dressing: In a small bowl, combine lime juice, oil, fish sauce, honey and pepper flakes. Set aside.

Drain noodles, rinse with cold water, drain again and transfer to a large bowl. Toss noodles with three-quarters of dressing, half of basil, half of mint and half of scallions.

Arrange noodles in individual bowls and top with carrot, cucumber, bell pepper, bean sprouts, chicken, remaining half of basil, mint, and scallions, and peanuts. Drizzle with remaining one-quarter of dressing.

Nutrition Information Per serving (2 cups): Calories: 426, Total Fat: 14 g, Sat. Fat: 2 g, Monounsaturated Fat: 4 g, Polyunsaturated Fat: 7 g, Carbs: 59 g, Fiber: 7 g, Sugars: 9 g, Protein: 19.5 g, Sodium: 352 mg, Cholesterol: 30 mg

HERBACEOUS HEALTH: Both basil and mint offer powerful health benefits: Basil contains flavonoids that help protect the body's chromosomes from radiation, while mint has relaxing properties to help soothe an upset stomach. Both herbs also have antibacterial properties.

Sweet & Spicy Beef Stir-Fry
with Asian Pear Sauce

A sticky, garlicky Asian pear sauce is the star of this stir-fry and what makes it taste so much like the one from your local takeout joint. This is one of our team's absolute favorite dishes of the issue–we highly recommend it!

INGREDIENTS

12 oz	lean beef sirloin, sliced thin (1½ inches x ¼ inch)
¼ cup	minced garlic, divided (about 12 cloves)
¼ cup	safflower oil, divided
2½ tbsp	reduced-sodium soy sauce, divided
1 large	Asian pear, peeled and cored
3 tbsp + 1 tsp	brown rice vinegar, divided
2 tbsp	raw honey
4 tsp	sriracha
4 small	heads baby bok choy
4 cups	soybean sprouts, rinsed

Serves **4.**
Hands-On Time: **35 Minutes.**
Total Time: **50 Minutes.**

INSTRUCTIONS

In a small bowl, toss beef with 1 tbsp garlic and 1½ tsp each oil and soy sauce. Let stand for 30 minutes.

Meanwhile, prepare sauce: Into a sieve set over a bowl, grate pear on the large holes of a box grater. Press to collect juice in bowl. In a small saucepan on medium, heat 1½ tsp oil. Add grated pear and 2 tbsp garlic and cook, stirring often, about 7 to 8 minutes, until lightly browned. Add 2 tbsp vinegar, honey, sriracha, remaining 2 tbsp soy sauce and ¼ cup reserved pear juice. Reduce heat to low and simmer for 8 to 10 minutes, until thickened. Keep warm.

Trim root end of bok choy until flat but leave intact with leaves attached. Slice lengthwise and place in a large bowl. Cover bok choy halves with cold water and soak to remove any dirt. Drain and rinse carefully to keep from breaking apart. Pat dry.

In an 11- to 12-inch sauté pan on medium, heat 1 tbsp oil. In pan, place bok choy halves cut side down and sprinkle with 2 tsp vinegar. Cover pan and cook for 3 to 5 minutes until tender and cut sides are caramelized. Transfer to a plate and keep warm.

To pan, add 1 tbsp oil and increase heat to medium-high; add sprouts, remaining 1 tbsp garlic and remaining 2 tsp vinegar and cook, stirring often, about 2 to 3 minutes, until lightly caramelized and tender. Transfer to plate.

To pan on medium-high, add remaining 1 tbsp oil. Add beef and cook, stirring, about 1 to 2 minutes, until starting to brown. Add ¼ cup Asian pear sauce and cook for 1 minute, until beef is cooked and sauce is heated through. To serve, mound ⅓ cup sprouts on each of 4 plates, top each with ½ cup beef, and cross 2 bok choy halves on top. Drizzle each with 1 tbsp of remaining sauce.

Nutrition Information Per serving (¼ of recipe): Calories: 381, Total Fat: 20 g, Sat. Fat: 2 g, Monounsaturated Fat: 4 g, Polyunsaturated Fat: 12 g, Carbs: 28 g, Fiber: 4 g, Sugars: 18 g, Protein: 27.5 g, Sodium: 578 mg, Cholesterol: 59 mg

Springtime Spaghetti
with Pesto, Asparagus & Zucchini

Bring spring to your dinner table with this garden-fresh spaghetti packed with seasonal herbs, asparagus and zucchini. If you have a shredder attachment for your food processor, save time and use it to shred the zucchini. Save the prettiest basil leaves from the bunch to sprinkle over each dish before serving.

INGREDIENTS

2 cups	packed fresh basil
½ cup	toasted unsalted walnuts
2 small	cloves garlic
1 tsp	ground black pepper, divided
½ tsp	sea salt, divided
¼ cup	extra-virgin olive oil
12 oz thin	asparagus spears, trimmed and cut into 2-inch lengths
1	zucchini, trimmed and cut into matchsticks or shredded
1 cup	frozen petite or baby peas, thawed
8 oz	whole-grain spaghetti
½ cup	grated or sliced Parmesan cheese
	zest of 1 lemon

Serves **4.**
Hands-On Time: **30 Minutes.**
Total Time: **35 Minutes.**

INSTRUCTIONS

In a food processor, pulse basil, walnuts, garlic, ½ tsp pepper and ¼ tsp salt, stopping to scrape down sides of bowl, until finely chopped. With processor running, slowly drizzle in oil, then ¼ cup water and blend until a chunky sauce forms.

Mist a large skillet with cooking spray and heat on medium-high. Add asparagus and cook, stirring frequently, for 2 minutes. Add ⅓ cup water and bring to a simmer. Cook, stirring occasionally, until asparagus is tender-crisp and no liquid remains, about 3 minutes. Add zucchini, peas and remaining ½ tsp pepper and ¼ tsp salt and cook, stirring frequently, until zucchini is tender, about 2 minutes.

Meanwhile, in a large pot, cook pasta al dente according to package directions. Drain, reserving 1 cup of the cooking water. Return pasta to pot.

Add asparagus mixture and basil mixture to pasta and heat on low, stirring gently to coat. Gradually stir in reserved cooking water, 1 tbsp at a time, until sauce reaches desired consistency. Divide among plates and top with Parmesan and lemon zest, dividing evenly.

Nutrition Information Per serving (2 cups): Calories: 493, Total Fat: 27 g, Sat. Fat: 5 g, Monounsaturated Fat: 13 g, Polyunsaturated Fat: 8 g, Carbs: 47 g, Fiber: 8 g, Sugars: 5 g, Protein: 18 g, Sodium: 486 mg, Cholesterol: 9 mg

ALL ABOUT THE GREENS: This pasta dish offers a wealth of vegetables and herbs including basil, asparagus and zucchini. Both asparagus spears and fragrant basil leaves are rich in bone-supportive vitamin K, while zucchini is packed with the carotenoids lutein and zeaxanthin. Studies have found that these potent antioxidants may help reduce your risk of age-related macular degeneration.

Chicken Parmesan
with Cheesy Eggplant Stacks

Baking the panko-crusted chicken on a wire rack lifts it away from the cooking juices, keeping the crust from getting soggy. Our eggplant stacks taste just as good as traditional eggplant Parm–but they're ready in a fraction of the time!

INGREDIENTS

Chicken

½ cup	whole-wheat panko bread crumbs
¼ cup	grated Parmesan cheese
1 tsp	dried oregano
½ tsp	each garlic powder and ground black pepper
1 large	egg white
2	boneless, skinless chicken breasts (about 1 lb), halved horizontally
2 tbsp	whole-wheat flour

Eggplant Stacks

1 large	eggplant (about 20 oz), trimmed, cut crosswise into 8 slices about ½ to ¾ inch thick
3	Roma tomatoes, cut crosswise into ¾-inch-thick rounds
3 tbsp	olive oil
1 tbsp	balsamic vinegar
1 tsp	dried oregano
½ tsp	each sea salt and ground black pepper
½ cup	shredded mozzarella cheese
¼ cup	loosely packed fresh basil leaves

Serves **4.**
Hands-On Time: **25 Minutes.**
Total Time: **45 Minutes.**

INSTRUCTIONS

Preheat oven to 425°F. Line a large rimmed baking sheet with foil or parchment paper. Arrange a wire rack over sheet; mist with cooking spray. Set aside.

Prepare chicken: In a large shallow plate, combine panko, Parmesan, oregano, garlic powder and pepper. In a separate shallow dish, whisk egg until frothy. Dust chicken with flour, shaking off excess. Working 1 piece at a time, dip chicken in egg, turning to coat. Press both sides into panko mixture. Transfer to rack; mist tops with cooking spray. Bake until no longer pink inside, about 15 minutes. Remove from oven; cover with foil.

Meanwhile, prepare stacks: Spread eggplant and tomatoes in a single layer on a separate rimmed parchment-lined sheet. Brush with oil and vinegar. Sprinkle with oregano, salt and pepper. Bake until eggplant is tender, about 15 minutes.

Preheat broiler; arrange rack 6 inches from top heat source. Sandwich tomato between eggplant slices to make 4 stacks; sprinkle with mozzarella. Broil until cheese melts, 1 minute. Sprinkle with basil. Serve with chicken.

Nutrition Information Per serving (¼ of recipe): Calories: 392, Total Fat: 18 g, Sat. Fat: 5 g, Monounsaturated Fat: 10 g, Polyunsaturated Fat: 2 g, Carbs: 26 g, Fiber: 6 g, Sugars: 7 g, Protein: 32 g, Sodium: 503 mg, Cholesterol: 78 mg

Polynesian Stir-Fry

Serves **2.**
Hands-On Time: **20 Minutes.**
Total Time: **1 Hour.**

INGREDIENTS

½ cup	brown rice
3 tbsp	fresh orange juice
2 tbsp	apple cider vinegar
1 tbsp	reduced-sodium tamari
1 tbsp	coconut sugar
½ tsp	sriracha, or to taste
2 tsp	grape seed oil, divided
1 cup	snap peas, halved diagonally
1 cup	cubed red bell pepper
¾ cup	fresh pineapple chunks (or frozen and thawed)
4	green onions, sliced into 1-inch lengths
1 5-oz	BPA-free can sliced water chestnuts
8 oz	extra-firm organic tofu, drained and cubed (½-inch cubes)
1 tsp	arrowroot mixed into 1 tsp water
1 tsp	toasted sesame oil

INSTRUCTIONS

To a small saucepan, add rice and 1 cup water and bring to a boil. Cover and reduce heat to a simmer; cook until tender, about 35 to 40 minutes.

Prepare sauce: in a small bowl, whisk together orange juice, vinegar, tamari, coconut sugar and sriracha; set aside.

In a wok or large nonstick skillet on high, heat 1 tsp grape seed oil. Add peas, bell pepper, pineapple, green onion and chestnuts. Stir-fry for 4 minutes, then transfer to a plate.

In the same wok on high, heat remaining 1 tsp grape seed oil. Add tofu and cook for 2 minutes per side, or until golden. Return vegetables to the pan and add sauce. When liquid starts to bubble, add arrowroot mixture. Let bubble, 15 seconds, and stir to coat all ingredients. Drizzle with sesame oil and serve on rice.

Nutrition Information Per serving (3 cups and ½ of rice): Calories: 516, Total Fat: 14.5 g, Sat. Fat: 2 g, Monounsaturated Fat: 4 g, Polyunsaturated Fat: 8 g, Carbs: 77 g, Fiber: 11 g, Sugars: 23 g, Protein: 20 g, Sodium: 399 mg, Cholesterol: 0 mg

Balsamic Cherry Pork Tenderloin
with Crispy Asparagus

Balsamic vinegar adds a heady hit of sweet-and-sour flavor to the cherries and keeps this sauce on the savory side. Pork tenderloin has a thin end that cooks faster than the rest of the roast; to keep it from overcooking, simply tuck it under so that the tenderloin is the same thickness throughout.

Serves **4.**
Hands-On Time: **25 Minutes.**
Total Time: **45 Minutes.**

INSTRUCTIONS

Preheat oven to 450°F. Line half of a large rimmed baking sheet with enough foil to leave a 2-inch overhang on sides. Bring edges of foil up, then fold over to create a 1-inch-tall border around half of sheet. (**NOTE:** *You can also use a smaller baking sheet and create foil border around the entire tray.*)

In a medium bowl, toss cherries with vinegar. Spoon into center of foil. In a small bowl, combine ½ tsp pepper, ¼ tsp salt and allspice; rub over pork. Arrange pork over top of cherry mixture, tucking in thin end of tenderloin. Bake until just a hint of pink remains in pork and temperature reaches 145°F when tested in thickest part, 25 to 30 minutes. (**TIP:** *If cherry juices begin to burn, fold sides of foil over to partially enclose pork.*)

Meanwhile, in a small food processor, pulse bread, almonds, thyme and remaining ¼ tsp each salt and pepper into coarse crumbs. Line a second large baking sheet with foil. In a large shallow bowl, beat eggs. Sprinkle 2 tbsp crumb mixture on a plate. Working 1 at a time, dip asparagus into egg, then dredge in crumb mixture, turning to coat lightly. When crumbs become too wet, wipe off plate and add 2 tbsp more of crumbs. (**NOTE:** *Wet crumbs will not stick to asparagus.*) Arrange in a single layer on prepared sheet. In last 5 minutes of pork baking time, add asparagus to oven.

Remove pork from oven and let pork rest on sheet for 5 minutes; keep asparagus in oven for 5 minutes more (for a total of 10 minutes baking time), until crispy. Transfer pork to cutting board and slice. Serve with cherry mixture and asparagus. Garnish pork with thyme sprigs (if using).

Nutrition Information Per serving (¼ of recipe): Calories: 268, Total Fat: 8 g, Sat. Fat: 2 g, Monounsaturated Fat: 4 g, Polyunsaturated Fat: 2 g, Carbs: 18 g, Fiber: 5 g, Sugars: 8 g, Protein: 32 g, Sodium: 389 mg, Cholesterol: 143 mg

INGREDIENTS

1¼ cups	frozen sour cherries, thawed but not drained; add juices to bowl along with cherries (**TIP:** *Or substitute with fresh pitted cherries.*)
4 tsp	balsamic vinegar
¾ tsp	ground black pepper, divided
½ tsp	sea salt, divided
½ tsp	ground allspice
1 lb	pork tenderloin, trimmed
1 slice	whole-grain crusty bread (about 1½ oz), torn into pieces
¼ cup	blanched unsalted slivered almonds
1 tbsp	packed chopped fresh thyme leaves + additional sprigs for garnish, optional
2 large	eggs
1 lb	thick asparagus spears, trimmed

ANTIOXIDANT-PACKED SPEARS: Asparagus contains anti-inflammatory and antioxidant compounds including the antioxidant glutathione (GSH), which helps prevent oxidative stress that can lead to premature aging and chronic diseases

Mixed Mushroom Stew
with Pork & Orzo

INGREDIENTS

2 cups	low-sodium chicken broth
1 oz	dried porcini mushrooms
1 tbsp	olive oil
6 oz	lean ground pork
1 large	zucchini, diced into ¼-inch pieces
3	cloves garlic, minced
8 oz	white mushrooms, sliced
10 oz	cremini mushrooms, sliced
1 4-oz	pkg gourmet mixed mushrooms (blend of portobellos, cremini, oysters and shiitakes), sliced
4 tbsp	white whole-wheat flour
6	green onions, chopped
1 tbsp	finely chopped fresh thyme
2 tsp	orange zest
1 tbsp	reduced-Sodium soy sauce
½ tsp	sea salt
¼ tsp	ground black pepper
4 cups	cooked whole-wheat orzo

Serves **8.**
Hands-On Time: **20 Minutes.**
Total Time: **45 Minutes.**

INSTRUCTIONS

In a small saucepan, bring broth to a boil on high heat. Add porcini mushrooms and simmer for 4 minutes. Strain mushrooms, reserving liquid. Set aside.

In a large saucepan, heat oil on medium-high. Add pork, stirring to break up meat. Cook until brown, about 3 to 4 minutes. Add zucchini and garlic and sauté for 2 minutes. Once zucchini is soft and begins to release liquid, add white, cremini and gourmet mushrooms. Cover and cook for about 4 minutes, until mushrooms begin to release liquid.

Stir in flour and cook, uncovered, for another 2 minutes. Add reserved porcini cooking liquid and bring to a boil. Mix in onion, thyme, orange zest, soy sauce, salt, pepper and porcini mushrooms. Simmer on medium-high heat for 3 to 4 minutes.

To serve, place ½ cup orzo in each soup bowl and top with 1 cup mushroom mixture.

Nutrition Information Per serving (1 cup mushroom stew and ½ cup orzo): Calories: 235, Total Fat: 7 g, Sat. Fat: 0.5 g, Carbs: 40 g, Fiber: 7 g, Sugars: 2 g, Protein: 12 g, Sodium: 198 mg, Cholesterol: 0 mg

Sesame Shrimp

INGREDIENTS

1 lb	jumbo shrimp, peeled, deveined and tails removed
2 tbsp	reduced-sodium soy sauce
¼ cup	peeled and minced ginger, divided
1 tbsp	rice vinegar
4 tsp	sesame oil, divided
5	cloves garlic, minced, divided
¼ tsp	ground black pepper
1 cup	quinoa, rinsed
1 cup	frozen shelled edamame
1 tbsp	extra-virgin olive oil
1	leek, halved and thinly sliced
1 bunch	bok choy, thinly sliced (about 6½ cups)
1	carrot, finely chopped
5	radishes, finely chopped
1½ tsp	arrowroot powder
1½ tbsp	sesame seeds

Serves **4.**
Hands-On Time: **30 Minutes.**
Total Time: **30 Minutes.**

INSTRUCTIONS

To a medium bowl, add shrimp, soy sauce, 2 tbsp ginger, vinegar, 3 tsp sesame oil, 2 cloves garlic and black pepper. Set aside to marinate at least 10 minutes and no longer than 30 minutes.

Meanwhile, in a medium saucepan on medium, heat remaining 1 tsp sesame oil. Add 1 clove garlic and quinoa and toast for 3 minutes, stirring often. Add 2 cups water, bring to a boil, reduce heat to low and simmer, covered, for about 15 minutes. During final 10 minutes of simmering, add edamame. Remove saucepan from heat and keep covered.

In a large sauté pan on medium, heat olive oil. Add leeks, remaining 2 tbsp ginger and remaining 2 cloves garlic and cook for 2 minutes, stirring, until softened. Add bok choy, carrot and radishes; sauté for 3 minutes more. Add shrimp and marinade from bowl; sauté for 4 to 5 minutes until shrimp is opaque throughout. Stir in arrowroot powder and cook until sauce thickens slightly, about 1 minute. Stir in sesame seeds.

To serve, spoon 1 cup quinoa-edamame mixture onto a plate and top with 1¼ cups shrimp and vegetables.

Nutrition Information Per serving (1¼ cups shrimp and vegetables and 1 cup quinoa): Calories: 438, Total Fat: 15 g, Sat. Fat: 2 g, Monounsaturated Fat: 6 g, Polyunsaturated Fat: 5 g, Carbs: 46 g, Fiber: 8 g, Sugars: 6 g, Protein: 33 g, Sodium: 516 mg, Cholesterol: 159 mg

Roasted Vegetable & Arugula Salad

with Chipotle Vinaigrette

Serves **5.**
Hands-On Time: **10 Minutes.**
Total Time: **50 Minutes.**

INGREDIENTS

1 lb	carrots, peeled and diced
1	medium yellow onion, diced
1 lb	beets, peeled and diced
½ cup	brewed black tea
1 tbsp	raw honey
1 tbsp	olive oil
2 tsp	apple cider vinegar
1 tsp	Dijon mustard
¼ tsp	chipotle chile powder
⅛ tsp	sea salt
5 cups	arugula
2½ oz	goat cheese, crumbled

INSTRUCTIONS

Preheat oven to 450°F. Mist a 9 x 13-inch roasting pan with cooking spray. On 1 side of pan, place carrots and onion; place beets on other side. Mist vegetables with cooking spray. Cover with foil and bake for 20 minutes. Uncover and cook for another 20 minutes.

In a small bowl, whisk together tea, honey, oil, vinegar, mustard, chipotle and salt. In a large bowl, add beets, carrots and onion. Pour dressing over top and gently toss to coat well. To serve, place 1 cup arugula on each of 5 plates, then top with 1 cup vegetables and ½ oz goat cheese.

Nutrition Information Per serving (1 cup vegetables, 1 cup greens, ½ oz goat cheese): Calories: 169, Total Fat: 6 g, Sat. Fat: 2.5 g, Monounsaturated Fat: 3 g, Polyunsaturated Fat: 1 g, Carbs: 25 g, Fiber: 6 g, Sugars: 16 g, Protein: 6 g, Sodium: 265 mg, Cholesterol: 6 mg

Turmeric-Roasted Vegetables

with Parsley Almond Gremolata

Serves **4.**
Hands-On Time: **25 Minutes.**
Total Time: **55 Minutes.**

INGREDIENTS

6 cups	broccoli florets (3 inch)
2	large carrots, cut diagonally into 1-inch chunks
1 tsp	ground turmeric
3 tbsp	coconut or olive oil, divided
	sea salt and ground black pepper, to taste
½ cup	raw unsalted almonds
1 large	shallot, minced
¼ cup	chopped fresh flat-leaf parsley
1 tsp	lemon zest + juice of ½ lemon, divided
1	clove garlic, minced

INSTRUCTIONS

Preheat oven to 425°F. Line 2 large rimmed baking sheets with parchment paper.

In a large bowl, toss broccoli, carrots, turmeric and 2 tbsp oil. Arrange in a single layer on prepared sheets. Season with salt and pepper. Roast until golden and tender, 30 to 35 minutes.

Meanwhile, in a food processor, process almonds until finely chopped. In a small skillet on medium-low, heat remaining 1 tbsp oil. Add shallot and sauté, stirring occasionally until tender, 4 to 5 minutes. Remove skillet from heat and stir in almonds, parsley, lemon zest and garlic.

Transfer roasted vegetables to a serving bowl. Top with gremolata and drizzle lemon juice over top.

Nutrition Information Per serving (¼ of recipe): Calories: 313, Total Fat: 26 g, Sat. Fat: 15 g, Monounsaturated Fat: 7 g, Polyunsaturated Fat: 3 g, Carbs: 16 g, Fiber: 6 g, Sugars: 5 g, Protein: 8 g, Sodium: 118 mg, Cholesterol: 0 mg

Spinach & Cauli-Rice Salad
with Cashew Dressing

INGREDIENTS

1	red onion, cut into ¼-inch wedges
8 oz	green beans
3 tbsp	extra-virgin olive oil or avocado oil, divided
1 tbsp	fresh thyme leaves
	sea salt and ground black pepper, to taste
3 cups medium	cauliflower florets (*TIP: Skip making cauliflower rice by purchasing fresh or frozen riced cauliflower.*)
6 oz	baby spinach

Dressing

6 tbsp	extra-virgin olive oil
3 tbsp	raw unsalted cashew butter
¼ tsp	lemon zest + 2½ tbsp fresh lemon juice
1	small garlic clove, minced
½ tsp	Dijon mustard
½ tsp	sea salt
	ground black pepper, to taste

Serves **4.**
Hands-On Time: **30 Minutes.**
Total Time: **40 Minutes.**

INSTRUCTIONS

Preheat oven to 400°F. Line 2 large baking sheets with parchment paper. Arrange onions and beans on sheets, drizzle with 2 tbsp oil and toss to coat. Sprinkle evenly with thyme and season with salt and pepper, to taste. Bake for 20 to 25 minutes, until beans are slightly golden and onions are caramelized.

Meanwhile, to a food processor, add cauliflower. Pulse about 15 times, until pieces are about the size of rice grains. (**NOTE:** *If you are using premade cauliflower rice, fresh or frozen, skip this step.*)

In a medium sauté pan on medium, heat 1 tbsp oil. Add riced cauliflower and toss to coat. Season with pinch salt. Sauté for 2 minutes, then cover and steam on low for 5 to 10 minutes, or until desired tenderness is achieved. (**TIP:** *If using frozen riced cauliflower, no need to cover and steam. Continue stirring frozen cauliflower until defrosted and excess water has evaporated.*)

Prepare dressing: In a glass jar, add all ingredients and 2 tbsp water and shake until well emulsified.

Assemble salad: Place spinach in a bowl. Add prepared cauliflower rice, roasted onions and green beans. Drizzle with enough dressing to coat lightly; toss. (**NOTE:** *Salad uses about three-quarters of dressing; use remaining dressing to drizzle over chicken or fish.*)

Nutrition Information Per serving (¼ of recipe): Calories: 405, Total Fat: 38 g, Sat. Fat: 6 g, Monounsaturated Fat: 28 g, Polyunsaturated Fat: 4 g, Carbs: 14.5 g, Fiber: 4 g, Sugars: 5 g, Protein: 5 g, Sodium: 337 mg, Cholesterol: 0 mg

TIP: If following our Meal Plan, keep dressing aside and toss before eating.

Lamb Roast

with Fava Bean Mash

INGREDIENTS

4	Yukon Gold potatoes, scrubbed and cut into 8 wedges
1 lb	lamb tenderloin, trimmed
¼ tsp	each sea salt and ground black pepper, divided
8	packed cups chopped beet greens
1	yellow onion, chopped into 1-inch pieces
1 cup	cooked fava beans or baby lima beans
1 tbsp	olive oil
2 tsp	lemon zest + juice of 1 lemon
2	cloves garlic

Serves **4.**
Hands-On Time: **10 Minutes.**
Total Time: **55 Minutes.**

INSTRUCTIONS

Preheat oven to 450°F. Mist a large roasting pan with cooking spray. Arrange potatoes in pan in a single layer; mist again with cooking spray. Bake potatoes, uncovered, for 15 minutes.

Meanwhile, heat a sauté pan on medium-high and mist with cooking spray. Sprinkle lamb with ⅛ tsp each salt and pepper. Sear lamb, browning meat, for 1 minute on each side. Remove lamb from pan and set aside. Add 1 cup water to pan. Deglaze pan by scraping up bits on bottom with a wooden spoon and cooking for about 30 seconds. Remove pan from heat.

Once potatoes are done, remove from oven and carefully push potatoes to 1 side of pan. Place lamb on other side. Add beet greens and onion over top of potatoes. Pour deglazing liquid over top of vegetables and lamb. Cover with foil and bake for 30 minutes or until a meat thermometer registers 145°F when placed in center of lamb. Remove pan from oven and uncover. Let rest for 5 minutes.

Meanwhile, place beans in the bowl of a food processor with oil, lemon juice and zest, garlic and remaining ⅛ tsp salt and ⅛ tsp pepper. Purée for 1 to 2 minutes or until smooth; set aside. (*Fava bean purée can be served warmed or at room temperature.*)

To serve, slice tenderloin into 1-oz pieces. On each plate, place ¼ cup bean purée, 4 slices lamb, 8 potato wedges and ½ cup beet green–onion mixture.

Nutrition Information Per serving (4 oz lamb, ¼ cup bean purée, 8 potato wedges, ½ cup greens mixture): Calories: 447, Total Fat: 11 g, Sat. Fat: 3.5 g, Monounsaturated Fat: 5.5 g, Polyunsaturated Fat: 0.5 g, Carbs: 54 g, Fiber: 8 g, Sugars: 4 g, Protein: 34 g, Sodium: 391 mg, Cholesterol: 73 mg

Zoodles
with Cilantro Pesto
& Grilled Chicken

INGREDIENTS

2 large or 4 small	zucchini, trimmed
¼ tsp	sea salt
1 cup	packed fresh cilantro
2 tbsp	chopped unsalted walnuts
2 tbsp	chopped shallot
1½ tbsp	Parmesan cheese
	zest and juice of ½ lemon
2	small cloves garlic
½ tsp	dried oregano
1 tbsp + ½ tsp	extra-virgin olive oil, divided
8 oz	chicken breast tenders
⅛ tsp	ground black pepper

Serves **2.**
Hands-On Time: **40 Minutes.**
Total Time: **1 Hour, 10 Minutes.**

INSTRUCTIONS

Working one at a time, secure zucchini in a spiral maker and turn crank to create "zoodles," long strands that resemble spaghetti. (***NOTE:*** *Always read directions for your spiral maker as directions vary by brand.*) Cut any zoodles that are very long in half. Line a large baking sheet with a double layer of paper towel and spread zoodles on sheet in a single layer. Gently squeeze with more paper towels. Sprinkle with salt; set aside 30 to 45 minutes. Working in batches, transfer to another sheet lined with paper towel; gently squeeze out moisture.

In a small food processor, pulse cilantro, walnuts, shallot, Parmesan, lemon zest and juice, garlic and oregano. With machine running, stream in 1 tbsp oil. Set aside.

Place chicken between 2 sheets of wax paper. Using a mallet, pound to 1-inch thickness. In a large skillet on medium-high, heat remaining ½ tsp oil. Season chicken with pepper. Cook for 4 to 6 minutes, turning once, until cooked through and golden. Transfer to a cutting board, let rest 5 minutes and then slice.

Mist same skillet with cooking spray and heat on medium-high. Add zoodles, cook for 2 to 3 minutes, until slightly softened. Remove from heat; toss with reserved pesto. Divide among plates; top with chicken.

__Nutrition Information__ Per serving (2 cups zoodles and ½ of chicken): Calories: 326, Total Fat: 17 g, Sat. Fat: 3 g, Monounsaturated Fat: 8 g, Polyunsaturated Fat: 5 g, Carbs: 16 g, Fiber: 4 g, Sugars: 9 g, Protein: 30 g, Sodium: 337 mg, Cholesterol: 66 mg

Shredded Brussels Sprout & Chicken Sauté

Serves **4.**
Hands-On Time: **25 Minutes.**
Total Time: **25 Minutes.**

INGREDIENTS

3 tbsp	extra-virgin olive oil or avocado oil
2	carrots, peeled and diced
1 large	yellow onion, diced
1	clove garlic, finely chopped
¾ tsp	each ground cumin and coriander
Pinch	ground cayenne pepper
1 lb	Brussels sprouts, trimmed, halved and thinly sliced
½ tsp	each sea salt and ground black pepper
10 oz	chicken breast, cooked and shredded (or chicken thighs)
	juice of ½ lemon

INSTRUCTIONS

In a large skillet on medium, heat oil. Add carrots, onions and garlic and sauté until onions are tender and translucent, about 6 minutes. Add cumin, coriander and cayenne and stir until fragrant, about 1 minute.

Add Brussels sprouts, salt and pepper and sauté until just tender, 3 to 4 minutes.

Stir in chicken and toss to combine. Stir in lemon juice.

Nutrition Information Per serving (¼ of recipe): Calories: 289, Total Fat: 14 g, Sat. Fat: 2 g, Monounsaturated Fat: 9 g, Polyunsaturated Fat: 2 g, Carbs: 17 g, Fiber: 6 g, Sugars: 5 g, Protein: 26 g, Sodium: 341 mg, Cholesterol: 60 mg

Red Curry Chicken Soup
with Rice Noodles

Curry paste brings the heat, and a little goes a long way–add it a teaspoon at a time until it's at your desired spice level. For a garnish, make a simple relish of diced mango dressed with lime juice, honey and sliced serrano chiles.

Serves **4.**
Hands-On Time: **20 Minutes.**
Total Time: **25 Minutes.**

INGREDIENTS

1 tbsp	coconut oil
12 oz	boneless, skinless chicken breast, cut into bite-size pieces
⅛ tsp	each sea salt and ground black pepper
1 13.5-oz	BPA-free can coconut milk
3–4 tsp	red curry paste
1 tbsp	fish sauce
1 cup	thinly sliced green bell pepper
2 oz	brown rice vermicelli noodles, broken

INSTRUCTIONS

In a saucepan on medium-high, heat oil. Sprinkle chicken with salt and pepper and add to pan. Sauté until browned, 4 to 5 minutes, stirring occasionally.

Add 2 cups water and coconut milk; bring to a boil. Stir in curry paste and fish sauce; simmer 2 to 3 minutes. Add bell pepper and noodles; return to a boil. (*TIP: For more manageable bites, break the rice noodles into smaller pieces before adding them to the soup.*) Simmer soup until noodles soften, 3 to 4 minutes.

Nutrition Information Per serving (¼ of soup): Calories: 348, Total Fat: 21 g, Sat. Fat: 19 g, Monounsaturated Fat: 1 g, Polyunsaturated Fat: 1 g, Carbs: 16 g, Fiber: 1 g, Sugars: 3 g, Protein: 23 g, Sodium: 539 mg, Cholesterol: 62 mg

Wild Mushroom & Lamb Ragout Pappardelle

Lamb is simmered with red wine, beef broth and wild mushrooms for a meal with deep umami flavor.

INGREDIENTS

10 oz	fresh whole-grain pasta sheets
1 tbsp	olive oil
¾ lb	boneless lamb loin roast, trimmed and cut into ½-inch-thick medallions (*Alternatively, you can also cut into ¼-inch-thick, 2-inch-long strips.*)
¼ tsp	each sea salt and ground black pepper
¾ lb	mixed wild mushrooms (such as chanterelle, oyster, shiitake and cremini), roughly chopped
3	cloves garlic, minced
2 cups	low-sodium beef broth
½ cup	dry red wine
8	sun-dried tomatoes (packed in oil), thinly sliced
2 tbsp	chopped fresh rosemary leaves

Serves **4.**
Hands-On Time: **25 Minutes.**
Total Time: **30 Minutes.**

INSTRUCTIONS

Slice pasta sheets lengthwise into 1-inch strips and gently separate into individual noodles. Lay on a flat surface.

In a large skillet on medium-high, heat oil. Season lamb with salt and pepper. Working in batches if necessary, add to skillet and sear, turning once, until browned on both sides, about 5 to 7 minutes for medium-rare or 7 to 9 minutes for medium. (If using lamb strips, cook for 5 minutes, turning frequently, until browned.) Transfer lamb to a plate and cover to keep warm. Reduce heat to medium, add mushrooms and cook, stirring frequently, until browned, about 7 to 10 minutes. Add garlic and cook, stirring, until fragrant, 30 seconds. Add broth and wine, scraping up browned bits from bottom of skillet. Bring to a simmer and cook until liquid is reduced by one-third, about 3 minutes.

To skillet, add pasta strips, nestling into liquid. Cover and simmer, stirring occasionally, until pasta is al dente, 4 to 5 minutes. Return lamb and any accumulated juices back to skillet and heat through, about 1 minute. Add tomatoes and rosemary and stir to combine. (***TIP:*** *If you don't have a lid for your skillet, cover it with a baking sheet.*)

Nutrition Information Per serving (¼ of recipe): Calories: 406, Total Fat: 13 g, Sat. Fat: 3.5 g, Monounsaturated Fat: 6 g, Polyunsaturated Fat: 2 g, Carbs: 42 g, Fiber: 7 g, Sugars: 2 g, Protein: 30 g, Sodium: 295 mg, Cholesterol: 131 mg

TIP: Fresh whole-grain pappardelle can be difficult to find, so we use flat lasagna sheets and slice them. If you can find fresh whole-grain pappardelle, fettuccine or linguine, substitute 10 oz here.

Halibut Pouches
with Basil Cucumber Salsa

INGREDIENTS

2 cups mustard greens or kale, stems removed

4 large fresh basil leaves

8 thin lime slices (from 1 to 2 limes)

4–5 radishes, trimmed and quartered

2 tsp olive oil

sea salt and ground black pepper, to taste

4 4-oz skinless halibut fillets

ground cayenne pepper, to taste, optional

Salsa

1½ cups diced cucumber

1½ tbsp finely chopped fresh basil leaves

2 tsp fresh lime juice

sea salt and ground black pepper, to taste

Serves **4.**
Hands-On Time: **20 Minutes.**
Total Time: **30 Minutes.**

INSTRUCTIONS

Preheat oven to 400°F. Tear 4 15 x 12-inch pieces of parchment paper and fold in half lengthwise like a book. Unfold pieces and lay on a work surface.

Place ½ cup mustard greens on 1 piece of parchment, just to the right of the fold going lengthwise in the same direction as the fold. Place 1 basil leaf over center of greens then 1 lime slice over top. Arrange one-quarter of radishes around greens. Drizzle ½ tsp oil over top and season with salt and black pepper. Place 1 halibut fillet on top. Season halibut lightly with salt, black pepper and cayenne (if using) and place another lime slice over top.

Fold parchment over and starting at one end, crimp paper around ingredients (similar to making a calzone). Seal paper tightly at the end by folding over and pinching. Repeat to make 3 more pouches. Place pouches on a large baking sheet and transfer to oven. Cook for 15 to 17 minutes, or until fish is opaque and flakes easily when tested with a fork.

Meanwhile, in a medium bowl combine all salsa ingredients.

Carefully make a cut in tops of pouches with scissors. Slowly tear pouches open, being careful to avoid steam. Spoon salsa over fish.

Nutrition Information Per serving (1 pouch and ¼ of salsa): Calories: 144, Total Fat: 4 g, Sat. Fat: 1 g, Carbs: 5 g, Fiber: 2 g, Sugars: 1 g, Protein: 22 g, Sodium: 206 mg, Cholesterol: 56 mg

Lemony Angel-Hair Pasta
with Chicken & Asparagus

Simple, wholesome ingredients and a speedy cook time make this dish a go-to weeknight comfort meal. You can customize this recipe using whatever ingredients you have on hand; broccoli makes a fine substitute for the asparagus, or you can omit the chicken and chicken broth and add mushrooms, fresh grated Parmesan and vegetable broth to make it vegetarian.

INGREDIENTS

4 oz	whole-grain angel-hair pasta, broken in half
12 oz	boneless, skinless chicken breast cutlets, sliced into 12 strips
¼ tsp	sea salt
⅛ tsp	ground black pepper
2 tsp	olive oil
½ cup	low-sodium chicken broth
3 tbsp	fresh lemon juice
2 tbsp	cold organic unsalted butter, cubed
1 bunch	asparagus (about 1 lb), trimmed and cut diagonally into 1½-inch lengths
½ cup	chopped fresh mint, divided

Serves **4.**
Hands-On Time: **15 Minutes.**
Total Time: **25 Minutes.**

INSTRUCTIONS

Cook pasta al dente according to package directions. Reserving ½ cup of the cooking liquid, drain pasta.

Meanwhile, season chicken with salt and pepper. In a large skillet, heat oil on medium. Add chicken and cook, turning once, until golden, 4 to 6 minutes. Stir in pasta, broth, lemon juice and butter and bring to a simmer. Add asparagus and cook, stirring, until asparagus is crisp-tender and chicken is no longer pink inside, 1 to 2 minutes. Stir in ¼ cup mint and enough of the reserved cooking liquid to make a thin sauce. Sprinkle with remaining ¼ cup mint.

Nutrition Information Per serving (¼ of recipe): Calories: 303, Total Fat: 11.5 g, Sat. Fat: 5 g, Monounsaturated Fat: 4 g, Polyunsaturated Fat: 1 g, Carbs: 26 g, Fiber: 4.5 g, Sugars: 2 g, Protein: 25 g, Sodium: 184 mg, Cholesterol: 77 mg

Chicken & Mushroom Quinoa-Crust Pizza
with Bell Pepper Sauce

Giving up gluten doesn't have to mean saying goodbye to your favorite foods like pizza. Here, we show you how to make your own crust using quinoa as a base, and we've piled heaps of mushrooms, cheese and chicken on top for a pizza that'll beat any delivery joint.

INGREDIENTS

1 tbsp +
2 tsp olive oil, divided

1 cup quinoa, rinsed and soaked overnight

½ tsp sea salt

½ tsp dried tarragon

½ tsp dried thyme

9-oz jar roasted red bell peppers, drained and roughly chopped

8 oz white mushrooms, sliced

¼ tsp ground black pepper

5 oz cooked and shredded boneless, skinless chicken breast (about 1¼ cups)

3 oz Manchego cheese, grated (about ¾ cup packed)

3 tbsp chopped fresh flat-leaf parsley leaves

Serves **4.**
Hands-On Time: **30 Minutes.**
Total Time: **50 Minutes.***
*Plus Overnight Soaking Time.

INSTRUCTIONS

Preheat oven to 450°F. Place a 10-inch ovenproof skillet (such as cast iron) on center rack until hot, about 10 minutes. Add 1 tbsp oil and heat in oven for 2 minutes. Meanwhile, rinse and drain soaked quinoa and transfer to a food processor. Add ½ cup + 2 tbsp water, ¼ tsp + ⅛ tsp salt, tarragon and thyme. Process until mixture resembles runny pancake batter, scraping down bowl as needed, 2 to 3 minutes. When oil is hot, remove skillet from oven and swirl to coat with oil. Pour quinoa mixture into skillet and bake until batter is set and golden brown, about 20 minutes.

Meanwhile, rinse out food processor. Add bell peppers and process until smooth; set aside. In a large skillet on medium-high, heat remaining 2 tsp oil and add mushrooms, black pepper and remaining ⅛ tsp salt. Cook, stirring frequently, until tender and lightly browned, about 10 minutes.

Spread bell pepper sauce over quinoa crust in skillet. Top with shredded chicken, mushrooms and cheese. Return to oven and bake until cheese is melted, 4 to 5 minutes. Let mixture rest in skillet for 5 minutes, then transfer to a cutting board and sprinkle with parsley. Cut into wedges.

Nutrition Information Per serving (¼ of pizza): Calories: 378, Total Fat: 17 g, Sat. Fat: 6 g, Monounsaturated Fat: 6 g, Polyunsaturated Fat: 3 g, Carbs: 33 g, Fiber: 5 g, Sugars: 1 g, Protein: 23 g, Sodium: 486 mg, Cholesterol: 53 mg

Sorghum Risotto

with Artichoke Hearts, Peas & Salmon Skewers

Considered an ancient grain, sorghum has a deliciously chewy texture that gives body to this colorful risotto topped with salmon skewers.

INGREDIENTS

3 tbsp	olive oil, divided
	zest of 2 lemons + 3 tbsp fresh lemon juice, divided
2 tbsp	Dijon mustard
⅓ cup	packed fresh dill, finely chopped
¼ cup	packed fresh mint leaves, finely chopped + 3 tbsp chopped for garnish
1 lb	skinless salmon fillet, cut into 1-inch cubes
3	artichokes
1	shallot, chopped
2	cloves garlic, chopped
1 cup	sorghum, rinsed and soaked overnight
4 cups	low-sodium vegetable or chicken broth, divided
1 cup	fresh shelled green peas (from about 1 lb with shells; frozen peas may be substituted, but do not thaw)
1 oz	grated Pecorino-Romano cheese (about ¼ cup packed)
2	red Fresno or Thai chiles, sliced and seeded, optional

Equipment:

4	metal or wooden skewers (if using wooden, soak for 30 minutes)

Serves **4.**
Hands-On Time: **40 Minutes.**
Total Time: **1 Hour.***
Plus Overnight Soaking Time and Marinating Time.

INSTRUCTIONS

In a small bowl, whisk together 2 tbsp oil, half the lemon zest, 1 tbsp lemon juice and mustard until combined. Add dill and mint and whisk to combine. Transfer to a large zip-top bag. Add salmon, then seal and massage the bag to coat salmon with marinade. Refrigerate for 1 to 4 hours.

Cut off top 2 inches of artichokes and discard any remaining spiky leaves. Cut off stems so that artichokes sit upright. Fill a large saucepan with about 1 inch water and place a metal steamer basket inside. Cover and bring to a boil. Place artichokes in basket, then cover and reduce heat to medium. Simmer until leaves can be easily plucked off and a fork inserted in the base comes out easily, 20 to 25 minutes. Transfer to a work surface. When cool enough to handle, remove all the outer leaves and scrape off the inedible "hairy" choke with a spoon; trim any tough bits off the base so you're left with just the hearts. Cut each heart into sixths and toss with 2 tbsp lemon juice in a small bowl to prevent discoloration. Set aside.

Meanwhile, in a large saucepan on medium, heat remaining 1 tbsp oil. Add shallot and garlic and cook, stirring frequently, until translucent, 1 to 2 minutes. Add sorghum and cook, stirring frequently, until lightly toasted, about 2 minutes. Add 3½ cups broth, then cover and bring to a boil. Reduce heat to medium-high and simmer, uncovered, stirring occasionally, until broth is almost completely absorbed and grains are tender but retain their naturally chewy texture, 35 to 55 minutes.

Add remaining ½ cup broth. When it comes to a simmer, add peas. Cook, stirring frequently, until peas are tender and broth is nearly absorbed, 3 to 4 minutes. Add cheese and reserved artichoke hearts and stir until heated through, about 1 minute. Remove from heat and stir in remaining half of lemon zest.

SUPER SORGHUM: A gluten-free grain that is considered safe for those with celiac disease, sorghum is rich in fiber and has shown promise in helping to maintain healthy cholesterol levels as well as managing diabetes and insulin resistance.

Meanwhile, place oven rack in upper-middle position and preheat broiler to high. Line a large rimmed baking sheet with foil and mist with cooking spray. Thread salmon onto skewers and place on baking sheet (discarding marinade). Broil until salmon flakes easily and is opaque in the center, 5 to 6 minutes, turning skewers halfway through. Divide sorghum among 4 plates and top with skewers. Garnish with remaining mint and chiles (if using).

Nutrition Information Per serving (1¼ cups sorghum and 1 skewer): Calories: 447, Total Fat: 14 g, Sat. Fat: 3 g, Monounsaturated Fat: 6 g, Polyunsaturated Fat: 3 g, Carbs: 50 g, Fiber: 9 g, Sugars: 7 g, Protein: 34 g, Sodium: 392 mg, Cholesterol: 62 mg

Sushi-Style Black Rice Salad
with Wasabi Vinaigrette

We've taken all your favorite sushi ingredients–nori, pickled ginger, rice and more–and put them in a salad tossed with a pungent wasabi dressing.

INGREDIENTS

1 cup	black Japonica rice
1 cup	frozen shelled edamame
6	radishes, trimmed and cut into wedges
2	scallions, sliced
3 cups	lightly packed baby spinach leaves
2 cups	seeded and chopped English cucumber
½ cup	chopped avocado, optional
¼ cup	pickled ginger, optional
1 sheet	toasted nori, cut into matchstick-size strips
1 tbsp	toasted sesame seeds

Vinaigrette

1 tbsp	wasabi paste
1 tbsp	olive oil mayonnaise
3 tbsp	rice vinegar
2 tbsp	reduced-sodium soy sauce
2 tsp	sesame oil

Serves **4.**
Hands-On Time: **15 Minutes.**
Total Time: **1 Hour, 10 Minutes.**

INSTRUCTIONS

Prepare vinaigrette: In a small bowl, whisk wasabi and mayonnaise until smooth; whisk in vinegar, soy sauce and oil. Set aside.

Cook rice according to package directions. Remove from heat and let stand, covered, for 10 minutes. Transfer to a large bowl and toss with half of vinaigrette. Let cool for 15 minutes.

Meanwhile, to a small pot of boiling water, add edamame and cook for 3 to 4 minutes, until tender. Drain and rinse with cold water; drain again.

To bowl with rice, add radish, scallions, spinach, cucumber, edamame, avocado and ginger (if using); toss gently to combine. Divide evenly among plates and drizzle with remaining dressing. Garnish with nori and sesame seeds.

Nutrition Information Per serving (2 cups): Calories: 373, Total Fat: 13 g, Sat. Fat: 2 g, Monounsaturated Fat: 3 g, Polyunsaturated Fat: 4 g, Carbs: 54 g, Fiber: 8 g, Sugars: 6 g, Protein: 16 g, Sodium: 428 mg, Cholesterol: 1 mg

Brown Rice Pork Pad Thai

Take a tip from Thai street vendors and have all your ingredients lined up next to the stove so you can work quickly and continue to move the ingredients around in the wok nonstop. Unsalted peanuts would make a crunchy topper to this dish for added texture.

INGREDIENTS

8 oz	brown rice pad Thai noodles
2 tbsp	tamarind purée
1 tbsp	fish sauce
1 tbsp	date sugar
1½ tbsp	coconut oil
2 large	cloves garlic, thinly sliced
1–2	red Thai chile peppers, finely chopped
8 oz	pork loin cutlets, trimmed and cut into ½-inch-wide strips
2 cups	chopped baby bok choy
1 small	red bell pepper, cut into thin strips
2 large	eggs, beaten
½ cup	thinly sliced green onions, divided
1 cup	fresh bean sprouts, divided
1 tbsp	dried shrimp, coarsely chopped
¼ cup	chopped fresh cilantro
1	lime, cut into quarters

Serves **4.**
Hands-On Time: **30 Minutes.**
Total Time: **30 Minutes.**

INSTRUCTIONS

In a large bowl, combine noodles with enough very hot tap water to cover. Soak until pliable, about 30 minutes. Drain and set aside.

In a small cup, combine tamarind, fish sauce, sugar and 1 tbsp hot water and stir to dissolve; set aside near the stove.

In a wok or large sauté pan on medium-high, heat oil. Add garlic and chile pepper and stir-fry until fragrant, 10 seconds. Add pork and stir-fry for 1 minute. Add bok choy and bell pepper and stir-fry until tender, 2 minutes.

Push meat and vegetables to the side of the wok. Add eggs and stir-fry until just cooked, 1 minute.

Add noodles and fish sauce mixture to the wok and stir-fry everything together until the noodles sear in places and soften a little, 1 to 2 minutes. Add ¼ cup onions, ½ cup bean sprouts and dried shrimp and stir-fry for 1 minute. Divide among bowls and top with remaining ¼ cup onions, ½ cup bean sprouts and cilantro. Serve with lime wedges.

Nutrition Information Per serving (1⅔ cups): Calories: 406, Total Fat: 11 g, Sat. Fat: 6.5 g, Monounsaturated Fat: 2 g, Polyunsaturated Fat: 1 g, Carbs: 56 g, Fiber: 6 g, Sugars: 8 g, Protein: 22 g, Sodium: 400 mg, Cholesterol: 133 mg

ENERGY-BOOSTING IRON: While it's not often the first meat to come to mind when it comes to lean protein, pork is a staple in Thai cooking for its rich flavor and versatility. Pork is high in iron, a mineral that's necessary for carrying oxygen to your body's cells in order to produce energy.

Lettuce-Wrapped Fish Cakes
with Sweet-Tart Sauce

Fish cakes in Thailand are often augmented with tapioca flour to make them sturdier; We opt for healthy, protein-rich quinoa instead. These make a great appetizer or can be served as a main course with noodles or rice. When preparing your quinoa for this recipe, use a ratio of 1 cup quinoa to 1⅔ cups water–this ensures your fish cakes don't get soggy. Do try the dipping sauce–just a little gives the fish cakes a sweet-tangy bite.

INGREDIENTS

1¼ lb	sea bass, rockfish or other mild white fish, boned and cut into 1-inch chunks
1	egg, beaten
½ cup	cooked quinoa
⅓ cup	finely chopped red bell pepper
¼ cup	finely chopped shallots, divided
3 tsp	minced lemongrass
2 tsp	finely minced lime leaf
2 tsp	finely chopped garlic
2 tsp	sriracha
3½ tsp	fish sauce, divided
¼ tsp	ground white pepper
½ cup	rice vinegar
¼ cup	finely chopped cucumber
2 tbsp	finely grated carrot
2 tbsp	date sugar
	Leaves from 1 head red or green leaf lettuce, core removed
2 tbsp	safflower oil or coconut oil

Makes **8 cakes.**
Hands-On Time: **25 Minutes.**
Total Time: **45 Minutes.**

INSTRUCTIONS

To a food processor, add fish and pulse until chopped. (**NOTE:** *Your largest piece should be about ¼ inch with some of the fish being very finely chopped and almost pastelike*.) Transfer to a large bowl and add egg, quinoa, bell pepper, 3 tbsp shallots, lemongrass, lime leaf, garlic, sriracha, 1½ tsp fish sauce and pepper. Stir thoroughly with a rubber spatula. Form into 8 cakes, each about 3½ to 4 inches in diameter. (Packing the mixture into a measuring cup or ice cream scoop will help to form the cakes.) Chill for 15 minutes.

Meanwhile, prepare sauce: Combine remaining 1 tbsp shallots, vinegar, cucumber, carrot, sugar and remaining 2 tsp fish sauce and stir to dissolve the sugar. Arrange lettuce on a serving platter.

In a large nonstick skillet on medium, heat oil. Working in batches, add fish cakes to pan and cook until golden brown on the outside and opaque white in center, about 3½ minutes per side. Arrange on platter with lettuce. To eat, wrap each cake in a lettuce leaf, drizzle with a little dipping sauce and eat taco-style.

Nutrition Information Per serving (1 cake with lettuce and sauce): Calories: 131, Total Fat: 5 g, Sat. Fat: 1 g, Monounsaturated Fat: 1 g, Polyunsaturated Fat: 3 g, Carbs: 10 g, Fiber: 1 g, Sugars: 6 g, Protein: 11 g, Sodium: 250 mg, Cholesterol: 42 mg

Chicken Fried Rice
with Pineapple

Fried rice in Thailand is made with cold leftover white jasmine rice, but we prefer the flavor and fiber of short-grain brown rice. The combination of sweet, fresh pineapple, salty fish sauce and spicy chile sauce is typical of Thai dishes. Leftovers are great for breakfast the next day with a fried egg on top.

INGREDIENTS

2 cups	short-grain brown rice
2 tbsp	minced lemongrass
4 tsp	fish sauce
2 tsp	reduced-sodium soy sauce
2 tsp	sriracha
8 oz	boneless, skinless chicken breast, thinly sliced
¼ tsp	ground white pepper
3 tbsp	coconut oil, divided
2 tbsp	minced fresh cilantro stems
4 tsp	chopped garlic
1½ cups	sliced green beans (1-inch slices)
1 cup	stemmed and thinly sliced shiitake mushrooms
1 cup	peeled and chopped fresh pineapple (½-inch pieces)
½ cup	chopped seeded tomato
¼ cup	thinly sliced green onions
1 cup	loosely packed torn fresh Thai basil

Serves **6.**
Hands-On Time: **25 Minutes.**
Total Time: **1 Hour, 10 Minutes.***
Plus Cooling Time.

INSTRUCTIONS

In a medium saucepan, bring rice, lemongrass and 4 cups water to a boil. Reduce heat to low, cover and simmer until rice is tender, about 45 minutes. Remove from heat and let rest, covered, for 5 minutes. Transfer rice to a rimmed baking sheet and refrigerate until cool to the touch, about 1 hour. (**NOTE:** *Don't skip the cooling step; using hot rice in the recipe will cause it to become overcooked and sticky.*)

In a small bowl, combine fish sauce, soy sauce and sriracha; set aside. Toss chicken with pepper. In a wok or large skillet on high, heat 1 tbsp oil. Add chicken and stir-fry until cooked through, about 2 minutes. Transfer to a plate.

In same wok on medium-high, heat 1 tbsp oil. Add cilantro stems and garlic and stir-fry for 20 seconds. Add beans and mushrooms and stir-fry until beans are crisp-tender, about 2 minutes. Push to the side of the wok.

Add remaining 1 tbsp oil to empty side of wok and add rice. Cook for 30 seconds without stirring to sear the rice slightly, and then stir-fry everything together for 30 seconds. Add chicken, pineapple, tomato, onions and fish sauce mixture and stir-fry for 1 minute. Remove wok from heat, add basil and toss once to combine.

Nutrition Information Per serving (1¼ cups): Calories: 346, Total Fat: 10 g, Sat. Fat: 6 g, Monounsaturated Fat: 2 g, Polyunsaturated Fat: 2 g, Carbs: 56 g, Fiber: 6 g, Sugars: 6 g, Protein: 15 g, Sodium: 382 mg, Cholesterol: 28 mg

Chicken Pho
with Pea Shoots

This flavorful broth-based Vietnamese-style soup is infused with fragrant ginger, garlic and whole spices, then piled high with fresh herbs and delicate pea shoots for a hit of freshness. If your shoots are longer than a few inches, snip them into shorter, bite-size pieces.

INGREDIENTS

4 cups	low-sodium chicken broth
2	¼-inch slices fresh ginger
1 large	shallot, thinly sliced
3	cloves garlic, sliced
4 tsp	fish sauce
2	green cardamom pods
1	star anise pod
½ stick	cinnamon
¼ tsp	ground turmeric
20 oz	boneless, skinless chicken breasts (about 2 large)
3 tbsp	fresh lime juice
¼ tsp	ground black pepper
4 oz	brown rice vermicelli noodles
1	jalapeño chile pepper, seeded and thinly sliced
3 cups	pea shoots
½ cup	each loosely packed chopped fresh cilantro and chopped fresh mint
2	green onions, white and light green parts, thinly sliced

Serves **4.**
Hands-On Time: **20 Minutes.**
Total Time: **45 Minutes.**

INSTRUCTIONS

In a Dutch oven or large saucepan, combine broth, ginger, shallot, garlic, fish sauce, cardamom, star anise, cinnamon, turmeric and 3 cups water; bring to a boil. Reduce heat to medium-low, cover and simmer for 10 minutes.

Reduce heat to low and add chicken. Simmer gently, uncovered, until chicken is no longer pink inside and reaches 165°F when tested with an instant-read thermometer in center, about 15 minutes. (**NOTE:** *Do not boil*.) Using tongs, transfer chicken to a cutting board; let cool slightly. Chop or shred into bite-size pieces. Set aside.

Arrange a fine-mesh sieve over a large bowl; strain broth mixture through sieve, discarding solids. Return liquid to Dutch oven and heat on low. Stir in chicken, lime juice and pepper and cook until heated through, about 3 minutes.

Meanwhile, cook noodles according to package directions; divide among bowls. Ladle broth mixture over top, dividing evenly. Sprinkle with jalapeño, pea shoots, cilantro, mint and green onions, dividing evenly.

Nutrition Information Per serving (¼ of recipe): Calories: 348, Total Fat: 6 g, Sat. Fat: 1.5 g, Monounsaturated Fat: 2 g, Polyunsaturated Fat: 1 g, Carbs: 33 g, Fiber: 5 g, Sugars: 4 g, Protein: 42 g, Sodium: 544 mg, Cholesterol: 104 mg

VITAMIN-RICH SHOOTS:

In addition to vitamin K, pea shoots are also jam-packed with vitamins A, C, and folate. Vitamin A supports bone growth and immune system health, while vitamin C is necessary for healing wounds and scar tissue. A type of B vitamin, folate is needed in adequate amounts to help ward off anemia and aid in tissue growth.

Steamed Clams
with Sorrel & Garlic Bread

Sorrel's lemony flavor is a perfect pairing for briny shellfish, such as clams. This recipe easily serves four as an elegant appetizer; to make it a meal, toss the clams and broth with 8 oz (4 cups cooked) whole-grain linguine.

INGREDIENTS

2 strips	organic bacon (about 2 oz), no added nitrites or nitrates, chopped
1 tbsp	olive oil
1 large	leek, white and light green parts only, halved lengthwise and thinly sliced
2	cloves garlic, thinly sliced
1 tbsp	chopped fresh thyme
1 cup	all-natural seafood stock
½ cup	dry white wine
½ tsp	ground black pepper
Pinch	red pepper flakes
2 lb	Manila or other small clams, rinsed and scrubbed (**NOTE:** *Opt for fresh, untreated clams as they are lower in sodium. Discard any clams with broken shells or ones that are open and do not close when tapped.*)
2 cups	sorrel, stemmed and roughly chopped

Garlic Bread

4 slices	whole-grain crusty bread (about 4 oz)
2 tsp	olive oil
1 large	clove garlic, halved lengthwise

Serves **4.**
Hands-On Time: **20 Minutes.**
Total Time: **30 Minutes.**

INSTRUCTIONS

Prepare garlic bread: Preheat oven to 350°F. On a baking sheet, arrange bread in a single layer and brush with 2 tsp oil. Bake until crisp and golden brown, about 10 minutes. Rub cut sides of garlic over bread; discard garlic. Cover bread with foil to keep warm.

Meanwhile, heat a large sauté pan on medium. Add bacon and cook, stirring often, until crisp, about 2 minutes. Using a slotted spoon, transfer bacon to a paper towel–lined plate; set aside. Drain fat from pan and discard.

In same pan, heat 1 tbsp oil on medium. Add leek and sauté, stirring often, until tender, about 3 minutes. Add garlic and thyme and sauté until fragrant, about 30 seconds.

Increase heat to medium-high and add stock, wine, black pepper, pepper flakes and 1 cup water, scraping up browned bits from bottom of pan with a wooden spoon. Bring to a simmer and add clams, arranging in a single layer. Cover and cook until clams have opened, about 6 minutes. Stir well and discard any unopened clams. Remove from heat and stir in bacon. Gently stir in sorrel until wilted. Serve with garlic bread.

Nutrition Information Per serving (1½ cups clam mixture and 1 slice bread): Calories: 210, Total Fat: 8 g, Sat. Fat: 1 g, Monounsaturated Fat: 5 g, Polyunsaturated Fat: 1 g, Carbs: 24 g, Fiber: 4 g, Sugars: 3 g, Protein: 11 g, Sodium: 564 mg, Cholesterol: 13 mg

Spice-Rubbed Pork Chops
with Escarole & Apple Sauté

Toasting the whole spices and grinding them yourself is the key to this dish's amazingly fragrant flavor. Choose a crisp, firm apple such as Braeburn or Fuji that will hold its shape when cooked with the slightly bitter greens. When prepping the escarole, trim just the very end of the root, keeping as much of the juicy white stem as possible–it's the best part.

INGREDIENTS

1 tsp	each fennel seeds and coriander seeds
½ tsp	sea salt, divided
½ tsp	ground black pepper
4 6-oz	boneless pork loin chops, trimmed
1 tbsp	olive oil
1	Braeburn or Fuji apple, cored and cut into ½-inch wedges
2 large	cloves garlic, thinly sliced
2 tsp	chopped fresh thyme
1 bunch	escarole (about 1 lb), trimmed and roughly chopped
1 tbsp	apple cider vinegar

Serves **4.**
Hands-On Time: **20 Minutes.**
Total Time: **30 Minutes.**

INSTRUCTIONS

Heat a large sauté pan on medium-low. Add fennel and coriander and cook, stirring frequently, until fragrant, about 2 minutes. Transfer to a clean spice grinder and add ¼ tsp salt and pepper; pulse until finely ground. (*Alternatively, transfer to a cutting board and crush spices with the bottom of a saucepan.*) Rub mixture all over pork.

Mist same sauté pan with cooking spray and heat on medium-high. Add pork and reduce heat to medium-low. Cook, undisturbed, until browned, about 4 minutes. Turn and cook, undisturbed, until just a hint of pink remains in centers and pork reaches 145°F when tested with an instant-read thermometer in thickest part, about 3 minutes. Transfer to a plate and cover loosely with foil to keep warm. Set aside.

In same sauté pan, heat oil on medium. Add apple and sauté, stirring occasionally, until beginning to brown, about 2 minutes. Add garlic and thyme and sauté until fragrant, about 1 minute. Gradually add escarole, tossing with tongs to wilt between additions. Stir in vinegar and remaining ¼ tsp salt, scraping up browned bits from bottom of pan with a wooden spoon. Serve with pork.

Nutrition Information Per serving (1 pork chop and 1 cup escarole mixture): Calories: 314, Total Fat: 13 g, Sat. Fat: 4 g, Monounsaturated Fat: 7 g, Polyunsaturated Fat: 1.5 g, Carbs: 11 g, Fiber: 5 g, Sugars: 5 g, Protein: 37 g, Sodium: 348 mg, Cholesterol: 96 mg

Kimchi Beef Burgers

New to kimchi? These Korean-inspired burgers are a great place to start. Most of the kimchi is mixed into the patties to infuse them with the spicy-sweet flavor of the fermented cabbage. The remaining is stirred into a mayo to make a tangy topping. If you have some on hand, you can add a couple of cloves of minced garlic and/or 2 tsp minced ginger to the patty mixture in Step 1 for added punch.

INGREDIENTS

12 oz	lean ground beef
5 tbsp	lightly drained finely chopped kimchi, divided
3 tbsp	olive oil mayonnaise, divided
2 tsp	sesame oil, divided
2 tsp	reduced-sodium soy sauce, divided
⅛ tsp	sea salt, or to taste
½ tsp	ground black pepper
1 tsp	brown rice vinegar
1	avocado, peeled, pitted and thinly sliced
4	whole-grain buns, toasted
4 oz	Persian cucumber, thinly sliced on the diagonal

Serves **4.**
Hands-On Time: **25 Minutes.**
Total Time: **25 Minutes.**

INSTRUCTIONS

In a large bowl, combine beef, 3 tbsp kimchi, 1 tbsp mayonnaise and 1 tsp each sesame oil and soy sauce. Shape into 4 ½-inch-thick patties. Season on both sides with salt and pepper. Mist a large nonstick skillet with cooking spray and heat on medium. Add patties and cook, turning once, until beef reads 160°F when tested with a thermometer, 5 to 7 minutes.(*Alternatively, if grilling, chill patties at least 30 minutes to firm up; cook on a greased grill for 5 to 7 minutes, turning halfway.*)

Meanwhile, in a small bowl, stir together vinegar, remaining 2 tbsp mayonnaise, 2 tbsp kimchi, 1 tsp sesame oil and 1 tsp soy sauce.

Lay avocado slices over cut side of each bun bottom. Top with patty, cucumber slices, sauce and bun top.

Nutrition Information Per serving (1 burger): Calories: 433, Total Fat: 27 g, Sat. Fat: 6 g, Monounsaturated Fat: 12 g, Polyunsaturated Fat: 8 g, Carbs: 28 g, Fiber: 7 g, Sugars: 5 g, Protein: 22 g, Sodium: 538 mg, Cholesterol: 55 mg.

Vietnamese Lettuce Wraps
with Seared Snapper
& Sweet Chile Sauce

Serve these noodle-filled lettuce wraps family-style with the toppings in separate small bowls so everyone can assemble their own at the table. Save any leftovers and enjoy as a salad the next day–simply chop the lettuce, toss with the toppings and drizzle with the sauce.

INGREDIENTS

8 oz brown rice vermicelli noodles

1 lb boneless, skinless snapper fillets (¾ to 1 inch thick), patted dry (**TIP:** *Use fish tweezers to remove bones or ask your fishmonger to do it for you.*)

½ tsp sea salt

1 tbsp grape seed oil

12 large leaves Boston or romaine lettuce

4 small carrots, cut into matchsticks

1 cup each fresh Thai basil (or regular basil), fresh cilantro and fresh mint

toasted unsalted peanuts, chopped, optional

Sauce

¾ cup white vinegar

3 tbsp organic evaporated cane juice (aka organic sugar)

3 tbsp fresh lime juice

1 tbsp fish sauce

½ Thai chile pepper or serrano chile, thinly sliced, or to taste (**NOTE:** *Remove the seeds for less heat.*)

Serves **4.**
Hands-On Time: **30 Minutes.**
Total Time: **30 Minutes.**

INSTRUCTIONS

Cook noodles according to package directions. Drain and rinse under cold water. Drain well and transfer to a bowl.

Meanwhile, cut fish into 3 x 1-inch strips. Sprinkle with salt. In a large nonstick skillet on medium, heat oil. Add fish and cook, turning often, until opaque and fish flakes easily when tested with a fork, 2 to 3 minutes. Transfer to a large plate.

Meanwhile, prepare sauce: In a small bowl, stir together all sauce ingredients until sugar is dissolved.

Spoon noodles into lettuce leaves and top with fish, carrots, basil, cilantro and mint, dividing evenly. Drizzle with sauce. (Alternatively, bring all ingredients to the table and have guests assemble their own wraps.) Garnish with peanuts (if using).

Nutrition Information Per serving (3 lettuce wraps): Calories: 423, Total Fat: 4 g, Sat. Fat: 1 g, Monounsaturated Fat: 1 g, Polyunsaturated Fat: 2 g, Carbs: 61 g, Fiber: 5 g, Sugars: 12 g, Protein: 30 g, Sodium: 633 mg, Cholesterol: 40 mg

CHOOSE WELL: Always use the Seafood Watch app when purchasing snapper as you'll find different sustainable varieties in your local fish store depending on your location. But avoid red snapper unless it's from a reputable fishmonger and is sustainably sourced, as a large percentage of fish sold as red snapper is mislabeled and may actually be illegally caught fish of various types.

Sesame Salmon Sushi Bowls

INGREDIENTS

1 cup	short-grain brown rice, rinsed
¾ tsp	sea salt, divided
2 tbsp	each black and white sesame seeds + additional for garnish
4 4-oz	boneless skin-on wild Alaskan salmon fillets (such as coho or sockeye; 1 inch thick), patted dry
¼ tsp	ground black pepper
2 tsp	grape seed oil
2 tsp	furikake* or toasted white sesame seeds
2 small	carrots, cut into ribbons (**TIP:** Use a vegetable peeler to cut the carrots lengthwise into ribbons.)
1	Persian, Japanese or other variety of small cucumber, thinly sliced
1	avocado, peeled, pitted and sliced (**TIP:** If slicing in advance, place in citrus juice to avoid browning.)
1	green onion, white and light green parts only, thinly sliced
4 tsp	drained jarred pickled sushi ginger
12 pieces	roasted seaweed snack, for serving (or substitute with nori sheets cut into 2-inch squares), optional

Soy Drizzle

2 tbsp	mirin
4 tsp	rice vinegar
1 tbsp	reduced-sodium soy sauce

All the flavor of salmon rolls, minus the finicky rolling–that's the beauty of these easy-to-make rice bowls. Furikake is a dry blend of sesame seeds, seaweed and dried fish. Look for it in specialty Asian grocery stores or make your own using our easy recipe; alternatively, you can simply substitute for sesame seeds. Run your finger along the flesh side of the salmon fillet to check for any pin bones. If you find any, pull them out with a clean set of tweezers.

Serves **4.**
Hands-On Time: **30 Minutes.**
Total Time: **50 Minutes.**

INSTRUCTIONS

In a saucepan, combine rice, ¼ tsp salt and enough water to cover by 3 inches. Bring to a boil; reduce heat to a simmer and cook until tender, about 45 minutes. Drain.

Meanwhile, spread black and white sesame seeds on a plate; set aside. Mist flesh side of fish with cooking spray; sprinkle with pepper and remaining ½ tsp salt. Gently press flesh side of fish into sesame seeds.

In a large nonstick skillet on medium, heat oil. Add fish, skin side up, and cook until golden brown, about 3 minutes. Turn and cook until skin is crispy and flesh is opaque and flakes easily when tested with a fork, about 4 minutes. Transfer to a large plate; peel off and discard skin. Cover to keep warm; set aside.

Whisk together all soy drizzle ingredients.

Divide rice among bowls; sprinkle with furikake. Top with carrots, cucumber, avocado, onion, pickled ginger, seaweed (if using) and fish, dividing evenly. Drizzle with soy mixture. Garnish with additional black and white sesame seeds.

Nutrition Information Per serving (¼ of recipe): Calories: 487, Total Fat: 20 g, Sat. Fat: 3 g, Monounsaturated Fat: 10 g, Polyunsaturated Fat: 7 g, Carbs: 50 g, Fiber: 10 g, Sugars: 7 g, Protein: 29 g, Sodium: 641 mg, Cholesterol: 53 mg

*You can purchase furikake, but we prefer to make our own to avoid preservatives. Simply combine 2 tbsp toasted white sesame seeds, 1 nori sheet, crumbled, ¼ tsp sea salt or to taste, and ¼ tsp organic evaporated cane juice, or to taste. Use in this recipe or as a seasoning for any Asian dish.

Chipotle Cauliflower Tacos
with Jalapeño Cilantro Sauce

Chipotle chile powder lends a smoky note to roasted cauliflower; if you prefer less heat but still want that smokiness, use smoked paprika instead. The real star of these tacos, though, is the creamy, herbaceous sauce, so don't skip it–some of our staff members ate it by the spoonful! Serve these veggie tacos with toppings of your choice: shredded cabbage, tomatoes, cilantro, hot sauce or salsa verde, and lime wedges for squeezing all work well here.

INGREDIENTS

Tacos

1 large	head cauliflower (about 2¼ lb), cut into bite-size florets
2 tbsp	olive oil
½ tsp	each sea salt, chipotle chile powder, garlic powder and organic evaporated cane juice (aka organic cane sugar)
¼ tsp	each chile powder, ground cumin and paprika
Pinch	ground black pepper
8	6-inch corn tortillas or large Bibb or Boston lettuce leaves

Sauce

1	jalapeño chile pepper, seeded and roughly chopped
1 cup	fresh cilantro (leaves and tender stems)
½ cup	olive oil mayonnaise
2 tbsp	fresh lime juice
1 tbsp	extra-virgin olive oil
1	clove garlic, roughly chopped
¼ tsp	sea salt
Pinch	ground black pepper

Serves **4.**
Hands-On Time: **25 Minutes.**
Total Time: **45 Minutes.**

INSTRUCTIONS

Preheat oven to 450°F. Line a large rimmed baking sheet with parchment paper. Set aside.

Prepare tacos: Bring a large saucepan of water to a boil. Add cauliflower and cook until just tender, 3 to 4 minutes. Drain well; transfer to a clean kitchen towel and pat dry. Set aside.

In a large bowl, stir together oil, salt, chipotle chile powder, garlic powder, cane juice, chile powder, cumin, paprika and black pepper. Add cauliflower and toss gently to coat. Arrange in a single layer on prepared sheet. Bake, turning once, until golden, 20 to 30 minutes.

Meanwhile, prepare sauce: In a blender or food processor, blend all ingredients until smooth.

Divide cauliflower among tortillas. Add desired toppings and drizzle with sauce, dividing evenly.

Nutrition Information Per serving (2 tacos): Calories: 331, Total Fat: 33 g, Sat. Fat: 5 g, Monounsaturated Fat: 15 g, Polyunsaturated Fat: 13 g, Carbs: 8 g, Fiber: 3 g, Sugars: 3 g, Protein: 3 g, Sodium: 559 mg, Cholesterol: 10 mg

Slow-Cooker Pulled Chicken Sandwiches
with Salsa Verde

Pile these sandwiches high with coleslaw, radishes, tomatoes, sour cream and hot sauce–we love eating them open-faced with a knife and fork Or, skip the buns and make a Mexican bowl!

INGREDIENTS

Chicken

2 lb	boneless, skinless chicken breasts or thighs
4	cloves garlic, minced
1 tsp	each chile powder, ground cumin and sea salt
½ tsp	chipotle chile powder
Pinch	ground black pepper
4	whole-grain buns, split and toasted (for serving open-faced; or 8 buns if you want to serve on full buns)

Salsa Verde

7	tomatillos, husked and rinsed
4	Anaheim chile peppers
1 large	shallot, roughly chopped
⅓ cup	fresh cilantro (leaves and tender stems)
2 large	cloves garlic, roughly chopped
1 tsp	sea salt
2 tbsp	olive oil

Serves **8.**
Hands-On Time: **40 Minutes.**
Total Time: **5 Hours.***
Plus Cooling Time.

INSTRUCTIONS

Prepare salsa: Preheat broiler to high and arrange oven rack 6 inches from heat source. Line a large rimmed baking sheet with foil and mist with cooking spray. Arrange tomatillos and chile peppers in a single layer on prepared sheet. Broil, turning once, until softened and slightly charred, about 10 minutes.

Transfer chile peppers to a large heat-proof bowl; cover bowl tightly with plastic wrap. Let stand for 15 minutes. Gently peel off skins and cut peppers in half; remove seeds and white pith. Discard skins, seeds and pith. Roughly chop peppers. (**TIP:** *Wear gloves when handling chile peppers to avoid irritation*.)

Meanwhile, transfer tomatillos to a blender or food processor; add shallot, cilantro, garlic and salt. Blend until smooth. Add chile peppers and blend until just combined.

In a large skillet on medium, heat oil. Add tomatillo mixture and bring to a simmer; cook, stirring often, for 5 minutes. Remove from heat; let cool completely.

Prepare chicken: In a 4- to 6-qt slow cooker, combine chicken, garlic, chile powder, cumin, salt, chipotle chile powder, black pepper and ½ cup salsa verde; stir to coat. Transfer remaining salsa verde to a bowl; cover and refrigerate until needed. Cover slow cooker and cook on high for 4 hours or on low for 7 hours.

Using tongs, transfer chicken to a separate large bowl. Using 2 forks, shred chicken into bite-size pieces. Return to slow cooker; stir to coat.

Meanwhile, in a small saucepan, heat reserved salsa verde on low, stirring occasionally, until warm. Divide chicken mixture among bun halves. Top with desired toppings and salsa verde, dividing evenly.

Nutrition Information Per serving (1 open-faced sandwich): Calories: 256, Total Fat: 8 g, Sat. Fat: 1 g, Monounsaturated Fat: 4 g, Polyunsaturated Fat: 1 g, Carbs: 16 g, Fiber: 3 g, Sugars: 3 g, Protein: 30 g, Sodium: 653 mg, Cholesterol: 83 mg

Mexican Cobb Salad

Queso fresco ("fresh cheese") puts a south-of-the-border spin on this American classic. The mild white cheese has a crumbly texture–perfect for sprinkling over salads. Try adding crumbled tortilla chips over top for added crunch. Or make tortilla strips easily by thinly slicing corn tortillas, tossing with oil and baking until crispy.

INGREDIENTS

6 strips	all-natural turkey bacon, no added nitrates or nitrites (about 8 oz total)
1	head romaine lettuce, trimmed and leaves torn or chopped
3 oz	queso fresco or feta cheese, crumbled
1–2	avocados, peeled, pitted and chopped
1 large	ear corn, husked and kernels removed (**TIP:** *Grill your corn for extra flavor.*)
2 cups	cherry or grape tomatoes, halved

Vinaigrette

¼ cup	extra-virgin olive oil
2 tbsp	red wine vinegar
1 tbsp	fresh lemon juice
1 medium to large	clove garlic, minced
1 tsp	Dijon mustard
½ tsp	sea salt
¼ tsp	ground black pepper
¼ cup	chopped fresh cilantro

Serves **6.**
Hands-On Time: **30 Minutes.**
Total Time: **45 Minutes.**

INSTRUCTIONS

Preheat oven to 375°F. Line a large rimmed baking sheet with parchment paper. Arrange bacon in a single layer on prepared sheet. Bake until tops of strips appear dry, about 15 minutes. Flip and bake until crisp, 8 to 10 minutes. Let cool enough to handle; roughly chop. (**TIP:** *Keep an eye on it as bacon brands can vary in thickness and take more or less time to cook*.)

Meanwhile, prepare vinaigrette: In a small bowl, whisk together oil, vinegar, lemon juice, garlic, mustard, salt and pepper. Whisk in cilantro.

In a large bowl, toss lettuce with three-quarters of the vinaigrette. Transfer to a large serving platter. Arrange bacon, cheese, avocados, corn and tomatoes over top of lettuce. Drizzle with remaining vinaigrette.

Nutrition Information Per serving (⅙ of recipe): Calories: 292, Total Fat: 22 g, Sat. Fat: 4 g, Monounsaturated Fat: 14 g, Polyunsaturated Fat: 3 g, Carbs: 15 g, Fiber: 7 g, Sugars: 5 g, Protein: 12 g, Sodium: 494 mg, Cholesterol: 35 mg

Baked Churros
with Chile Chocolate Sauce

This Latin American street food is traditionally deep-fried, but we prefer this lighter, baked version–plus your friends and family will never guess they're whole grain! Be sure to serve the churros immediately to prevent them from getting soggy.

INGREDIENTS

7 tbsp	organic unsalted butter, divided
6 tbsp	coconut sugar or organic evaporated cane juice (aka organic sugar), divided
½ tsp	sea salt
1 cup	whole-wheat pastry flour
2 large	eggs
½ tsp	pure vanilla extract
1 tsp	ground cinnamon

Chocolate Sauce

½ cup	dark chocolate chips
¼ cup	heavy whipping cream (35%)
¼ cup	whole milk
Pinch	ground cayenne pepper

Makes **16 to 18 Churros.**
Hands-On Time: **40 Minutes.**
Total Time: **45 Minutes.**

INSTRUCTIONS

Preheat oven to 425°F. Line a large rimmed baking sheet with parchment paper. Set aside.

In a large saucepan, bring 5 tbsp butter, 2 tbsp coconut sugar, salt and 1 cup water to a boil, whisking often. Remove from heat; stir in flour. Continue stirring until a large dough ball forms, about 2 minutes.

Transfer dough to a stand mixer fitted with paddle attachment. Beat on low for 1 minute. In a small bowl, whisk eggs and vanilla. Working in 3 additions, add egg mixture, beating well after each, until dough is smooth, elastic and slightly sticky.

Transfer dough to a pastry bag fitted with a 1-inch star tip. Pipe dough onto prepared sheet into 5-inch strips, 2 inches apart. Bake, turning once, until golden but still slightly soft, 13 to 15 minutes.

Meanwhile, prepare sauce: In a heat-proof bowl set over a saucepan of gently simmering water, heat chocolate chips, stirring often, until melted. Whisk in cream, milk and cayenne until smooth. Cover to keep warm.

Meanwhile, in a separate small bowl, combine cinnamon and remaining ¼ cup coconut sugar. Melt remaining 2 tbsp butter. Remove churros from oven; immediately brush all over with butter and sprinkle with cinnamon mixture. Serve with sauce.

Nutrition Information Per serving (1 churro and 2 tsp sauce): Calories: 149, Total Fat: 9 g, Sat. Fat: 5 g, Monounsaturated Fat: 3 g, Polyunsaturated Fat: 0.5 g, Carbs: 15.5 g, Fiber: 1 g, Sugars: 8 g, Protein: 2 g, Sodium: 67 mg, Cholesterol: 37 mg

DON'T HAVE A PASTRY BAG? Transfer the dough to a large zip-top bag and snip one corner to make a 1-inch opening. Pipe into strips as directed, then run the tines of a fork over the surface of each to make ridges.

Balsamic Roasted Strawberry Clafouti

Fresh strawberries are roasted with balsamic vinegar in this French-style baked dessert.

INGREDIENTS

1 lb	strawberries, trimmed and quartered (If large, cut into sixths.), divided
⅓ cup + 1 tbsp	maple sugar, divided
1 tbsp	balsamic vinegar
3 large	eggs
1 cup	whole milk
½ cup	white whole-wheat flour
1 tsp	pure vanilla extract
¼ tsp	sea salt
2 tbsp	organic unsalted butter, melted and cooled slightly

Serves **6.**
Hands-On Time: **10 Minutes.**
Total Time: **1 Hour, 20 Minutes.**

INSTRUCTIONS

Preheat oven to 350°F. Transfer half of berries to an 8 x 8-inch baking dish; stir in 1 tbsp maple sugar and vinegar. Roast about 10 minutes, until tender but not mushy, stirring halfway. Let cool for 10 minutes.

Over a medium bowl, set a fine mesh sieve and pour in roasted strawberries and their liquid. Set aside to drain for about 10 minutes. To a small bowl, transfer roasted berries. Stir in remaining uncooked berries to bowl with strawberry liquid. (**MAKE AHEAD:** *This can be done up to 1 day ahead; cover and refrigerate. Before proceeding, bring to room temperature.*)

Preheat oven to 350°F. Mist a 9-inch cast iron skillet or 9-inch pie plate with cooking spray. To a blender, add eggs, milk, remaining ⅓ cup maple sugar, flour, vanilla and salt. Blend on high for 20 seconds.

Add butter and blend on high for 45 seconds more. Pour into prepared skillet or pie plate, then scatter roasted strawberries over batter. Bake in center of oven until puffed, edges are golden and center is set but slightly jiggly, about 30 minutes. Cool on a wire rack for 10 minutes. Cut into wedges and top with fresh berries.

Nutrition Information Per serving (⅙ of clafouti): Calories: 190, Total Fat: 8 g, Sat. Fat: 4 g, Monounsaturated Fat: 2.5 g, Polyunsaturated Fat: 1 g, Carbs: 23 g, Fiber: 2 g, Sugars: 14 g, Protein: 6 g, Sodium: 136 mg, Cholesterol: 107 mg

Chile Chocolate Cupcakes
with Cinnamon Buttercream Frosting

INGREDIENTS

2 large	eggs
1 cup	unsalted creamy almond butter
2 tsp	pure vanilla extract
¾ cup	coconut sugar
⅓ cup	unsweetened cocoa powder
1 tsp	ground cinnamon
1 tsp	baking soda
½ tsp	each ground nutmeg and ginger
¼ tsp	each sea salt and ground cayenne pepper

Frosting

½ cup	coconut sugar
1	stick (½ cup) organic unsalted butter
1 tbsp	plain unsweetened almond or coconut milk
2 tsp	ground cinnamon
1 tsp	pure vanilla extract

Makes **8 Cupcakes.**
Hands-On Time: **25 Minutes.**
Total Time: **40 Minutes.**

INSTRUCTIONS

Prepare cupcakes: Preheat oven to 325°F. In a large bowl, whisk eggs. Stir in almond butter and 2 tsp vanilla and mix until well combined. In a medium bowl, mix together ¾ cup coconut sugar, cocoa powder, 1 tsp cinnamon, baking soda, nutmeg, ginger, salt and cayenne. Add dry ingredients to wet and stir until well combined. Line 8 muffin tins with baking cups and fill three-quarters full with batter. Bake for 25 to 30 minutes, or until a toothpick inserted into center comes out clean. Set aside to cool completely in pan.

Prepare buttercream: In a blender, blend ½ cup coconut sugar on high for about 1 minute, until mostly powdery. Using a stand mixer or a hand mixer, beat butter and powdered coconut sugar on low until combined, then beat on high until light and airy, about 4 minutes. Stir in milk, 2 tsp cinnamon and 1 tsp vanilla and beat on high for 1 minute more. Spread buttercream over cooled cupcakes. (***MAKE AHEAD:*** *Store cupcakes in the refrigerator for up to 4 days; bring to room temperature before serving.*)

Nutrition Information Per serving (1 cupcake): Calories: 467, Total Fat: 31 g, Sat. Fat: 9 g, Monounsaturated Fat: 14 g, Polyunsaturated Fat: 5 g, Carbs: 47 g, Fiber: 5 g, Sugars: 39 g, Protein: 9 g, Sodium: 256 mg, Cholesterol: 77 mg

Basil Lime Sorbet

We don't typically think of them in desserts, but herbs go really well with all kinds of fruit flavors. Here, basil complements lime for a sweet-tart treat.

INGREDIENTS

20	limes, divided
1¼ cups	organic evaporated cane juice (aka organic cane sugar)
½ cup	packed fresh basil leaves
Pinch	sea salt

Makes **3½ Cups.**
Hands-On Time: **25 Minutes.**
Total Time: **45 Minutes.***
Plus Chilling and Freezing Time.

INSTRUCTIONS

Zest 3 limes. In a food processor, combine lime zest, cane juice and basil and pulse a few times. (**NOTE:** *By breaking up basil in the food processor, we're "bruising" it, which allows the basil to release its flavors into the sugar syrup.*) Transfer mixture to a medium saucepan, then add 1 cup water and bring to a boil on medium-high, stirring to dissolve cane juice. Remove from heat and set aside for 30 minutes.

Meanwhile, juice zested limes plus enough additional limes to yield 2 cups juice.

Strain cane juice mixture through a fine mesh sieve into a large bowl, pressing on the solids. Stir in lime juice and salt. Thoroughly chill in fridge, then freeze in an ice cream maker according to manufacturer's instructions. (Alternatively, pour chilled sorbet mixture into a shallow pan and freeze, stirring and breaking up with a fork every hour for 3 to 4 hours. Once solid, set aside at room temperature for about 10 minutes, then transfer to a food processor. Pulse until smooth, then transfer to a container and refreeze.)

Nutrition Information Per serving (¼ cup): Calories: 73, Total Fat: 0 g, Sat. Fat: 0 g, Carbs: 20 g, Fiber: 0 g, Sugars: 18 g, Protein: 0 g, Sodium: 9 mg, Cholesterol: 0 mg

The Baja Grilled
Peach Salad

with Spicy Cashew Dressing
(See recipe, p. 202)

Summer Recipes

Almond Biscotti Energy Balls

Makes **24 Balls.**
Hands-On Time: **15 Minutes.**
Total Time: **45 Minutes.**

INGREDIENTS

1 cup	almond meal
½ cup	natural unsalted crunchy almond butter
⅓ cup	dried goji berries
¼ cup	pure maple syrup
2 tbsp	sesame seeds
2 tbsp	unsalted pepitas
2 tsp	pure almond extract, optional
1 tsp	pure vanilla extract
½ cup	old-fashioned rolled oats
3 tbsp	sliced unsalted almonds

INSTRUCTIONS

To a food processor, add almond meal, almond butter, goji berries, maple syrup, sesame seeds, pepitas, almond extract (if using) and vanilla extract; process on high for 1 minute. Add oats and almonds; process for 30 seconds. Remove mixture from processor and roll into a large ball; wrap in plastic wrap and freeze for 30 minutes.

Remove dough ball from freezer, remove plastic, divide and roll dough into 24 1-inch balls. Place in an airtight container and refrigerate.

Nutrition Information Per serving (2 balls): Calories: 189, Total Fat: 13 g, Sat. Fat: 1 g, Monounsaturated Fat: 7 g, Polyunsaturated Fat: 3 g, Carbs: 15 g, Fiber: 3 g, Sugars: 8 g, Protein: 6 g, Sodium: 40 mg, Cholesterol: 0 mg

TIP: If following our Two-Week Meal Plan, refrigerate 6 balls and freeze 8 balls. Defrost and use when called for.

Raspberry Lime Squares

Makes **16 Squares.**
Hands-On Time: **25 Minutes.**
Total Time: **25 Minutes.***
Plus Soaking and Freezing Time.

INGREDIENTS

2 cups	raw unsalted cashews
1 cup	raw unsalted almonds
½ cup	pitted Medjool dates
½ cup	unsweetened shredded coconut
⅛ tsp	sea salt
	zest and juice of 1 lime, divided
6 tbsp	coconut oil, melted
2 tbsp	pure maple syrup
½ tsp	pure vanilla extract
1½ cups	raspberries, divided (**TIP:** *Frozen can be substituted; thaw completely and drain first.*)

INSTRUCTIONS

Place cashews in a bowl and cover with water. Soak in the refrigerator for at least 3 hours. Drain and rinse.

Prepare base: To a food processor or high-powered blender, add almonds, dates, coconut and salt. Pulse until crumbly and slightly chunky, 15 to 30 seconds. If needed, add 2 to 4 tsp water and process until it holds together when rolled into a ball. Press into an 8 x 8-inch baking pan. Chill in freezer.

Meanwhile, prepare filling: In processor or blender, place cashews, lime juice, coconut oil, maple syrup and vanilla; process until very smooth.

Remove chilled base from freezer and top with two-thirds of filling in an even layer. Add 1 cup raspberries to remaining filling in processor or blender and process until smooth. Pour over filling and top with lime zest; cover and freeze until solid, about 5 hours.

Cut into 16 squares and garnish with remaining ½ cup raspberries. Store bars in freezer. Thaw in refrigerator for 2 hours or at room temperature for 20 minutes before eating.

Nutrition Information Per serving (1 square): Calories: 218, Fat: 17.5 g, Sat. Fat: 7 g, Monounsaturated Fat: 7 g, Polyunsaturated Fat: 2 g, Carbs: 14 g, Fiber: 3 g, Sugars: 7 g, Protein: 5 g, Sodium: 18 mg, Cholesterol: 0 mg

Mocha Smoothie Bowl

INGREDIENTS

¼ cup	plain unsweetened almond milk
6 oz	organic firm tofu
2 tbsp	raw cashew butter
4 tsp	raw cacao powder or unsweetened cocoa powder
1½ tsp	instant coffee granules
2	pitted dates
½ tsp	pure vanilla extract
½ cup	ice
Pinch	sea salt
1 tsp	lucuma powder, optional*

Optional toppings:

Pinch	ground cinnamon
1 tbsp	toasted chopped unsalted hazelnuts
¾ tsp	chia seeds
1 tbsp	goji berries

INSTRUCTIONS

To a blender or food processor, add all ingredients; blend until smooth. Serve with toppings of your choice.

Nutrition Information Per serving (1 recipe): Calories: 613, Total Fat: 26 g, Sat. Fat: 6 g, Monounsaturated Fat: 12 g, Polyunsaturated Fat: 7 g, Carbs: 80 g, Fiber: 16 g, Sugars: 50 g, Protein: 23 g, Sodium: 209 mg, Cholesterol: 0 mg

*OPTIONAL SUPERFOOD BOOST:

Lucuma is a low-glycemic fruit, which not only has a subtle sweetness, but also contains iron, zinc, calcium, protein and fiber.

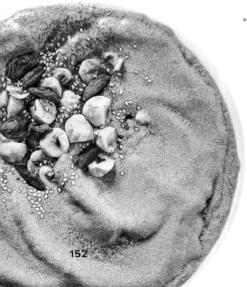

Mint Chip Smoothie Bowl

INGREDIENTS

¼ cup	plain unsweetened almond milk
1½	frozen bananas
⅓	avocado
1 cup	packed baby spinach
¼ tsp	pure vanilla extract
1 to 2 drops	pure peppermint extract
¼ tsp	chlorella, optional*
1 tbsp	cacao nibs or carob chips

Optional toppings:

2 tsp	raw almond butter (*TIP: You can bring to room temperature and squeeze out of a zip-top bag with the corner snipped off.*)
1 tsp	raw cacao nibs or carob chips
1 tsp	hemp seeds

INSTRUCTIONS

To a blender or food processor, add all ingredients except cacao nibs; blend until smooth. Transfer to a bowl and fold in cacao nibs. Serve with toppings of your choice.

Nutrition Information Per serving (1 recipe): Calories: 366, Total Fat: 16 g, Sat. Fat: 4 g, Monounsaturated Fat: 8 g, Polyunsaturated Fat: 2 g, Carbs: 55 g, Fiber: 17 g, Sugars: 22 g, Protein: 7 g, Sodium: 99 mg, Cholesterol: 0 mg

*OPTIONAL SUPERFOOD BOOST:

An amazing detoxifier and immune booster, chlorella is rich in vitamin B12, chlorophyll and protein.

Pink Pitaya
Smoothie Bowl

INGREDIENTS

¼ **cup**	plain unsweetened almond milk
1	3.5-oz frozen pitaya packet
1	frozen banana
½ **cup**	frozen blueberries
1 **tsp**	maqui berry powder, optional*

Optional toppings:

¼ **cup**	all-natural granola
½ **tsp**	bee pollen
	Several blueberries

INSTRUCTIONS

To a blender or food processor, add all ingredients; blend until smooth. Serve with toppings of your choice.

Nutrition Information Per serving (1 recipe): Calories: 214, Total Fat: 2 g, Sat. Fat: 0 g, Carbs: 50 g, Fiber: 8 g, Sugars: 29 g, Protein: 3 g, Sodium: 47 mg, Cholesterol: 0 mg

*OPTIONAL SUPERFOOD BOOST: Maqui berry powder is rich in antioxidants, such as vitamin C, and also contains calcium, iron and phytonutrients that are antiaging and anti-inflammatory.

Mango Sunshine
Smoothie Bowl

INGREDIENTS

6 **tbsp**	plain unsweetened almond milk
1½ **cups**	frozen mango chunks
½ **cup**	chilled cooked cauliflower
2 **tbsp**	coconut butter
1	pitted date
¼ **tsp**	ground turmeric, optional*

Optional toppings:

¼ **cup**	blueberries
1 **tbsp**	unsweetened shredded coconut or shaved fresh coconut
1 **tbsp**	toasted sliced unsalted almonds

INSTRUCTIONS

To a blender or food processor, add all ingredients; blend until smooth. Serve with toppings of your choice.

Nutrition Information Per serving (1 recipe): Calories: 450, Total Fat: 19.5 g, Sat. Fat: 16 g, Monounsaturated Fat: 2 g, Polyunsaturated Fat: 1.5 g, Carbs: 74 g, Fiber: 14 g, Sugars: 59 g, Protein: 6 g, Sodium: 92 mg, Cholesterol: 0 mg

*OPTIONAL SUPERFOOD BOOST: Turmeric is incredibly anti-inflammatory and can help lower cholesterol, plus it's an antioxidant, wound healer, digestive stimulant and liver detoxifier.

Savory Potato Noodle & Chive Waffles

A cross between a latke and a hash brown, these crispy waffles made from spiralized potatoes are a must-try. We love them with a little yogurt and maple syrup, but you can also load them up with salmon and dill for a heartier meal.

INGREDIENTS

4 small	Russet potatoes (or use 2 Russet and 2 sweet potatoes), scrubbed
½ tbsp	extra-virgin olive oil
¼ tsp	each garlic powder and sea salt
⅛ tsp	ground black pepper
2 large	eggs, beaten
3 tbsp	chopped fresh chives

Optional toppings
Greek yogurt
Pure maple syrup

Makes **2 8-Inch Waffles.**
Hands-On Time: **25 Minutes.**
Total Time: **45 Minutes.**

INSTRUCTIONS

Secure potatoes in a spiralizer and turn crank to create noodles, about the thickness of linguine. Pat dry with a clean towel.

In a large skillet on medium, heat oil. Add noodles and season with garlic powder, salt and pepper. Cover and cook for 5 minutes, or until noodles are tender and cooked through (work in batches, if necessary). Transfer to a large bowl; set aside to cool for 5 to 10 minutes. Add eggs and chives and toss to combine.

Preheat an 8-inch waffle iron and mist with cooking spray. Pack in half of potato mixture and close lid firmly. Cook until waffle is golden brown and crispy, about 15 minutes. (If your waffle maker has a timer, you may have to ignore it as it will go off early; keep a close eye to avoid burning.) Repeat with remaining waffle. Top with desired toppings.

Nutrition Information Per serving (1 waffle): Calories: 258, Total Fat: 9 g, Sat. Fat: 2 g, Monounsaturated Fat: 5 g, Polyunsaturated Fat: 1.5 g, Carbs: 35 g, Fiber: 3 g, Sugars: 3 g, Protein: 10 g, Sodium: 319 mg, Cholesterol: 186 mg

Granola-topped Apricot & Plum Bowl
with Tahini Yogurt Dressing

Inspired by the Middle Eastern tradition of mixing sweet fruits with savory foods like tahini, this summer bowl would be ideal served at your next barbecue. Garnish with a little citrus zest for extra brightness.

INGREDIENTS

Granola

½	egg white (about 1 tbsp)
1 tsp	raw honey
1 tsp	extra-virgin olive oil
¼ cup	unsalted shelled pistachios, chopped
3 tbsp	rolled oats
1 tbsp	sesame seeds
½ tsp	ground coriander
¼ tsp	sea salt
Pinch	ground cayenne pepper

Bowl

1½ tsp	tahini paste
2 tbsp	full-fat plain yogurt
2 tsp	fresh lemon juice
2	apricots or peaches, pitted and cut into thin wedges
2	plums, pitted and cut into thin wedges

Serves **4.**
Hands-On Time: **15 Minutes.**
Total Time: **30 Minutes.**

INSTRUCTIONS

Prepare granola: Preheat oven to 350°F. Line an 8- or 9-inch pie plate with parchment paper. In a medium bowl, whisk egg white, honey and oil until combined. Add pistachios, oats, sesame seeds, coriander, salt and cayenne. Spread evenly on pie plate and bake, stirring halfway, until golden brown, about 15 minutes. (**MAKE AHEAD:** *Granola can be made up to 1 week ahead and stored in an airtight container.*)

Meanwhile, prepare dressing: In a medium bowl, whisk together tahini and 4 tsp water until smooth. Add yogurt and lemon juice; whisk until smooth.

Divide apricots and plums among bowls. Drizzle with dressing and sprinkle with granola.

Nutrition Information Per serving (¼ of recipe): Calories: 129, Total Fat: 8 g, Sat. Fat: 1 g, Monounsaturated Fat: 4 g, Polyunsaturated Fat: 2 g, Carbs: 13 g, Fiber: 2 g, Sugars: 1 g, Protein: 4 g, Sodium: 132 mg, Cholesterol: 1 mg

Honeydew & Blackberry Bowl
with Basil & Lime Drizzle

The herbal taste of basil with lime juice and a touch of salt and
pepper make the fruits in this bowl taste even sweeter. Mix and
match with your favorite melons and berries.

INGREDIENTS

1 lb honeydew melon,
seeded, peeled and
cut into chunks (about
½ small melon)

1 cup blackberries, divided

1 tsp finely grated lime
zest + 2 tbsp fresh
lime juice

1 tbsp organic evaporated
cane juice (aka organic
cane sugar)

¼ cup chopped fresh basil
leaves, divided

Pinch each sea salt and
ground black pepper

Serves **4.**
Hands-On Time: **15 Minutes.**
Total Time: **20 Minutes.***
*Plus cooling time.

INSTRUCTIONS

To a serving bowl, add melon and ½ cup blackberries (or divide among
individual bowls); refrigerate.

To a small saucepan on low, add lime zest and juice, cane juice and 2 tbsp
water, stirring occasionally, until cane juice dissolves, about 5 minutes. Cool
to room temperature.

In a small bowl, combine remaining ½ cup blackberries, lime juice mixture,
2 tbsp basil, salt and pepper. Mash until berries are broken down and
mixture looks saucy; drizzle over fruit. Garnish with remaining 2 tbsp basil.

Nutrition Information Per serving (¼ of recipe): Calories: 48, Total Fat: 0 g, Sat. Fat: 0 g,
Carbs: 12 g, Fiber: 2 g, Sugars: 9 g, Protein: 1 g, Sodium: 39 mg, Cholesterol: 0 mg

THE OTHER MEMORY-BOOSTING BERRY: Blueberries usually
get all the glory when it comes to brain health, but blackberries deserve some
attention, too. They contain the same dark-pigmented flavonoids that blueberries
do, called anthocyanins, which protect the brain from free radical damage and
therefore may help prevent cognitive decline.

No-Pasta Mediterranean Zucchini Salad

Zucchini noodles stand in for wheat noodles in this gluten- and grain-free take on a pasta salad that's packed to the brim with chickpeas, olives and feta.

INGREDIENTS

Salad

2	zucchini, trimmed
½ small	red onion, sliced
1 14-oz	BPA-free can quartered artichoke hearts, drained
1 14.5-oz	BPA-free can unsalted diced tomatoes, drained
1 cup	BPA-free canned chickpeas, drained and rinsed
½ cup	halved pitted Kalamata olives
½ cup	crumbled full-fat feta cheese

Dressing

¼ cup	extra-virgin olive oil
2 tbsp	red wine vinegar
1 tbsp	fresh lemon juice
1 tsp	dried oregano flakes
1 tsp	Dijon mustard
½ tsp	each dried parsley, garlic powder and sea salt
¼ tsp	ground black pepper

Serves **6.**
Hands-On Time: **30 Minutes.**
Total Time: **30 Minutes.**

INSTRUCTIONS

Prepare dressing: In a medium bowl, whisk together all dressing ingredients.

Secure zucchini in a spiralizer and turn crank to create noodles, about the thickness of linguine. Pat dry with a clean towel; trim noodles to desired length.

To a large bowl, add zucchini noodles, onion, artichokes, tomatoes, chickpeas, olives and feta. Pour dressing over top and toss well to combine.

Nutrition Information Per serving (⅙ of recipe): Calories: 210, Total Fat: 14 g, Sat. Fat: 3.5 g, Monounsaturated, Fat: 9 g, Polyunsaturated Fat: 1 g, Carbs: 16 g, Fiber: 3 g, Sugars: 5 g, Protein: 6 g, Sodium: 733 mg, Cholesterol: 11 mg

Coconut Chicken Corn Chowder

Coconut milk and fresh basil lend Thai-inspired taste to this all-American classic. Simmering the corn cobs with the broth after you remove the kernels is the secret for adding tons of flavor at no extra cost! To toast the coconut flakes, simply add them to a dry skillet on medium heat, stirring occasionally, until golden.

INGREDIENTS

2 large	ears corn, husked
1 tsp	coconut oil
1 cup	finely diced celery (about 4 stalks)
1 bunch	green onions, thinly sliced on the diagonal, light and dark green parts divided
3	cloves garlic, minced
½ tsp	sea salt, divided
⅛ tsp	ground white or black pepper
3 cups	low-sodium chicken broth
1 cup	full-fat coconut milk
2	boneless, skinless chicken breasts (about 14 oz), diced
½	sweet potato (about 5 oz), peeled and diced
½ cup	thinly sliced fresh basil
¼ cup	unsweetened coconut flakes (or shredded coconut), toasted

Serves **4.**
Hands-On Time: **30 Minutes.**
Total Time: **40 Minutes.**

INSTRUCTIONS

Cut kernels from corn, reserving cobs. In a large saucepan, heat oil on medium. Add corn kernels, celery and light parts of onions and cook, stirring often, until celery and onions are translucent, 6 to 8 minutes. Add garlic, ¼ tsp salt and pepper and cook, stirring, until fragrant, about 30 seconds.

Meanwhile, snap reserved corn cobs in half. In a separate saucepan, bring corn cobs and broth to a boil. Reduce heat to medium-low, cover and cook for 5 minutes. Strain through a fine-mesh sieve into corn kernel mixture; discard corn cobs. Bring to a boil. Reduce heat to low and cook, stirring occasionally, until corn kernels are tender, 8 to 10 minutes.

Using a slotted spoon, transfer about 1 cup of the corn kernel mixture to a blender; add coconut milk and purée until smooth.

Stir chicken and sweet potato into broth mixture. Increase heat to medium, cover and cook, stirring occasionally, until chicken is cooked through and sweet potato is tender, 3 to 5 minutes.

Stir in coconut milk mixture and cook until heated through. Remove from heat and stir in dark green parts of onions, basil and remaining ¼ tsp salt. To serve, top with coconut flakes.

Nutrition Information Per serving (¼ of recipe): Calories: 375, Total Fat: 18 g, Sat. Fat: 14 g, Monounsaturated Fat: 2 g, Polyunsaturated Fat: 1 g, Carbs: 25 g, Fiber: 4 g, Sugars: 7 g, Protein: 31 g, Sodium: 388 mg, Cholesterol: 72 mg

Cucumber Kale Wraps
with Zesty Peanut Sauce

This plant-based version of lettuce wraps introduces crisp and refreshing cucumber noodles. A sweet-tart peanut sauce is drizzled inside the wrap and also used as a flavorful dip.

INGREDIENTS

2 large	cucumbers
½ tsp + pinch	sea salt, divided
4 large	curly kale leaves, washed, patted dry and tough stems removed
1 cup	BPA-free canned chickpeas, drained and rinsed
2 pinches	each ground black pepper and chile powder, divided
Pinch	ground cumin
1	orange bell pepper, finely chopped
1⅓ cups	shredded purple cabbage
¼ cup	chopped cherry tomatoes
¼ cup	fresh alfalfa sprouts
3 tbsp	finely chopped fresh cilantro leaves
1 small	clove garlic, minced
½ cup	natural unsalted creamy peanut butter
1 tbsp	reduced-sodium tamari sauce
2 tsp	fresh lime juice
1½ tsp	raw honey
Pinch	ground ginger

Serves **4**.
Hands-On Time: **20 Minutes.**
Total Time: **20 Minutes.**

INSTRUCTIONS

Slice ends off cucumbers. Working one at a time, secure cucumber in a spiral slicer and turn the crank to create noodles. Place noodles in a colander over a bowl; sprinkle with ½ tsp salt and let sit for 10 minutes to drain liquid.

On a flat surface, lay each kale leaf flat. In a medium bowl, mash chickpeas with a fork and season with pinch each salt, black pepper, chile powder and cumin. Divide chickpea mixture among kale leaves and spread in an even layer to within 1 inch of edges.

Over chickpea mixture, layer cucumber noodles, bell pepper, cabbage, tomatoes, sprouts and cilantro.

To a mini food processor or blender, add garlic, peanut butter, tamari, lime juice, honey, ground ginger and remaining pinch each black pepper and chile powder. Add 1 tbsp water; process until smooth. Add more water, 1 tbsp at a time, and process until sauce reaches desired consistency.

Drizzle 1 tsp peanut sauce over ingredients on each kale leaf. Fold in sides of each kale leaf and roll up like a burrito; secure with a toothpick. Slice each wrap in half and serve with remaining peanut sauce.

Nutrition Information Per serving (1 wrap and 2½ tbsp peanut sauce): Calories: 298, Total Fat: 16 g, Sat. Fat: 1 g, Monounsaturated Fat: 9 g, Polyunsaturated Fat: 6 g, Carbs: 30 g, Fiber: 7g, Sugars: 9 g, Protein: 14 g, Sodium: 441 mg, Cholesterol: 0 mg

Chilled Green Goddess Soup
with Open-Face Shrimp Lettuce Cups

Flavorful, gorgeously hued Green Goddess dressing was the inspiration for this fresh and tangy chilled soup that features kefir, a type of fermented milk drink. It pairs nicely with orange-scented shrimp lettuce cups for a well-rounded spring lunch.

INGREDIENTS

1 small	avocado, peeled and pitted
1 small	shallot, roughly chopped
1	lime, juiced
½ tbsp	orange zest + 1 large navel orange, juiced, divided
1½ cups	plain whole-milk kefir
1½ cups	loosely packed fresh flat-leaf parsley
1 cup	low-sodium chicken broth
½ cup	loosely packed fresh tarragon
¼ tsp	each sea salt and ground black pepper, divided
¼ cup	plain whole-milk yogurt
1 tbsp	grainy Dijon mustard
½ tbsp	white wine vinegar
6 oz small	wild shrimp, thawed if frozen and drained, patted dry
1	stalk celery, finely chopped
½ large	red bell pepper, finely chopped
2–4	leaves Bibb, Boston or romaine lettuce
1 tbsp	chopped fresh dill
1 tbsp	chopped fresh chives
½ slice	whole-grain bread
1	clove garlic

Serves **2.**
Hands-On Time: **25 Minutes.**
Total Time: **25 Minutes.**

INSTRUCTIONS

Prepare soup: In a blender, place avocado, shallot, lime juice, orange juice, kefir, parsley, broth, tarragon and ⅛ tsp each salt and black pepper. Blend until smooth; transfer to refrigerator to chill.

Prepare sandwiches: In a large bowl combine yogurt, Dijon, vinegar, orange zest and remaining ⅛ tsp each salt and black pepper. Add shrimp, celery and bell pepper; toss gently to coat. Divide shrimp mixture among lettuce leaves (1 to 2 per person) and sprinkle with dill and chives.

Toast bread until golden brown. Slice garlic clove in half lengthwise and rub cut sides against toasted bread. Cut toast into ¼-inch cubes.

To serve, divide soup between 2 bowls; top with toast cubes and serve with shrimp lettuce cups.

Nutrition Information Per serving (1½ cups soup and 1 to 2 lettuce cups): Calories: 461, Total Fat: 21 g, Sat. Fat: 7 g, Monounsaturated Fat: 10 g, Polyunsaturated Fat: 2 g, Carbs: 36 g, Fiber: 9 g, Sugars: 18 g, Protein: 35 g, Sodium: 721 mg, Cholesterol: 191 mg

Unbundled Spring Rolls
with Raspberry Ginger Sauce

This hearty bowl is a staff favorite–we just love the pairing of the sweet and tangy raspberry sauce over savory chicken and crunchy vegetables.

INGREDIENTS

5 oz	glass noodles (such as mung bean noodles) or brown rice vermicelli
2	boneless, skinless chicken breasts (about 1 lb total)
¾ tsp	sea salt
½ tsp	paprika
	ground black pepper, to taste
4	Persian or other small cucumbers, julienned
1–2 large	avocados, peeled, pitted and thinly sliced
2 cups	shredded red cabbage
2 cups	grated or shredded carrots
½ cup	fresh cilantro leaves

Raspberry Ginger Sauce

2 cups	raspberries (or use frozen, defrosted)
½ cup	rice vinegar
¼ cup	unpasteurized organic white miso
¼ cup	extra-virgin olive oil
1 tbsp	raw honey
2 tsp	peeled and finely grated ginger
1–2 tsp	sriracha, optional

Serves **6.**
Hands-On Time: **30 Minutes.**
Total Time: **30 Minutes.**

INSTRUCTIONS

Cook noodles according to package directions; drain.

Heat a grill to medium-high. Season chicken with salt, paprika and pepper. Grill chicken until cooked through, 4 to 6 minutes per side. Set aside until cool enough to handle, then cut into 1-inch slices.

Meanwhile, prepare Raspberry Ginger Sauce: In a blender, purée all ingredients plus 1 tbsp water to desired consistency.

Divide noodles, chicken, cucumbers, avocado, cabbage, carrots and cilantro among bowls. Drizzle with sauce.

Nutrition Information Per serving (⅙ of recipe): Calories: 428, Total Fat: 20 g, Sat. Fat: 3 g, Monounsaturated Fat: 14 g, Polyunsaturated Fat: 3 g, Carbs: 44 g, Fiber: 8 g, Sugars: 12 g, Protein: 19 g, Sodium: 600 mg, Cholesterol: 42 mg

Shredded Carrot & Chicken Salad
with Raisins, Jicama & Citrus Yogurt Dressing

Jicama is a crunchy, mild vegetable that's common in Mexican cuisine. It looks a little intimidating because of its size and odd shape, but once you peel it, the cool flesh is easy to slice and adds a crisp texture to salads. Use any cooked chicken you have on hand in this salad–make some extra next time you have the grill going. We love this salad with a drizzle of sriracha sauce.

Serves **6.**
Hands-On Time: **30 Minutes.**
Total Time: **30 Minutes.**

INSTRUCTIONS

Make dressing: In a small bowl, whisk together all dressing ingredients until combined. Set aside.

Make salad: In a large bowl, combine corn, jicama, carrots, cabbage, raisins, parsley, mint and hemp hearts. Add chicken and dressing; toss to coat.

Nutrition Information Per serving (⅙ of recipe): Calories: 296, Total Fat: 15 g, Sat. Fat: 3 g, Monounsaturated Fat: 8 g, Polyunsaturated Fat: 4 g, Carbs: 27 g, Fiber: 5 g, Sugars: 14 g, Protein: 16 g, Sodium: 241 mg, Cholesterol: 29 mg

INGREDIENTS

Dressing

½ cup	whole-milk plain Greek yogurt
¼ cup	extra-virgin olive oil
3 tbsp	fresh lemon juice
2 tbsp	white wine vinegar
1 tbsp	fresh orange juice
1 tbsp	Dijon mustard, optional
1	small clove garlic, minced
½ tsp	sea salt
Pinch	ground black pepper

Salad

1	ear corn (grilled, boiled or fresh), kernels removed
½	jicama, peeled and julienned
3 cups	shredded or grated carrots
1½ cups	shredded red cabbage
½ cup	unsulfured green raisins or organic golden raisins
⅓ cup	fresh flat-leaf parsley, chopped
¼ cup	fresh mint, chopped
¼ cup	hemp hearts
10 oz	cooked chicken breast (preferably grilled)

Grilled Fontina & Blackberry Sandwiches

Serves **6.**
Hands-On Time: **30 Minutes.**
Total Time: **30 Minutes.**

1 loaf	hearty whole-grain bread, cut into 12 slices
2 tbsp	extra-virgin olive oil
12 oz	blackberries
6 oz	fontina cheese, shredded
1 tbsp	fresh thyme leaves
1 tbsp	raw honey, or to taste

INSTRUCTIONS

Preheat a griddle or heavy-bottomed skillet on medium. Brush 1 side of each slice of bread with oil.

In a medium bowl, gently smash blackberries with a fork or potato masher to a coarse texture.

Prepare sandwiches: Spread about 3 tbsp crushed blackberries on the non-oiled side of one slice of bread. Top with 1 oz shredded cheese and ½ tsp thyme. Drizzle with ½ tsp honey. Place a slice of bread on top, oil side up. Repeat with remaining sandwiches.

Working in batches, add sandwiches to griddle and cook until golden brown on underside, about 5 to 6 minutes. Flip and cook until other side is golden brown and cheese is melted, 5 minutes more.

Nutrition Information Per serving (1 sandwich): Calories: 407, Total Fat: 17 g, Sat. Fat: 7 g, Monounsaturated Fat: 7 g, Polyunsaturated Fat: 3 g, Carbs: 45 g, Fiber: 9 g, Sugars: 11 g, Protein: 19 g, Sodium: 542 mg, Cholesterol: 33 mg

Vietnamese Shrimp Salad
with Mint Chile Dressing

This salad has a nice bit of heat to it thanks to the fresh chile. Fiery, sweat-inducing capsaicin is found mostly in the white pith (and the seeds that come into contact with the pith), so devein and seed the chile if you want to cut back on spiciness. For added flavor, you can add chopped fresh mint, cilantro or Thai basil to the salad.

INGREDIENTS

Dressing

⅓ cup	fresh mint
¼ cup	extra-virgin olive oil
3 tbsp	diced red onion
2 tbsp	fresh lime juice
1 tbsp	rice vinegar
1 tsp	fish sauce
1 small	clove garlic, peeled
¼ tsp	raw honey
⅛ tsp	chile paste

Salad

1 tbsp	extra-virgin olive oil
12 oz	medium shrimp, peeled and deveined
¼ tsp	sea salt
Pinch	ground black pepper
6 cups	chopped romaine or butter lettuce
2 cups	bean sprouts or julienned zucchini
2	Persian cucumbers (or ½ English cucumber), diced or thinly sliced
1 large	carrot, julienned or grated
1	red Thai bird's-eye chile or red finger chile, thinly sliced
½ cup	raw unsalted peanuts, toasted

Serves **6.**
Hands-On Time: **30 Minutes.**
Total Time: **30 Minutes.**

INSTRUCTIONS

Make dressing: In a blender or food processor, purée dressing ingredients until smooth. (Or, for a chunkier texture, mince the garlic, chop the mint and whisk all ingredients together.) Set aside.

Make salad: In a medium skillet on medium, heat oil. Add shrimp and sprinkle with salt and pepper. Cook, turning halfway, until shrimp are pink and opaque, about 4 minutes.

In a large bowl, combine lettuce, sprouts, cucumbers, carrot, chile and peanuts. Top with shrimp and drizzle with dressing; toss to coat.

Nutrition Information Per serving (⅙ of salad): Calories: 234, Total Fat: 17 g, Sat. Fat: 2 g, Monounsaturated Fat: 11 g, Polyunsaturated Fat: 3 g, Carbs: 9 g, Fiber: 4 g, Sugars: 4 g, Protein: 14 g, Sodium: 205 mg, Cholesterol: 68 mg

Eggplant Hero

INGREDIENTS

1 tbsp + ¾ tsp	dried rosemary, divided
½ tsp	ground cumin, divided
8 tsp	sliced unsalted almonds
7 tbsp	nutritional yeast seasoning, divided
2 tbsp	garlic powder
2 tbsp + 1 tsp	dried parsley, divided
1 tsp	ground black pepper
½ tsp + ⅛ tsp	ground cayenne pepper, divided
2	eggs
1¼ lb	eggplant, sliced in ¼-inch rounds
1 14.5-oz	BPA-free can fire-roasted diced tomatoes
¼ cup	chopped fresh basil leaves
2	cloves garlic, minced
1	bay leaf
2 tsp	extra-virgin olive oil
1	green bell pepper, sliced
1 large	onion, peeled and sliced
4	whole-wheat hoagie rolls, split and toasted

Serves **4.**
Hands-On Time: **35 Minutes.**
Total Time: **1 Hour, 10 Minutes.**

INSTRUCTIONS

Arrange oven racks in top and middle position; preheat to 300°F. In a small bowl, combine ½ tsp rosemary and ¼ tsp cumin. Lightly wet almonds with about ¼ tsp water and toss with spice mixture. Spread out on a small baking sheet. Bake on top rack for 5 minutes, until golden. Set aside. Increase oven temperature to 400°F.

In a small flat baking dish, combine 5 tbsp yeast seasoning, garlic powder, 2 tbsp parsley, 1 tbsp rosemary, black pepper and ½ tsp cayenne.

Line 2 large baking sheets with parchment paper. In a medium bowl, beat eggs. Working 1 at a time, dip eggplant in egg, turning to coat both sides and letting excess drip back into bowl. Press both sides of eggplant in mixture in baking dish. Place coated eggplant on sheet. Repeat with remaining eggplant. Bake on middle rack for 40 minutes, turning halfway.

Meanwhile, prepare sauce: In a blender, combine tomatoes, basil and garlic until smooth. Transfer to a medium saucepan on medium. Stir in remaining ¼ tsp rosemary and cumin, 1 tsp parsley, 1/8 tsp cayenne and bay leaf. Cover and simmer on low for 10 minutes. Remove and discard bay leaf. Stir in remaining 2 tbsp yeast seasoning. Cover and keep warm on low.

In a medium skillet on medium, heat oil. Sauté bell pepper for 3 minutes. Add onion and sauté 10 minutes more, until onions and peppers are soft.

To assemble sandwiches, spread 2 tbsp tomato sauce on bottom half of each roll. Layer 4 to 5 eggplant slices over sauce. Spoon another 2 tbsp tomato sauce over eggplant and top with about ½ cup sautéed peppers and onions. Sprinkle 2 tsp spiced almonds over each sandwich.

Nutrition Information Per serving (1 roll, 5 oz eggplant, ½ cup peppers and onions, ¼ cup sauce, 2 tsp almonds): Calories: 395, Total Fat: 10 g, Sat. Fat: 2 g, Monounsaturated Fat: 5 g, Polyunsaturated Fat: 3 g, Carbs: 60 g, Fiber: 14 g, Sugars: 16 g, Protein: 17 g, Sodium: 400 mg, Cholesterol: 93 mg

TIP: If following our Meal Plan, refrigerate 1 serving of eggplant, sauce and sautéed peppers and onions separately as leftovers. Set aside 1 bun and 2 tsp almonds. Reheat and assemble when called for.

Vegetarian Taco Salad
with Chunky Pico Dressing

You definitely won't miss the chicken or beef in this substantial vegetarian version of a taco salad. We use pico de gallo in the dressing for a chunkier texture, but you can pulse it in the food processor if you prefer a smoother dressing.

INGREDIENTS

Vinaigrette

1 cup	fresh pico de gallo or salsa
3 tbsp	extra-virgin olive oil
2–3 tsp	raw honey or pure maple syrup
¾ tsp	sea salt
¼ tsp	chile powder
Pinch	ground black pepper

Salad

8 cups	chopped romaine lettuce
1 15-oz	BPA-free can unsalted pinto beans, drained and rinsed (or 1½ cups drained home-cooked beans)
1 cup	thinly sliced radishes of your choice (4–6 medium)
1 cup	shredded Monterey Jack or Mexican cheese blend, optional
⅓ cup	fresh cilantro, roughly chopped
1	avocado, sliced or cubed
1 oz	whole-grain corn tortilla chips, crumbled, optional

Serves **6.**
Hands-On Time: **25 Minutes.**
Total Time: **25 Minutes.**

INSTRUCTIONS

Make vinaigrette: In a small bowl, whisk together all dressing ingredients until combined. Set aside.

Make salad: To a large bowl, add lettuce, beans, radishes, cheese (if using), cilantro and avocado. Drizzle with dressing and toss to coat. Sprinkle tortilla strips (if using) over top.

Nutrition Information Per serving (⅙ of recipe): Calories: 208, Total Fat: 12 g, Sat. Fat: 2 g, Monounsaturated Fat: 9 g, Polyunsaturated Fat: 1 g, Carbs: 22 g, Fiber: 8 g, Sugars: 5 g, Protein: 5 g, Sodium: 661 mg, Cholesterol: 31 mg

Middle Eastern Chicken & Rice Salad

with Tahini Dill Dressing

A key ingredient in many Middle Eastern salads, mint gives this recipe a wonderful freshness. Simply seasoned chicken bumps up the protein content, making this a filling main dish. Using leftover cooked rice speeds up dinner prep – just make extra the night before.

INGREDIENTS

Dressing

¼ cup	fresh dill
¼ cup	extra-virgin olive oil
3 tbsp	fresh lemon juice
2 tbsp	fresh mint
2 tbsp	tahini paste
¾ tsp	sea salt
Pinch	ground black pepper

Salad

2 6-oz	boneless, skinless chicken breasts
½ tsp	paprika
½ tsp	sea salt
Pinch	ground black pepper
6 cups	lightly packed baby spinach
1 cup	diced roasted red peppers
1 cup	cooked and cooled brown rice (**TIP:** Use a frozen cooked brown rice, thawed.)
½ cup	pitted green olives, halved
¼ cup	unsalted pine nuts, optional, toasted
6	Medjool dates, pitted and chopped

Serves **6.**
Hands-On Time: **20 Minutes.**
Total Time: **30 Minutes.**

INSTRUCTIONS

Make dressing: In a blender or food processor, blend together all dressing ingredients until smooth. Set aside.

Make salad: Preheat a grill to medium-high. Sprinkle chicken with paprika, salt and pepper. Grill until no longer pink inside, about 5 to 6 minutes per side. Transfer to a cutting board.

In a large bowl, combine spinach, red peppers, rice, olives, pine nuts (if using) and dates. Slice chicken and add to bowl. Drizzle with dressing; toss to coat.

Nutrition Information Per serving (⅙ of recipe): Calories: 299, Total Fat: 15 g, Sat. Fat: 2 g, Monounsaturated Fat: 10 g, Polyunsaturated Fat: 3 g, Carbs: 28 g, Fiber: 4 g, Sugars: 14 g, Protein: 14 g, Sodium: 661 mg, Cholesterol: 31 mg

Grilled Watermelon Skewers
with Feta & White Bean Salad

INGREDIENTS

1½ cups	cooked cannellini beans, rinsed (or BPA-free canned beans, drained and rinsed)
2 cups	packed arugula
1 large	shallot, thinly sliced
3 tbsp	chopped sun-dried tomatoes
½ tbsp	extra-virgin olive oil
2 oz	feta cheese, crumbled
	sea salt and ground black pepper, to taste
1	seedless watermelon, rind removed and cut into 2-inch square chunks (about 20 chunks)
½ cup	balsamic vinegar

EQUIPMENT:

4	metal skewers (14 to 18 inches each)

Serves **4.**
Hands-On Time: **35 minutes.**
Total Time: **35 minutes.**

INSTRUCTIONS

In a large bowl, combine beans, arugula, shallot, tomatoes and oil. Add cheese and mix gently. Season with salt and pepper. Divide among 4 plates.

Preheat a grill to medium. (Alternatively, you can set a broiler to high.) Thread 5 chunks watermelon onto each skewer. Place skewers directly on grill grates and cook, turning 2 or 3 times, until light grill marks appear, 6 to 10 minutes total. (If broiling, place skewers on a broiler pan and cook 8 to 10 inches from heat, turning 2 or 3 times, until light browning is visible, 10 to 14 minutes total.) Rest 1 skewer over top of each salad.

In a small covered saucepan on medium-high, bring vinegar to a simmer. Uncover and reduce heat to medium-low to maintain a steady simmer. Cook, swirling pan occasionally, until vinegar coats bottom of pan when tilted and is slightly thickened, 6 to 8 minutes. Remove from heat and immediately drizzle vinegar over salads and watermelon, dividing evenly.

Nutrition Information Per serving (½ cup salad and 1 watermelon skewer): Calories: 219, Total Fat: 5 g, Sat. Fat: 2 g, Carbs: 36 g, Fiber: 5 g, Sugars: 18 g, Protein: 10 g, Sodium: 320 mg, Cholesterol: 4 mg

ANTIOXIDANT BOOST: Watermelon may be everyone's favorite summer thirst quencher, but it's also an antioxidant powerhouse. Like tomatoes, it contains lycopene, which is being studied for its anticarcinogenic effects. Plus, the melon's red flesh contains rich stores of beta-carotene, a carotenoid that may help reduce the risk of heart attack, stroke, osteoarthritis and rheumatoid arthritis.

Mixed Berry Burrata Salad

Serves **6**.
Hands-On Time: **15 Minutes**.
Total Time: **15 Minutes.**

2	8-oz rounds burrata cheese
1 cup	strawberries, hulled and sliced
½ cup	blackberries
½ cup	blueberries
½ cup	raspberries
3 tbsp	basil leaves, thinly sliced + additional leaves for garnish
¼ tsp	sea salt (***TIP:*** Try a flaky sea salt such as Maldon.)
	ground black pepper, to taste
2–3 tsp	extra-virgin olive oil
4 tsp	aged balsamic vinegar

INSTRUCTIONS

Pull burrata apart with your hands; arrange on a platter.

Arrange berries around and on top of the cheese. Sprinkle with sliced basil, salt and pepper, then drizzle with oil and vinegar. Garnish with additional basil.

Nutrition Information Per serving (⅙ of recipe):
Calories: 241, Total Fat: 17 g, Sat. Fat: 10 g, Monounsaturated Fat: 6 g, Polyunsaturated Fat: 1 g, Carbs: 7 g, Fiber: 2 g, Sugars: 4 g, Protein: 15 g, Sodium: 258 mg, Cholesterol: 44 mg

Lemon Tahini-Smothered Broccolini
with Crunchy Seeds

The long, slender stems of broccolini are completely edible, so don't ditch them. Add a serving of whole grains such as freekeh, bulgur or millet to complete this vegetarian meal, or serve the vibrant greens alongside grilled fish or chicken.

INGREDIENTS

1 tbsp	unsalted sunflower seeds
2 tsp	sesame seeds
1½ tbsp	chia seeds
⅓ cup	tahini paste
1½ tsp	finely grated lemon zest + 2 tbsp fresh lemon juice
½ tsp	sea salt
Pinch	ground cayenne pepper
1½ tbsp	extra-virgin olive oil
2	bunches (7 oz each) broccolini, trimmed, or 14 oz broccoli crowns cut into long slices with stems attached

Serves **4.**
Hands-On Time: **15 Minutes.**
Total Time: **25 Minutes.**

INSTRUCTIONS

In a small skillet on medium, toast sunflower and sesame seeds, stirring frequently, until golden, 3 minutes. Add chia; set aside.

In a small bowl, whisk together tahini, ¼ cup boiling water, lemon zest, lemon juice, salt and cayenne until smooth. Whisk in olive oil and set aside. (**NOTE:** *If mixture is very thick, add more water to adjust consistency.*)

In a steamer basket over boiling water, steam broccolini until crisp-tender, 4 to 5 minutes. Arrange broccolini on a platter. Drizzle with tahini dressing and sprinkle with toasted seed mixture.

Nutrition Information Per serving (¼ of recipe): Calories: 246, Total Fat: 19 g, Sat. Fat: 3 g, Monounsaturated Fat: 9 g, Polyunsaturated Fat: 7 g, Carbs: 14 g, Fiber 4 g, Sugars: 3 g, Protein: 8 g, Sodium: 276 mg, Cholesterol: 0 mg

Rainbow Salad

with Beets, Kale & Avocado Dressing

The fresh crunch of beets and kale pairs wonderfully with this creamy homemade avocado dressing. Adjust the amount of honey, salt or black pepper to your taste. If you'd like more color, use both red and golden beets.

INGREDIENTS

2 large	red and/or golden beets, peeled
2 cups	loosely packed finely chopped kale
2 tbsp	shelled unsalted whole pistachios
2 tbsp	soft goat cheese, crumbled
1 tsp	unsalted sunflower seeds

Avocado Dressing

2	cloves garlic
1 large	avocado, peeled, pitted and chopped
	Juice of 1 lime
1½ tbsp	extra-virgin olive oil
1½ tbsp	apple cider vinegar
1 tbsp	chopped fresh basil leaves + additional for garnish
2 tsp	raw honey
Pinch	each sea salt and ground black pepper

Serves **4.**
Hands-On Time: **20 Minutes.**
Total Time: **25 Minutes.**

INSTRUCTIONS

Slice ends off beets. Working one at a time, secure beets in a spiral slicer and turn the crank to create noodles.

In a large bowl, combine beet noodles, kale, pistachios, cheese and seeds.

To a mini food processor or blender, add all dressing ingredients plus 1 tbsp water; process until smooth. Add more water, 1 tbsp at a time, and process until dressing reaches desired consistency.

Pour dressing over kale and beet mixture; toss to combine. Let sit for 5 minutes to allow dressing flavors to permeate the ingredients; toss again before serving. Garnish with additional basil (if using).

Nutrition Information Per serving (1 cup): Calories: 244, Total Fat: 18 g, Sat. Fat: 3 g, Monounsaturated Fat: 12 g, Polyunsaturated Fat: 2.5 g, Carbs: 18 g, Fiber: 7 g, Sugars: 8 g, Protein: 5.5 g, Sodium: 119 mg, Cholesterol: 3 mg

Open-Faced Veggie Melts
with Smoked Mozzarella

Any kind of bread will work well in this recipe, but for best-ever veggie melts, start with a nice thick slice of your favorite artisan (or homemade) whole-grain loaf. We love the mild, smoky flavor of smoked mozzarella, but you can substitute with your favorite cheese: Gouda, provolone or smoked cheddar are great options. Don't worry if your fennel bulb doesn't come with the fronds attached–sprinkle the melts with fresh parsley or dill instead.

INGREDIENTS

- **2 tsp** olive oil
- **1** fennel bulb, quartered, cored and thinly sliced (fronds reserved)
- **1** yellow bell pepper, thinly sliced
- **1** bunch broccolini, florets quartered and stems halved crosswise and quartered lengthwise
- **4 tsp** balsamic vinegar
- **⅛ tsp** each sea salt and ground black pepper
- **4** slices whole-grain bread
- **4 oz** smoked mozzarella cheese, shredded, divided

Serves **4.**
Hands-On Time: **25 Minutes.**
Total Time: **30 Minutes.**

INSTRUCTIONS

Preheat oven to 400°F. In a large nonstick skillet, heat oil on medium. Add fennel slices and bell pepper and sauté, stirring often, until lightly browned, about 5 minutes.

Add broccolini florets and stems, increase heat to medium-high and sauté until tender, 5 to 7 minutes. Reduce heat to low and stir in vinegar, salt and pepper.

On a rimmed baking sheet, arrange bread in a single layer and sprinkle with half of the cheese, dividing evenly. Top with fennel mixture and remaining cheese, dividing evenly. Bake until cheese melts, 5 to 8 minutes. Sprinkle with fennel fronds.

Nutrition Information Per serving (1 veggie melt): Calories: 278, Total Fat: 10.5 g, Sat. Fat: 4.5 g, Monounsaturated Fat: 4 g, Polyunsaturated Fat: 1 g, Carbs: 32 g, Fiber: 7.5 g, Sugars: 8 g, Protein: 15 g, Sodium: 457 mg, Cholesterol: 22 mg

Grilled Steak & Romaine Hearts

with Tangy Date Sauce

A quick turn in the grill pan or on the outdoor grill gives romaine hearts a mouthwatering smoky flavor and crisp-tender texture that makes it worthy of succulent grilled tenderloin.

INGREDIENTS

8 oz	haricots verts or small green beans, trimmed
12	pitted dates
1½ tsp	yellow mustard seeds
¼ cup	apple cider vinegar
4 tsp	olive oil, divided
3 tbsp	shaved Parmesan cheese, divided
2 6-oz	beef tenderloin or top sirloin medallions
¼ tsp	each sea salt and ground black pepper, divided
2	romaine lettuce hearts, halved lengthwise (root end intact)

Serves **4.**
Hands-On Time: **25 Minutes.**
Total Time: **30 Minutes.**

INSTRUCTIONS

In a steamer basket set over a saucepan of simmering water, cook haricots verts until crisp-tender, 2 to 3 minutes. Drain and run under cold water. In a blender, purée dates, mustard seeds and ½ cup hot water. Add vinegar and 2 tsp oil and blend until combined. Toss haricots verts with ¼ cup date sauce and 2 tbsp cheese. Set aside.

Heat a grill pan on medium-high and brush with ½ tsp oil (or heat a greased outdoor grill to medium-high). Season beef with ⅛ tsp each salt and pepper and cook, turning once, until desired doneness, 10 to 12 minutes for medium-rare. (***TIP:*** *If beef begins to over brown, reduce heat to medium.*) Transfer to a cutting board, cover loosely with foil and let rest for 5 minutes. Thinly slice against the grain.

While beef is resting, brush romaine with remaining 1½ tsp oil and sprinkle with remaining ⅛ tsp each salt and pepper. Working in batches if necessary, place romaine, cut sides down, on grill pan or grill. Cover and cook until tender and grill-marked, 4 to 5 minutes. Turn, cover and cook for 2 more minutes. To serve, top romaine with beef, remaining 1 tbsp cheese and date sauce, dividing evenly. Serve with haricots verts.

Nutrition Information Per serving (¼ of recipe): Calories: 294, Total Fat: 12 g, Sat. Fat: 3.5 g, Monounsaturated Fat: 6 g, Polyunsaturated Fat: 1 g, Carbs: 25 g, Fiber: 4 g, Sugars: 20 g, Protein: 22 g, Sodium: 221 mg, Cholesterol: 57 mg

TIP: The bottom cores of romaine hearts help the lettuce hold its shape while grilling, but they can taste bitter. To avoid the bitter flavor, cut off 1 inch from the root end after grilling.

Spicy Lentil Meatball Tacos
with Lime Pepita Cream

INGREDIENTS

1 cup	unsalted pepitas
5 tbsp	fresh lime juice (about 3 limes)
¼ tsp	coarse sea salt
1½ cups	lentils, rinsed
2½ cups	vegetable broth
1	bay leaf
2 tsp	olive oil spread
½ cup	finely chopped carrot
1¾ cups	finely chopped yellow onion, divided
2	cloves garlic, minced
2	eggs
¾ cup	old-fashioned rolled oats
½ cup	chopped fresh cilantro leaves, divided
1 tbsp	chile powder
1 tsp	ground cumin
¼ tsp	ground cayenne pepper
8	6-inch corn tortillas
½ cup	chopped avocado
¼ cup	chopped tomatoes

Serves **4 (Plus Leftovers).**
Hands-On Time: **25 Minutes.**
Total Time: **45 Minutes.***
Plus Soaking Time.

INSTRUCTIONS

In a bowl, soak pepitas in water for 3 hours; drain. In a blender, combine pepitas, 1 cup water, lime juice and salt. Blend until mixture is the consistency of cream.

Preheat oven to 400°F. In a medium saucepan, bring lentils, broth and bay leaf to a boil. Reduce heat to medium-low and simmer for 20 minutes. Drain and transfer to a large bowl; discard bay leaf.

In a medium skillet on medium-high, heat oil spread. Add carrot and 1½ cups onion and sauté for 3 minutes. Add garlic and sauté for 2 minutes more. Add to bowl with lentils. To bowl, add eggs, oats, ¼ cup cilantro, chile powder, ground cumin and cayenne. Stir until well combined.

Line a large baking sheet with parchment paper. Using wet hands, shape mixture into 2-inch balls, making 18 balls total. Place on baking sheet. Bake for 18 to 20 minutes.

Slice 12 lentil balls in half (reserve remaining 6 for use in Meal Plan). Place 3 lentil ball halves on each of 8 tortillas. Top each taco with 1½ tbsp pepita cream. Divide avocado, tomato and remaining ¼ cup each onion and cilantro over tacos.

Nutrition Information Per serving (2 tacos and 3 tbsp cream): Calories: 508, Total Fat: 20 g, Sat. Fat: 4.5 g, Monounsaturated Fat: 7.5 g, Polyunsaturated Fat: 5 g, Carbs: 64 g, Fiber: 18 g, Sugars: 7 g, Protein: 23 g, Sodium: 267 mg, Cholesterol: 62 mg

TIP: If following our Meal Plan, refrigerate leftover ingredients to make 1 serving of 2 tacos, plus refrigerate an additional 6 lentil balls and leftover pepita cream. Reserve leftover lime juice lime juice and use when called for.

Curried Apricot Pan-Roasted Chicken

with Broccolini Amandine

INGREDIENTS

4 5-oz	boneless, skinless chicken breasts
⅛ tsp	each sea salt and ground black pepper + additional, to taste
3 tbsp	olive oil, divided
2	bunches broccolini, trimmed (1 lb)
4	chopped green onions, white and green parts, divided
2 tbsp	minced fresh ginger
2 tbsp	minced garlic, divided
2 tsp	curry powder
½ tsp	red pepper flakes
4 cups	sliced fresh apricots (8 apricots)
¼ cup	dry white wine
¾ cup	low-sodium chicken broth
2 tbsp	raw honey
	minced zest of ½ orange
2 tbsp	organic unsalted butter, diced
¼ cup	unsalted chopped or slivered almonds

Serves **4.**
Hands-On Time: **30 Minutes.**
Total Time: **30 Minutes.**

INSTRUCTIONS

Preheat oven to 400°F. Season chicken with ⅛ tsp each salt and pepper. In a large sauté pan on high, heat 2 tbsp oil. Add chicken and sear until browned on 1 side, 4 minutes. Flip and transfer pan to oven. Roast until cooked through, about 10 minutes, then transfer to a plate and tent with foil. Meanwhile, blanch broccolini in a pot of boiling water until nearly fork tender, 3 to 4 minutes. Drain, transfer to ice water to cool, drain again. Set aside.

To same pan with chicken drippings on medium heat, add whites of onions, ginger, 1 tbsp garlic, curry powder and pepper flakes; sweat until onions soften, about 1 minute.

Stir in apricots, increase heat to medium-high, cover and sauté for 3 minutes. Add wine and scrape up browned bits from pan with a wooden spoon. When wine has evaporated, stir in broth, honey and orange zest; cook until sauce thickens, 5 to 6 minutes.

Stir in butter until emulsified. Stir in greens of onions; season with additional salt and pepper. Cover to keep warm.

In a large sauté pan on medium, heat remaining 1 tbsp oil. Add remaining 1 tbsp garlic and cook for 30 seconds. Add broccolini and cook until heated, 3 minutes. Stir in almonds and additional salt and pepper. Serve sauce over chicken and broccolini alongside.

Nutrition Information Per serving (1 chicken breast with sauce and ¼ of broccolini): Calories: 529, Total Fat: 24 g, Sat. Fat: 6 g, Monounsaturated Fat: 12.5 g, Polyunsaturated Fat: 3 g, Carbs: 41 g, Fiber: 8 g, Sugars: 27 g, Protein: 40.5 g, Sodium: 244 mg, Cholesterol: 119 mg

Vegetable & Tempeh Coconut Curry

INGREDIENTS

1 cup	farro
2 tsp	olive oil spread
16 oz	tempeh (plain or flax variety), chopped into ½-inch cubes
1	large onion, chopped
1	each small red bell pepper and orange bell pepper, chopped
1 large	yellow summer squash, chopped
2 tbsp	peeled and minced fresh ginger
2	cloves garlic, minced
2 tbsp	curry powder
1 tbsp	ground turmeric
½ tsp	ground cayenne pepper
2 cups	vegetable broth
9 oz	coconut milk
2½ cups	snap peas
1½ tbsp	rice vinegar
1 tbsp	reduced-sodium tamari sauce
5 tbsp	chopped fresh cilantro leaves
5 tbsp	chopped scallions

Serves **5.**
Hands-On Time: **35 Minutes.**
Total Time: **40 Minutes.**

INSTRUCTIONS

Cook farro according to package directions.

Meanwhile, in a large skillet on medium-high, heat oil spread. Add tempeh and onion and sauté for 3 minutes, until onion begins to soften. Stir in bell peppers, squash, ginger, garlic, curry powder, turmeric and cayenne; sauté for 3 minutes, stirring often. Add broth, coconut milk and snap peas. Cover and simmer for 10 minutes. Before serving, stir in vinegar and tamari.

Divide farro between bowls and top each with 1½ cups curry mixture and 1 tbsp each cilantro and scallions.

Nutrition Information Per serving (1½ cups): Calories: 511, Total Fat: 21.5 g, Sat. Fat: 11 g, Monounsaturated Fat: 5 g, Polyunsaturated Fat: 4 g, Carbs: 56 g, Fiber: 18 g, Sugars: 7 g, Protein: 25 g, Sodium: 211 mg, Cholesterol: 0 mg

TIP: If following our Meal Plan, refrigerate 2 servings (1½ cups each) for leftovers. Also, refrigerate remaining coconut milk from can and use when called for.

Ginger Chicken Fajitas
with Cashew Sour Cream

INGREDIENTS

2 tsp	grape seed oil, divided
1	yellow onion, thinly sliced
1	red bell pepper, thinly sliced
10 oz	boneless, skinless chicken breasts, cut into thin strips
1	1-inch piece fresh ginger, peeled and minced
2	cloves garlic, minced
1 tsp	ground cumin
½–1 tsp	ground cayenne pepper
¼ tsp	red pepper flakes, optional
Pinch	each sea salt and ground black pepper
2 tbsp	fresh lime juice
6 large	Swiss chard leaves, stems removed

Cashew Sour Cream

¾ cup	raw unsalted cashews
2 tsp	nutritional yeast
1 tsp	apple cider vinegar
1 tsp	fresh lime juice
⅛ tsp	sea salt

Serves **3.**
Hands-On Time: **30 Minutes.**
Total Time: **30 Minutes.***
Plus Soaking Time.

INSTRUCTIONS

Prepare cashew sour cream: In a bowl, soak cashews in water for at least 3 hours in the refrigerator. Drain and rinse. In a high-powered blender or small food processor, place cashews, ⅓ cup water and remaining sour cream ingredients. Blend until very smooth. Refrigerate until ready to serve.

Prepare fajitas: In a large nonstick skillet on medium, heat 1 tsp oil. Add onion and sauté for 3 minutes. Add bell pepper and sauté for 3 minutes, until onion starts to brown. Transfer mixture to a bowl; set aside.

In same skillet on medium, heat remaining 1 tsp oil. Add chicken and cook until lightly browned, about 4 minutes. Return onion and bell pepper to skillet. Add ginger, garlic, cumin, cayenne, pepper flakes (if using) and pinch each salt and black pepper. Cook and stir until spices are fragrant and chicken is cooked through, about 2 minutes. Add 2 tbsp lime juice and stir up browned bits from bottom of skillet.

To serve, divide fajita mixture and cashew cream among chard leaves.

Nutrition Information Per serving (2 chard leaves, 1½ cups fajita mixture, ⅓ of cream): Calories: 350, Fat: 18.5 g, Sat. Fat: 3 g, Monounsaturated Fat: 8 g, Polyunsaturated Fat: 5 g, Carbs: 19 g, Fiber: 4 g, Sugars: 6 g, Protein: 29 g, Sodium: 272 mg, Cholesterol: 69 mg

TIP: If following our Meal Plan, store leftover chicken and sour cream in separate containers in refrigerator. Wrap remaining leaves in damp paper towel and store in a bag in refrigerator.

Sweet Pepper Sirloin Salad

with Fresh Horseradish Vinaigrette & Blue Cheese

INGREDIENTS

1 lb	boneless top sirloin steak, about ¾ inch thick, trimmed
5 oz	mixed spring greens
½	each yellow and orange bell pepper, sliced
1 cup	grape tomatoes, halved
½ cup	thinly sliced red onion
1½ oz	crumbled blue cheese

Vinaigrette

⅓ cup	white balsamic or white wine vinegar
2 tbsp	fresh grated horseradish
1 tbsp	safflower or olive oil
2	cloves garlic, minced
½ tsp	each sea salt and coarse ground black pepper

Serves **4.**
Hands-On Time: **15 Minutes.**
Total Time: **25 Minutes.**

INSTRUCTIONS

Heat a large grill pan or grill on medium-high and lightly grease grates. Add steak and cook, turning once, to desired doneness, 6 to 8 minutes for medium-rare (internal temperature of 145°F when tested with an instant-read thermometer) and 7 to 10 minutes for medium (160°F). Transfer to a cutting board and let rest for 10 minutes; thinly slice against grain into 12 to 16 slices.

Meanwhile, in a small bowl, whisk together all vinaigrette ingredients.

In a large bowl, combine greens, bell peppers, tomatoes and onion. Top with steak, vinaigrette and cheese, dividing evenly.

Nutrition Information Per serving (3 oz steak, 2½ cups greens mixture, 2 tbsp vinaigrette): Calories: 221, Total Fat: 10 g, Sat. Fat: 3 g, Monounsaturated Fat: 4.5 g, Polyunsaturated Fat: 1 g, Carbs: 13 g, Fiber: 2 g, Sugars: 7 g, Protein: 21 g, Sodium: 441 mg, Cholesterol: 36 mg

PEPPERS FOR YOUR PEEPERS: The addition of bell peppers makes this salad a vitamin C superstar–providing 167% of your daily value (DV). A water-soluble vitamin, vitamin C is renowned for its importance to good eyesight, helping to prevent cataracts and macular degeneration.

Cauliflower & Quinoa Patties
with Mediterranean Salad

Parmesan, garlic and herbs add big flavor to these easy patties while a fresh, feta-topped tomato and olive salad is served alongside.

INGREDIENTS

6 cups	cauliflower florets (about 1 small cauliflower)
2	cloves garlic, minced
1 large	egg
1 large	egg white, beaten
1 cup	cooked quinoa
2 tbsp	finely chopped fresh flat-leaf parsley leaves
¾ cup	whole-wheat flour
½ cup	grated Parmesan cheese
¾ tsp	baking powder
½ tsp	dried oregano
	sea salt and ground black pepper, to taste
2 tbsp	grape seed or safflower oil, divided

Mediterranean Salad

4	plum tomatoes, finely chopped
2	scallions, thinly sliced
½ cup	chopped pitted Kalamata olives
¼ cup	chopped fresh mint leaves
2 tbsp	fresh lemon juice
½ cup	crumbled feta cheese

Serves **6.**
Hands-On Time: **30 Minutes.**
Total Time: **55 Minutes.***
Plus Cooling Time.

INSTRUCTIONS

Prepare salad: In a small bowl, combine tomatoes, scallions, olives, mint and lemon juice; stir in feta. Set aside.

In a large saucepan of boiling salted water, add cauliflower and cook until very tender, about 8 minutes. Drain well and transfer to a large bowl. Roughly mash cauliflower with a potato masher to pea-size pieces; let cool for 15 minutes.

Stir in garlic, egg and egg white, quinoa and parsley. In a separate bowl, whisk flour, Parmesan, baking powder, oregano, salt and pepper; stir flour mixture into quinoa mixture until just combined.

Using ¼ cup mixture for each, roll into balls, then flatten slightly to form ¾-inch-thick round patties. Repeat with remaining mixture to make a total of 18 patties.

In a large nonstick skillet on medium, heat 1 tbsp oil. Add half of patties and cook for about 8 minutes, using 2 utensils to help turn them halfway, until golden and cooked through. Transfer to a paper towel–lined plate and repeat with remaining 1 tbsp oil and other half of patties. Serve with salad.

Nutrition Information Per serving (3 patties and ¾ cup salad): Calories: 269, Total Fat: 14 g, Sat. Fat: 4 g, Monounsaturated Fat: 4 g, Polyunsaturated Fat: 4.5 g, Carbs: 26 g, Fiber: 5.5 g, Sugars: 4 g, Protein: 12 g, Sodium: 571 mg, Cholesterol: 48 mg

Mediterranean Quinoa
with Red Beets

INGREDIENTS

1 cup	quinoa, rinsed
2 tbsp	olive oil
3 cups	peeled, diced red beets (1 lb)
1	bunch green onions, sliced, white and green parts, divided
2 tbsp	minced garlic
1 tbsp	minced lemon zest + 2 tbsp fresh lemon juice, divided
1 cup	chopped fresh flat-leaf parsley
1 cup	chopped unsalted walnuts, toasted
¼ tsp	each sea salt and ground black pepper, or to taste
	balsamic vinegar, to taste
6 tbsp	crumbled feta cheese

Serves **6.**
Hands-on time: **20 minutes.**
Total time: **30 minutes.**

INSTRUCTIONS

In a large nonstick skillet, cook quinoa according to package directions; transfer to a bowl and set aside.

In same skillet on medium-high, heat oil. Add beets and whites of onion and sauté until beets are fork-tender, 10 minutes. Add garlic and cook for 1 minute more. Stir in quinoa, greens of onions, lemon zest and juice, parsley and walnuts; season with salt, pepper and vinegar. Garnish each serving with 1 tbsp feta.

Nutrition Information Per serving (1 cup): Calories: 344, Total Fat: 21 g, Sat. Fat: 3.5 g, Monounsaturated Fat: 6 g, Polyunsaturated Fat: 11 g, Carbs: 32 g, Fiber: 6 g, Sugars: 7 g, Protein: 10 g, Sodium: 234 mg, Cholesterol: 8 mg

Smoky-Sweet Beer Can Chicken

with Grilled Veggies

If you've never made a beer can chicken, don't be daunted–it's an easy, tasty and fun way to roast a chicken. We've added a maple-chile rub plus a pile of summery grilled zucchini. Use any leftovers to make chicken and zucchini soft tacos.

INGREDIENTS

2 tbsp	maple sugar
1½ tbsp	smoked paprika
2 tsp	each garlic powder and onion powder
1½ tsp	chile powder
½ tsp	sea salt
1 3½-lb	chicken
1 12-oz	can organic beer
3 small	zucchini, halved lengthwise
3 small	golden zucchini or crookneck squash, halved lengthwise
1	scallion, thinly sliced

Serves **4.**
Hands-On Time: **40 Minutes.**
Total Time: **1 Hour, 30 Minutes.**

INSTRUCTIONS

In a small bowl, combine maple sugar, smoked paprika, garlic powder, onion powder, chile powder and salt. Set aside 1 tbsp of spice mixture. Place chicken on a work surface, gently slip fingers under skin and work in remaining spice mixture over meat. Pour ¾ cup beer into an 8 x 8-inch baking pan. Place can with remaining beer upright in pan. Slide chicken upright over can, with legs and can forming a tripod to balance chicken. Tuck in wings.

Prepare a grill for indirect medium heat (to maintain a temperature of about 350°F). Place a double layer of foil, about 12 inches square, over the cooler part of the grate. Place pan with chicken on foil, cover and cook for 15 minutes.

Baste chicken with pan juices. Continue to cook, brushing with pan juices every 15 or 20 minutes, until a thermometer inserted in thickest part of thigh reads 165°F, about 1 hour total cooking time. (Cover chicken loosely with foil if skin starts to get too brown.) Remove chicken from grill and set aside to rest 10 minutes.

While chicken is resting, increase heat to medium-high. Sprinkle both sides of zucchini with reserved spice mixture and grill until tender and lightly charred, 3 to 4 minutes per side. Transfer zucchini to plates or a platter and sprinkle with scallions.

Carefully carve chicken while it's still on the can. Remove skin and serve, with zucchini and pan juices alongside.

Nutrition Information Per serving (6 oz chicken, 1½ zucchini, 1½ tbsp sauce): Calories: 314, Total Fat: 10 g, Sat. Fat: 3 g, Monounsaturated Fat: 3.5 g, Polyunsaturated Fat: 3 g, Carbs: 15 g, Fiber: 4 g, Sugars: 8 g, Protein: 40 g, Sodium: 388 mg, Cholesterol: 115 mg

Smoky Cauliflower Steaks
with Tomato Sauce & Microgreens

There's a new steak in town–and, surprisingly, it's made from cauliflower. Here, we cut the cruciferous veggie into thick steaks, coat it with spices then roast it 'til golden for maximum caramelization (read: flavor).

INGREDIENTS

2 large	heads cauliflower (25 to 30 oz each)
3 tbsp	olive oil + additional for drizzling
2 tsp	smoked paprika, divided
½ tsp	ground black pepper
¼ tsp	sea salt + additional as needed
1½–2 cups	unsalted tomato sauce
½ cup	microgreens, for garnish
2 tbsp	unsalted pine nuts, toasted
1 tsp	sesame seeds, toasted

Serves **4.**
Hands-On Time: **25 Minutes.**
Total Time: **55 Minutes.**

INSTRUCTIONS

Preheat oven to 425°F. Line a large rimmed baking sheet with foil.

Trim stems of cauliflower heads so that cauliflower sits flat upright. Cut each cauliflower vertically into two ¾-inch-thick steaks, making 4 steaks total. (Reserve remaining cauliflower for another use.) Arrange on prepared baking sheet.

In a small bowl, stir together oil, 1 tsp paprika, pepper and salt; brush half of mixture over cauliflower. Roast for 10 minutes. Turn and brush with remaining oil mixture; roast until tender and golden brown, about 25 minutes.

Meanwhile, in a small saucepan, combine tomato sauce, remaining 1 tsp smoked paprika and additional salt as needed; heat on low until warmed. Place 1 cauliflower steak on each plate and garnish with microgreens, pine nuts and sesame seeds. Drizzle each with additional oil.

Nutrition Information Per serving (1 steak with sauce and garnishes): Calories: 220, Total Fat: 18 g, Sat. Fat: 2 g, Monounsaturated Fat: 11 g, Polyunsaturated Fat: 3 g, Carbs: 15 g, Fiber: 5.5 g, Sugars: 7 g, Protein: 5 g, Sodium: 678 mg, Cholesterol: 0 mg

The Baja Grilled Peach Salad
with Spicy Cashew Dressing

Sweet, juicy grilled peaches add a lovely warm-weather flair to this salad packed to the brim with beautiful vegetables. The true star of this meal, though, is the creamy cashew dressing spiked with just a touch of cayenne. If you have time, we suggest making the candied pecans as they add an addictive sweet-salty crunch.

INGREDIENTS

1½ lb	boneless, skinless chicken breasts (about 2)
½ tsp	sea salt
½ tsp	paprika
	ground black pepper, to taste
3	peaches, pitted and quartered
3	ears sweet corn, husked
1 tbsp	olive oil
6–7 oz	mixed greens
4	green onions, thinly sliced
1 large	avocado, peeled, pitted and cubed
⅓ cup	toasted unsalted pecans, chopped*

Spicy Cashew Dressing

¼ cup	raw unsalted cashews, soaked in water for 1 to 4 hours (depending on the strength of your blender), and drained
¼ cup	apple cider vinegar
2 tbsp	extra-virgin olive oil
2 tsp	Dijon mustard
2 tsp	raw honey
½ tsp	sea salt
Pinch	ground cayenne pepper

Serves **6.**
Hands-On Time: **25 Minutes.**
Total Time: **30 Minutes.***
Plus Soaking Time.

INSTRUCTIONS

Preheat a grill to medium and lightly oil grates. Season chicken with ½ tsp salt, paprika and pepper. Brush peaches and corn lightly with olive oil. Grill peaches, chicken and corn until peaches have light grill marks (about 4 minutes per side), chicken is cooked through (about 5 to 6 minutes per side) and corn has light grill marks (8 to 10 minutes, turning occasionally). Slice chicken into 1-inch slices; cut corn kernels off the cob.

Meanwhile, prepare dressing: In a blender, add all dressing ingredients along with ¼ cup water; blend until smooth and creamy.

To a bowl, add mixed greens. Add corn and onions; drizzle dressing to lightly coat and toss. Arrange on a platter and top with chicken, peaches, avocados and pecans. Drizzle with remaining dressing.

*If time allows, make your own candied pecans (optional): In a skillet on medium, toast pecans until fragrant. Add 1 tbsp pure maple syrup and pinch salt and stir constantly until syrup is caramelized, 3 to 4 minutes.

Nutrition Information Per serving (⅙ of recipe): Calories: 410, Total Fat: 23 g, Sat. Fat: 3.5 g, Monounsaturated Fat: 14 g, Polyunsaturated Fat: 4 g, Carbs: 27 g, Fiber: 7 g, Sugars: 12 g, Protein: 28.5 g, Sodium: 469 mg, Cholesterol: 63 mg

Charred Corn & Tomato Salad
with Halloumi Cheese

Sweet summer corn and tomatoes are elevated with a fragrant tarragon dressing and flavor-packed halloumi. The firm Mediterranean cheese holds up well to heat, making it ideal for grilling. Look for halloumi in the deli section of your supermarket– it's often sold alongside feta and bocconcini.

INGREDIENTS

1	lemon, halved
¼ cup	fresh tarragon
2½ tbsp	olive oil, divided
1 tbsp	red wine vinegar
1 tsp	Dijon mustard
¼ tsp	each sea salt and ground black pepper
8	plum tomatoes, halved lengthwise
2	ears corn, husked
4 oz	halloumi cheese, cut in ¼-inch-thick slices
1	avocado, peeled, pitted and sliced
1	green onion, thinly sliced

Serves **4.**
Hands-On Time: **30 Minutes.**
Total Time: **30 Minutes.**

INSTRUCTIONS

Heat a grill to medium-high and brush grates with cooking oil. Place lemon halves, cut sides down, on grill. Close lid and grill until lemon is grill-marked, 1 to 2 minutes. Let cool enough to handle. Squeeze juice from lemon into a small bowl; discard lemon.

Prepare dressing: In a small food processor, blend lemon juice, tarragon, 1½ tbsp olive oil, vinegar, mustard, salt and pepper until well combined. Set aside.

Brush tomatoes, corn and halloumi all over with remaining 1 tbsp olive oil. Place corn on grill. Close lid and grill, turning often, until bright yellow and grill-marked, 7 to 8 minutes. Transfer to a cutting board and let cool enough to handle.

Meanwhile, place halloumi on grill. Close lid and grill, turning once, until grill-marked, about 4 minutes. Place tomatoes, cut side down, on grill. Close lid and grill, without turning, until slightly softened and grill-marked, about 2 minutes.

Halve each tomato piece lengthwise to make wedges. Cut kernels from corn. Divide tomatoes and avocado among plates. Top with corn, halloumi, onion and dressing.

Nutrition Information Per serving (2 cups): Calories: 318, Total Fat: 23.5 g, Sat. Fat: 7 g, Monounsaturated Fat: 13 g, Polyunsaturated Fat: 2.5 g, Carbs: 21 g, Fiber: 6 g, Sugars: 7.5 g, Protein: 11 g, Sodium: 510 mg, Cholesterol: 18 mg

Beet & Beef Burgers
with Tomato Relish

We've spiked these beef burgers with grated beet and carrot to add a hint of sweetness and a healthy dose of fiber. Any whole-grain bun or lettuce wrap works well with this burger–then add your favorite toppings such as tomatoes, onion and lettuce.

INGREDIENTS

1	head garlic
½ tsp	olive oil
2	plum tomatoes, halved lengthwise and seeded
1 tsp	red wine vinegar
1 tsp	raw honey
¼ tsp	ground allspice
1 lb	lean ground beef
1	red beet, peeled and grated (about 1 cup)
1 large	carrot, peeled and grated (about 1 cup)
1 large	egg
½ cup	whole-grain bread crumbs
¼ cup	each finely chopped fresh basil and parsley
¼ tsp	each sea salt and ground black pepper

Serves **6.**
Hands-On Time: **35 Minutes.**
Total Time: **50 Minutes.**

INSTRUCTIONS

Preheat a grill to medium. Fold a 24-inch-long sheet of heavy-duty foil in half crosswise to make a 12-inch square. Slice off top third of garlic head to expose cloves; place head in center of foil and drizzle with oil. Fold up edges of foil to create a pouch, pinching to seal. Place on grill, close lid and grill until cloves are soft and golden brown, about 30 minutes. Let cool enough to handle.

Meanwhile, place tomatoes, cut side down, on grill. Close lid and grill, turning once, until lightly grill-marked, about 2 minutes. Transfer to a food processor. Squeeze garlic cloves into processor. Add vinegar, honey and allspice and pulse until coarsely chopped. Scrape into a small bowl; set aside.

Meanwhile, in a large bowl, mix together beef, beet, carrot, egg, bread crumbs, basil, parsley, salt and pepper. Shape into 6 patties.

Lightly grease grill grates. Place patties on grill, close lid and grill on medium heat, turning once, until an instant-read thermometer reaches 160°F when inserted in thickest part, 8 to 10 minutes. Serve with relish.

Nutrition Information Per serving (1 patty and 2 tsp relish): Calories: 176, Total Fat: 7 g, Sat. Fat: 3 g, Monounsaturated Fat: 3 g, Polyunsaturated Fat: 1 g, Carbs: 10 g, Fiber: 2 g, Sugars: 3 g, Protein: 19 g, Sodium: 166 mg, Cholesterol: 81 mg

Cucumber Dill Salmon Patties
with Lemon Caper Mayo

Looking for tasty new ways to put your cucumber crop to good use? Add them to burgers! Here, we've mixed small, sweet Persian cucumbers into healthy salmon patties to make them extra juicy. Serve with tomato slices on a large, sturdy lettuce leaf, such as Boston lettuce or radicchio, or on a whole-grain bun.

INGREDIENTS

2 small	Persian cucumbers, roughly chopped
¼ large	red onion, diced (about ¼ cup)
1 tbsp	fresh lemon juice
1 lb	boneless, skinless salmon fillet
1 large	egg
½ cup	whole-grain bread crumbs
2 tbsp	chopped fresh dill
1 tsp	Dijon mustard
1 tsp	wasabi paste
¼ tsp	each sea salt and ground black pepper

Lemon Caper Mayo

¼ cup	olive oil mayonnaise
2 tbsp	capers, drained, rinsed and chopped
2 tsp	lemon zest

Serves **6.**
Hands-On Time: **25 Minutes.**
Total Time: **1 Hour.**

INSTRUCTIONS

In a food processor, pulse cucumbers, onion and lemon juice until finely chopped. Add salmon and pulse until coarsely chopped. Add egg, bread crumbs, dill, mustard, wasabi paste, salt and pepper and pulse until just combined.

Line a large plate with parchment paper. Shape salmon mixture into 6 patties and arrange in a single layer on plate. Refrigerate for 30 minutes.

Preheat a grill to high and lightly brush grates with cooking oil. Place patties on grill, close lid and grill until bottoms are grill-marked, about 5 minutes. Turn, close lid and grill until an instant-read thermometer reaches 145°F when inserted in thickest part, about 4 minutes.

Meanwhile, prepare lemon caper mayo: In a small bowl, stir together mayonnaise, capers and lemon zest. Serve with patties.

Nutrition Information Per serving (1 patty and 2 tsp mayo): Calories: 187, Total Fat: 11 g, Sat. Fat: 2 g, Monounsaturated Fat: 4 g, Polyunsaturated Fat: 5 g, Carbs: 4 g, Fiber: 1 g, Sugars: 1 g, Protein: 17 g, Sodium: 293 mg, Cholesterol: 70 mg

Asparagus & Zucchini Pappardelle
with Parmesan

Zucchini are full of moisture, which means they often steam instead of sear in your pan. To get a proper golden sear, the trick is to not overcrowd the pan. Cook the slices in small batches in a single layer in your skillet and avoid the temptation to stir too often; they need time to brown.

INGREDIENTS

8 oz	whole-grain pappardelle (dried or fresh pasta)
1 tbsp	olive oil
2	yellow zucchini, halved lengthwise and thinly sliced crosswise
3	cloves garlic, minced
1 lb	asparagus, trimmed and cut into 1½-inch lengths
¼ tsp	each sea salt and ground black pepper
1 large	lemon, zested and juiced, divided
½ cup	grated Parmesan cheese
3 tbsp	finely chopped fresh mint
¼ cup	toasted unsalted pine nuts, optional

Serves **4.**
Hands-On Time: **30 Minutes.**
Total Time: **30 Minutes.**

INSTRUCTIONS

Bring a large saucepan of water to a boil. Add pasta and cook al dente according to package directions. Reserving ¼ cup cooking liquid, drain pasta.

Meanwhile, in a large skillet on medium-high, heat oil. Working in small batches, sauté zucchini, stirring frequently, until softened and golden brown, 2 to 3 minutes.

Return all zucchini to skillet. Add garlic and sauté until fragrant, about 30 seconds. Add asparagus, salt, pepper and lemon juice. Reduce heat to medium-low; cook, stirring occasionally and scraping up any browned bits from bottom of pan, until asparagus is tender and bright green, 2 to 3 minutes.

Remove from heat. Add pasta, lemon zest and cheese; toss to combine. If necessary, add enough reserved pasta-cooking water to reach desired consistency. Sprinkle with mint and pine nuts (if using).

Nutrition Information Per serving (2 cups): Calories: 289, Total Fat: 8 g, Sat. Fat: 2 g, Monounsaturated Fat: 3 g, Polyunsaturated Fat: 2 g, Carbs: 46 g, Fiber: 8 g, Sugars: 5 g, Protein: 15 g, Sodium: 322 mg, Cholesterol: 9 mg

Thai Mango Zucchini Noodle Salad
with Chicken

Zucchini and carrot spirals are a lighter and lower-carb alternative to grain-based noodles. Here, they are tossed with a spicy mango dressing and topped with chicken and crunchy cashews.

INGREDIENTS

10 oz	boneless, skinless chicken breasts (2 breasts)
1½ cups	low-sodium chicken broth
1	clove garlic, thinly sliced
1½ tsp	minced fresh ginger
½	avocado, pitted and peeled
2½ cups	frozen mango chunks, thawed
6 tbsp	loosely packed fresh cilantro leaves, divided
2 tbsp	fresh lime juice
1 tsp	reduced-sodium tamari sauce
¼ tsp	sriracha sauce
3 large	zucchini, ends trimmed
1 large	carrot, ends trimmed and peeled
¼ cup	raw unsalted cashews

Serves **6.**
Hands-On Time: **20 minutes.**
Total Time: **40 minutes.***
Plus Cooling Time.

INSTRUCTIONS

In a small saucepan, place chicken in a single layer. Pour in broth, then add garlic and ginger. Cover and bring to a boil on medium-high. Reduce heat to a simmer, covered, until chicken is no longer pink, 8 to 10 minutes. Transfer to a cutting board. When cool enough to handle, shred or chop.

Meanwhile, increase heat to high and boil broth mixture, uncovered, until liquid is reduced to ¼ cup, 6 to 8 minutes. Let cool to room temperature.

In a blender, combine avocado, mango, 4 tbsp cilantro, lime juice, tamari, sriracha and broth mixture; blend on high speed until creamy and smooth.

Working with 1 piece at a time, place zucchini into a spiral slicer and turn crank to create long strands that resemble spaghetti noodles. Repeat with carrot. (**NOTE:** *Always read directions for your spiral slicer as instructions may vary by brand.*) In a large bowl, place zucchini and carrot strands and toss with mango mixture to coat. Let stand for 5 minutes. Add chicken to bowl, tossing to coat. Sprinkle with cashews and remaining 2 tbsp cilantro.

Nutrition Information Per serving (2 cups): Calories: 205, Total Fat: 7 g, Sat. Fat: 1 g, Monounsaturated Fat: 3 g, Polyunsaturated Fat: 1 g, Carbs: 24 g, Fiber: 5 g, Sugars: 16 g, Protein: 16 g, Sodium: 106 mg, Cholesterol: 35 mg

TIP: No spiral slicer? Use a julienne peeler or vegetable peeler to make ribbons, then stack and thinly slice by hand.

Garlic Shrimp Spaghetti
with Buttery Kale

You can easily pull off this protein-packed meal on busy weeknights–all you really need is a bunch of kale and a handful of freezer and pantry staples. Be sure to cut the tough stems from the kale–an easy way is to fold the leaf in half lengthwise and run your knife or kitchen scissors along the inner edge of the stem to remove. Omit the chile pepper (or scrape out the seeds) for a milder pasta.

INGREDIENTS

8 oz	whole-grain spaghetti
10 oz large	shrimp, peeled and deveined
½ tsp	ground black pepper
¼ tsp	sea salt
1 tbsp	olive oil
4 large	cloves garlic, sliced
1 tsp	dried parsley
¼ tsp	red pepper flakes
2 tsp	lemon zest
2 tbsp	organic unsalted butter
4 cups	finely sliced stemmed kale
1	red finger chile pepper (or other hot red chile such as cherry bomb, cayenne or Thai), thinly sliced

Serves **4.**
Hands-On Time: **25 Minutes.**
Total Time: **25 Minutes.**

INSTRUCTIONS

Bring a large saucepan of water to a boil. Add pasta and cook al dente according to package directions. Drain.

Meanwhile, in a large bowl, toss shrimp with pepper and salt to coat; set aside. In a large skillet on medium-high, heat oil. Add garlic, parsley and pepper flakes and cook, stirring constantly, until fragrant, 30 to 45 seconds. Add shrimp and sauté, stirring frequently, until shrimp are pink and opaque throughout, 3 to 4 minutes. Stir in lemon zest. Transfer to a plate and cover to keep warm.

In same skillet, heat butter on medium-high. Add kale and sauté until wilted, about 1 minute. Add pasta, shrimp mixture and chile pepper and toss to combine.

Nutrition Information Per serving (2 cups): Calories: 384, Total Fat: 12 g, Sat. Fat: 4.5 g, Monounsaturated Fat: 4.5 g, Polyunsaturated Fat: 2 g, Carbs: 51 g, Fiber: 7 g, Sugars: 2 g, Protein: 23 g, Sodium: 209 mg, Cholesterol: 115 mg

Roasted Grape & Salmon Kale Salad

with Cider Maple Vinaigrette & Gorgonzola

INGREDIENTS

Vinaigrette

1 small	shallot, minced
5 tbsp	extra-virgin olive oil
3 tbsp	apple cider vinegar
2 tbsp	unsweetened apple juice
2 tsp	pure maple syrup (**TIP:** *We prefer Grade A maple syrup here for its light flavor that won't overpower other ingredients in the dressing.*)
1 tsp	Dijon mustard, optional
½ tsp	sea salt
Pinch	ground black pepper

Salad

2 cups	red grapes
1 tbsp	olive oil, divided (**TIP:** *Remember when choosing olive oils for high-heat cooking, you can go with a regular olive oil or a high-quality extra-virgin that can withstand the heat.*)
¼ tsp + pinch	sea salt, divided
⅛ tsp	ground black pepper, divided
1 18-oz	wild salmon fillet
12 cups	stemmed, sliced and lightly packed kale
½ cup	sliced unsalted almonds
⅓ cup	crumbled Gorgonzola cheese

To keep prep quick, roast the salmon at the same time as red grapes all on one baking sheet for quick cleanup. The cooked fruit gives the salad a sweet-tart tang that balances the richness of the cheese and fish. Sprouts or microgreens make a nice garnish on this dish.

Serves **6.**
Hands-On Time: **15 Minutes.**
Total Time: **30 Minutes.**

INSTRUCTIONS

Preheat oven to 425°F. Make vinaigrette: In a small bowl, whisk together all vinaigrette ingredients. Set aside.

Make salad: Line a large rimmed baking sheet with parchment paper. In a medium bowl, toss grapes with 2 tsp oil; sprinkle with pinch each salt and pepper. Transfer onto half of prepared pan. Arrange salmon on other half of pan; drizzle with remaining 1 tsp oil and sprinkle with remaining ¼ tsp salt and pinch pepper. Roast until salmon is rare in center but edges flake easily when tested with a fork, 10 to 13 minutes. Remove salmon from pan; let cool. Continue roasting grapes until slightly shriveled, 7 to 10 minutes more. Let cool.

Meanwhile, in a large bowl, massage kale with half of vinaigrette until well coated.

Break salmon into chunks; add to kale mixture along with roasted grapes, almonds and cheese. Drizzle with remaining vinaigrette.

Nutrition Information Per serving (⅙ of salad): Calories: 359, Total Fat: 23 g, Sat. Fat: 4 g, Monounsaturated Fat: 15 g, Polyunsaturated Fat: 3 g, Carbs: 16 g, Fiber: 3 g, Sugars: 11 g, Protein: 22 g, Sodium: 401 mg, Cholesterol: 45 mg

HEART HELPERS: Both almonds and salmon provide heart-healthy fats to this kale salad. Almonds are high in monounsaturated fats that support your ticker, while studies have shown that omega-3s, such as those found in salmon, may reduce your risk of cardiovascular disease because of their ability to reduce inflammation.

Halibut Ceviche
with Tomato Gazpacho

The high acidity in citrus juice denatures, or rearranges, the proteins in fish in the same way heat does, so while it's not technically "cooked," it's not raw either. The halibut can become too firm if you let it sit for too long in the juice, so be sure to serve it right after bringing it to room temperature. Give the gazpacho a quick stir or whirl in the blender before serving if it looks like it has separated.

INGREDIENTS

Ceviche

1 lb	boneless, skinless halibut fillets, cut into ¼-inch chunks (or substitute with cod) (**NOTE:** *For the easiest slicing, pop the fish in the freezer for 10 to 15 minutes to firm up first.*)
1 small	jalapeño chile pepper, seeded and finely chopped
¾ cup	fresh lime juice
¼ cup	fresh lemon juice
½ tsp	sea salt
1	green onion, thinly sliced
½ large	red bell pepper, finely chopped
6 tbsp	extra-virgin olive oil
¼ cup	chopped fresh cilantro
¼ tsp	ground black pepper

Gazpacho

7	vine-ripened tomatoes (about 1 lb), seeded and roughly chopped
2	Persian, Japanese or other variety of small cucumbers (about 8 oz), peeled and roughly chopped
1	shallot, quartered
½ large	red bell pepper, roughly chopped
3 tbsp	sherry vinegar or red wine vinegar
1½ tsp	sea salt
¼ cup	extra-virgin olive oil

Serves **4 to 6.**
Hands-On Time: **30 Minutes.**
Total Time: **45 Minutes.**

INSTRUCTIONS

Prepare ceviche: To a large bowl, add fish and jalapeño. Stir in lime juice, lemon juice and salt. Stir until well combined, pressing down to submerge fish in liquid. Cover surface directly with plastic wrap. Refrigerate for 8 to 10 minutes.

Remove plastic wrap; stir well and press down on fish to submerge in liquid. Cover surface directly with plastic wrap. Refrigerate until fish is white and opaque throughout, 8 to 10 minutes more. Drain, discarding liquid. Return to bowl. Stir in onion, bell pepper, oil, cilantro and black pepper. Set aside at room temperature for about 10 minutes.

Meanwhile, prepare gazpacho: In a blender, combine all gazpacho ingredients except oil; blend until smooth. Remove stopper from lid; gradually drizzle in oil, blending until combined. Refrigerate until needed.

Divide gazpacho among bowls. Top with fish mixture, dividing evenly.

Nutrition Information Per serving (⅙ of recipe): Calories: 311, Total Fat: 25 g, Sat. Fat: 4 g, Monounsaturated Fat: 18 g, Polyunsaturated Fat: 2.5 g, Carbs: 7 g, Fiber: 2 g, Sugars: 4 g, Protein: 15 g, Sodium: 558 mg, Cholesterol: 37 mg

Chicken Enchiladas
with Corn & Cape Gooseberry Salsa

Sweet corn stands out in the tangy, spicy chicken filling in these enchiladas. And because no Mexican-inspired meal should go without cheese, we smother it in piping-hot, bubbling mozzarella.

INGREDIENTS

2 6-oz	boneless, skinless chicken breasts
	sea salt, to taste
1	white onion, divided
4 cups	stemmed and skinned cape gooseberries
2	jalapeño chile peppers, stemmed and seeded
¾ cup	lightly packed coarsely chopped fresh cilantro, divided
2 tbsp	fresh lime juice
⅔ cup	fresh corn kernels (from about 1 ear)
½	red bell pepper, seeded and diced
2 tsp	chile powder
1 tsp	ground cumin
10	6-inch corn tortillas
½ cup	shredded mozzarella cheese
3	green onions, thinly sliced, optional
1	plum tomato, diced, optional

Nutrition Information Per serving (2 enchiladas): Calories: 325, Total Fat: 5 g, Sat. Fat: 1 g, Carbs: 47 g, Fiber: 10 g, Sugars: 3.5 g, Protein: 25 g, Sodium: 224 mg, Cholesterol: 43 mg

Serves **5.**
Hands-On Time: **45 Minutes.**
Total Time: **1 Hour, 15 Minutes.**

INSTRUCTIONS

Arrange 1 oven rack in highest and 1 rack in lowest position. Preheat oven to 425°F. Mist chicken with cooking spray and season with salt. Arrange on a tray and roast on bottom rack for 15 to 20 minutes, until an instant-read thermometer reaches 165°F when inserted in center of chicken. Let cool to room temperature.

Meanwhile, slice half of onion into ¼-inch-thick slices. Dice remaining half; reserve diced onion. Arrange gooseberries, sliced onion and jalapeños in a single layer on a large parchment-lined baking sheet. Transfer to top rack of oven (at same time as chicken) and cook until gooseberries are blistered and split open, about 10 minutes. Let cool to room temperature. Reduce oven to 375°F.

Meanwhile, finely shred chicken and transfer to a large bowl. Set aside.

Prepare salsa: In a food processor, combine gooseberry-jalapeño mixture and any accompanying juices, ½ cup cilantro and lime juice. Pulse for about 30 seconds, until almost smooth. Transfer to a medium bowl, add additional salt and set aside. (**MAKE AHEAD:** *Prepare salsa up to 48 hours in advance, cover and refrigerate until needed*.)

Heat a large skillet on medium-high and mist with cooking spray. Add diced onion, corn and bell pepper and cook, stirring frequently, until onion is translucent, 3 to 4 minutes. Stir in chile powder and cumin and cook for 1 minute, until fragrant. Add to chicken and stir to combine. Stir in ¾ cup salsa and additional salt.

Arrange tortillas in a stack, wrap in a double layer of foil and warm in oven for 5 to 6 minutes, until softened. Spread ½ cup salsa over bottom of a 9 x 13-inch casserole dish. Spoon ¼ cup chicken mixture into center of each tortilla. Roll tortillas over chicken mixture and place seam side down in dish. (**NOTE:** *Simply roll into a tube; do not fold in sides.*) Drizzle remaining salsa over enchiladas and sprinkle with mozzarella, dividing evenly. Bake until mozzarella is bubbling and filling is hot, about 25 minutes. Top with remaining ¼ cup cilantro, and if using, green onions and tomato.

Herbed Skirt Steak Tacos
with Beet & Fresno Chile Salsa

Red beet and chile pepper salsa makes for a striking and flavorful topper on these oregano and sriracha-marinated steak tacos. Because this salsa requires a little baking time to cook the beet, you can make it entirely up to 1 day in advance and refrigerate until serving.

INGREDIENTS

2 tbsp	sriracha
2 tbsp	chopped fresh oregano
2 tbsp	fresh lime juice
¼ tsp	ground black pepper
14 oz	skirt steak, trimmed
8	6-inch corn tortillas
2 cups	shredded romaine lettuce

Salsa

1 large (10 oz)	red beet
3	green onions, chopped
1	Fresno (red jalapeño) or jalapeño chile pepper, finely chopped
2 tbsp	fresh orange juice
1 tbsp	fresh lime juice
1 tsp	extra-virgin olive oil
¼ tsp	sea salt

Serves **4.**
Hands-On Time: **30 Minutes.**
Total Time: **1 Hour, 15 Minutes.**

INSTRUCTIONS

Prepare salsa: Preheat oven to 400°F. Wrap beet in foil and place on a baking sheet. Bake until a paring knife slips easily into center of beet, about 45 minutes. Unwrap beet, and when cool enough to handle, push skin off with your fingers and discard. Finely chop beet and combine with remaining salsa ingredients; set aside.

Meanwhile, in a glass or stainless steel bowl or a zip-top bag, combine sriracha, oregano, lime juice and black pepper. Add steak and rub marinade into meat. Marinate in the refrigerator for 30 minutes, or up to 3 hours.

Heat a grill or grill pan on medium-high. Grill tortillas in batches until warm and pliable, about 1 minute per side. Stack tortillas and wrap in foil; set aside.

Remove steak from marinade, shaking off excess. To grill or grill pan on medium-high, add steak and grill until medium-rare, 2 to 3 minutes per side. Let steak rest on a cutting board for 5 minutes. Thinly slice against the grain, then chop into small pieces. Divide steak, lettuce and salsa among tortillas.

Per serving (2 tacos with toppings): Calories: 365, Total Fat: 15 g, Sat. Fat: 4 g, Monounsaturated Fat: 8 g, Polyunsaturated Fat: 1 g, Carbs: 33 g, Fiber: 5 g, Sugars: 8 g, Protein: 26 g, Sodium: 317 mg, Cholesterol: 69 mg

Baked Goat Cheese Salad
with Caramelized Onions, Strawberries & Pecans

Impress your guests with this bold-flavored, restaurant-style salad. Strawberries add sweetness to offset the tangy goat cheese and sharp citrusy dressing.

INGREDIENTS

2 large	Spanish onions, thinly sliced
¾ cup	whole-wheat panko bread crumbs
1 tsp	chopped fresh thyme
	sea salt and ground black pepper, to taste
4	egg whites
4 oz	chèvre or spreadable goat cheese
3 tbsp	fresh lemon juice
2 tsp	Dijon mustard
3 tbsp	chopped raw unsalted pecans
12 cups	baby arugula
2 cups	thinly sliced strawberries

Serves **4.**
Hands-On Time: **1 Hour, 10 Minutes.**
Total Time: **1 Hour, 10 Minutes.**

INSTRUCTIONS

Caramelize onions: Heat a large nonstick skillet on medium-high and lightly mist with cooking spray. Add onions and cook, stirring frequently, until fragrant, 1 to 2 minutes. (**NOTE:** *Skillet will be quite full to start, but onions shrink as they cook.*) Reduce heat to medium-low and cook, stirring occasionally, until very soft, sticky and light caramel in color, about 1 hour. Remove from heat, transfer to a large plate and let cool at room temperature for 10 minutes.

Meanwhile, preheat oven to 425°F. In a medium bowl, combine panko, thyme, salt and pepper. In a separate medium bowl, lightly beat egg whites; set aside. With your hands, gently press goat cheese into 4 1-oz balls and flatten each into ½-inch-thick patties. Dip patties in egg, turning to coat, then gently press both sides into panko mixture; repeat process to coat each patty twice. Transfer to a small tray, cover loosely with plastic wrap and freeze for 20 minutes.

Meanwhile, prepare dressing: In a small bowl, whisk lemon juice, mustard, salt and pepper; set aside.

Line a medium baking sheet with foil and mist with cooking spray. Arrange cheese patties in a single layer on half of sheet and mist tops with cooking spray. Bake for 6 minutes. Flip patties and bake for 6 more minutes, until golden. Turn oven heat off and remove sheet from oven. Add pecans to remaining half of sheet. Return to oven until pecans are warm, about 3 minutes.

In a large bowl, combine arugula, strawberries and dressing. Toss gently to coat and divide among plates. Top with onions, pecans and cheese patties, dividing evenly.

Nutrition Information Per serving (¼ of salad and 1 cheese patty): Calories: 252, Total Fat: 11 g, Sat. Fat: 5 g, Monounsaturated Fat: 4 g, Polyunsaturated Fat: 2 g, Carbs: 27 g, Fiber: 6 g, Sugars: 9 g, Protein: 14 g, Sodium: 284 mg, Cholesterol: 13 mg

Sirloin Steaks

with Cabernet Blackberry Sauce & Grilled Fennel

Sweet blackberry sauce pairs perfectly with hearty steaks and spicy black pepper. Lightly grilled fennel adds a delicate touch and makes this easy dish taste like it was made by a pro!

INGREDIENTS

4	cloves garlic, minced, divided
2 tbsp	balsamic vinegar
4 tsp	chopped fresh thyme, divided
1½ tsp	coarse ground black pepper + additional, to taste
1 tbsp	Dijon mustard
1 tsp	safflower oil + additional for oiling grill
1 lb	top sirloin, cut into 4 1-inch-thick steaks
2	shallots, minced
½ cup	Cabernet Sauvignon wine
1 cup	low-sodium beef broth
4 cups	fresh blackberries, divided
	juice of ½ lemon
2	bulbs fennel, fronds removed and sliced through the stem into quarters
	sea salt, to taste
½ tsp	kosher salt
2 tsp	cold organic unsalted butter

Serves **4.**
Hands-On Time: **40 Minutes.**
Total Time: **50 Minutes.***
Plus Marinating Time.

INSTRUCTIONS

In a small bowl, combine half of garlic, vinegar, 3 tsp thyme, pepper, Dijon and oil. Rub mixture on all sides of steaks, transfer to resealable container, cover and refrigerate for 4 to 24 hours.

Heat a medium saucepan on medium-high and mist with cooking spray. Add shallots and sauté, stirring frequently, until soft and light golden, about 2 minutes. Stir in wine, broth and 3 cups blackberries and bring to a boil. Reduce heat to medium and simmer, stirring occasionally, for 10 minutes, until berries are very soft and liquid is reduced by about half. Remove from heat.

Over a small bowl, strain blackberry mixture through a fine-mesh sieve, gently pressing on solids with a ladle to extract juice from berries; discard solids. Rinse saucepan; return blackberry sauce to pan over low heat, cover and keep warm.

Heat a grill or grill pan on medium-high and lightly brush with oil. In a large bowl, combine remaining half of garlic, 1 tsp thyme and lemon juice. Add fennel and toss to combine. Mist with cooking spray and toss gently to coat. Season with sea salt and pepper, to taste. Add fennel to grill and cook, turning once, until golden brown and lightly charred on the edges, 8 to 10 minutes. Set aside and cover to keep warm.

Season steaks with kosher salt and grill for about 3 minutes per side, until an instant-read thermometer registers 145°F when inserted in center of steak. Let steak rest for 3 minutes. Return sauce to medium heat and stir in butter until melted. (**NOTE:** *Do not use oil or premelted butter, as it will not emulsify.*) Divide steak and fennel among serving plates. Top with blackberry sauce and remaining blackberries, dividing evenly.

Nutrition Information Per serving (¼ of recipe): Calories: 328, Total Fat: 9 g, Sat. Fat: 3 g, Monounsaturated Fat: 3 g, Polyunsaturated Fat: 1 g, Carbs: 31 g, Fiber: 11 g, Sugars: 9 g, Protein: 28 g, Sodium: 489 mg, Cholesterol: 47 mg

Peaches & Coconut Cream Ice Cream

INGREDIENTS

2 cups	sliced peaches (fresh or frozen)
2 tsp	pure vanilla extract, divided
¼ tsp	sea salt, divided
2 13.5-oz	BPA-free cans coconut milk, refrigerated overnight (**NOTE:** *It's important to use a brand without fillers and gums for this recipe.*)
3 tbsp	raw honey

Serves **8.**
Hands-On Time: **15 minutes.**
Total Time: **25 minutes.***
**Plus Cooling and Freezing Time.*

INSTRUCTIONS

Chill a large mixing bowl and beaters (for an electric hand mixer) in the refrigerator for 15 minutes.

Meanwhile, in a small pot on medium-low, bring peaches, ¼ cup water, 1 tsp vanilla and ⅛ tsp salt to a simmer. Cover and simmer, stirring occasionally, for 10 minutes, using a spoon to crush and break up pieces until texture is a chunky purée. Remove from heat and cool completely.

Meanwhile, scoop solid white cream from coconut milk cans into chilled bowl; reserve liquid for another use. Using hand mixer, beat cream for 1 minute, until light and fluffy, then add remaining 1 tsp vanilla, ⅛ tsp salt and honey. Beat on high for 1 additional minute. Fold peach purée into coconut mixture, then pour into a parchment-lined loaf pan, spreading so that top is even. Freeze for 3 to 4 hours, stirring vigorously every 30 minutes.

To serve, let stand at room temperature for 20 minutes, then slice into individual servings using a warmed knife, or use a warmed ice cream scoop (run under hot water for 20 seconds).

Nutrition Information Per serving (⅛ of recipe): Calories: 196, Total Fat: 16 g, Sat. Fat: 15 g, Monounsaturated Fat: 0.5 g, Polyunsaturated Fat: 0.5 g, Carbs: 10 g, Fiber: 1 g, Sugars: 10 g, Protein: 2 g, Sodium: 74 mg, Cholesterol: 0 mg

Grilled Stone Fruit Salad
with Coconut Crème Anglaise

Serve fruit warm off the grill, or grill in advance and serve at room temperature.

INGREDIENTS

1 cup	coconut milk
1	vanilla bean, split (**TIP:** *If you don't have a whole vanilla bean, substitute with 2 tsp pure vanilla extract.*)
2 tbsp	organic evaporated cane juice (aka organic cane sugar), divided
2 large	egg yolks
	high-heat cooking oil (such as grape seed or safflower), as needed
2	peaches, halved and pitted
2	nectarines, halved and pitted
2	plums, halved and pitted
2 cups	cherries
¼ cup	coarsely torn fresh basil

Serves **4.**
Hands-On Time: **25 minutes.**
Total Time: **25 minutes.***
Plus Chilling Time.

INSTRUCTIONS

In a small saucepan on medium, heat milk, vanilla bean and 1 tbsp cane juice until just steaming and small bubbles form around edges, stirring occasionally, about 3 minutes. In a medium heat-proof bowl, whisk egg yolks with remaining 1 tbsp cane juice. Once milk is warmed, very slowly pour milk mixture into egg mixture in a very thin stream, whisking constantly. Stir mixture back into saucepan and return to medium heat, stirring constantly with a wooden spoon or spatula until steaming and thick enough to coat the back of a spoon, about 8 to 10 minutes.

Strain mixture through a fine mesh sieve into a bowl. Using a knife, scrape any remaining vanilla out of pod and stir into crème anglaise, discarding pod. Place plastic wrap directly on surface and refrigerate until cold, at least 1 hour or up to 3 days.

Preheat a grill to medium-high and brush grates with oil. Add peaches, nectarines and plums to grill, cut side down, and grill for 3 to 4 minutes, until warm and lightly charred. Flip and grill for about 2 minutes more. Transfer to a cutting board. When cool enough to handle, cut each half lengthwise into 2 pieces. Drizzle crème anglaise over each plate and divide peaches, nectarines and plums over top. Garnish evenly with cherries and basil.

Nutrition Information Per serving (¼ of recipe): Calories: 285, Total Fat: 15 g, Sat. Fat: 11.5 g, Monounsaturated Fat: 2 g, Polyunsaturated Fat: 1 g, Carbs: 39 g, Fiber: 4 g, Sugars: 30 g, Protein: 5 g, Sodium: 12 mg, Cholesterol: 92 mg

Grilled Dark Cherry Crumble

It really doesn't get any easier than this foil-packet cherry crumble! For the fastest prep, opt for frozen cherries, which are already pitted, and thaw them overnight in the fridge. Be sure to drain any cherry juices after thawing to keep your crumble from becoming soggy. We love the tangy taste of Greek yogurt, but if you prefer a sweeter topping, try vanilla ice cream or frozen yogurt.

INGREDIENTS

3 cups fresh or frozen pitted dark sweet cherries, thawed (**TIP:** *You can also use sour cherries if you prefer. You'll need to add an additional 2 tbsp coconut sugar into the cherry mixture in Step 2.*)

1 tsp each pure vanilla and pure almond extract

½ cup coconut sugar, divided

3 tbsp whole-wheat flour, divided

¾ cup old-fashioned rolled oats

¼ cup chopped raw unsalted almonds

¼ cup cold organic unsalted butter, cubed

⅓ cup whole-milk Greek yogurt, optional

Serves **8.**
Hands-On Time: **10 Minutes.**
Total Time: **30 Minutes.**

INSTRUCTIONS

Heat a grill to medium-high. Line a 24-inch-long piece of heavy-duty foil with parchment paper.

In a large bowl, toss together cherries, vanilla extract, almond extract, ¼ cup sugar and 1 tbsp flour. In a separate bowl, stir together oats, almonds and remaining ¼ cup sugar and 2 tbsp flour; using a pastry blender or 2 knives, cut in butter until crumbly.

Spoon cherry mixture into center of parchment and sprinkle with oat mixture. Bring short edges of foil together, then fold inward a few times along each long edge to seal packet. Place on grill and reduce heat to medium-low. Close lid and cook until cherries are softened and oats are lightly browned, about 20 minutes. Serve with yogurt (if using).

Oven Variation: Bake packet on a rimmed baking sheet in a 350°F oven until cherries are softened and oats are lightly browned, about 20 minutes.

Nutrition Information Per serving (⅛ of recipe): Calories: 208, Total Fat: 9 g, Sat. Fat: 4 g, Monounsaturated Fat: 3 g, Polyunsaturated Fat: 1 g, Carbs: 32 g, Fiber: 3 g, Sugars: 23 g, Protein: 3 g, Sodium: 7 mg, Cholesterol: 15 mg

Strawberry Pistachio Frozen Yogurt

INGREDIENTS

1 lb	strawberries, hulled and quartered (about 4 cups)
½ cup + 2 tbsp	coconut sugar, divided
1½ tsp	pure vanilla extract
⅛ tsp	sea salt
3	large egg yolks
1 cup	buttermilk
1 cup	plain whole-milk Greek yogurt
½ cup	full-fat sour cream
⅓ cup	unsalted pistachios, roughly chopped

Makes **6 Cups.**
Hands-On Time: **20 Minutes.**
Total Time: **1 Hour, 20 Minutes.***
Plus Freezing Time.

INSTRUCTIONS

In a large bowl, combine strawberries, ½ cup coconut sugar, vanilla and salt. Toss to coat and set aside until juices start to run out of berries, at least 1 hour or up to 3 hours.

In a small saucepan, vigorously whisk egg yolks and remaining 2 tbsp coconut sugar until thickened, 1 minute. Add buttermilk and whisk to combine. Set over medium-low heat and cook, stirring constantly with a wooden spoon, until mixture thickens and coats back of spoon, 5 to 7 minutes (do not boil). Set aside to cool to room temperature.

In a blender, combine strawberries and juice, buttermilk mixture, yogurt and sour cream. Purée until smooth, 30 to 45 seconds.

Pour mixture into an 8 x 8 x 3-inch metal baking pan and transfer to freezer. Stir every 30 minutes. When mixture thickens (about 1 hour), stir in pistachios and return to freezer. Continue stirring mixture every 30 minutes until firm enough to scoop, about 2½ to 3 hours total freezing time. (Alternatively, process in an ice cream maker according to manufacturer's instructions.)

(**NOTE:** *This recipe is best eaten fresh after the last stirring. However, you can freeze it for up to 1 week, removing from freezer a few minutes before serving to let it soften slightly.*)

Nutrition Information Per serving (½ cup): Calories: 144, Total Fat: 7 g, Sat. Fat: 3.5 g, Monounsaturated Fat: 2 g, Polyunsaturated Fat: 1 g, Carbs: 18 g, Fiber: 1 g, Sugars: 16.5 g, Protein: 4 g, Sodium: 58 mg, Cholesterol: 56 mg

Chocolate Caramel Peanut Butter Pie

INGREDIENTS

Crust

1 cup	dried unsweetened shredded coconut
½ cup	packed pitted Medjool dates
½ cup	raw unsalted walnuts
½ cup	raw unsalted almonds
5 tbsp	unsweetened cocoa powder
1 tsp	pure vanilla extract

Mousse

2 cups	coconut cream (from about 2 13.5-oz BPA-free cans) (***TIP:** Refrigerate cans overnight and scoop out the thick white cream that separates the next day, reserving water for another use.*)
1 cup	creamy all-natural unsalted peanut butter
2 tbsp	pure maple syrup
½ tsp	pure vanilla extract
⅛ tsp	sea salt

Drizzle

1 13.5-oz	BPA-free can coconut milk
½ cup	coconut sugar
1 tsp	pure vanilla extract
1 tbsp	coconut oil

Serves **14.**
Hands-On Time: **30 Minutes.**
Total Time: **1 Hour.***
**Plus Chilling and Freezing Time.*

INSTRUCTIONS

Prepare crust: In a food processor, combine all crust ingredients and process for 3 minutes, until mixture sticks together and forms a large single mass. Line a 9-inch round pie pan with parchment paper on bottom and up the sides. Press crust mixture into pan; use your fingers to press it in firmly, pushing up the edges of the pan to form the crust's edge. Transfer to freezer to set.

Meanwhile, prepare mousse: Using an electric hand or stand mixer, beat coconut cream on high until very smooth, about 1 minute. Add peanut butter, maple syrup, ½ tsp vanilla and salt and beat on high for 1 minute more. Remove crust from freezer and spread peanut butter mousse evenly inside crust, then return to freezer to set for at least 4 hours.

Prepare drizzle: In a medium saucepan on medium-high, mix together coconut milk and coconut sugar. Bring just to a boil, stirring frequently, then reduce heat to medium or low so that mixture stays at a gentle simmer. Cook for 30 minutes, stirring occasionally, until it's reduced by about half and turned a rich, deep brown. Remove from heat and vigorously stir in 1 tsp vanilla and coconut oil. Refrigerate for at least 1 hour before serving.

To serve, remove pie from freezer and let sit at room temperature for 10 minutes before slicing. Drizzle sliced pie with caramel sauce. Pie can be stored in freezer for up to 1 month; caramel sauce keeps in a tightly covered container for 4 to 5 days in the refrigerator.

Nutrition Information Per serving (¼₄ of pie): Calories: 394, Total Fat: 32 g, Sat. Fat: 18 g, Monounsaturated Fat: 7 g, Polyunsaturated Fat: 6 g, Carbs: 22 g, Fiber: 4 g, Sugars: 16 g, Protein: 8 g, Sodium: 42 mg, Cholesterol: 0 mg

Peach Upside-Down Cake on the Grill

There's so much going on with this scrumptious dessert: juicy peaches, buttery-sweet topping, cardamom-laced cake and even a touch of rum. Best of all, it's easy to put together. Try it with other stone fruits such as nectarines, plums, apricots or a combination.

INGREDIENTS

¼ cup	organic unsalted butter
½ cup + 6 tbsp	organic evaporated cane juice (aka organic cane sugar), divided
2 large or 3 small	peaches (12 to 14 oz), pitted and cut into ½-inch wedges
1 cup	white whole-wheat flour
¼ cup	almond flour/meal
1½ tsp	ground cardamom
1¼ tsp	baking powder
¼ tsp	sea salt
2 large	eggs
6 tbsp	whole milk
2 tbsp	safflower or grape seed oil
2 tbsp	dark or spiced rum, optional

Serves **12.**
Hands-On Time: **30 Minutes.**
Total Time: **1 Hour, 10 Minutes.**

INSTRUCTIONS

Mist a 9-inch round baking pan with cooking spray and set aside.

In a small saucepan on the stove top on medium, melt butter. Remove from heat and stir in 6 tbsp cane juice. Transfer mixture to prepared baking pan, spreading it out evenly, then top with peaches, arranging wedges in concentric circles. Set aside.

In a medium bowl, whisk together flours, cardamom, baking powder and salt. Set aside.

In the bowl of an electric stand mixer, use a handheld whisk to lightly beat eggs. Add remaining ½ cup cane juice, milk and oil and beat with paddle attachment on medium speed until light and frothy, about 3 minutes. (**NOTE:** *A handheld electric mixer will also work here.*) On low speed, add flour mixture in 3 additions, mixing until just incorporated after each. Transfer batter to pan, spreading evenly over peaches.

Prepare a grill for indirect medium heat (to maintain a temperature of about 325°F). Place a double layer of foil, about 12 inches square, over the cooler part of the grate. Place pan with cake batter on foil, cover and cook until edges are separating from the pan and a toothpick comes out clean, 35 to 40 minutes. Remove cake from the grill and let stand for 5 minutes.

Place a serving plate on top of the pan and carefully invert, then slowly lift pan off cake. Rearrange any peaches that stick to the pan. Drizzle rum (if using) over cake 1 tbsp at a time, letting it soak in between additions. Serve warm or at room temperature.

Nutrition Information Per serving (¹⁄₁₂ of cake): Calories: 184, Total Fat: 9 g, Sat. Fat: 3 g, Monounsaturated Fat: 2.5 g, Polyunsaturated Fat: 2.5 g, Carbs: 24 g, Fiber: 2 g, Sugars: 17 g, Protein: 3.5 g, Sodium: 113 mg, Cholesterol: 42 mg

Grilled Berry Cobbler

If you're lucky enough to grow fresh berries in your backyard, this super-simple recipe is sure to become your go-to summer dessert! Sprinkle with additional lemon zest and serve with a generous dollop of yogurt and a drizzle of sweet honey.

INGREDIENTS

1 cup	stemmed and quartered strawberries
1 cup	blueberries
½ cup	each blackberries (halved) and raspberries
1	lemon, zested and juiced
1 cup	whole-grain spelt flour
½ cup	coconut sugar
2 tsp	baking powder
½ tsp	ground cinnamon
¼ tsp	sea salt
½ cup	whole milk
¼ cup	organic unsalted butter, melted

Serves **8.**
Hands-On Time: **15 Minutes.**
Total Time: **40 Minutes.**

INSTRUCTIONS

Preheat a grill to medium-high. Mist a 10-inch cast-iron skillet with cooking spray. In a large bowl, stir together strawberries, blueberries, blackberries, raspberries, lemon zest and lemon juice.

In a separate bowl, whisk together flour, sugar, baking powder, cinnamon and salt. Stir in milk and butter until just combined. Scrape into skillet and sprinkle with berry mixture.

Turn off heat on 1 side of grill. Place skillet on unheated side, close lid and grill until cake is set and edges are golden, 25 to 30 minutes. Let cool slightly. Cut into wedges.

Nutrition Information Per serving (⅛ of cobbler): Calories: 195, Total Fat: 7 g, Sat. Fat: 4 g, Monounsaturated Fat: 2 g, Polyunsaturated Fat: 1 g, Carbs: 34 g, Fiber: 3 g, Sugars: 20 g, Protein: 3 g, Sodium: 212 mg, Cholesterol: 17 mg

Curried Cauliflower Rice Bowls
with Crispy Chickpeas
(See recipe, p. 279)

Fall Recipes

Superfood Scones

Light, flaky whole-wheat pastry and antioxidant-loaded superfoods–such as hemp, cacao nibs and pecans–make this a healthy alternative to a baked good from your local coffee shop.

INGREDIENTS

1½ cups	whole-wheat pastry flour or spelt flour + additional for dusting
1½ tsp	baking powder
¾ tsp	orange zest
⅜ tsp (¼ + ⅛ tsp)	baking soda
¼ tsp	sea salt
6 tbsp	cold organic unsalted butter (**TIP:** *Keep in fridge until ready to use.*)
½ cup	unsweetened raisins or currants
¼ cup	chopped unsalted pecans
¼ cup	raw cacao nibs (or use ¼ cup dark chocolate chunks and reduce maple syrup to 2 tbsp)
2 tbsp	hemp hearts
½ cup	cold buttermilk + additional as needed
2½ tbsp	pure maple syrup (preferably Grade A)
½ tsp	pure vanilla extract

Serves **6.**
Hands-On Time: **30 Minutes.**
Total Time: **45 Minutes.**

INSTRUCTIONS

Preheat oven to 450°F. Line a baking sheet with parchment paper.

In a large mixing bowl, whisk together flour, baking powder, orange zest, baking soda and salt. Cut butter into pieces and use a pastry cutter or your fingertips to work butter into flour mixture, making a coarse meal with a few larger chunks.

Add raisins, pecans, cacao nibs and hemp hearts to bowl and stir to combine.

In a separate mixing bowl, whisk together buttermilk, maple syrup and vanilla. Slowly add buttermilk mixture to flour-butter mixture, stirring to combine, just until mixture begins to form clumps. (**NOTE:** *If any dry flour remains, add more buttermilk as necessary, 1 tbsp at a time, until flour is incorporated.*)

Transfer mixture to baking sheet. Lightly dust your hands with flour and gather mixture into a ball, squeezing to form a dough (it may still crumble slightly).

Flatten dough to 1-inch thickness and fold in half. Flatten and fold once more. Gently shape into a 1-inch-thick, 6-inch-diameter round. Cut into 6 wedges, then arrange them ½ inch apart. (Alternatively, shape into a rectangle and cut into squares.)

Brush tops with buttermilk. Bake scones until puffed, golden brown on top and hollow sounding when tapped on bottoms, 15 to 18 minutes. Let cool slightly on a wire rack.

Nutrition Information Per serving (1 scone): Calories: 377, Total Fat: 20 g, Sat. Fat: 9 g, Monounsaturated Fat: 6 g, Polyunsaturated Fat: 3 g, Carbs: 44 g, Fiber: 9 g, Sugars: 20 g, Protein: 6 g, Sodium: 281 mg, Cholesterol: 33 mg

Almond Raspberry Thumbprint Cookies

These easy, portable gluten-free cookies are the perfect solution for busy days when you need an energy boost that fit into your meal plans without weighing you down..

INGREDIENTS

1 ½ cups	almond flour
½ cup	unsweetened shredded coconut
¼ cup	ground flaxseeds
1 tsp	baking soda
¼ tsp	sea salt
¼ cup	coconut oil, melted
¼ cup	pure maple syrup
1 tsp	pure vanilla extract
1/2 tsp	pure almond extract
6 tbsp	all-natural raspberry jam

Serves **12.**
Hands-On Time: **15 Minutes.**
Total Time: **35 Minutes.**

INSTRUCTIONS

Preheat oven to 350°F. In a large bowl, combine flour, coconut, flaxseeds, baking soda and salt.

To dry mixture, stir in oil, maple syrup, vanilla and almond extract.

Scoop dough onto a large rimmed parchment-lined baking sheet in 2-tbsp mounds, about ½ inch apart, making about 12 cookies. With your knuckle, press a dent into the middle of each. Fill each dent with jam, being careful not to overflow, about ½ tablespoon per cookie. Bake for 18 to 20 minutes, until golden brown. Set aside to cool on sheet.

Nutrition Information (2 cookies), Calories: 186, Carbs: 12 g, Fat: 5 g, Fiber: 3 g, Protein: 4 g, Sat. Fat: 6.5 g, Sodium: 149 mg, Sugar: 8 g, Polyunsaturated Fat Content: 2.5 g

Slow-Cooker Pumpkin Pie Breakfast Sorghum

Serves **4.**
Hands-On Time: **10 Minutes.**
Total Time: **8 Hours, 10 Minutes.**

INGREDIENTS

1 cup	sorghum, rinsed
1 cup	unsweetened almond milk
¾ cup	pumpkin purée (not pumpkin pie filling)
2 tbsp	pure maple syrup
1 tbsp	pumpkin pie spice
1 tsp	pure vanilla extract

INSTRUCTIONS

In a 3- to 4-quart slow cooker, combine all ingredients and 2 cups water. Stir well. Cover and cook on low for 8 hours, until sorghum is tender and liquid is absorbed.

NOTE: *This dish can be refrigerated in a covered container and individual servings can be scooped out and reheated. To reheat, transfer to a small saucepan, add a splash of almond milk or water and cook over medium heat until heated through.*

Nutrition Information Per serving (1 heaping cup): Calories: 221, Total Fat: 3 g, Sat. Fat: 0 g, Carbs: 47 g, Fiber: 5 g, Sugars: 10 g, Protein: 6.5 g, Sodium: 52 mg, Cholesterol: 0 mg

MORE USES FOR SORGHUM: Toss cooked sorghum with roasted veggies and your favorite vinaigrette for a hearty grain salad, or pop on the stove top as you would pop popcorn.

Apple Pie Overnight Oats

Kefir adds creaminess to this overnight oat recipe while also imparting a boost of gut-friendly probiotics. We love this dish cold, which best preserves the benefits of kefir, but you can also warm it up on the stove top, if preferred.

Serves **6.**
Hands-On Time: **15 Minutes.**
Total Time: **15 Minutes.***
*Plus Overnight Refrigeration.

INGREDIENTS

2	apples, grated
2 cups	old-fashioned rolled oats
1¾ cups	unsweetened almond milk
1¾ cups	full-fat plain kefir or yogurt
½ cup	unsweetened raisins
½ cup	unsweetened apple juice
½ cup	chopped raw walnuts
4 tsp	fresh lemon juice
1 tsp	ground cinnamon
⅛ tsp	ground nutmeg
	raw honey or stevia, to taste, optional

Optional toppings:

additional walnuts, chopped apple or bee pollen

INSTRUCTIONS

Prepare oats the night before: In a large bowl, mix all ingredients except honey and optional toppings. Cover; refrigerate overnight.

In the morning, stir or drizzle in honey (if using). Divide among bowls and top with additional toppings (if using).

Nutrition Information Per serving (⅙ of recipe): Calories: 325, Total Fat: 12 g, Sat. Fat: 2.5 g, Monounsaturated Fat: 3 g, Polyunsaturated Fat: 6 g, Carbs: 49 g, Fiber: 6 g, Sugars: 26 g, Protein: 8 g, Sodium: 89 mg, Cholesterol: 10 mg

Black Bean Tacos
with Maqui Berry Salsa

INGREDIENTS

2 cups	blackberries, coarsely chopped
2 tbsp	fresh lime juice
2 tsp	maqui powder
½ large	red onion, minced, divided
1 tbsp	olive oil
1 15-oz	BPA-free can unsalted black beans
¼ tsp	each chipotle powder and sea salt
8	6-inch corn tortillas, warmed (or 8 large romaine leaves)
1	orange bell pepper, sliced into matchsticks
¼ cup	fresh cilantro leaves
¼ cup	unsalted macadamia nuts, finely chopped

Serves **4.**
Hands-On Time: **30 Minutes.**
Total Time: **45 Minutes.**

INSTRUCTIONS

Prepare salsa: In a small bowl, combine blackberries, lime juice, maqui powder and 2 tbsp onion. Cover and refrigerate until ready to serve.

In a small saucepan on medium, heat oil. Add remaining onion and sauté for 7 to 8 minutes, until onion is very soft, stirring occasionally. Add beans and their liquid, chipotle and salt. Reduce heat to medium-low and simmer for 15 minutes.

Using a slotted spoon, drain a scoop of beans and add to center of each tortilla. Top with bell pepper, salsa, cilantro and nuts. Serve any remaining salsa on the side.

Nutrition Information Per serving (2 tacos): Calories: 361, Total Fat: 12.5 g, Sat. Fat: 2 g, Monounsaturated Fat: 9 g, Polyunsaturated Fat: 1 g, Carbs: 54 g, Fiber: 16 g, Sugars: 6 g, Protein: 12 g, Sodium: 151 mg, Cholesterol: 0 mg

BEAUTY BOOST: Maqui berry, or "rainforest blueberry," hailing from the Patagonian region of Chile, is noticeably rich in purple pigment–an indication of its exceptionally high concentration of anthocyanin antioxidants, making it one of the most antioxidant-rich foods found in nature. These anthocyanins are behind the growing interest in maqui among the medical community, particularly with regard to the berry's link to enhanced respiratory and cardiovascular health. Combined with its wealth of vitamin C, maqui is an effective tool for skin rejuvenation, collagen production and overall healthy, graceful aging.

Harvest Squash & Quinoa Salad

Greet fall with this hearty salad layered in a Mason jar for easy transporting. For extra flavor and vibrant color, we've simmered the quinoa with beets.

INGREDIENTS

1 small	butternut squash (about 1 lb) peeled, seeded and cut into ½-inch cubes
¼ tsp	each sea salt, ground black pepper and ground cinnamon
1	beet, peeled and shredded
½ cup	quinoa, rinsed
6 tbsp	balsamic vinegar
¼ cup	whole-grain mustard
2 tbsp	pure maple syrup
¼ cup	chopped unsalted walnuts
1½ cups	pomegranate arils
2 oz	crumbled goat cheese
6 cups	packed chopped kale

Equipment:

4	1-qt jars

Serves **4.**
Hands-On Time: **30 Minutes.**
Total Time: **1 Hour, 10 Minutes.***
Plus Cooling Time.

INSTRUCTIONS

Preheat oven to 400°F. Arrange squash on a large rimmed baking sheet. Mist with cooking spray, sprinkle with salt, pepper and cinnamon; toss to coat. Roast for 40 to 45 minutes, turning halfway, until tender. Cool to room temperature.

Meanwhile, in a small saucepan, bring 1 cup water to a boil. Add beet and quinoa. Cover, reduce heat to a simmer and cook for 15 minutes, until liquid is absorbed. Remove from heat and let stand, covered, for 5 minutes, before fluffing with a fork. Cool to room temperature.

Prepare dressing: In a small bowl, whisk together vinegar, mustard and maple syrup. Divide evenly among jars, about 3 tbsp per jar. Divide squash, quinoa mixture, walnuts, pomegranate arils, cheese and kale among jars. Cover jars and refrigerate until ready to serve, up to 5 days. When ready to serve, shake in jar to distribute dressing or transfer to a bowl and toss.

Nutrition Information Per serving (1 jar): Calories: 304, Total Fat: 10 g, Sat. Fat: 3 g, Monounsaturated Fat: 2 g, Polyunsaturated Fat: 4.5 g, Carbs: 46.5 g, Fiber: 7 g, Sugars: 17 g, Protein: 10 g, Sodium: 410 mg, Cholesterol: 7 mg

Beet, Orange & Burrata Salad
with Herb Toasts

A fresh, soft cheese made from mozzarella and cream, burrata helps give this colorful salad an air of sophistication.

INGREDIENTS

2	beets (about 11 oz), ends trimmed
1	clove garlic, minced
1 tbsp	extra-virgin olive oil, divided
1 tsp	finely chopped fresh flat-leaf parsley leaves
2	oranges
2 tbsp	white or regular balsamic vinegar
¼ tsp	Dijon mustard
¼ tsp	sea salt, or to taste
	ground black pepper, to taste
6 oz	fresh-baked whole-wheat bread, cut into 4 slices
5 cups	(5 oz) baby arugula
6 oz	fresh burrata or mozzarella cheese, broken into about 8 pieces

Serves **4.**
Hands-On Time: **30 Minutes.**
Total Time: **1 Hour, 10 Minutes.**

INSTRUCTIONS

Position racks in center and top third of oven and preheat to 425°F. Wrap beets in foil and roast on center rack until tender when pierced with a fork, about 1 hour. Set aside to cool. Peel and cut each beet into 12 slices. Keep oven on.

Meanwhile, in a small bowl, whisk together garlic, 2 tsp oil and parsley; set aside.

Use a sharp knife to slice peel off oranges. Cut each orange into 6 round slices. Squeeze pieces of orange peel (there should be some flesh still attached) to yield about 2 tbsp juice. Whisk in vinegar, 2 tsp water, remaining 1 tsp oil, mustard, salt and pepper.

On a small baking sheet, place bread and bake on top rack until golden, about 10 minutes. Brush with garlic, oil and sprinkle with pinch salt.

In a large bowl, toss arugula with 3 tbsp orange vinaigrette. Divide among plates and top with oranges, beets and cheese. Drizzle with remaining vinaigrette. Serve with toasts.

Nutrition Information Per serving (¼ of salad): Calories: 319, Total Fat: 14 g, Sat. Fat: 6 g, Monounsaturated Fat: 4 g, Polyunsaturated Fat: 1 g, Carbs: 37 g, Fiber: 6 g, Sugars: 12 g, Protein: 15 g, Sodium: 533 mg, Cholesterol: 25 mg

Mushroom Cashew Lettuce Wraps

Serves **4.**
Hands-On Time: **25 Minutes.**
Total Time: **25 Minutes.**

INGREDIENTS

1½ tbsp	reduced-sodium tamari
1 tbsp	coconut sugar
1½ tsp	peeled and grated ginger
Pinch	ground cayenne pepper
1½ tbsp	sesame oil
3 large	cloves garlic, thinly sliced
4 cups	chopped shiitake and/or maitake mushrooms
½ cup	raw unsalted cashews
2	green onions, thinly sliced, divided
8–12	butter lettuce leaves
	sriracha sauce, to taste
1	lime, cut into wedges

INSTRUCTIONS

In a small bowl, combine tamari, sugar, ginger and cayenne. Set aside.

In a large nonstick skillet on medium, heat oil. Add garlic and cook for 30 seconds. Stir in mushrooms and cook for 3 to 4 minutes more, stirring occasionally. Mix in cashews and half of green onions, then add tamari mixture and stir well. Cook, stirring constantly, until excess liquid has evaporated, 1 to 2 minutes.

To serve, scoop mushroom filling into the center of lettuce leaves. Drizzle with sriracha, and sprinkle with remaining half of green onions and a squeeze of lime.

Nutrition Information Per serving (2 to 3 wraps): Calories: 186, Total Fat: 12 g, Sat. Fat: 2 g, Monounsaturated Fat: 5 g, Polyunsaturated Fat: 3 g, Carbs: 18 g, Fiber: 3 g, Sugars: 8 g, Protein: 5.5 g, Sodium: 372 mg, Cholesterol: 0 mg

Bangkok Curry Bowls
with Rice Noodles & Vegetables

Remember those packages of preservative-laden dehydrated noodles you probably ditched when you started eating clean? The beauty of those packages was their simplicity–just add boiling water and eat. We've recreated the convenience with this layered noodle bowl with mushrooms, carrots, edamame and bok choy. Simply prepare the broth before leaving the house, store in a heat-proof container and pour over top when you're ready.

INGREDIENTS

½ cup	coconut milk
¼ cup	fresh lime juice
4 tsp	red curry paste
1 tsp	fish sauce
4 oz	brown rice vermicelli noodles
1 large	carrot, peeled and grated
½ large	bunch bok choy (about 8 leaves), thick stems removed and thinly sliced
1⅓ cups	sliced mushrooms
1 cup	shelled, frozen edamame
1 lb	boneless, skinless chicken breasts, cooked, cooled and chopped into bite-size pieces (**NOTE:** *Use any cooked chicken you have on hand, or season with salt and pepper and roast in the oven or poach.*)
¼ cup	chopped fresh cilantro leaves
4 cups	low-sodium chicken broth, for serving

Equipment:

4 1-qt	heat-proof jars or containers
	insulated thermos

Serves **4.**
Hands-On Time: **20 Minutes.**
Total Time: **45 Minutes.**

INSTRUCTIONS

In a small bowl, whisk together coconut milk, lime juice, curry paste and fish sauce. Cover and refrigerate.

Divide noodles, carrot, bok choy, mushrooms, edamame, chicken and cilantro evenly among jars. Cover and refrigerate until ready to serve, up to 4 days.

To serve, empty the contents of one jar into a heat-proof thermos. In a small saucepan, bring 1 cup broth and 1 cup water to a boil; add one-quarter of coconut milk mixture (about 3½ tbsp) and heat through. Pour into thermos and keep covered until ready to eat. Alternatively, heated broth mixture can be transported separately in thermos and added to jar just before serving; let stand for 5 minutes before eating. A microwave may also be used to heat the broth mixture.

Nutrition Information Per serving (1 jar): Calories: 391, Total Fat: 13 g, Sat. Fat: 7 g, Monounsaturated Fat: 2 g, Polyunsaturated Fat: 1 g, Carbs: 35 g, Fiber: 5 g, Sugars: 4 g, Protein: 38 g, Sodium: 427 mg, Cholesterol: 67 mg

Triple Green Soup
with Cannellini Beans
& Spiced Pepitas

We've packed this soup with a triple-punch of greens–kale, Swiss chard and spinach. These greens contain antioxidants that help fight against oxidative stress and may help in the prevention of cancer. We've also added a finishing touch of pepitas (also known as pumpkin seeds), toasted with aromatic turmeric and ginger.

INGREDIENTS

3 tbsp	extra-virgin olive oil, divided
1 small	yellow onion, chopped
2	cloves garlic, chopped
½ tsp	red pepper flakes, optional
4 cups	low-sodium vegetable broth
2 cups	jarred, boxed or BPA-free canned unsalted chopped tomatoes
4 oz	Lacinato kale (aka Tuscan or dinosaur kale), stems and ribs discarded, chopped (about 2 packed cups)
4 oz	Swiss chard, stems and ribs discarded, chopped (about 2 packed cups)
3 oz	spinach leaves (about 3 packed cups)
1 15-oz	BPA-free can unsalted cannellini beans, drained and rinsed
¼ cup	unsalted pepitas (aka pumpkin seeds)
½ tsp	each ground turmeric and ginger
2 tbsp	chopped fresh basil

Serves **4.**
Hands-On Time: **30 Minutes.**
Total Time: **30 Minutes.**

INSTRUCTIONS

In a large saucepan on medium, heat 1 tbsp oil. Add onion and cook, stirring occasionally, until translucent, about 5 minutes. Add garlic and pepper flakes (if using). Stir until fragrant, about 1 minute. Add broth, 1 cup water and tomatoes. Cover, then increase heat to medium-high and bring to a simmer.

Add kale and simmer, covered, 3 minutes. Add chard and continue simmering, covered, until greens are tender, 3 minutes more. Add spinach and beans; cover and simmer until heated through, 1 to 2 minutes.

Meanwhile, in a medium skillet on medium, heat 2 tsp oil. Add pepitas, turmeric and ginger. Toss well to combine and cook until spices are fragrant and pepitas are toasted, stirring occasionally, 4 to 6 minutes. Divide soup among 4 bowls and top with pepitas and basil. Drizzle 1 tsp of remaining oil over each bowl.

Nutrition Information Per serving (2 cups soup and 1 tbsp pepitas): Calories: 282, Total Fat: 15 g, Sat. Fat: 2 g, Monounsaturated Fat: 9 g, Polyunsaturated Fat: 2 g, Carbs: 28 g, Fiber: 10 g, Sugars: 8 g, Protein: 10 g, Sodium: 244 mg, Cholesterol: 0 mg

Quinoa & Veggie Sushi
with Miso Ginger Sauce

Protein-rich quinoa replaces rice in this homemade sushi that will keep you going all day long with energy to spare. Our miso dipping sauce is to die for–you'll want to make extra to use as a dip or to drizzle over chicken, tofu or your favorite grain bowls.

INGREDIENTS

4	sheets toasted nori (**NOTE:** *This recipe works best with larger sheets of nori measuring 8 x 7½ inches.*)
2⅔ cups	cooked quinoa
1 large	cucumber, julienned
2 large	carrots, julienned
1 large	avocado, sliced thinly lengthwise

Miso Ginger Sauce

6 tbsp	rice vinegar
¼ cup	organic white miso
¼ cup	extra-virgin olive oil
¼ cup	peeled and chopped ginger
1 tbsp	raw honey
2	cloves garlic, peeled
1 tsp	sriracha or pinch ground cayenne pepper

Serves **4.**
Hands-On Time: **40 Minutes.**
Total Time: **40 Minutes.**

INSTRUCTIONS

Prepare sauce: Purée all sauce ingredients and 1 tbsp water in a blender until smooth.

Prepare sushi: Lay 1 sheet of nori on a clean, flat surface. Spread ⅔ cup cooked quinoa onto sheet, leaving a ½-inch border on the top and bottom of the paper. Take 1 tbsp of sauce and spread in a horizontal line across the center of quinoa. Lay one-quarter of each cucumber and carrots over sauce. Arrange avocado slices evenly over cucumber and carrots, making sure ingredients extend all the way to the left and right sides of the nori.

Starting at the edge closest to you, gently roll the nori away from you, tucking as you go, until it is rolled up all the way. Dab edge with water if necessary to seal. Repeat with remaining ingredients. Slice into 1-inch pieces or slice in half and eat as a hand roll. Serve with remaining sauce. Sauce can be made 3 to 4 days ahead and stored in the fridge. Roll ingredients can be prepped ahead and assembled just before eating or up to 1 day in the fridge.

Nutrition Information Per serving (1 large roll and ¼ of sauce): Calories: 480, Total Fat: 26 g, Sat. Fat: 4 g, Monounsaturated Fat: 18 g, Polyunsaturated Fat: 4 g, Carbs: 53 g, Fiber: 10 g, Sugars: 15 g, Protein: 10 g, Sodium: 586 mg, Cholesterol: 0 mg

Root Vegetable–Baked Quinoa
with Kale & Goat Cheese

INGREDIENTS

4	carrots, peeled and sliced
4 to 5	parsnips, peeled and sliced
1 tbsp	olive oil
½ tsp	dried thyme
½ tsp	ground black pepper, divided
¼ tsp	sea salt
2 cups	low-sodium vegetable broth
1½ cups	tricolor quinoa
8 oz	curly kale, ribs discarded, leaves chopped (5 packed cups)
	zest of 1 small lemon
5 oz	grated mozzarella cheese
4 oz	goat cheese, crumbled
2 tbsp	chopped basil

Serves **8.**
Hands-On Time: **30 Minutes.**
Total Time: **1 Hour, 10 Minutes.**

INSTRUCTIONS

Preheat oven to 425°F. Line a large rimmed baking sheet with foil and mist with cooking spray. To a large bowl, add carrots, parsnips, oil, thyme, ¼ tsp pepper and salt. Stir to coat vegetables evenly and spread on baking sheet. Bake for 15 minutes, then toss with a spatula and continue baking until golden brown and tender, about 10 minutes more. Reduce oven temperature to 350°F.

Meanwhile, in a large saucepan, bring broth and 1½ cups water to a boil. Stir in quinoa, cover and return to boil. Add kale to pan on top of quinoa (don't stir it in). Cover and reduce heat to medium low. Simmer until quinoa and kale are tender and most of liquid has absorbed, 15 to 18 minutes. (Keep pan covered for the first 10 minutes of cooking, then stir once or twice to ensure quinoa cooks evenly.)

To a large bowl, add quinoa mixture, vegetables, lemon zest, mozzarella and remaining ¼ tsp black pepper; stir gently. Mist a 9 x 13-inch baking dish with cooking spray and add quinoa mixture. Crumble goat cheese evenly over top. Bake at 350°F until goat cheese is heated through, 12 to 14 minutes. Let rest for 5 minutes. Sprinkle with basil.

Nutrition Information Per serving (1¼ cups): Calories: 273, Total Fat: 11 g, Sat. Fat: 5 g, Monounsaturated Fat: 4 g, Polyunsaturated Fat: 2 g, Carbs: 32 g, Fiber: 6 g, Sugars: 4 g, Protein: 13 g, Sodium: 305 mg, Cholesterol: 21 mg

Swiss Chard Wraps
with Almond Lime Dip

INGREDIENTS

Wraps

2	carrots, peeled and grated
1 large	beet, peeled and grated
1 tsp	extra-virgin olive oil
¼ tsp	sea salt, divided
2	avocados, peeled, pitted and chopped
¼ cup	chopped fresh cilantro leaves
3 tbsp	fresh lime juice
¼ tsp	ground black pepper
2	bunches Swiss chard (about 16 leaves)
1 cup	packed pea shoots or sprouts (such as alfalfa, radish or broccoli)

Sauce

¼ cup	natural unsalted almond butter
2 tbsp	raw honey
2 tbsp	fresh lime juice
2 tsp	reduced-sodium tamari

Serves **4.**
Hands-On Time: **30 Minutes.**
Total Time: **30 Minutes.**

INSTRUCTIONS

Prepare sauce: In a small bowl, combine all sauce ingredients until smooth; set aside.

In a medium bowl, combine carrots, beet, oil and ⅛ tsp salt. In another medium bowl, combine avocados, cilantro, 3 tbsp lime juice, remaining ⅛ tsp salt and pepper; lightly mash to a chunky consistency.

Remove spine of each chard leaf starting about two-thirds of way up without splitting leaves in half. Add about 1 inch water to a large saucepan fitted with a steamer basket. Cover and bring to a boil. Reduce heat to medium-high and add leaves to basket. Cover and steam until leaves are tender, 3 to 4 minutes. Using tongs, carefully remove leaves from basket and lay on a paper towel–lined plate. Gently blot with more paper towels.

Assemble wraps: Place about 2 tbsp carrot mixture, 1 tbsp pea shoots and 1 rounded tbsp avocado mixture at stem end of each leaf. Roll up to enclose filling, tucking in sides as you roll. Repeat with remaining leaves and filling. Serve with dip. (**TIP:** *Wraps can be made up to 5 hours ahead.*)

Nutrition Information Per serving (4 wraps and 2 tbsp sauce): Calories: 364, Total Fat: 25 g, Sat. Fat: 3 g, Monounsaturated Fat: 16 g, Polyunsaturated Fat: 4 g, Carbs: 34 g, Fiber: 13 g, Sugars: 16 g, Protein: 9 g, Sodium: 533 mg, Cholesterol: 0 mg

Ginger Soy Cod en Papillote
with Shiitakes & Green Onions

En papillote is French for "in parchment"–a classic technique that holds in moisture and cooks food by the steam created inside the packet.

INGREDIENTS

1 cup	long-grain brown rice
1½ tbsp	reduced-sodium soy sauce
2 tsp	mirin
1 tbsp	peeled and minced fresh ginger
2 tsp	chopped garlic
1 tsp	raw honey
1 tsp	toasted sesame oil
3 oz	shiitake mushrooms, stemmed and sliced (1¼ cups)
1 cup	chopped bok choy
4 6-oz	skinless cod fillets
	ground black pepper, to taste
2	green onions, thinly sliced

Serves **4.**
Hands-On Time: **25 Minutes.**
Total Time: **55 Minutes.**

INSTRUCTIONS

Preheat oven to 400°F. Cook rice according to package directions.

In a medium bowl, combine soy sauce, mirin, ginger, garlic, honey and oil; set aside.

Cut 4 14-inch squares of parchment paper. Divide mushrooms and bok choy in the center of parchment sheets. Place 1 cod fillet over each mound of vegetables. Season cod with pepper and spoon soy sauce mixture over each fillet. To seal packets, working one at a time, bring opposite edges of parchment together and fold down toward fillet in ½-inch sections. Next, fold each side of parchment in toward fillings in ½-inch sections. (**NOTE:** *Packets should be securely closed but not too tight.*)

Carefully place packets on a rimmed baking sheet and bake for 12 to 14 minutes, until fish is opaque throughout and flakes easily with a fork.

Transfer packets to plates and tear paper open, being careful to avoid escaping steam. Serve with rice and garnish cod with green onions.

Nutrition Information Per serving (1 fillet, ½ cup vegetables, ¾ cup rice): Calories: 331, Total Fat: 3 g, Sat. Fat: 1 g, Monounsaturated Fat: 1 g, Polyunsaturated Fat: 1 g, Carbs: 41 g, Fiber: 4 g, Sugars: 4 g, Protein: 35 g, Sodium: 445 mg, Cholesterol: 78 mg

Veggie BLT
with Coconut Bacon, Caramelized Leeks & Roasted Tomato

Homemade coconut bacon with smoked paprika and maple syrup is the star of these piled-high sandwiches. We suggest making extra coconut bacon to use on salads, pastas or to eat out of hand– you're going to want to put it on everything!

INGREDIENTS

4 cups	grape tomatoes
2 tsp	grape seed oil, divided
1	leek, white and light green parts, thinly sliced
⅛ tsp	sea salt
¼ cup	Dijon mustard
12	slices whole-grain bread or corn bread (**TIP:** Try pairing with our homemade Maple Corn Bread recipe from cleaneating.com.)
1	avocado, peeled, pitted and sliced

Coconut Bacon

1 cup	unsweetened dried sliced coconut or coconut flakes
1 tbsp	pure maple syrup
1½ tsp	reduced-sodium tamari
1 tsp	smoked paprika
½ tsp	grape seed oil

Serves **6.**
Hands-On Time: **20 Minutes.**
Total Time: **1 Hour, 20 Minutes.**

INSTRUCTIONS

Preheat oven to 325°F. In a medium bowl, toss tomatoes and 1 tsp oil. Spread on a large parchment-lined baking sheet and roast for 1 hour, or until slightly shriveled and sweet.

To a medium bowl, add all coconut bacon ingredients and toss well to coat. Spread on a second large parchment-lined baking sheet. Bake until crispy. (**NOTE:** This can take anywhere from 8 to 18 minutes, depending on the size of your coconut, so check often to avoid burning.)

Meanwhile, in a medium skillet on medium, add remaining 1 tsp oil. Add leeks and sauté until golden brown, about 8 minutes, stirring occasionally. Reduce heat to low and cook for 8 to 10 minutes more, until caramelized. Stir in salt and set aside.

To assemble, spread mustard on one side of all bread slices. Divide coconut bacon, tomatoes, leeks and avocado over 6 bread slices; sandwich with remaining 6 bread slices.

Nutrition Information Per serving (1 sandwich): Calories: 519, Total Fat: 29 g, Sat. Fat: 10 g, Monounsaturated Fat: 6 g, Polyunsaturated Fat: 11 g, Carbs: 61 g, Fiber: 10 g, Sugars: 17 g, Protein: 9 g, Sodium: 525 mg, Cholesterol: 0 mg

Spaghetti Alla Melanzane
with Tomatoes & Chickpeas

INGREDIENTS

1½ cups	cooked chickpeas
1 lb	eggplant, diced (5 cups)
1 lb	vine tomatoes, seeded and chopped (2 cups)
½ cup + ⅓ cup	chopped fresh basil, divided
6 tbsp	balsamic vinegar
2 tbsp + 2 tsp	extra-virgin olive oil, divided
1 tsp	raw honey
1½ tsp	red pepper flakes
½ tsp	ground black pepper
6 oz	whole-wheat spaghetti
3	cloves garlic, minced
6 oz	baby spinach, chopped (6 cups)
¾ cup	crumbled feta cheese

Serves **4.**
Hands-On Time: **25 Minutes.**
Total Time: **1 Hour, 30 Minutes.**

INSTRUCTIONS

In a large bowl, combine chickpeas, eggplant, tomatoes and ½ cup basil. In a small bowl, whisk together vinegar, 2 tbsp oil, honey, pepper flakes and black pepper. Pour over chickpea mixture and set aside to marinate for 30 minutes.

Cook spaghetti according to package directions. Drain, reserving ½ cup cooking water.

Meanwhile, in a large skillet, heat remaining 2 tsp oil on medium-high. Sauté garlic for 1 to 2 minutes. Add spinach and sauté for 2 minutes. Reduce heat to medium and add chickpea mixture; cook for 10 minutes or until eggplant is softened. Slowly stir in reserved cooking water.

Return chickpea mixture to large bowl along with spaghetti. Stir in feta cheese. Top with remaining ⅓ cup basil.

Nutrition Information Per serving (2 cups): Calories: 492, Total Fat: 18 g, Sat. Fat: 6 g, Monounsaturated Fat: 9 g, Polyunsaturated Fat: 2 g, Carbs: 68 g, Fiber: 15.5 g, Sugars: 16 g, Protein: 19 g, Sodium: 312 mg, Cholesterol: 25 mg

TIP: If following our Meal Plan, refrigerate 2 servings (4 cups) spaghetti; reheat when called for.

Pumpkin Turkey Lasagna
with Spinach & Béchamel Sauce

INGREDIENTS

1½ lb	ground turkey breast
¾ tsp	sea salt, divided
½ tsp	ground black pepper, divided
¼ tsp	red pepper flakes, optional
5 tbsp	unsalted organic butter, divided
2	cloves garlic, finely chopped
12 oz	baby spinach
2½ cups	pumpkin purée (not pumpkin pie filling)
4 tsp	chopped fresh sage
6 tbsp	white whole-wheat flour
4 cups	whole milk
¼ tsp	ground nutmeg
12	whole-wheat no-boil lasagna noodles
5 oz	grated mozzarella cheese
1 oz	grated Parmesan cheese

NOTE: If following our Meal Plan, refrigerate 1 serving and freeze 6 slices in an airtight container; when called for, defrost each slice then bake, covered, in a 375°F oven until heated through, 15 to 25 minutes.

Serves **8.**
Hands-On Time: **40 Minutes.**
Total Time: **1 Hour, 15 Minutes.***
*Plus Cooling Time.

INSTRUCTIONS

Preheat oven to 400°F and mist a 9 x 13-inch baking dish with cooking spray.

Mist a large skillet with cooking spray and heat on medium-high. Add turkey, ¼ tsp each salt and black pepper, and pepper flakes (if using). Cook, stirring and crumbling turkey with a spatula, until no longer pink, 5 to 8 minutes. Transfer to a medium bowl and set aside.

Using same skillet, reduce heat to medium and melt 1 tbsp butter. Add garlic and cook, stirring constantly, until fragrant, about 1 minute. Add spinach and cook, stirring occasionally, until leaves are wilted and any liquid released is completely evaporated, 4 to 5 minutes. Transfer to a cutting board. Let cool then roughly chop.

Mist same skillet with cooking spray and heat on medium. Add pumpkin, ¼ tsp salt and remaining ¼ tsp black pepper. Cook, stirring frequently, until excess water evaporates and pumpkin thickens slightly, about 5 minutes. Transfer to a medium bowl and stir in sage; set aside.

In a large saucepan, melt remaining ¼ cup butter on medium. When butter begins to foam, add flour and stir until slightly toasted, about 2 minutes. Slowly pour milk into pan while you whisk. Increase heat to high and bring to a steady simmer, whisking frequently. Reduce heat to medium and simmer until slightly thickened, 2 to 3 minutes. Whisk in nutmeg and remaining ¼ tsp salt. Remove from heat.

Spread one-third of the sauce (about 1⅓ cups) in prepared baking dish. Top with 4 noodles, half of pumpkin, half of turkey, half of spinach and 2 oz mozzarella. Repeat layers, starting with sauce and ending with mozzarella. Top with remaining 4 noodles, remaining one-third of sauce, remaining 1 oz mozzarella and Parmesan. Cover with nonstick foil. Bake in center of oven until sauce is bubbling and cheese is melted, about 30 minutes. Remove foil and switch to broil on high. With lasagna still in center of oven, broil until cheese is lightly browned, 4 to 5 minutes. Cool on a wire rack for 15 minutes.

Nutrition Information Per serving (⅛ of lasagna): Calories: 459, Total Fat: 19 g, Sat. Fat: 10 g, Monounsaturated Fat: 5 g, Polyunsaturated Fat: 2 g, Carbs: 38 g, Fiber: 6 g, Sugars: 9 g, l Protein: 34 g, Sodium: 543 mg, Cholesterol: 97 mg

Kung Pao Chickpea Stir-Fry over Sesame-Fried Millet

Fiber-rich chickpeas stand in for meat in this colorful stir-fry with a spicy-sweet sauce–all served over millet sautéed in sesame oil and speckled with green onions.

INGREDIENTS

2 cups	cooked or BPA-free canned chickpeas, drained and rinsed
1 tbsp	sesame oil, divided
2	stalks celery, sliced
1 large	carrot, peeled and sliced
4	cloves garlic, minced
3 cups	white or cremini mushrooms, sliced
1	red bell pepper, sliced
1 cup	sugar snap peas, strings removed
3 cups	cooked millet
¼ cup	sliced green onions
⅛ tsp	sea salt
⅓ cup	toasted unsalted almonds or peanuts, chopped
2 tbsp	toasted sesame seeds

Sauce

3 small	red chiles, minced
¼ cup	rice vinegar
¼ cup	reduced-sodium tamari
¼ cup	low-sodium vegetable broth
2 tbsp	natural unsalted almond or peanut butter
2 tbsp	tapioca starch
1 tbsp	pure maple syrup
2 tsp	sesame oil

Serves **6.**
Hands-On Time: **30 Minutes.**
Total Time: **30 Minutes.**

INSTRUCTIONS

In a medium bowl, whisk together all sauce ingredients. Add chickpeas and set aside.

In a large wok or skillet on high, heat 1 tsp oil. Add celery and carrots and sauté for 3 minutes. Add garlic and mushrooms and sauté for 2 minutes. Add bell pepper and peas and sauté for another 2 minutes. Add chickpea-sauce mixture and cook for 1 minute. Set aside.

Prepare millet: In a large skillet on high, heat remaining 2 tsp oil. Add millet and sauté for 3 minutes. Add green onions and sauté for 2 minutes. Remove from heat and stir in salt. Serve chickpea mixture over millet. Top with nuts and seeds.

Nutrition Information Per serving (1 cup stir-fry and ½ cup millet): Calories: 387, Total Fat: 15 g, Sat. Fat: 2 g, Monounsaturated Fat: 7 g, Polyunsaturated Fat: 5 g, Carbs: 51 g, Fiber: 9 g, Sugars: 10 g, Protein: 14 g, Sodium: 546 mg, Cholesterol: 0 mg

Supercharged Chicken Parm

INGREDIENTS

2	vine-ripened tomatoes, each sliced into 4 ¼-inch rounds
½ large	red onion, sliced into 4 ½-inch rounds
2 tsp	Italian seasoning, divided
⅛ tsp	sea salt
1 tsp	olive oil
½ tsp	balsamic vinegar
1	egg, beaten
⅓ cup	ground flaxseeds
¼ cup	whole-wheat bread crumbs
3 tbsp	nutritional yeast
2 tbsp	chia seeds
¾ tsp	garlic powder, divided
½ tsp	ground black pepper
4 4-oz	chicken breasts (or 2 8-oz breasts, halved crosswise)
2 cups	pasta sauce
3 oz	wild sardines packed in oil with lemon, minced (or use regular sardines and marinate briefly with ¼ tsp lemon zest and 1 tbsp lemon juice)
½ cup	sliced fresh basil

Serves **4.**
Hands-On Time: **25 Minutes.**
Total Time: **45 Minutes.**

INSTRUCTIONS

Preheat oven to 375°F. On a large rimmed baking sheet, arrange tomato and onion. Sprinkle with ½ tsp Italian seasoning and salt, and drizzle with oil and vinegar. Roast for 25 minutes.

Meanwhile, prepare chicken: In a shallow dish, place egg. In a separate shallow dish, combine flax, bread crumbs, yeast, chia, remaining 1½ tsp Italian seasoning, ½ tsp garlic powder and pepper. Dip chicken in egg, letting excess drip off, then dip in flax mixture, turning to coat both sides; place in a glass baking dish misted with cooking spray. Bake for 15 to 18 minutes, until no longer pink inside and juices run clear.

Meanwhile, heat pasta sauce in a saucepan on medium-high; stir in sardines and remaining ¼ tsp garlic powder. Heat gently.

To serve, on each plate, layer 1 onion slice and 2 tomato slices; top with 1 chicken piece and ½ cup sauce. Sprinkle with basil.

Nutrition Information Per serving (1 chicken breast, ½ cup sauce, 2 tomato slices, 1 onion slice): Calories: 380, Total Fat: 13 g, Sat. Fat: 2 g, Monounsaturated Fat: 5 g, Polyunsaturated Fat: 5 g, Carbs: 28.5 g, Fiber: 10 g, Sugars: 12 g, Protein: 39 g, Sodium: 524 mg, Cholesterol: 123 mg

TIP: If following our Meal Plan, refrigerate 1 serving and freeze 2 servings. (Store chicken, roasted vegetables and sauce separately; heat and assemble before eating.) Refrigerate remaining sardines for Wednesday's snac

Zucca Spaghetti
with Walnut Ginger Pesto & Lemon Shrimp

Walnut pesto with pungent ginger and fragrant fresh basil is the hero that brings this dish together. Walnuts have the highest concentration of antioxidants among nuts, while also containing essential fatty acids, so keep them on hand and snack on them often! In this dish, spaghetti squash is a carotenoid-rich stand-in for pasta, while protein-packed shrimp is among the seafood picks with the least amount of mercury.

INGREDIENTS

1 4-lb	spaghetti squash, halved lengthwise
2	packed cups fresh basil leaves + 2 tbsp chopped basil for garnish
½ cup	toasted unsalted walnuts (2 oz)
1	1-inch piece fresh ginger, peeled and roughly chopped
½ tsp	sea salt, divided
6 tbsp	extra-virgin olive oil, divided
3	cloves garlic, chopped
1 tsp	ground black pepper, divided
1 lb large	shrimp, peeled and deveined
	zest and juice of 1 lemon

Serves **4.**
Hands-On Time: **20 Minutes.**
Total Time: **50 Minutes.**

INSTRUCTIONS

Preheat oven to 400°F. Place squash cut side down in a large baking dish. Add enough water to cover bottom of dish in a thin layer. Cover with foil and bake until flesh is tender when pierced with a fork, 30 to 40 minutes. Transfer to a work surface and use a fork to scrape out flesh in spaghetti-like strands; add to a large bowl.

Meanwhile, prepare pesto: In a food processor, combine basil leaves, walnuts, ginger and ⅛ tsp salt. Pulse until finely chopped, scraping down sides of bowl as needed. With processor running, slowly pour in ¼ cup oil through the feed tube. Scrape down sides of bowl; run processor again and slowly pour ¼ cup water through the feed tube. (**NOTE:** *If you prefer a thinner texture, add more water, 1 tbsp at a time.*)

In a large skillet on medium, heat 1 tbsp oil. Add garlic and cook, stirring frequently, until fragrant, 1 minute. Add squash, ⅛ tsp salt and ½ tsp pepper and cook, stirring gently, until heated through, 3 to 4 minutes. Divide among 4 plates. Top each plate of squash evenly with pesto. Wipe out skillet.

In same skillet on medium, heat remaining 1 tbsp oil on medium. Season shrimp with remaining ¼ tsp salt and ½ tsp pepper. Add to skillet and cook, turning once or twice, until lightly browned and opaque in the center, about 4 minutes. Top plates evenly with shrimp. Drizzle lemon juice over top and garnish with lemon zest and chopped basil.

Nutrition Information Per serving (1 cup squash, ¼ of shrimp and pesto): Calories: 484, Total Fat: 33 g, Sat. Fat: 4 g, Monounsaturated Fat: 18 g, Polyunsaturated Fat: 10 g, Carbs: 10 g, Fiber: 7 g, Sugars: 10 g, Protein: 26 g, Sodium: 415 mg, Cholesterol: 26 mg

Loaded Beef Gyro Bowl
with Tzatziki

INGREDIENTS

½ cup	peeled, quartered and thinly sliced cucumber
⅜ tsp	(¼ tsp + ⅛ tsp) sea salt, divided
1 cup	plain whole-milk Greek yogurt
1	clove garlic, minced
¾ tsp	lemon zest + ½ tsp fresh lemon juice, divided
½ tsp	freeze-dried dill (or chopped fresh dill)
½ cup	quinoa, rinsed
2	portobello mushroom caps, stems and gills removed and reserved
1 tsp	olive oil
½ lb	95% lean ground beef
1½ tsp	Italian seasoning
1 tsp	dried rosemary
¼ tsp	ground cumin
⅛ tsp	ground black pepper
2 cups	chopped baby spinach

Toppings

½ cup	peeled and chopped cucumber
½ cup	halved grape tomatoes
½ cup	red bell pepper strips
2 tbsp	diced red onion
2 tbsp	chopped, toasted unsalted walnuts
8	Kalamata olives

Serves **2.**
Hands-On Time: **30 Minutes.**
Total Time: **30 Minutes.**

INSTRUCTIONS

In a medium bowl, toss sliced cucumber with ¼ tsp salt; set aside for 20 minutes. Drain liquid from bowl, then stir in yogurt, garlic, ¼ tsp lemon zest, lemon juice and dill. Cover and refrigerate.

Cook quinoa according to package directions.

Meanwhile, brush mushroom caps with oil and sprinkle with remaining ½ tsp lemon zest and pinch salt on inside and outside of caps. In a skillet on medium-high, cook mushroom caps for 3 to 5 minutes per side. Slice into quarters and set aside.

In same skillet on medium-high, cook beef, Italian seasoning, rosemary, cumin, pepper and remaining pinch salt. Cook for 4 to 5 minutes, breaking up beef with a wooden spoon, until browned.

To serve, in a bowl, layer half of quinoa, spinach and beef mixture. Top with half of each of quartered mushrooms and toppings; top each with ¼ cup tzatziki.

Nutrition Information Per serving (1 gyro bowl): Calories: 569, Total Fat: 26 g, Sat. Fat: 9 g, Monounsaturated Fat: 9.5 g, Polyunsaturated Fat: 6 g, Carbs: 45 g, Fiber: 8 g, Sugars: 8 g, Protein: 40 g, Sodium: 637 mg, Cholesterol: 80 mg

TIP: If following our Meal Plan, refrigerate tzatziki, quinoa, beef and topping leftovers separately; assemble when called for. Refrigerate mushroom stems for Saturday's breakfast.

Charred Lettuce & Grilled Flank Steak Salad
with Orange Shallot Vinaigrette

INGREDIENTS

8	fingerling potatoes, scrubbed and halved lengthwise (about 10 oz)
½ tsp	dried oregano
	sea salt and ground black pepper, to taste
2 cups	grape tomatoes, halved lengthwise
	zest and juice of 1 large orange
1	shallot, minced
2 tbsp	white balsamic vinegar
1 tbsp	olive oil
2 tsp	raw honey
1 tsp	Dijon mustard
1 tbsp	chopped fresh tarragon leaves
8 oz	flank steak, trimmed
4	hearts romaine lettuce
¼ cup	toasted unsalted walnut pieces
⅓ cup	crumbled blue cheese

Serves **4.**
Hands-On Time: **40 Minutes.**
Total Time: **1 Hour.**

INSTRUCTIONS

Preheat oven to 425°F. Mist potatoes with cooking spray and season with oregano, salt and pepper. Arrange potatoes cut side down on 1 side of a parchment-lined baking sheet and roast for 10 minutes.

Add tomatoes to second side of sheet, mist with cooking spray and season with salt and pepper. Return sheet to oven and roast for 25 minutes more, until potatoes are fork-tender and golden and tomatoes are lightly charred and shriveled. Set aside.

Meanwhile, prepare vinaigrette: Whisk together orange zest and juice, shallot, vinegar, oil, honey, Dijon and tarragon. Season with salt and pepper.

Mist a grill pan with cooking spray or grease a grill and heat to medium-high. Mist steak with cooking spray and season with salt and pepper. Grill steak to desired doneness, turning once; about 8 minutes for medium-rare or 10 minutes for medium. Transfer to a cutting board or plate and cover loosely with foil to rest. Keep grill pan on medium-high.

Trim a small piece from root end of romaine, keeping leaves attached to root, then cut romaine in half lengthwise. Brush or toss romaine with about half of vinaigrette. Working in batches if necessary, add romaine to pan cut sides down, turning occasionally, until charred on all sides, about 4 minutes.

Thinly slice steak across the grain. Arrange 2 romaine heart halves on each plate, cut sides up, and top evenly with steak, potatoes and tomatoes. Drizzle with remaining dressing and garnish evenly with walnuts and blue cheese.

Nutrition Information Per serving (¼ of recipe): Calories: 321, Total Fat: 15 g, Sat.Fat: 5 g, Monounsaturated Fat: 6 g, Polyunsaturated Fat: 4 g, Carbs: 28 g, Fiber: 4 g, Sugars: 10 g, Protein: 19 g, Sodium: 286 mg, Cholesterol: 43 mg

Harvest Chicken Salad
with Pomegranate Seeds & Feta

INGREDIENTS

8	shallots, halved lengthwise
8	Brussels sprouts, trimmed and halved lengthwise
3	parsnips, peeled and cut into ½-inch chunks
2	sweet potatoes, peeled and cut into ½-inch chunks
¼ cup	fresh lemon juice, divided
2 tsp	chile powder
1 tsp	ground cumin
¼ tsp	ground cinnamon
	sea salt and ground black pepper, to taste
10 oz	cooked shredded, boneless chicken breasts, cooled
2 tbsp	finely chopped fresh chives
1 tbsp	olive oil
½ cup	pomegranate seeds
½ cup	crumbled feta cheese
3 tbsp	toasted unsalted pumpkin seeds

Serves **4.**
Hands-On Time: **25 Minutes.**
Total Time: **1 Hour, 10 Minutes.**

INSTRUCTIONS

Position oven racks in top and bottom thirds of oven and preheat to 425°F. In a large bowl, toss shallots, Brussels sprouts, parsnips and potatoes. Drizzle with 3 tbsp lemon juice and season with chile powder, cumin, cinnamon, salt and pepper; toss to coat. Arrange in a single layer on 2 parchment-lined baking sheets, and mist with cooking spray. Roast for about 45 minutes, until vegetables are lightly browned and fork-tender, switching and turning trays and tossing vegetables halfway through. Set aside to cool for about 5 minutes, or until just warm.

Transfer vegetables to a large bowl and toss with remaining 1 tbsp lemon juice, chicken, chives and oil. Season with salt and pepper. Transfer to a platter and top with pomegranate, feta and pumpkin seeds.

Nutrition Information Per serving (¼ of recipe): Calories: 392, Total Fat: 12 g, Sat. Fat: 3 g, Monounsaturated Fat: 5 g, Polyunsaturated Fat: 2 g, Carbs: 41 g, Fiber: 9 g, Sugars: 15 g, Protein: 32 g, Sodium: 413 mg, Cholesterol: 65 mg

Almond-Crusted Cod
with Green Olive Salsa

Mild-tasting cod is served over nutty arugula and earthy lentils, and topped off with a piquant salsa. The textures and flavors in this easy dish play off each other beautifully.

INGREDIENTS

½ cup	green lentils, rinsed
¼ cup	diced red onion + 2 tbsp minced, divided
¼ tsp	sea salt
¼ cup	coarsely chopped green pimento-stuffed olives (martini olives)
¼ cup	chopped fresh flat-leaf parsley
1 tbsp	chopped drained capers
1 tbsp	red wine vinegar
2 tbsp + 4 tsp	extra-virgin olive oil, divided
4 5-oz	skinless cod fillets, about ¾ inch thick
1 large	egg white, lightly beaten
¼ cup	sliced unsalted almonds
4 cups	loosely packed arugula

Serves **4.**
Hands-On Time: **30 Minutes.**
Total Time: **1 Hour, 5 Minutes.**

INSTRUCTIONS

To a small saucepan on medium-high, add lentils, diced onion, salt and 1 cup water and bring to a boil. Reduce to a simmer, cover and cook until lentils are tender, about 25 minutes. Drain and set aside to cool.

Meanwhile, in a medium bowl, combine minced onion, olives, parsley, capers, vinegar and 2 tbsp oil; set aside.

Brush top (skinless side) of fish with egg white. Press almonds evenly over top of fish. In a very large skillet on medium, heat remaining 4 tsp oil. Add fish, crusted side down, and cook until almonds are toasted, 2 to 3 minutes. Carefully turn and continue cooking until fish is cooked through, 3 to 4 minutes.

Arrange arugula on plates or a platter and top with lentils. Arrange fish over lentils and spoon on olive mixture.

Nutrition Information Per serving (1 fish fillet, 1 cup arugula, ¼ cup lentils, 2½ tbsp olive mixture): Calories: 344, Total Fat: 16 g, Sat. Fat: 2 g, Monounsaturated Fat: 11 g, Polyunsaturated Fat: 2.5 g, Carbs: 18 g, Fiber: 5 g, Sugars: 2 g, Protein: 31 g, Sodium: 477 mg, Cholesterol: 54 mg

Moroccan Red Lentil Stew
with Parsnip Fries

Tomatoes and an array of fragrant spices commingle with lentils and chickpeas for a satisfying bowl of comfort. Save some for tomorrow's lunch–it's even better the next day!

Serves **8.**
Hands-On Time: **25 Minutes.**
Total Time: **45 Minutes.**

INGREDIENTS

1 tbsp	olive oil
2	carrots, thinly sliced
1	yellow onion, chopped
3	cloves garlic, minced
1 tsp	each ground cumin, ground ginger and ground turmeric
¼ tsp	each ground cayenne pepper and ground cinnamon
	sea salt and ground black pepper, to taste
1 28-oz	BPA-free can unsalted diced tomatoes
2 cups	low-sodium vegetable broth
2 cups	peeled, seeded and cubed butternut squash (about ½ lb)
2 cups	dry red lentils
1 cup	cooked or BPA-free canned chickpeas
2 tbsp	fresh lemon juice
¼ cup	chopped fresh flat-leaf parsley leaves

Parsnip Fries

8	parsnips (about 3 lb), trimmed and peeled
1 tbsp	olive oil
1 tsp	ground coriander
	sea salt and ground black pepper, to taste
1 tbsp	chopped fresh flat-leaf parsley leaves
1 tsp	finely grated lemon zest

INSTRUCTIONS

Prepare parsnip fries: Preheat oven to 450°F. Cut parsnips in half crosswise. Halve (or quarter) lengthwise to make fries of roughly the same size.

In a large bowl, toss parsnips with 1 tbsp oil, coriander, salt and pepper. Spread parsnips on a large, rimmed parchment-lined baking sheet. Bake, tossing once or twice, until golden brown and tender, about 30 minutes.

Meanwhile, in a Dutch oven on medium-high, heat 1 tbsp oil; add carrots, onion and garlic and cook, stirring occasionally, until softened, about 6 minutes. Add cumin, ginger, turmeric, cayenne, cinnamon, salt and pepper; cook, stirring, for 1 minute.

Stir in tomatoes, broth, squash, lentils and chickpeas; bring to a boil. Reduce heat, cover and simmer until lentils and squash are tender, 10 to 15 minutes. Stir in lemon juice and ¼ cup parsley; simmer for 1 minute. Toss fries with 1 tbsp parsley and lemon zest. Serve with stew.

Nutrition Information Per serving (1¼ cups stew and ¾ cup fries): Calories: 393, Total Fat: 6 g, Sat. Fat: 1 g, Monounsaturated Fat: 3 g, Polyunsaturated Fat: 1 g, Carbs: 73 g, Fiber: 17 g, Sugars: 13 g, Protein: 17 g, Sodium: 111 mg, Cholesterol: 0 mg

SMALL BUT MIGHTY LENTILS: Lentils are packed with folate, or vitamin B9, which plays an important role in the health of your nervous system. Additionally, folate, along with other B vitamins, helps to regulate homocysteine, an amino acid that is linked to an increase in the risk of cardiovascular disease when present in high concentrations.

Dijon Chicken & Quinoa Skillet

with Baby Kale & Cranberries

A zesty maple Dijon sauce tops this protein-packed skillet meal that's loaded with good-for-you kale and studded with cranberries for a pop of tart-sweetness.

INGREDIENTS

5 tsp	olive oil, divided
1 lb	boneless, skinless chicken breasts, cut into 2-inch pieces
¼ + ⅛ tsp	sea salt, divided
½ tsp	ground black pepper
1 cup	quinoa, rinsed
5 oz	baby kale (about 5 packed cups)
3 tbsp	Dijon mustard
2 tbsp	pure maple syrup
1 tbsp	fresh lemon juice
⅓ cup	dried unsweetened cranberries

Serves **4.**
Hands-On Time: **25 Minutes.**
Total Time: **45 Minutes.**

INSTRUCTIONS

In a large skillet or sauté pan on medium-high, heat 2 tsp oil. Add chicken, season with ¼ tsp salt and pepper and cook, stirring occasionally, until lightly browned, 3 to 4 minutes. Stir in quinoa, 1¾ cups water and remaining ⅛ tsp salt. Increase heat to high, cover and bring to a boil. Reduce heat to medium and simmer, covered, stirring occasionally, for about 15 minutes.

Add about half of kale and cover skillet to let it wilt slightly, about 1 minute. Add remaining half of kale and stir to combine. Cover and simmer until kale is tender and liquid is absorbed, 4 to 6 minutes. (**NOTE:** *If all the liquid absorbs before kale finishes cooking, add more water as needed*.) Remove from heat.

In a small bowl, whisk together mustard, maple syrup, lemon juice and remaining 3 tsp oil. To skillet, add about half of mustard sauce and the cranberries and stir to combine. Divide among plates and drizzle evenly with remaining mustard sauce.

Nutrition Information Per serving (1¾ cups): Calories: 392, Total Fat: 11 g, Sat. Fat: 2 g, Monounsaturated Fat: 6 g, Polyunsaturated Fat: 2.5 g, Carbs: 39 g, Fiber: 5.5 g, Sugars: 7 g, Protein: 33 g, Sodium: 380 mg, Cholesterol: 83 mg

Smoky Chicken Breasts & Crispy Chickpeas

Humble chicken breasts are dressed up by fragrant spices and deliciously roasted Brussels sprouts, grapes and chickpeas. We were wowed by the sweet and smoky flavor combination of this dish–who knew Brussels sprouts and grapes would go so perfectly together?

INGREDIENTS

1½ tsp	each mild chile powder (such as ancho) and ground cumin, divided
1 tsp	ground black pepper, divided
½ tsp	sea salt, divided
4	bone-in, skin-on chicken breasts (about 2 lb)
1 lb	Brussels sprouts, trimmed and halved lengthwise
2 cups	red seedless grapes (about ¾ lb)
2 tbsp	olive oil, divided
½ tsp	dried thyme
1 15-oz	BPA-free can chickpeas, drained, rinsed and dried

Serves 4.
Hands-On Time: **25 Minutes.**
Total Time: **55 Minutes.**

INSTRUCTIONS

Preheat oven to 400°F. Mist a large rimmed nonstick baking sheet with cooking spray. In a small bowl, stir together 1 tsp each chile powder and cumin, ½ tsp pepper and ¼ tsp salt. Lightly mist chicken with cooking spray and rub chile powder mixture all over, gently lifting the skin and seasoning the meat underneath (do not remove skin). Place on prepared sheet and roast for 10 minutes; remove from oven.

Meanwhile, to a large bowl, add Brussels sprouts, grapes, 4 tsp oil, thyme, remaining ½ tsp black pepper and remaining ¼ tsp salt. Toss gently to combine. In a small bowl, stir together chickpeas, remaining ½ tsp each chile powder and cumin and remaining 2 tsp oil.

To baking sheet with chicken, add Brussels sprout mixture and chickpeas, spreading around chicken in as close to a single layer as possible. Return to oven and roast for 30 to 35 minutes more, tossing Brussels sprout mixture and chickpeas halfway, until chicken is no longer pink in thickest part and internal temperature reaches 165°F, sprouts are browned and tender and grapes have burst and become soft and juicy.

Nutrition Information Per serving (1 chicken breast and 1¼ cups Brussels sprout mixture): Calories: 520, Total Fat: 20 g, Sat. Fat: 4 g, Monounsaturated Fat: 10 g, Polyunsaturated Fat: 4 g, Carbs: 39 g, Fiber: 9.5 g, Sugars: 16 g, Protein: 49 g, Sodium: 461 mg, Cholesterol: 111 mg

CHICKPEA POWER: Also called garbanzo beans, chickpeas are rich in molybdenum, a mineral that aids the body in metabolizing fats and carbohydrates. Chickpeas are also a good plant-based source of nonheme iron, providing you with 26% of your daily value (DV) of iron per 1-cup serving. The absorption of nonheme iron is strongly enhanced by vitamin C, which the Brussels sprouts in this dish provides.

Spiced Edamame Falafel Wraps
with Papaya Chutney

We've swapped out chickpeas for edamame in this twist on typical falafel. Served with a homemade sweet and sour papaya chutney and creamy yogurt, this is a full meal in a wrap. For a kick of heat, try a quick spicy tahini sauce instead of yogurt–simply whiz up tahini paste, water, lemon zest and juice, and a red chile in a food processor and you've got another element to add to these wraps!

Serves **8.**
Hands-On Time: **30 Minutes.**
Total Time: **50 Minutes.**

INGREDIENTS

1 tbsp	ground flaxseeds
1 tbsp	grape seed oil, divided
1 small	onion, diced
2	cloves garlic, minced
1 tsp	each ground cumin, coriander and turmeric
4 cups	edamame, shelled and cooked
⅓ cup	fresh flat-leaf parsley, finely chopped
½ tsp	sea salt
2 large	beets, grated
2 large	carrots, grated
½ cup	plain coconut or regular yogurt
8 6-inch	whole-grain pitas (***TIP:*** *For a lower-carb meal, substitute 8 large collard green leaves for the pitas.*)

Papaya Chutney

1 tsp	grape seed oil
3	cloves garlic, minced
1	jalapeño chile pepper, seeded and minced
1 tsp	ground coriander
1 small	papaya, cut into ¼-inch cubes (about 3 cups)
	juice and zest of 1 lime
1 tbsp	apple cider vinegar
1 tbsp	peeled and minced fresh ginger
1 tbsp	pure maple syrup
⅛ tsp	sea salt

INSTRUCTIONS

Prepare chutney: In a medium saucepan on medium, heat 1 tsp oil. Add 3 cloves garlic, jalapeño and coriander and sauté until fragrant, about 1 minute. Add remaining chutney ingredients except for the salt, and stir. Bring to boil, reduce heat and simmer for 20 minutes, stirring occasionally. When the chutney has reduced by one-third and has thickened, remove from heat and stir in ⅛ tsp salt. Chutney can be served warm, at room temperature or chilled.

Meanwhile, in a small bowl, combine flaxseeds and 2 tbsp water. Set aside for at least 10 minutes.

In a small skillet on medium, heat 1 tsp oil. Add onions and sauté until translucent, about 4 minutes. Add 2 cloves garlic, cumin, coriander and turmeric and sauté until fragrant, about 1 minute. Set aside.

To a food processor, add edamame, parsley and ½ tsp salt and process until thoroughly combined but only to a coarse, mealy texture. To a large bowl, add edamame mixture along with onion-spice mixture and flaxseeds. Using your hands, thoroughly combine. Using a 1-tbsp measure, form mixture into small balls and arrange on a large parchment-lined baking sheet, making about 32 balls in total.

In a large skillet on medium, heat ½ tsp oil. Add 8 balls. Using your spatula, flatten each ball slightly, cover and cook for about 2 minutes, or until golden brown. Flip, cover and cook for another 2 minutes on the other side. Repeat with remaining oil and balls.

Divide falafels, beet and carrot, yogurt and papaya chutney among pitas.

Nutrition Information Per serving (1 wrap): Calories: 371, Total Fat: 10 g, Sat. Fat: 2 g, Monounsaturated Fat: 2 g, Polyunsaturated Fat: 4 g, Carbs: 60 g, Fiber: 12 g, Sugars: 13 g, Protein: 16 g, Sodium: 484 mg, Cholesterol: 0 mg

Potato, Celery Root & Pear Gratin

This comforting vegetable dish is easy to put together for a weeknight meal but impressive enough to serve for company.

INGREDIENTS

1 tbsp	olive oil
1	leek, white and light green parts only, thinly sliced
2	cloves garlic, minced
1 12-oz	BPA-free can evaporated milk
1 tbsp	chopped fresh thyme leaves
¼ tsp	ground nutmeg
	sea salt and ground black pepper, to taste
1	celery root (about 1½ lb), peeled and sliced ⅛ inch thick
2	yellow-fleshed potatoes (about ½ lb each), peeled and sliced ⅛ inch thick
2	firm ripe pears (about ½ lb each), peeled, cored, and sliced crosswise into ⅛-inch-thick rounds
¼ cup	grated Parmesan cheese

Serves **6.**
Hands-On Time: **20 Minutes.**
Total Time: **1 Hour, 45 Minutes.**

INSTRUCTIONS

Preheat oven to 375°F. Mist an 8 x 10-inch baking dish with cooking spray.

In a medium saucepan on medium, heat oil; add leeks and garlic and cook, stirring occasionally, until softened, about 5 minutes. Stir in milk, thyme, nutmeg, salt and pepper, and bring to a boil (still on medium). Remove from heat.

Reserving most of milk mixture, line base of dish with leeks using a slotted spoon. Arrange alternating slices of celery root, potatoes and pears, starting with edges of dish then filling center with slices to fit.

Pour milk mixture evenly over top. Loosely cover with foil and bake for 1 hour. Remove cover, sprinkle with cheese and continue baking until tender and golden brown, 20 to 30 minutes more. Let stand for 5 minutes before serving.

Nutrition Information Per serving (⅙ of gratin): Calories: 268, Total Fat: 9 g, Sat. Fat: 4 g, Monounsaturated Fat: 4 g, Polyunsaturated Fat: 1 g, Carbs: 41 g, Fiber: 5 g, Sugars: 16 g, Protein: 9 g, Sodium: 262 mg, Cholesterol: 21 mg

THE GOOD ROOT: A member of the Apiaceae family of vegetables, celery root (aka celeriac) is a plentiful source of essential minerals such as phosphorus, iron, copper and calcium. Necessary for cell metabolism, phosphorus is a component of the energy-carrying molecule adenosine triphosphate (ATP) while both iron and copper help prevent anemia–plus calcium is essential for strong bones and teeth.

Arctic Char
with Watercress, Fennel & Orange Sauté

Sweet sautéed fennel and orange juice mellow the peppery taste of watercress in this company-worthy dish. For the best flavor, add the watercress and orange zest to the sauté at the very last minute. If the sauté is done cooking before the fish, simply take it off the heat and stir in the greens and zest when you're ready to serve. Use clean tweezers to remove the pin bones from the fish, or ask your fishmonger to do it for you.

INGREDIENTS

1	navel orange
4 5-oz	skin-on arctic char fillets, pin bones removed
1 tbsp + 1 tsp	olive oil, divided
¼ tsp	each sea salt and ground black pepper, divided
1 large	bulb fennel, trimmed, cored and thinly sliced (about 4 cups)
1½ large	shallots, thinly sliced (about ¾ cup)
1 large	clove garlic, thinly sliced
½ cup	dry white wine
1 bunch	watercress, trimmed (**NOTE:** *Leave 1 inch of stems attached*.)

Serves **4.**
Hands-On Time: **30 Minutes.**
Total Time: **30 Minutes.**

INSTRUCTIONS

Preheat oven to 400°F. Zest orange; set zest aside. Cut 4 thin slices from orange and cut each slice in half; set slices aside. Juice remaining orange; set aside.

Line a small baking sheet with parchment paper and mist with cooking spray. Arrange fish, skin side down, on sheet. Brush tops with 1 tsp oil and sprinkle with ⅛ tsp each salt and pepper. Arrange orange slices over top. Bake until fish flakes easily when tested with a fork, about 10 minutes.

Meanwhile, in a large sauté pan, heat remaining 1 tbsp oil on medium-high. Add fennel, shallots and remaining ⅛ tsp each salt and pepper and sauté, stirring often, until fennel and shallots are golden brown, about 5 minutes. Add garlic and sauté until fragrant, about 30 seconds.

Reduce heat to medium and stir in wine and orange juice. Bring to a simmer and cook until fennel is tender and liquid is reduced by half, about 3 minutes. Remove from heat and add watercress and orange zest; toss just until watercress is slightly wilted. Serve with arctic char.

Nutrition Information Per serving (1 piece fish and ¾ cup fennel mixture): Calories: 330, Total Fat: 16 g, Sat. Fat: 4 g, Monounsaturated Fat: 7 g, Polyunsaturated Fat: 3 g, Carbs: 16 g, Fiber: 4 g, Sugars: 8 g, Protein: 33 g, Sodium: 295 mg, Cholesterol: 50 mg

GET YOUR OMEGAS: One of the most sustainable fish you can find, arctic char's high fat content means it is brimming with omega-3 fatty acids, which help protect against cardiovascular disease, improve mood and boost brain function.

SUPERFOOD BOOST: Goji berries are a surprising source of the essential amino acids your body needs to form a complete protein–not bad for a berry! They're high in more than 20 vitamins and minerals–to name a couple, they pack 140% of your daily vitamin A intake and 20% of your daily vitamin C intake in just one 1-oz serving.

Curried Cauliflower Rice Bowls

with Crispy Chickpeas

Pulsing cauliflower in your food processor turns the veggie into a versatile rice substitute that's lower in calories and carbs than rice. Here, we sauté it with Indian spices and serve with crispy chickpeas and a rich curry sauce.

INGREDIENTS

1 15-oz	BPA-free can unsalted chickpeas, drained and rinsed
2 tbsp	coconut oil, divided
½ tsp	each sea salt and ground black pepper, divided
¼ tsp	ground cumin 1 head cauliflower, cut into florets
½	yellow onion, finely chopped
3	cloves garlic, minced
½ tsp	ground turmeric
3 tbsp	unsweetened dried goji berries, optional
8 cups	packed baby spinach
2 tsp	fresh lemon juice
2	carrots, thinly sliced into rounds, optional
½	head purple cabbage, shredded, optional
½ cup	raw unsalted cashews, chopped, optional

Curry Sauce

1 cup	full-fat coconut milk
1 tbsp	Thai red curry paste
1 tsp	curry powder
½ tsp	ground cumin

Serves **4.**
Hands-On Time: **45 Minutes.**
Total Time: **50 Minutes.**

INSTRUCTIONS

Prepare curry sauce: In a small saucepan, whisk together all sauce ingredients. Bring to a boil; reduce heat to low and simmer, whisking occasionally, until slightly thickened, about 5 minutes. Cover; set aside.

Meanwhile, preheat oven to 400°F. Using a clean towel, pat chickpeas dry, discarding any loosened skins. Melt 1 tbsp oil and pour into a large bowl. Add chickpeas, ¼ tsp each salt and pepper and cumin and toss to coat. Spread on a parchment-lined rimmed baking sheet and bake, stirring occasionally, until golden brown and crispy, 25 to 30 minutes. Let cool on sheet for 10 minutes.

Meanwhile, in a food processor, pulse cauliflower into rice-sized pieces. In a large skillet, heat remaining 1 tbsp oil on medium. Add onion and garlic and sauté, stirring occasionally, until softened, 4 to 5 minutes. Stir in cauliflower, turmeric and remaining ¼ tsp each salt and pepper and sauté until cauliflower is softened and no liquid remains, about 10 minutes. Remove from heat and stir in goji berries (if using). Cover to keep warm.

In a large saucepan on medium, heat ½ cup curry sauce. Add spinach and cook, tossing, until wilted and bright green, 2 to 3 minutes. Remove from heat; stir in lemon juice. Divide cauliflower mixture, spinach mixture and chickpeas among bowls. If using, top with carrots, cabbage and cashews. Drizzle bowls with remaining curry sauce.

Nutrition Information Per serving (¼ of recipe): Calories: 338, Total Fat: 17 g, Sat. Fat: 15 g, Monounsaturated Fat: 1 g, Polyunsaturated Fat: 0 g, Carbs: 33 g, Fiber: 10.5 g, Sugars: 6 g, Protein: 13 g, Sodium: 510 mg, Cholesterol: 0 mg

PROTEIN BOOST:
Amp up the protein by adding baked and sliced chicken breast to this brimming bowl—as we did on the cover.

Miso, Almond & Mushroom Soba Noodle Bowls

You won't miss the meat in these Asian-style bowls, thanks to a generous dose of satisfying umami, a savory, meat-like taste found in mushrooms and miso paste. Serve this dish warm or chilled; if serving cold, be sure to rinse the noodles under cold water once they're done cooking.

Serves **4.**
Hands-On Time: **35 Minutes.**
Total Time: **35 Minutes.**

INGREDIENTS

2 tbsp	grape seed oil, divided
2	portobello mushrooms, cut into ¼-inch-thick slices
2–4	baby bok choy, halved and cored
2 cups	sugar snap peas, trimmed
1	red bell pepper, cut into matchsticks
⅛ tsp	sea salt
8 oz	cooked soba noodles or whole-wheat spaghetti
4	carrots, shredded or cut into matchsticks, divided
¼ cup	sliced raw unsalted almonds
4	scallions, thinly sliced on the bias, optional
2 tbsp	hemp seeds, optional
1 tbsp	black sesame seeds, optional

Sauce

⅓ cup	fresh orange juice
3 tbsp	smooth roasted almond butter
3 tbsp	rice vinegar
1 tbsp	cordyceps powder, optional
2½ tsp	white miso paste
1 tsp	garlic powder
¼ tsp	onion powder
⅛ tsp	ground cayenne pepper

INSTRUCTIONS

Prepare sauce: In a bowl, whisk together all sauce ingredients until smooth. Set aside.

In a large skillet, heat ½ tbsp oil on high. Add half of the portobellos in a single layer and cook, turning once, until golden brown, 2 to 4 minutes. Transfer to a plate. Repeat with ½ tbsp oil and remaining portobellos and add to plate.

In same skillet, heat remaining 1 tbsp oil on medium. Add bok choy, cut sides down. Add peas and bell pepper and stir-fry until bok choy is slightly wilted, bell pepper is crisp-tender and peas are bright green, about 1 minute. Remove from heat and sprinkle with salt.

In a separate bowl, toss together noodles, half of the carrots and ½ cup of the sauce. Divide noodle mixture, mushrooms, bok choy mixture, remaining half of carrots and almonds among bowls. If using, top with scallions, hemp seeds and sesame seeds. Drizzle bowls with remaining sauce.

Nutrition Information Per serving (¼ of recipe): Calories: 320, Total Fat: 18 g, Sat. Fat: 2 g, Monounsaturated Fat: 8 g, Polyunsaturated Fat: 7.5 g, Carbs: 35 g, Fiber: 6 g, Sugars: 12 g, Protein: 10 g, Sodium: 279 mg, Cholesterol: 0 mg

SUPERFOOD BOOST: Far from your average mushroom, cordyceps stimulates cells in your immune system, helping your body fight off infections. It may also help boost stamina and fight fatigue, making it a popular energy supplement among athletes.

INGREDIENTS

⅓ cup	hemp hearts
2 tbsp	apple cider vinegar
1 tbsp	nutritional yeast
½ tsp	sea salt, divided
¼ tsp	chipotle chile powder
1	yellow onion, quartered lengthwise
2	cloves garlic (peel on)
2	Roma tomatoes
1 tbsp	olive oil
8 oz	organic tempeh, crumbled
2 cups	cremini or white button mushrooms, coarsely chopped
2 tbsp	chile powder
1 tbsp	pure maple syrup
2 tsp	cacao powder, optional
2 tsp	each ground cumin and dried oregano
2 cups	cooked brown rice
1	head romaine lettuce, halved lengthwise, cored and thinly sliced crosswise
2	radishes, trimmed and thinly sliced, optional
1	avocado, peeled, pitted and sliced, optional
2 tbsp	chopped fresh cilantro, optional

Salsa

1	lime, zested and juiced
1 tsp	pure maple syrup
	Pinch sea salt
1	mango, peeled, pitted and diced
½	red bell pepper, finely chopped
1	scallion, white and light green parts only, thinly sliced

Tempeh Taco Bowl
with Mango Salsa

We're bringing back the taco bowl with this meatless take on the classic. Tempeh, made from fermented soybeans, has a nutty, mushroom-like taste and is one of our favorite vegetarian substitutes for ground beef. We've even cracked the code on a dairy-free chile cheese sauce–who knew hemp, nutritional yeast and chile could taste so good together?

Serves **4.**
Hands-On Time: **50 Minutes.**
Total Time: **50 Minutes.**

INSTRUCTIONS

Prepare salsa: In a bowl, whisk together lime zest and juice, 1 tsp maple syrup and salt. Add mango, red pepper and scallion and toss to coat. Set aside.

In a blender, combine hemp seeds, vinegar, nutritional yeast, ¼ tsp salt, chipotle chile powder and 3 tbsp water and blend until completely smooth. Scrape into a separate bowl and set aside. Clean blender.

Heat a large skillet on medium-high. Add onion, garlic and tomatoes and cook, turning occasionally, until dark brown and blistered, 5 to 7 minutes for garlic and 10 minutes for onion and tomatoes. Peel garlic and add to blender. To blender, add onion and tomatoes and purée until smooth. In same skillet, heat oil on medium. Add onion mixture and cook, stirring constantly, until beginning to darken, about 2 minutes.

Meanwhile, in a separate bowl, stir together tempeh, mushrooms, chile powder, 1 tbsp maple syrup, cacao powder (if using), cumin, oregano and remaining ¼ tsp salt. Add to onion mixture and cook, stirring often, until thickened, 5 to 7 minutes.

Divide rice and lettuce among bowls. Top with tempeh mixture, drizzle with hemp mixture and sprinkle with salsa. If using, top with radishes, avocado and cilantro.

Nutrition Information Per serving (¼ of recipe): Calories: 477, Total Fat: 17.5 g, Sat. Fat: 3 g, Monounsaturated Fat: 5 g, Polyunsaturated Fat: 8 g, Carbs: 63 g, Fiber: 10 g, Sugars: 21.5 g, Protein: 24 g, Sodium: 419 mg, Cholesterol: 0 mg

SUPERFOOD BOOST: Boost this bowl with cacao powder! Made from ground roasted cacao beans, cacao powder contains high levels of flavonoids that can decrease your risk of cardiovascular disease when consumed regularly and in moderation. It's also a source of iron and magnesium, both of which can help reduce food cravings.

Creamy Chicken Enchilada Casserole

This enchilada-inspired casserole has a mild heat that's balanced by cooling yogurt. If you already have cooked chicken on hand, you can skip the first step–if doing so, you'll need 2 cups broth.

INGREDIENTS

1 lb	boneless, skinless chicken breasts (If breasts are very large, cut in half crosswise.)
6	cloves garlic (smash 2 cloves and mince 4 cloves), divided
4 cups	low-sodium chicken broth, or as needed
2 tbsp	olive oil
2	white onions, quartered and sliced
2	red bell peppers, quartered and sliced
2	poblano or pasilla peppers, quartered, seeded and sliced
2	jalapeño peppers, halved, seeded and thinly sliced
2 tsp	each ground coriander and cumin
6 tbsp	white whole-wheat flour
3½ cups	plain whole-milk greek yogurt, divided
5 tbsp	chopped fresh cilantro, divided
	sea salt, to taste
12	6-inch corn tortillas, halved
1 cup	shredded Monterey Jack cheese
¼ cup	thinly sliced red onion, optional

Serves **8.**
Hands-On Time: **1 hour.**
Total Time: **2 Hours, 10 Minutes.**

INSTRUCTIONS

In a medium saucepan, combine chicken, smashed garlic and enough broth to cover chicken by ½ inch. Bring to a gentle boil on medium, reduce to simmer and cook for 5 minutes. Remove from heat, cover and set aside for 10 minutes, or until chicken is cooked. Transfer chicken to a plate. Strain broth; reserve 2 cups (save remaining broth for another use).

Preheat oven to 375°F. Mist a 9 x 13-inch baking pan with cooking spray; set aside.

Meanwhile, in a large saucepan on medium, heat oil. Add white onions and cook, stirring occasionally, for 1 minute. Add bell, poblano and jalapeño peppers and cook, stirring occasionally, until tender, about 8 minutes. Stir in minced garlic, coriander and cumin and cook, stirring, until fragrant, 30 to 60 seconds. Add flour; stir to combine. Add reserved 2 cups broth; bring to a boil, stirring to smooth out lumps. Cook until thickened slightly, 1 minute. Remove from heat; stir in 3 cups yogurt, ¼ cup cilantro and salt. Set aside.

Shred chicken. Arrange 8 tortilla halves in bottom of prepared pan. Spread one-third of pepper mixture over tortillas and top with one-half of chicken. Repeat layers. Top with remaining tortilla halves and remaining pepper mixture. Sprinkle with cheese, cover with foil and bake for 20 minutes.

Remove foil and bake until cheese begins to brown and casserole is heated through, about 20 minutes. Let stand 10 minutes.

Sprinkle with red onion (if using) and remaining 1 tbsp cilantro. Top each serving with a dollop of remaining ½ cup yogurt.

Nutrition Information Per serving (⅛ of casserole and 1 tbsp yogurt): Calories: 421, Total Fat: 21 g, Sat. Fat: 12 g, Monounsaturated Fat: 6 g, Polyunsaturated Fat: 2 g, Carbs: 30 g, Fiber: 5 g, Sugars: 6 g, Protein: 28 g, Sodium: 207 mg, Cholesterol: 72 mg

Braised Spiced Chickpeas
with Swiss Chard & Sweet Potatoes

INGREDIENTS

3 tbsp	extra-virgin olive oil
2	yellow onions, finely chopped
2	small fennel bulbs, cored and finely chopped
¼ tsp	kosher salt or sea salt + additional to taste
7 large	cloves garlic, minced
1 tbsp	orange zest
1 tsp	each ground cumin and coriander
½ tsp	ground cinnamon
1 lb	sweet potatoes, peeled and cut into ½-inch cubes
2 15-oz	BPA-free cans unsalted chickpeas (aka garbanzo beans), rinsed and drained
2 oz	each dried unsweetened apricots, plums and figs (**NOTE:** *Roughly chop apricots and plums; remove tough stems of figs and chop into quarters.*)
3 cups	low-sodium chicken broth
1 tbsp	raw honey
1 lb	rainbow chard (leaves and stems), roughly chopped
	ground black pepper, to taste
	fresh cilantro leaves, for garnish

Serves **6.**
Hands-On Time: **30 Minutes.**
Total Time: **55 Minutes.**

INSTRUCTIONS

To a 5.5-qt Dutch oven (or larger) or a large pot on medium, add oil, onions, fennel and salt and cook, stirring occasionally, until soft and translucent, 10 to 12 minutes. Add the garlic, zest, cumin, coriander and cinnamon. Stir and cook until fragrant, 1 minute.

2. Add potatoes, chickpeas, apricots, plums, figs, broth and honey. Cover, increase heat to medium-high and bring to a boil. Reduce heat to medium-low; cook for 10 minutes, until potatoes are barely tender. Stir in the chard. Cook, uncovered, for 8 to 10 minutes, until greens are tender. Season with additional salt and pepper and garnish servings with cilantro. (***TIP:*** *Can be served on its own or over couscous or rice, or with chicken over top.*)

Nutrition Information Per serving (⅙ of recipe): Calories: 393, Total Fat: 11 g, Sat. Fat: 1 g, Monounsaturated Fat: 6 g, Polyunsaturated Fat: 2 g, Carbs: 67 g, Fiber: 14 g, Sugars: 28 g, Protein: 13 g, Sodium: 423 mg, Cholesterol: 0 mg

FIBERFUL CHICKPEAS: Chickpeas (also known as garbanzo beans) get a lot of praise for their high protein content of 15 grams per cooked cup. But it's their impressive amount of fiber–12 grams per cooked cup, or nearly half of the recommended daily value (DV) for women and nearly one-third of the recommended DV for men that is linked to most of their health benefits. Because most of this fiber is in the insoluble form, studies have shown chickpeas help lower the more harmful form of LDL cholesterol, reduce risk of heart disease and help balance blood sugar level. A broad set of vitamins and minerals, including calcium, vitamin K, magnesium and zinc, also means chickpeas help promote strong bones.

Watercress & Spinach Soup
with Cheesy Thyme Crisps

INGREDIENTS

1 1-lb	bag chopped frozen spinach (or 1 lb fresh spinach, roughly chopped)
8 oz	watercress
2 tbsp	extra-virgin olive oil
2	yellow onions, finely chopped
1¼ tsp	kosher salt (or 1 tsp fine sea salt), divided + additional to taste
3 large	cloves garlic, roughly chopped
4 cups	low-sodium vegetable broth
¼ cup	fresh mint leaves
3 tbsp	cold organic unsalted butter
1½ tbsp	fresh lemon juice
¼ tsp	ground black pepper + additional to taste
	Crème fraîche, for serving, optional

Cheesy Thyme Crisps (Optional)

1 cup	finely grated Parmigiano-Reggiano
½ cup	grated Gruyère cheese
½ tbsp	white whole-wheat flour, sifted
¾ tsp	finely chopped fresh thyme
Pinch	ground black pepper

Serves **4 to 6.**
Hands-On Time: **30 Minutes.**
Total Time: **1 Hour.***
*Plus Cooling Time.

INSTRUCTIONS

Prepare thyme crisps (if making): Preheat oven to 350°F. In a large bowl, toss all crisp ingredients. Place 6 1-tbsp mounds of mixture, evenly spaced apart, on a large parchment-lined baking sheet. Pat the mounds, using your fingers, into 3½- to 4-inch rounds.

Bake for 8 minutes until crisps are light brown. Set aside to cool on sheet for 5 minutes, then use a metal spatula to transfer to a wire rack to cool completely. Using a cool baking sheet, repeat to cook remaining crisps.

Meanwhile, fill a small pot halfway with water and bring to a boil. Add spinach and cook until thawed, about 2 minutes. Add watercress and continue to cook just 2 minutes more. Drain and cool quickly under cold running water. Continue to drain in strainer, squeezing out as much water from spinach and watercress as possible. (**NOTE:** *If using fresh spinach instead of frozen, blanch for only 2 minutes at the same time as watercress.*)

In a large saucepan on medium-low, heat oil. Add onion and ¼ tsp salt and cook for 6 to 7 minutes, stirring occasionally, until onion is soft and beginning to turn golden. Add garlic, stir, and cook until fragrant, 1 minute. Add broth, increase heat to high and bring to a simmer; remove from heat.

To a blender, add spinach, watercress, mint and stock mixture. Blend until smooth. Add butter, lemon juice, pepper and remaining 1 tsp salt; continue to blend until fully incorporated. Season to taste with additional salt and pepper. Serve soup in individual bowls. If using, add a dollop of crème fraîche and a few cheesy thyme crisps.

Nutrition Information Per serving (¼ of soup): Calories: 224, Total Fat: 16.5 g, Sat. Fat: 6.5 g, Monounsaturated Fat: 8 g, Polyunsaturated Fat: 1 g, Carbs: 16 g, Fiber: 6 g, Sugars: 5 g, Protein: 6.5 g, Sodium: 853 mg, Cholesterol: 23 mg

Creamy Mushroom & Tarragon Chicken
with Green Beans

Sherry adds a rich nutty note to this mushroom sauce, which we've made extra-creamy by stirring in tangy cream cheese.

INGREDIENTS

4 6-oz	boneless, skinless chicken breasts
½ tsp	each sea salt and ground black pepper
1 tbsp	olive oil
8 oz	cremini or white button mushrooms, sliced
½	yellow onion, finely chopped
2	cloves garlic, thinly sliced
1 tsp	dried tarragon
2 tbsp	whole-wheat flour
¼ cup	dry sherry or dry white wine
½ cup	low-sodium chicken broth
¼ cup	full-fat cream cheese
1 lb	green beans, trimmed

Serves **4.**
Hands-On Time: **25 Minutes.**
Total Time: **30 Minutes.**

INSTRUCTIONS

Season chicken with salt and pepper. Mist a large nonstick skillet with cooking spray and heat on medium-high. Add chicken and cook, turning once, until golden brown, about 6 minutes. Transfer to a plate.

In same skillet on medium-high, heat oil. Add mushrooms and onion and sauté, stirring often, until no liquid remains and mushrooms are beginning to brown, about 3 minutes. Add garlic and tarragon and sauté until fragrant, about 45 seconds. Add flour and stir until well combined.

Add sherry and cook, scraping up browned bits from bottom of pan, until reduced by half, about 30 seconds. Stir in broth. Return chicken and any juices to skillet. Reduce heat to low, cover and cook, turning chicken halfway through, until chicken is no longer pink inside, about 10 minutes. Whisk in cream cheese until smooth. Cover and keep warm.

Meanwhile, in a steamer basket set over a saucepan of simmering water, cook beans until crisp-tender, about 4 minutes. Divide beans among plates and top with chicken and mushroom sauce.

Nutrition Information Per serving (1 breast with ¼ of sauce and beans): Calories: 362, Total Fat: 14 g, Sat. Fat: 4.5 g, Monounsaturated Fat: 5 g, Polyunsaturated Fat: 2 g, Carbs: 16 g, Fiber: 4 g, Sugars: 6 g, Protein: 44 g, Sodium: 387 mg, Cholesterol: 139 mg

Cauliflower Chickpea Korma

Korma is one of the mildest Indian curries out there, but we've kicked it up a notch with fiery fresh chiles. You can take the cayenne down to ¼ tsp if you prefer a slightly milder version. A combination of soaked and blended cashews and yogurt give this satisfying vegetarian main an ultra-creamy texture. Serve with whole-grain naan.

INGREDIENTS

½ cup	raw unsalted cashews, roughly chopped
2 tsp	each coriander seeds and cumin seeds
1 tsp	each garam masala, turmeric and paprika
½ tsp	ground cayenne pepper
2	green finger chile peppers (or serrano pepper), seeded and roughly chopped
1½ cups	jarred unsalted puréed strained tomatoes (aka passata), divided
¼ cup	fresh cilantro + additional for garnish
1	2-inch piece ginger, peeled and roughly chopped
2	cloves garlic, halved
¼ tsp	sea salt
1 tbsp	safflower oil
1 large	yellow onion, finely chopped
1 large	head cauliflower, trimmed and cut into bite-size florets (about 6 cups)
1	carrot, thinly sliced (**TIP:** *Halve larger carrots lengthwise and thinly slice crosswise.*)
1 15-oz	BPA-free can unsalted chickpeas (aka garbanzo beans), drained and rinsed
1¾ cups	low-sodium vegetable or chicken broth
¾ cup	whole-milk plain yogurt

Serves **4.**
Hands-On Time: **35 Minutes.**
Total Time: **1 Hour, 10 Minutes.**

INSTRUCTIONS

To a heat-proof bowl, add cashews and enough boiling water to cover. Let stand for 30 to 45 minutes. Drain, reserving 2 tbsp soaking water.

Meanwhile, heat a Dutch oven or large heavy-bottomed saucepan on medium-low. Add coriander, cumin, garam masala, turmeric, paprika and cayenne pepper and cook, stirring often, until fragrant, about 2 minutes. Transfer to a food processor.

To food processor with spices, add cashews and reserved soaking water and process until finely ground. Add chile peppers, 3 tbsp strained tomatoes, cilantro, ginger, garlic and salt. Pulse, stopping to scrape down side of bowl, until a smooth paste forms, 2 to 3 minutes. Set aside.

Wipe out Dutch oven. In Dutch oven on medium-low, heat oil. Add onion and cook, stirring often, until soft and light golden, 6 to 7 minutes. Stir in cashew mixture, cauliflower, carrot and chickpeas.

Add broth and remaining strained tomatoes; bring to a boil. Reduce heat to a gentle simmer and cook, stirring occasionally, until cauliflower and carrot are tender, 10 to 12 minutes. Remove from heat; gradually stir in yogurt, a spoonful at a time, until smooth. Garnish with additional cilantro.

Nutrition Information Per serving (¼ of recipe): Calories: 367, Total Fat: 14 g, Sat. Fat: 3 g, Monounsaturated Fat: 5 g, Polyunsaturated Fat: 4 g, Carbs: 47 g, Fiber: 12 g, Sugars: 14 g, Protein: 17 g, Sodium: 272 mg, Cholesterol: 6 mg

Spiced Pumpkin Mousse

Serves **10.**
Hands-On Time: **20 Minutes.**
Total Time: **2 Hours, 20 Minutes**
(Includes Chilling).

INGREDIENTS

2	15-oz cans BPA-free unsweetened pumpkin purée
1 1-lb pkg	organic silken tofu, drained well
½ cup	pure maple syrup
1½ tsp	ground cinnamon
¾ tsp	ground ginger
¼ tsp	each ground nutmeg, ground cloves and sea salt
½ cup	plain Greek yogurt
1 oz	dark chocolate, cut into thin shards (about ¼ cup)

INSTRUCTIONS

In a food processor, combine pumpkin and tofu. Process until smooth, about 30 seconds. Add maple syrup, cinnamon, ginger, nutmeg, cloves and salt. Process until combined, about 30 seconds more.

Transfer mousse to a resealable container, cover and refrigerate for at least 4 hours.

Drain any water that has accumulated from mousse. Give it a quick stir and scoop ½ cup mousse into each of 10 small glasses or ramekins. (You may have some mousse left over.)

Top each serving with yogurt and chocolate. Keep refrigerated until ready to serve.

Nutrition Information Per serving (½ cup mousse, 2 tsp yogurt, 1 tsp chocolate): Calories: 130, Total Fat: 3.5 g, Sat. Fat: 1.5 g, Carbs: 22 g, Fiber: 4 g, Sugars: 14 g, Protein: 4 g, Sodium: 60 mg, Cholesterol: 0 mg

TIME-SAVING TIP: You can prepare pumpkin mousse through Step 2 up to 1 day ahead. Put mousse in glasses and top with yogurt and chocolate up to 5 hours before serving.

Individual Apple & Pecan Crumbles

Serves **10.**
Hands-On Time: **30 Minutes.**
Total Time: **1 Hour, 40 Minutes.**

INGREDIENTS

½ cup	white whole-wheat flour
2 tbsp	organic unsalted butter, cut into 3 or 4 pieces
½ cup	rolled oats
2 tbsp	chopped unsalted pecans
⅓ cup plus 2 tbsp	organic evaporated cane juice (aka organic cane sugar), divided
¼ tsp + pinch	sea salt, divided
2½ lb	sweet-tart apples (such as McIntosh), peeled, cored and thinly sliced (about 5 apples)
1 tbsp	fresh lemon juice
¼ cup	crème fraîche

INSTRUCTIONS

Mist 10 ½-cup ramekins with cooking spray and arrange on a large, rimmed baking sheet.

Prepare crumble topping: In a medium bowl, combine flour and butter, working butter into flour with a pastry cutter, a fork or your fingertips until mixture resembles a coarse meal. Stir in oats, pecans, ⅓ cup cane juice and ¼ tsp salt. Set aside.

In a large bowl, combine apples, lemon juice, remaining 2 tbsp cane juice and pinch salt. Transfer fruit to ramekins.

Preheat oven to 375°F. Sprinkle crumble topping over apples and bake for 60 minutes, until fruit is tender and topping is golden brown. Set aside to cool 10 minutes. Top each crumble with crème fraîche, dividing evenly.

Nutrition Information Per serving (1 crumble with crème fraîche): Calories: 180, Total Fat: 5 g, Sat. Fat: 3 g, Monounsaturated Fat: 1 g, Polyunsaturated Fat: 1 g, Carbs: 32 g, Fiber: 4 g, Sugars: 20 g, Protein: 2 g, Sodium: 66 mg, Cholesterol: 12 mg

SUBSTITUTION GUIDE

The next time you're missing an ingredient or want to transform a Meal Plan to make it meatless, Paleo, dairy-free, or gluten-free, don't panic. Our recipes and Meal Plans are flexible and will come out delicious even when you improvise.

Use our suggestions below as a starting point, and start asking yourself questions such as:

- What do I really want this dish to taste like?
- What textures do I like?
- Why did the recipe developer put all of these ingredients in here, anyway?

Here are some general guidelines about making substitutions in recipes:

- Try to keep ingredients within the same ethnic category. Ethnic flavor combinations have been developed over centuries and blend together naturally. If you want to make over a Mexican dish without meat, for example, use traditional Mexican proteins and starches such as pinto beans, black beans and posole (hominy), not Asian mung beans or Indian lentils.

- Dissect the basic flavors of the dish. If you're missing a certain flavoring, ask yourself if it is basically sweet, salty, sour, bitter or spicy. Think of something from your cupboard in the same category. Substituting starches and proteins makes less of a difference in overall taste than spices and flavorings.

- Try the pantry approach to cooking: If you find yourself continually missing key ingredients, analyze your pantry and consider restocking it. Assemble complementary herbs, spices and flavorings in groupings in your pantry. That way, when you are experimenting with a dish—Italian, for example—your Italian seasonings, such as basil, parsley, garlic and oregano, will be grouped together, and you can substitute accordingly.

- Consider the following groupings for pantry organization: baking goods; oils and vinegars; beans and grains; and sauces and broths. Try to keep these stocked so that you don't have to run out to the store at the last minute.

Make It Meatless

Ingredient: MEAT
Substitute: Beans; cheese; organic tofu

Ingredient: MEAT/SEAFOOD BROTHS
Substitute: Vegetable broth; water in which beans, pasta or vegetables have been cooked; vegetable bouillon cubes or miso paste diluted with water

Ingredient: GELATIN
Substitute: Agar (powder or flakes); arrowroot (powder); kudzu powder

Make It Vegan

Ingredient: BUTTERMILK
Substitute: Clabbered soy milk (1 cup soy milk mixed with 2 tsp lemon juice or white vinegar)

Ingredient: CHEESE
Substitute: Nut-based cheese; nutritional yeast

Ingredient: CHEESE OR RICOTTA CHEESE
Substitute: Crumbled organic tofu; nut-based ricotta

Ingredient: MILK
Substitute: Nut milk; rice milk; soy milk; coconut milk

Make It Allergen-Free

Ingredient: BUTTER
Substitute: Ghee (milk solids have been removed, but ghee shouldn't be used in the case of a serious dairy allergy); olive oil; sesame oil; coconut oil

Ingredient: CHOCOLATE
Substitute: Carob

Ingredient: COW'S MILK
Substitute: Goat's milk; rice milk; nut milk

Ingredient: COW'S MILK CHEESE
Substitute: Goat cheese; sheep's milk cheese; nut cheese

Ingredient: EGGS
Substitute: 1 mashed banana or ¼ cup applesauce per egg (for baked goods); 1 tbsp ground flaxseeds or chia to 3 tbsp water per egg (let sit for 10 minutes); 3 tbsp aquafaba (water from a can of chickpeas) per egg; for egg whites, substitute 1 tbsp agar flakes whisked into 1 tbsp water per egg white (chill for 5 minutes)

Ingredient: PEANUTS OR PEANUT BUTTER
Substitute: Almonds or almond butter

Make It Gluten-Free

Ingredient: WHOLE-WHEAT FLOUR
Substitute: Buckwheat flour; gluten-free oat flour; brown rice flour; quinoa flour

Ingredient: BREAD CRUMBS
Substitute: Cooked quinoa or almond flour (as a binder); cassava flour or almond flour (as a breading for chicken or fish)

Ingredient: WHOLE-WHEAT PASTA
Substitute: Pasta made from rice, quinoa, beans or lentils

Everyday Swaps for Exotic Ethnic

ORIGIN: AMERICAS
Ingredient: CACTUS PADS (NOPALES)
Substitute: Green beans; okra

Ingredient: CHAYOTE SQUASH
Substitute: Yellow or green pattypan squash; zucchini

Ingredient: POBLANO OR ANAHEIM CHILES
Substitute: Minced jalapeño chiles; green bell pepper

ORIGIN: ASIAN
Ingredient: BOK CHOY (CHINESE WHITE CABBAGE)
Substitute: Beet greens; kale; Swiss chard

Ingredient: CHINESE COOKING WINE
Substitute: Dry sherry

Ingredient: CHINESE FIVE-SPICE POWDER
Substitute: Mixture of anise seed or star anise, fennel seed, cinnamon, black peppercorns and cloves

Ingredient: GALANGAL (THAI GINGER)
Substitute: Fresh ginger

Ingredient: LEMONGRASS
Substitute: Lemon zest

Ingredient: LOTUS ROOT
Substitute: Jicama; water chestnuts

Ingredient: MIRIN (JAPANESE RICE WINE)
Substitute: Sweet white wine

Ingredient: NAM PLA
Substitute: Soy sauce and lime juice

Ingredient: RICE VINEGAR
Substitute: Apple cider vinegar; white wine vinegar

Ingredient: SESAME OIL
Substitute: 1 tbsp sesame seeds cooked in ½ cup grape seed or safflower oil

Ingredient: THAI BASIL
Substitute: Italian basil

Ingredient: WATER CHESTNUTS
Substitute: Jicama

ORIGIN: INDIAN
Ingredient: CHANA DAL
Substitute: Split yellow peas

Ingredient: CURRY POWDER
Substitute: Mixture of ground ginger, cumin, coriander, fenugreek, turmeric and fennel

Ingredient: GARAM MASALA
Substitute: Mixture of 1 tsp cardamom seeds, 1 tbsp cumin seed, 1 tbsp coriander seed, 2 tsp black peppercorns, 1 tsp cinnamon, 1 tsp cloves and 1 tsp nutmeg

Ingredient: JAGGERY (COARSE PALM SUGAR)
Substitute: Date sugar; coconut sugar

Ingredient: TOOR DAL, URAD DAL, MUNG DAL
Substitute: Red lentils

ORIGIN: MEDITERRANEAN
Ingredient: BROCCOLI RABE
Substitute: Broccoli plus arugula or dandelion greens

Ingredient: CANNELLINI BEANS
Substitute: Great northern beans; navy beans; red kidney beans

Ingredient: FAVA BEANS
Substitute: Lima beans; butter beans

Ingredient: FENNEL
Substitute: Celery plus some fennel seeds or anise seeds

Ingredient: PARMESAN CHEESE
Substitute: Any hard, aged grating cheese such as Asiago, Romano or aged Monterey Jack

Ingredient: PINE NUTS
Substitute: Walnuts; a mixture of walnuts and almonds

Make It Alcohol-Free

Ingredient: RED WINE
Substitute: Pomegranate juice; ½ cup water with 2 tsp balsamic vinegar

Ingredient: WHITE WINE
Substitute: Vegetable broth; apple juice; carrot juice

Ingredient: WINE OR BEER
Substitute: Nonalcoholic wine or beer

YOUR 1- AND 2-WEEK SEASONAL MEAL PLANS

Whether you want a little extra pep in your step, you're eschewing meat for a while or you're curious about Paleo, we've got 14 weeks of delicious daily clean-eating menus to choose from, and we've done all the work for you. Here's how to use them:

First, select the plan of your choice then go to **cleaneating.com/booklists** to download and print the corresponding shopping list. Your pre-made lists will have further ingredient details and clean brand recommendations, and you can reprint the lists again and again, keeping your beautiful book intact. You'll notice that some plans are 1-week plans while others are 2 weeks; this provides some flexibility depending on your commitment level and time frame. If you happen to really like a particular 2-week plan but only want a 1-week commitment, be sure to adjust the grocery list so that you're not over-shopping and ending up with food waste. We've included many of the recipes found in the cookbook in the meal plans, and there are also mini recipes at the end of the plans, all of which are listed by page number. Feel free to remove or add snacks and reduce or increase serving sizes according to your needs. And don't forget that you're always free to make swaps using the handy substitutions found on page 296. These plans are yours to customize and enjoy.

Coconut Chicken
Corn Chowder
(See recipe, p. 164)

Monday

Breakfast: 1 bar *No-Cook Almond Cherry Bars* (p. 2) and 1 cup green tea

Snack: *Cottage Cheese Parfait:* Top ½ cup cottage cheese with ½ cup thawed frozen wild blueberries and 1 tsp pumpkin seeds

Lunch: 1½ cups *Orange Carrot Soup* (p. 314); 4 crackers with ½ avocado, sliced and ¼ cup fresh salsa verde

Snack: 3 cups Parmesan Popcorn (p. 314)

Dinner: *Greek-Style Salmon:* Rub a 3-oz salmon fillet with ¼ tsp EVOO and sprinkle with 2 tsp Za'atar; cook in a skillet with cooking spray; serve over 1 cup steamed spinach with tzatziki (below)

Tzatziki: Combine ½ cup yogurt with 1 clove minced garlic, ¼ shredded cucumber, 1 tsp chopped mint and pinch each salt and pepper

1 piece *Dark Chocolate Bark* (p. 314)

NUTRIENTS: Calories: 1,765, Fat: 83 g, Sat. Fat: 16 g, Carbs: 197 g, Fiber: 44 g, Sugars: 86 g, Protein: 76 g, Sodium: 2,057 mg, Cholesterol: 76 mg

Tuesday

Breakfast: *Tex-Mex Egg & Salsa:* 1 poached egg, ½ avocado, sliced, 2 tbsp salsa on 1 slice toast

Snack: Top ½ cup yogurt with 1 pear, chopped, and ½ tsp honey

Lunch: *Mediterranean Fusilli:* Heat ⅔ cup tomato sauce with ¼ cup pitted black olives, sliced, pinch red pepper flakes, 1 tsp capers, 3 oz tuna and 1 chopped carrot; toss with ½ cup cooked pasta

Snack: 1 oz *Spiced Walnuts* (p. 315) and ½ orange (leftover from Orange Carrot Soup)

Dinner: 1 serving *Persian-Style Chicken Stew with Walnuts & Pomegranate Molasses* (p. 20) with ½ cup cooked quinoa

1 piece *Dark Chocolate Bark*

NUTRIENTS: Calories: 1,729, Fat: 80 g, Sat. Fat: 14 g, Carbs: 166 g, Fiber: 30 g, Sugars: 63 g, Protein: 98 g, Sodium: 1,964 mg, Cholesterol: 359 mg

Wednesday

Breakfast: 1 bar *No-Cook Almond Cherry Bars* (leftovers, p. 2) and 1 cup green tea

Snack: Top ½ cup yogurt with ½ pear, chopped and ½ tsp honey

Lunch: 1½ cups *Orange Carrot Soup* (leftovers, p. 314); 2 oz tuna on 1 slice bread

Snack: 3 cups *Parmesan Popcorn*

Dinner: 1 serving *Persian-Style Chicken Stew with Walnuts & Pomegranate Molasses* (leftovers, p. 2) with ½ cup cooked quinoa

1 cup mixed baby greens with 1 tsp each EVOO and ACV

NUTRIENTS: Calories: 1,801, Fat: 76 g, Sat. Fat: 10 g, Carbs: 205 g, Fiber: 40 g, Sugars: 91 g, Protein: 87 g, Sodium: 1,356 mg, Cholesterol: 130 mg

Thursday

Breakfast: *Cinnamon Pear Toast:* 1 slice bread topped with ½ cup cottage cheese, ½ pear, sliced, and sprinkled with cinnamon; toast or broil

Snack: ½ pear, sliced, with 1 tbsp almond butter

Lunch: *Supercharged Winter Salad* (p. 20)

4 crackers

Snack: ½ bar *No-Cook Almond Cherry Bars* (leftovers, p. 2)

1 cup green tea

Dinner: *Quick Pasta Fagioli Soup:* Simmer 2 cups vegetable broth, ⅓ cup each uncooked pasta, diced carrots, celery and onions, until pasta is cooked, about 8 minutes; add ½ cup chickpeas, 1 handful baby spinach and 2 tbsp chopped parsley; simmer 1 minute and remove from heat; sprinkle with a drizzle of EVOO and 1 tsp Parmesan

1 piece *Dark Chocolate Bark*

NUTRIENTS: Calories: 1,728, Fat: 71 g, Sat. Fat: 12 g, Carbs: 227 g, Fiber: 45 g, Sugars: 81 g, Protein: 56 g, Sodium: 1,663 mg, Cholesterol: 13 mg

Friday

Breakfast: 1 recipe *Purple Power Smoothie* (p. 314)

Snack: 1 oz *Spiced Walnuts* (leftovers, p. 315)

Lunch: 1 serving *Persian-Style Chicken Stew with Walnuts & Pomegranate Molasses* (leftovers, p. 20) with ½ cup cooked quinoa

Snack: 3 cups *Parmesan Popcorn*

Dinner: *Bison Avocado Slider:* Form 4 oz bison or beef into a patty and grill or cook in nonstick pan; top with 2 oz avocado and handful of fresh baby spinach on 1 slice toasted bread; serve with 1 carrot and ½ cucumber, sliced

1 piece *Dark Chocolate Bark*

NUTRIENTS: Calories: 1,775, Fat: 75 g, Sat. Fat: 14 g, Carbs: 201 g, Fiber: 36 g, Sugars: 78 g, Protein: 87 g, Sodium: 1,107 mg, Cholesterol: 140 mg

Saturday

Breakfast: *Wild Blueberry Toast:* 1 slice bread with ½ cup cottage cheese, ½ cup wild blueberries and cinnamon; toast or broil

Snack: ½ bar *No-Cook Almond Cherry Bars* (leftovers, p. 20) and 1 cup green tea

Lunch: *Black Bean Bowl:* Heat 1 can black beans with ½ tsp each cumin, garlic powder, chile powder and smoked paprika; roast 1 sweet potato; serve ½ of bean mixture, ½ of sweet potato, sliced, with squeeze lime, ⅓ avocado over ½ cup cooked rice; top with 1 tbsp pumpkin seeds and 2 tbsp salsa verde

Snack: 1 oz Spiced Walnuts

Dinner: *Quick Pasta Fagioli Soup:* Simmer 2 cups vegetable broth, ⅓ cup each uncooked pasta, diced carrots, celery and onions, until pasta is cooked, about 8 minutes; add ½ cup chickpeas, 1 handful baby spinach and 2 tbsp chopped parsley; simmer 1 minute and remove from heat; sprinkle with a drizzle of EVOO and 1 tsp Parmesan

1 piece *Dark Chocolate Bark*

NUTRIENTS: Calories: 1,700, Fat: 66 g, Sat. Fat: 12 g, Carbs: 225 g, Fiber: 52 g, Sugars: 63 g, Protein: 62 g, Sodium: 1,836 mg,

Sunday

Breakfast: 1 recipe *Purple Power Smoothie* (p. 314)

Snack: Top ½ cup yogurt with ½ pear, sliced and ½ tsp honey

Lunch: *Supercharged Winter Salad* (p. 315)

4 crackers

Snack: 3 cups *Parmesan Popcorn*

Dinner: *Black Bean Bowl* (leftovers): Serve reserved bean mixture and sweet potato, sliced, with squeeze lime, ⅓ avocado over ½ cup cooked brown rice; top with 1 tbsp pumpkin seeds and 2 tbsp salsa verde

1 piece *Dark Chocolate Bark*

NUTRIENTS: Calories: 1,796, Fat: 60 g, Sat. Fat: 13 g, Carbs: 278 g, Fiber: 51 g, Sugars: 101 g, Protein: 53 g, Sodium: 1,900 mg, Cholesterol: 10 mg

WEEK 2

Monday

Breakfast: *Arugula Omelette:* Sauté 2 tbsp chopped yellow onion, ¼ cup grape tomatoes, halved, in 1 tsp coconut oil; add 4 eggs, whisked with 1 tsp water and pinch salt, and cook until almost set; add 1 cup arugula and pinch oregano, fold over and cook until set (eat half; save leftovers)

¼ avocado, sliced, with pinch salt

Snack: 1 orange, ½ oz walnuts

Lunch: *Tuna Salad:* Combine 2 cups arugula, ¼ cup grape tomatoes, 2 tbsp chopped yellow onion, 3 oz tuna and ½ oz almonds, chopped, with 1 tsp EVOO, 1 tbsp ACV and pinch each salt and pepper flakes

Snack: ½ bell pepper, sliced, with ¼ cup baba ghanoush

Dinner: 1 serving *Mexican Chicken Stuffed Peppers* (p. 26; save leftovers)

Baked Sweet Potato: Bake 2 sweet potatoes (eat 1 with pinch salt and ¼ tsp EVOO; save leftovers)

Pecan Cinnamon Apple (p. 316)

NUTRIENTS: Calories: 1,567, Fat: 89 g, Sat. Fat: 18 g, Carbs: 109 g, Fiber: 27 g, Sugars: 56 g,Protein: 89 g, Sodium: 1,298 mg, Cholesterol: 613 mg

Tuesday

Breakfast: *Arugula Omelette* (leftovers)

½ oz walnuts

Snack: 1 *Pecan Cinnamon Apple* (leftovers)

Lunch: 1 serving *Mexican Chicken Stuffed Peppers* (leftovers, p. 26)

Side Salad: Toss 1 cup arugula, ½ avocado, chopped, ¼ cup grape tomatoes and 1 tbsp chopped yellow onion with ½ tsp EVOO, 2 tsp ACV and pinch each salt and pepper

Snack: ½ bell pepper, sliced, with 2 tbsp baba ghanoush

1 Paleo-friendly bar

Dinner: *Orange Ginger Cod:* Season 1 cod fillet with pinch each salt and pepper; sauté in 1 tsp coconut oil with ½ tsp grated ginger; drizzle with 1 tbsp orange juice

Spiced Cauliflower: Cut ½ head cauliflower into florets, toss with 1 tsp coconut oil and 1 tsp Mexican seasoning (leftovers, p. 26); roast until lightly browned (eat half; save leftovers)

NUTRIENTS: Calories: 1,792, Fat: 105 g, Sat. Fat: 26 g, Carbs: 109 g, Fiber: 29 g, Sugars: 62 g, Protein: 115 g, Sodium: 1,158 mg, Cholesterol: 655 mg

Wednesday

Breakfast: 1 serving *Sweet Cherry Almond Flaxseed Smoothie* (p. 3; save leftovers)

1 hard-boiled egg with pinch salt

Snack: 1 Pecan Cinnamon Apple (leftovers)

Lunch: *Stuffed Sweet Potato:* 1 baked sweet potato (leftovers), reheated and stuffed with ¼ avocado, chopped, 4 grape tomatoes, halved, 2 tbsp baba ghanoush, 2 pinches salt and pinch pepper ¼ cup sauerkraut

Snack: ½ bell pepper, sliced, ½ oz walnuts

Dinner: 1 serving *Orange-Scented Asparagus & Beef Stir-Fry* (p. 21; save leftovers)

Spiced Cauliflower (leftovers)

1 serving *Lemon, Coconut & Cayenne Mousse* (make ahead) (p. 2; save leftovers)

NUTRIENTS: Calories: 1,784, Fat: 111.5 g, Sat. Fat: 48 g, Carbs: 151 g, Fiber: 34 g, Sugars: 88 g, Protein: 60 g, Sodium: 991 mg, Cholesterol: 370 mg

Thursday

Breakfast: 1 serving *Sweet Cherry Almond Flaxseed Smoothie* (leftovers, p. 3)

Snack: ½ bell pepper, sliced

2 tbsp baba ghanoush

¼ cup sauerkraut

Lunch: 1 serving *Orange-Scented Asparagus & Beef Stir-Fry* (leftovers)

1 apple

Snack: 1 serving *Lemon, Coconut & Cayenne Mousse* (leftovers, p.2) with ½ oz walnuts, chopped

Dinner: *Paleo Schnitzel:* Grind 1 cup almonds to a flour; mix with ½ tsp each salt and oregano, ¼ tsp granulated garlic and pepper, to taste; pound 3 chicken breasts, dip in 2 eggs, whisked, and dredge in almond mixture; pan sear in 2 tsp coconut oil in a nonstick ovenproof skillet on medium for 1 minute, turn gently then transfer to oven, covered, until cooked through (eat 1 breast; save leftovers)

Tex-Mex Kale Chips (p. 315)

NUTRIENTS: Calories: 1,776, Fat: 110 g, Sat. Fat: 48 g, Carbs: 124 g, Fiber: 27.5 g, Sugars: 78 g, Protein: 85 g, Sodium: 1,113 mg, Cholesterol: 380 mg

Friday

Breakfast: *Spinach Omelette:* Sauté 1 tbsp chopped yellow onion, 4 grape tomatoes, halved, in ½ tsp coconut oil; add 2 eggs, whisked with ½ tsp water and pinch salt; cook until almost set; add ½ cup spinach and pinch oregano, fold over and cook until set

1 orange

Snack: ½ banana and 1 oz almonds

Lunch: 1 serving *Paleo Schnitzel* (leftovers), 1 cup cauliflower florets, 2 tbsp baba ghanoush

Snack: 1 serving *Tex-Mex Kale Chips* (leftovers)

Dinner: 1 serving *Orange-Scented Asparagus & Beef Stir-Fry* (leftovers)

1 sweet potato, baked, with ¼ tsp EVOO and pinch salt

¼ cup sauerkraut

NUTRIENTS: Calories: 1,497, Fat: 82 g, Sat. Fat: 25 g, Carbs: 107 g, Fiber: 28 g, Sugars: 48 g, Protein: 94 g, Sodium: 1,527 mg, Cholesterol: 659 mg

Saturday

Breakfast: *Cocoa Almond Sipper:* Blend 1 cup almond milk, ½ banana, ½ oz almonds, ground, 1½ tsp cocoa powder, 1 tsp each coconut oil and maple syrup, ⅛ tsp cinnamon and ice, as desired

Snack: 1 serving *Tex-Mex Kale Chips* (leftovers), 1 orange, ½ oz almonds

Lunch: 1 serving *Mexican Chicken Stuffed Peppers*, thawed and reheated (leftovers, p. 26)

1 cup cauliflower florets

¼ cup sauerkraut

Snack: 1 Paleo-friendly bar

Dinner: Sauté 1 cod fillet in 1 tsp EVOO with pinch each salt, pepper, oregano; drizzle with 2 tsp lemon juice

Maple Chile Squash: Toss 10 oz butternut squash with 2 tsp each coconut oil and maple syrup and pinch each salt and pepper flakes; roast and divide into 3 servings (eat 1 serving; save leftovers)

NUTRIENTS: Calories: 1,514, Fat: 75 g, Sat. Fat: 18 g, Carbs: 120 g, Fiber: 27 g, Sugars: 64 g, Protein: 109 g, Sodium: 1,270 mg, Cholesterol: 273 mg

Sunday

Breakfast: *Cinnamon Banana Pancakes:* Mash 1 banana; beat in 2 eggs and pinch cinnamon; heat 1 tsp coconut oil in a nonstick pan and dollop mixture into 2-inch-wide pancakes; cook until set, turning once; sprinkle with ½ tsp flaxseeds

Snack: 2 carrots, sliced

1 apple

Lunch: 1 serving *Orange-Scented Asparagus & Beef Stir-Fry* (leftovers)

Spinach Salad: Toss together 2 cups spinach, ½ orange, segmented, 2 tbsp chopped yellow onion, ½ oz almonds, chopped, with 1 tsp EVOO, 1 tbsp ACV and 2 pinches salt

Snack: Remaining ½ orange (from lunch)

½ oz walnuts

Dinner: 1 serving *Paleo Schnitzel* (leftovers)

1 serving *Maple Chile Squash* (leftovers)

¼ cup sauerkraut

NUTRIENTS: Calories: 1,573, Fat: 84 g, Sat. Fat: 29 g, Carbs: 129 g, Fiber: 30 g, Sugars: 70 g, Protein: 89 g, Sodium: 1,360 mg, Cholesterol: 654 mg

EVOO = extra-virgin olive oil
ACV = apple cider vinegar

Monday

Breakfast: 1 serving *Sweet Cherry Almond Flaxseed Smoothie* (p. 3; save leftovers)

Snack: 1 hard-boiled egg

2 carrots, sliced

Lunch: *Salmon Squash Salad:* Toss 2 cups spinach, 3 oz salmon, 2 tbsp chopped onion and 1 serving Maple Chile Squash (leftovers) with 1 tsp EVOO, 1 tbsp ACV and pinch each salt and pepper

Snack: 1 orange

½ oz walnuts

Dinner: 1 serving *Chicken Adobo with Orange & Wilted Spinach* (p. 24; save leftovers)

Bake 2 sweet potatoes (eat 1 with ¼ tsp EVOO and pinch salt; save leftovers)

½ cup broccoli with *Lemon Tahini Dip:* Whisk together ½ cup tahini, 3 tbsp lemon juice, 1 minced clove garlic and ⅓ cup water, or to desired consistency; season with pinch salt, or to taste, and stir in ¼ cup chopped parsley; divide into 4 servings (eat 1 serving; save leftovers)

NUTRIENTS: Calories: 1,520, Fat: 79.5 G, Sat. Fat: 15 g, Carbs: 130 g, Fiber: 31 g, Sugars: 64 g, Protein: 81 g, Sodium: 1,121 mg, Cholesterol: 347 mg

Tuesday

Breakfast: 1 serving *Sweet Cherry Almond Flaxseed Smoothie* (leftovers, p. 3)

Snack: 2 carrots, sliced

½ cup broccoli florets

1 serving Lemon *Tahini Dip* (leftovers)

Lunch: 1 serving *Chicken Adobo with Orange & Wilted Spinach* (leftovers)

½ apple, sliced

½ oz almonds

Snack: 1 Paleo-friendly bar

Dinner: *Salmon Salad:* Toss 2 cups spinach, 3 oz salmon, 2 tbsp chopped onion, remaining ½ apple, sliced, with 1 tsp EVOO, 1 tbsp ACV and pinch each salt and pepper

Chocolate Orange Pudding: In a food processor, blend 2 bananas, 1 avocado, ¼ cup cocoa powder, 2 tbsp maple syrup and 1 tsp orange zest; divide into 4 ramekins and chill before eating (eat 1 ramekin; save leftovers)

NUTRIENTS: Calories: 1,734, Fat: 90 g, Sat. Fat: 14 g, Carbs: 161 g, Fiber: 37 g, Sugars: 95 g, Protein: 90 g, Sodium: 1,036 mg, Cholesterol: 160 mg

Wednesday

Breakfast: *Eggs 'n' Greens:* 2 eggs, scrambled in ½ tsp coconut oil with pinch salt with 2 cups spinach, sautéed in ½ tsp coconut oil with pinch salt; 1 orange

Snack: 1 serving *Chocolate Orange Pudding* (leftovers)

Lunch: 1 baked sweet potato (leftovers), heated, stuffed with ½ cup steamed broccoli and 1 serving *Lemon Tahini Dip* (leftovers)

1 oz walnuts

Snack: 1 carrot, sliced

½ cup broccoli florets

Dinner: 1 serving *Chicken Adobo with Orange & Wilted Spinach* (leftovers)

1⅓ cups *Thai Kabocha Squash Soup* (p.18; save leftovers)

Sweet Roasted Pineapple: Toss 2 cups pineapple, thawed, with 2 tsp maple syrup and ¼ tsp cinnamon; roast and divide into 3 servings (eat 1 serving with ½ tsp flaxseeds; save leftovers)

Make *Chia Bowl* for tomorrow

NUTRIENTS: Calories: 1,536, Fat: 82.5 G, Sat. Fat: 23 g, Carbs: 147 g, Fiber: 32 g, Sugars: 68 g, Protein: 70 g, Sodium: 1,298 mg, Cholesterol: 502 mg

Thursday

Breakfast: *Chia Bowl* (with ¼ cup cherries, thawed and heated, ½ banana, sliced, pinch cinnamon and drizzle maple syrup, if desired (save leftovers)

Snack: 2 hard-boiled eggs with pinch salt

¼ cup sauerkraut

Lunch: 1⅓ cups *Thai Kabocha Squash Soup* (leftovers, p. 18)

2 carrots, sliced, with 1 serving *Lemon Tahini Dip* (leftovers)

Snack: 1 orange and 1 oz walnuts

Dinner: *Beef "Tacos":* 8 oz beef, sliced, tossed in ½ tsp *Mexican Seasoning* (leftovers, p. 26) and ⅛ tsp salt; stir-fry with ½ bell pepper, sliced, and ½ onion, sliced (eat ½; save leftovers); serve in 2 to 3 leaves lettuce with ¼ avocado, chopped and juice of ½ lime

1 cup broccoli, steamed and tossed with ½ tsp EVOO, 1 minced garlic clove and pinch salt

1 serving *Sweet Roasted Pineapple* (leftovers) with ½ tsp flaxseeds

NUTRIENTS: Calories: 1,560, Fat: 91.5 g, sat. Fat: 23 g, Carbs: 137 g, Fiber: 38 g, Sugars: 60.5 g, Protein: 67 g, Sodium: 1,636 mg, Cholesterol: 458 mg

Friday

Breakfast: *Chia Bowl* (leftovers) topped with ¼ cup cherries, thawed and heated, ½ banana, sliced, pinch cinnamon and drizzle maple syrup, if desired; 1 hard-boiled egg

Snack: 2 carrots, sliced and 1 oz walnuts

Lunch: 1 serving *Chicken Adobo with Orange & Wilted Spinach* (leftovers), ½ bell pepper

Snack: 1 serving *Sweet Roasted Pineapple* (leftovers) with ½ tsp flaxseeds

Dinner: *Beef "Tacos"* (leftovers); serve in 2 to 3 leaves lettuce with ¼ avocado, chopped and juice of ½ lime

1 cup broccoli florets, steamed and tossed with ½ tsp EVOO and pinch each salt and pepper flakes

Spicy Paprika Kale Chips: Remove stems from 1 large bunch kale; toss leaves with 1 tsp EVOO, ½ tsp paprika and pinch cayenne; bake on a tray until lightly browned and divide into 3 servings (eat 1 serving; save leftovers)

NUTRIENTS: Calories: 1,469, Fat: 81 g, Sat. Fat: 15.5 g, Carbs: 114 g, Fiber: 37.5 g, Sugars: 50 g,Protein: 82 g, Sodium: 909 mg, Cholesterol: 401 mg

Saturday

Breakfast: *Cinnamon Banana Pancakes:* Mash 1 banana, beat with 2 eggs and pinch cinnamon; heat 1 tsp coconut oil in a nonstick pan and dollop mixture into 2-inch-wide pancakes; cook until set, turning once; sprinkle with ½ tsp flaxseeds

Snack: 2 carrots, sliced and ½ oz walnuts

Lunch: 1⅓ cups *Thai Kabocha Squash Soup* (leftovers, p. 18)

2 oz sardines

1 serving *Spicy Paprika Kale Chips* (leftovers)

Snack: *Green Goddess Smoothie* (P. 314)

Dinner: 1 serving *Mexican Chicken Stuffed Peppers*, thawed and reheated (leftovers, p. 26)

Side Salad: Toss 2 cups chopped lettuce, with ½ bell pepper, chopped, and 2 tbsp each chopped onion and carrot with 1 tsp EVOO, 1 tbsp ACV and pinch each salt and pepper

1 serving *Chocolate Orange Pudding* (leftovers)

NUTRIENTS: Calories: 1,733, Fat: 93 g, Sat. Fat: 26.5 g, Carbs: 153 g, Fiber: 38 g, Sugars: 67 g, Protein: 94 g, Sodium: 1,476 mg, Cholesterol: 648 Mg

Sunday

Breakfast: *Green Goddess Smoothie* (P. 314)

Snack: 2 carrots, sliced, with 2 tbsp tahini

¼ cup sauerkraut

Lunch: *Sardine Salad:* Toss 2 cups chopped lettuce, 2 oz sardines, 2 tbsp each chopped onion and carrot, and ½ bell pepper, sliced, with 1 tsp EVOO, 1 tbsp ACV, pinch each salt and pepper flakes

1 serving *Chocolate Orange Pudding* (leftovers)

Snack: 1 apple, cored and baked with pinch cinnamon; with 1 tsp flaxseeds

Dinner: *Oregano Chicken:* Sprinkle 5 oz chicken with pinch each oregano, salt and pepper flakes and ½ tsp EVOO; bake

1⅓ cups *Thai Kabocha Squash Soup* (leftovers, p. 63)

1 serving *Spicy Paprika Kale Chips* (leftovers)

NUTRIENTS: Calories: 1,335, Fat: 65 g, Sat. Fat: 16 g, Carbs: 138 g, Fiber: 37 g, Sugars: 64 g, Protein: 70 g, Sodium: 1,619 mg, Cholesterol: 159 mg

WEEK 1

Monday

Breakfast: 1 *Sweet Green Smoothie* (p. 83)

Snack: ¼ cup baba ghanoush with 2 carrots, sliced, and 1 oz crackers

Lunch: 2 slices *Avocado Sweet Potato Toast* (p. 315) with 2 hard-boiled eggs sliced over top; ½ cup bell pepper slices

Snack: 1 *Cinnamon Maca Bliss Bar* (p. 70; save leftovers)

Dinner: Roast 2 5-oz chicken breasts with 1 tsp EVOO, ¼ tsp salt and ⅛ tsp black pepper; slice; eat 1 breast (save leftovers) over 1 serving *Spinach & Cauli-Rice Salad* (p. 104; save leftovers)

½ cup blueberries

NUTRIENTS: Calories: 1,600, Fat: 96.5 g, Sat. Fat: 17 g, Carbs: 119 g, Fiber: 29.5 g, Sugars: 52 g, Protein: 72 g, Sodium: 1,549 mg, Cholesterol: 461 mg

Tuesday

Breakfast: 2 slices *Cashew Banana Sweet Potato Toast* (p. 315)

Snack: 1 serving *Chile-Roasted Walnuts* (p. 83; save leftovers)

Lunch: 1 serving *Spinach & Cauli-Rice Salad* (leftovers, p. 104); 1 cooked chicken breast (leftovers)

½ cup blueberries

Snack: ¼ cup baba ghanoush with 2 carrots and 2 stalks celery, sliced

Dinner: *Piled-High Burger:* Form 5 oz ground beef into a patty; sprinkle with pinch each salt and pepper; grill with 1 portobello mushroom brushed with ¼ tsp EVOO; top mushroom with patty, 1 tsp mustard, 2 tbsp chopped onion, 2 thin slices avocado and 2 tbsp sauerkraut

1 cup green beans, steamed, with pinch salt

NUTRIENTS: Calories: 1,633, Fat: 103.5 g, Sat. Fat: 19 g, Carbs: 103.5 g, Fiber: 28 g, Sugars: 41 g, Protein: 81 g, Sodium: 1,563 mg, Cholesterol: 175 mg

Wednesday

Breakfast: 1 *Sweet Green Smoothie* (p. 314)

Snack: ¼ cup baba ghanoush with 2 carrots and 2 stalks celery, sliced

Lunch: 1 baked sweet potato; top with ¼ avocado smashed with 2 tsp lime juice and pinch salt, ½ tsp hemp seeds; 1 oz crackers with 2 tbsp cashew butter

Snack: 1 *Cinnamon Maca Bliss Bar* (leftovers, p. 70)

Dinner: 1 serving *Spinach & Cauli-Rice Salad* (leftovers, p. 104)

Cook 5 oz halibut in skillet with 1 tsp olive oil with ⅛ tsp salt; drizzle with 1 tbsp lemon juice and serve over salad

½ banana, sprinkled with cinnamon

NUTRIENTS: Calories: 1,699, Fat: 101 g, Sat. Fat: 17 g, Carbs: 149 g, Fiber: 33 g, Sugars: 65 g, Protein: 62 g, Sodium: 1,606 mg, Cholesterol: 78 mg

Thursday

Breakfast: *Berry Chia Pudding* (make ahead): Whisk 1 cup coconut milk, 3 tbsp chia and ¼ tsp vanilla, divide among 2 small bowls or Mason jars; refrigerate overnight; eat 1 bowl (save leftovers) with ¼ cup blueberries and pinch cinnamon

Snack: 1 *Sweet Green Smoothie* (p. 83)

Lunch: 1 serving *Spinach & Cauli-Rice Salad* (leftovers, p. 104)

1 hard-boiled egg, sliced

Snack: 1 oz crackers with ¼ avocado, smashed with 2 tsp lime juice and 2 pinches salt

2 carrots, sliced

Dinner: 1 serving *Red Curry Chicken Soup with Zoodles* (p. 315; save leftovers)

½ cup red bell pepper slices

NUTRIENTS: Calories: 1,525, Fat: 110 g, Sat. Fat: 51 g, Carbs: 92.5 g, Fiber: 26 g, Sugars: 32 g, Protein: 58 g, Sodium: 1,499 mg, Cholesterol: 249 mg

Friday

Breakfast: 2 slices Avocado Sweet Potato Toast (p. 83) with 2 hard-boiled eggs sliced over top

Snack: 1 serving *Berry Chia Pudding* (leftovers), topped with ½ banana, sliced, and pinch cinnamon

Lunch: *Salmon Salad Lettuce Wraps:* Toss 6 oz canned salmon with 2 tbsp lemon juice, 1 tsp EVOO, 2 tbsp each chopped onion and celery and pinch each salt and pepper; serve ½ on 1 to 2 romaine lettuce leaves (save leftover salmon salad)

Snack: 1 serving *Chile-Roasted Walnuts* (leftovers, p. 314)

2 stalks celery, sliced

Dinner: 1 serving *Red Curry Chicken Soup with Zoodles* (leftovers, p. 315)

2 cups baby spinach sautéed in ½ tsp EVOO with 1 clove garlic, chopped and pinch salt

½ banana, sliced, with pinch cinnamon

NUTRIENTS: Calories: 1,466, Fat: 101 g, Sat. Fat: 50 g, Carbs: 81.5 g, Fiber: 23 g, Sugars: 26 g, Protein: 74 g, Sodium: 1,548 mg, Cholesterol: 506 mg

Saturday

Breakfast: 2 slices *Cashew Banana Sweet Potato Toast* (p. 315)

Snack: 1 *Sweet Green Smoothie* (p. 315)

Lunch: 1 serving *Red Curry Chicken Soup with Zoodles* (leftovers, p. 315)

1 oz crackers

Tomato-Cucumber Salad: Toss 1 tomato, chopped, ½ cup chopped cucumber, 2 tbsp lemon juice, 1 tbsp EVOO and ⅛ tsp each salt and pepper

Snack: 1 serving *Chile-Roasted Walnuts* (leftovers, p. 314)

Dinner: *Salmon Salad* (leftovers) on 1 to 2 romaine lettuce leaves

1 cup green beans, steamed, drizzled with ½ tsp EVOO, and sprinkled with pinch salt; top with 2 tbsp almonds, chopped

NUTRIENTS: Calories: 1,590, Fat: 101.5 g, Sat. Fat: 31 g, Carbs: 108 g, Fiber: 23 g, Sugars: 37.5 g, Protein: 81 g, Sodium: 1,589 mg, Cholesterol: 133 mg

Sunday

Breakfast: *Rise & Shine Salad:* Toss 1 tomato, chopped, ½ cup chopped cucumber, 1 tbsp each chopped onion and mint, 2 tbsp lemon juice, 1 tbsp EVOO and ⅛ tsp each salt and pepper; top with 2 sunny-side-up eggs cooked in 1 tsp EVOO; top with 1 tbsp baba ghanoush

Snack: 1 serving *Chile-Roasted Walnuts* (leftovers, p. 314)

Lunch: 1 serving *Red Curry Chicken Soup with Zoodles* (leftovers, p. 315)

Snack: 1 *Cinnamon Maca Bliss Bar* (leftovers, p. 70)

Dinner: *Piled-High Burger:* Form 5 oz ground beef into a patty; sprinkle with pinch salt and pepper; grill, with 1 portobello mushroom brushed with ¼ tsp EVOO; top mushroom with patty, 1 tsp mustard, 2 tbsp chopped onion, 2 thin slices avocado and 2 tbsp sauerkraut

2 cups baby spinach sautéed in ½ tsp EVOO with 1 clove garlic, chopped, and pinch salt

½ banana, sprinkled with cinnamon

NUTRIENTS: Calories: 1,621, Fat: 112 g, Sat. Fat: 38 g, Carbs: 82 g, Fiber: 21 g, Sugars: 43 g, Protein: 82 g, Sodium: 1,756 mg, Cholesterol: 521 mg

EVOO = extra-virgin olive oil
ACV = apple cider vinegar

Monday

Breakfast: *Coco-Berry Shake* (p. 314)

Snack: *Tahini Dip:* Whisk 2 tbsp tahini, 1 tbsp lemon juice, pinch salt and cayenne and water to thin; 1 oz crackers; ½ cup cucumber slices

Lunch: *Herbed Scramble:* Sauté 2 tbsp chopped shallot in 1 tsp EVOO; add 2 eggs, whisked, and ⅛ tsp salt and cook, stirring in 2 tbsp each chopped parsley and dill; ½ small avocado, smashed with 1 tbsp lemon juice and pinch salt

1 tomato, sliced, with pinch salt

Snack: 1 serving *Cinnamon Maca Bliss Bar* (leftovers, p. 70)

1 carrot, sliced

Dinner: 1 serving *Shredded Brussels Sprouts & Chicken Sauté* (p. 107; save leftovers) with 2 tbsp almonds, chopped, over top

1 kiwi, sliced

NUTRIENTS: Calories: 1,587, Fat: 91.5 g, Sat. Fat: 18 g, Carbs: 138 g, Fiber: 35 g, Sugars: 62 g, Protein: 74 g, Sodium: 1,401 mg, Cholesterol: 432 mg

Tuesday

Breakfast: 2 slices *Cashew Banana Sweet Potato Toast* (p. 314)

1 boiled egg with pinch salt

Snack: 1 serving *Chile-Roasted Walnuts* (leftovers, p. 314)

Lunch: 1 serving *Shredded Brussels Sprouts & Chicken Sauté* (leftovers, p. 107)

1 carrot, sliced

Snack: ½ small avocado, smashed with 1 tbsp lemon juice and pinch salt

1 oz crackers

Dinner: Cook 5 oz sole in a skillet with 1 tsp EVOO and 2 pinches each salt and pepper; squeeze 1 tsp lime juice over top; sprinkle with 1 tsp chopped dill; eat with 1 serving *Berry Salsa* (p. 314)

1 cup broccoli, steamed

1 *Cinnamon Maca Bliss Bar* (leftovers, p. 70)

NUTRIENTS: Calories: 1,609, Fat: 96 g, Sat. Fat: 16 g, Carbs: 131 g, Fiber: 32 g, Sugars: 46 g, Protein: 74.5 g, Sodium: 1,741 mg, Cholesterol: 302 mg

Wednesday

Breakfast: *Coco-Berry Shake* (p. 314)

Snack: 2 slices *Cashew Banana Sweet Potato Toast* (p. 315)

Lunch: *Shredded Brussels Sprouts & Chicken Sauté* (leftovers, p. 107)

Snack: 3 oz sliced turkey

Berry Salsa (leftovers) and 1 oz crackers

Dinner: *Turmeric Roasted Vegetables* (p. 102; save leftovers)

Form 5 oz ground beef into a patty, sprinkle with salt and pepper; grill; serve with veggies and 1 tsp mustard

1 pitted date stuffed with 1 walnut

NUTRIENTS: Calories: 1,544, Fat: 76 g, Sat. Fat: 24 g, Carbs: 125 g, Fiber: 27 g, Sugars: 46 g, Protein: 101 g, Sodium: 1,474 mg, Cholesterol: 185 mg

Thursday

Breakfast: *Editor's Special* (p. 314)

Snack: ½ banana with 1 tbsp cashew butter and pinch cinnamon

Lunch: *Turmeric Roasted Vegetables* (leftovers, p. 102) with 1 sunny-side-up egg, cooked in 1 tsp EVOO with pinch each salt and pepper

Berry Salsa (p. 314 leftovers) with 1 oz crackers

Snack: 1 *Cinnamon Maca Bliss Bar* (leftovers, p. 70)

Dinner: *Shredded Brussels Sprouts & Chicken Sauté* (leftovers, p. 107)

Quick Golden Milk: Heat 1 cup coconut milk beverage with pinch each turmeric and cinnamon (or more to taste) and ¼ tsp vanilla; stir in ½ tsp honey

NUTRIENTS: Calories: 1,595, Fat: 98 g, Sat. Fat: 26 g, Carbs: 125 g, Fiber: 32 g, Sugars: 56 g, Protein: 71 g, Sodium: 1,641 mg, Cholesterol: 264 mg

Friday

Breakfast: *Coco-Berry Shake* (p. 314)

1 boiled egg with pinch cayenne

Snack: 1 serving *Chile-Roasted Walnuts* (leftovers, p. 314)

1 kiwi, sliced

Lunch: *Turkey-Avo Wraps:* Divide 4 oz turkey and ½ avocado between 2 romaine leaves; top each wrap with 1 tbsp each chopped tomatoes and yellow onions, 1 tsp sauerkraut, ½ tsp each capers and mustard

1 carrot, sliced

Snack: 1 chopped sweet potato, tossed with 1 tsp coconut oil then baked; drizzle with 2 tbsp tahini mixed with 1 tbsp lemon juice, pinch salt and water to thin

Dinner: *Turmeric Roasted Vegetables* (leftovers, p. 102)

5 oz sole, cooked in skillet with 1 tsp EVOO and 2 pinches each salt and pepper; squeeze 1 tsp lemon juice over top and sprinkle with 2 tsp chopped dill

2 pitted dates each stuffed with 1 walnut

NUTRIENTS: Calories: 1,548, Fat: 89 g, Sat. Fat: 25 g, Carbs: 124 g, Fiber: 33.5 g, Sugars: 56 g, Protein: 79 g, Sodium: 1,944 mg, Cholesterol: 291 mg

Saturday

Breakfast: *Editor's Special* (p. 83)

Snack: 1 *Cinnamon Maca Bliss Bar* (leftovers, p. 89)

1 carrot, sliced

Lunch: *Turmeric-Roasted Vegetables* (leftovers, p. 87) with 2 sunny-side-up eggs, cooked in 1 tsp EVOO with pinch each salt and pepper

Snack: 1 serving *Chile-Roasted Walnuts* (leftovers, p. 83)

Dinner: *Mediterannean Chop:* Toss 1 cup chopped lettuce, ½ cup each chopped tomato and cucumber, ¼ cup chopped parsley, 1 tbsp chopped shallot, 1 tbsp each EVOO and lemon juice and pinch each salt and pepper; topped with 1 5-oz chicken breast, sprinkled with ⅛ tsp salt, and pinch each pepper and turmeric, grilled

1 kiwi, sliced

NUTRIENTS: Calories: 1,559, Fat: 103.5 g, Sat. Fat: 24 g, Carbs: 92 g, Fiber: 29 g, Sugars: 47 g, Protein: 82 g, Sodium: 1,716 mg, Cholesterol: 468 mg

Sunday

Breakfast: *Middle Eastern Benny* (p. 314)

Snack: 1 serving *Chile-Roasted Walnuts* (leftovers, p. 314)

1 kiwi, sliced

Lunch: *Turkey Wraps:* Divide 4 oz turkey between 2 romaine leaves; top each wrap with 1 tbsp each chopped tomatoes and yellow onions, 1 tsp sauerkraut and ½ tsp each capers and mustard; ½ cup cucumber slices

1 date stuffed with 1 walnut

Snack: 2 slices *Avocado Sweet Potato Toast* (p. 315)

Dinner: *Burger & Greens:* Form 5 oz ground beef into a patty; sprinkle with pinch each salt and pepper and grill; toss 2 cups chopped lettuce with ¼ cup each chopped parsley and tomato and 2 tbsp chopped shallot with 2 tbsp each EVOO and lemon juice and pinch each salt and pepper; top with 2 tbsp almonds, chopped

NUTRIENTS: Calories: 1,585, Fat: 112 g, Sat. Fat: 19 g, Carbs: 69 g, Fiber: 22 g, Sugars: 22 g, Protein: 85 g, Sodium: 1,691 mg, Cholesterol: 509 mg

WEEK 1

Monday

Breakfast: ¾ cup cooked hot cereal with ½ cup milk, 1 sliced banana and 1 tsp honey

Snack: 1 apple and 2 tbsp peanut butter

Lunch: *Salmon Arugula Salad:* 4 oz salmon, broiled, with 1 tbsp strawberry jam, 3 cups arugula, 10 pecans, ½ cup each chopped cucumber and carrots, 2 tsp apple cider vinegar and 1 tsp EVOO

8 crackers

Snack: ½ mango, peeled and diced, with ½ cup Greek yogurt

Dinner: 1 serving *Spinach & Potato Puffs* (p. 81; save leftovers)

1 cup corn and vegetable soup

1 cup blackberries

NUTRIENTS: Calories: 1,740, Fat: 70 g, Sat. Fat: 23 g, Carbs: 214 g, Fiber: 33 g, Sugars: 102 g, Protein: 73 g, Sodium: 1,256 mg, Cholesterol: 212 mg

Tuesday

Breakfast: ¾ cup cold cereal with 1 cup milk and 1 cup sliced strawberries

Snack: ½ mango, peeled and diced, with 1 cup cooked black beans and 2 tbsp chopped cilantro

Lunch: *Turkey Sandwich:* 3 oz sliced turkey breast, 2 thin slices avocado, 1 tsp Dijon mustard and 2 slices toasted bread

Fennel Salad: 1 cup sliced fennel with ¼ cup diced red bell pepper, 2 tsp apple cider vinegar and 1 tsp EVOO

Snack: 1 peeled and sliced kiwi

¼ cup pistachios

Dinner: 1 serving *Chicken Parmesan with Cheesy Eggplant Stacks* (see recipe, p. 96)

NUTRIENTS: Calories: 1,667, fat: 54 g, sat. Fat: 13 g, Carbs: 202.5 g, Fiber: 45 g, Sugars: 67 g, Protein: 102 g, Sodium: 1,126 mg, Cholesterol: 171 mg

Wednesday

Breakfast: 1 tbsp peanut butter mixed with ½ cup ricotta, ¼ tsp cinnamon and 1 tsp honey and spread on 1 toasted English muffin

1 apple

Snack: 1 cup sliced strawberries and 10 pecans

Lunch: 1 serving *Spinach & Potato Puffs* (leftovers, p. 87)

4 cups chopped romaine lettuce, 1 chopped hard-boiled egg and 2 slices red onion with 2 tsp apple cider vinegar and 1 tsp EVOO

Snack: 1 cup corn and vegetable soup with 8 crackers

1 cup blackberries

Dinner: 1 serving *Roasted Vegetable & Arugula Salad* (p. 102; save leftovers)

4 oz chicken breast, broiled, topped with 2 slices lemon; 15 red grapes

NUTRIENTS: Calories: 1,750, Fat: 71 g, sat. Fat: 23.5 g, Carbs: 192 g, Fiber: 38 g, Sugars: 88 g, Protein: 96 g, Sodium: 1,689 mg, Cholesterol: 479 mg

Thursday

Breakfast: ¾ cup cooked hot cereal mixed with 1 cup blackberries, 1 tsp honey and 10 chopped almonds

Snack: 1 sliced banana and 1½ oz goat cheese

Lunch: 1 serving *Roasted Vegetable & Arugula Salad* (leftovers, p. 102) with 1½ cups cooked black beans, 2 tbsp chopped cilantro and ¼ cup Greek yogurt

Snack: 1 apple and ¼ cup hummus

Dinner: *Basil Shrimp & Peas:* ½ lb shrimp, cooked, 2 cups each cooked brown rice and cooked peas, 1 cup shredded basil, 2 tsp lemon zest and juice 1 lemon tossed with 1 diced yellow onion, sautéed (eat half; save leftovers)

NUTRIENTS: Calories: 1,786, Fat: 42 g, Sat. Fat: 16.5 g, Carbs: 279 g, Fiber: 66 g, Sugars: 75.5 G, Protein: 89 g, Sodium: 1,112 mg, Cholesterol: 171 mg

Friday

Breakfast: ½ cup ricotta puréed with 1 tbsp strawberry jam, ½ mashed banana, 1 tbsp flaxseed

Snack: ¼ cup pistachios

10 cherries with ½ cup Greek yogurt

Lunch: 1 serving *Curried Chicken Salad with Mango & Cashews* (p. 80)

Snack: 1 cup *Kiwi Smoothie* (p. 314)

1 oz cheddar cheese

Dinner: 1 serving *Roasted Vegetable & Arugula Salad* (leftovers, p. 102) mixed with 3 oz pork tenderloin, cooked and diced, and 1 large baked white potato, diced

NUTRIENTS: Calories: 1,911, Fat: 92 g, Sat. Fat: 35.5 g, Carbs: 186 g, Fiber: 29 g, Sugars: 75 g, Protein: 100 g, Sodium: 1,019 mg, Cholesterol: 250 mg

Saturday

Breakfast: ¾ cup cold cereal with ½ cup milk and 10 halved cherries

Snack: ½ sliced red bell pepper with 2 tbsp hummus

Lunch: *Chicken Spinach Salad:* 1 cup chicken breast, cooked and diced, 4 cups chopped raw spinach, 1 cup each shredded carrot and cucumber; whisk 2 tbsp peanut butter, 1 tbsp water, 2 tsp apple cider vinegar and 1 tsp honey and toss over veggies

Snack: 8 crackers

15 red grapes

Dinner: 4 oz lean sirloin steak, broiled, topped with ½ oz goat cheese and 2 cups cooked Swiss chard sautéed with 1 minced clove garlic and ½ tsp olive oil

1 large baked white potato topped with 1 tbsp Greek yogurt

1 cup blackberries

NUTRIENTS: Calories: 1,706, Fat: 52 g, Sat. Fat: 15 g, Carbs: 211 g, Fiber: 39 g, Sugars: 63 g, Protein: 114 g, Sodium: 1,737 mg, Cholesterol: 214 mg

Sunday

Breakfast: 2 eggs scrambled in 1 tsp olive oil

1 toasted English muffin with 2 tbsp strawberry jam

Snack: 1 cup *Kiwi Smoothie* (p. 314)

10 cherries

10 whole almonds

Lunch: *Basil Shrimp & Peas* (leftovers)

Snack: ½ cup Greek yogurt with 1 sliced banana and ½ cup sliced strawberries

Dinner: 4 oz chicken breast, broiled, topped with 1 cup cooked carrots, puréed, with 1 tsp EVOO, 1 tsp honey and a dash of chipotle chile powder 1 cup sliced fennel bulb and 1 cup sliced red onion, sautéed with 1 tsp olive oil

1½ cups sliced baked beets

NUTRIENTS: Calories: 1,847, Fat: 52 g, Sat. Fat: 17 g, Carbs: 256 g, Fiber: 47 g, Sugars: 114 g, Protein: 106 g, Sodium: 1,158 mg, Cholesterol: 617 mg

EVOO = extra-virgin olive oil
ACV = apple cider vinegar

Monday

Breakfast: *Berry Parfait:* ½ cup Greek yogurt puréed with ½ cup ricotta and topped with 1 cup raspberries and ¼ cup cold cereal, crushed

Snack: 1 cup sliced apricots; 1 granola bar

Lunch: *Mushroom Cheese Sandwich* Sauté 1 cup sliced cremini mushrooms with 1 tsp olive oil and ¼ cup chopped yellow onion; top 1 slice bread, toasted, with ¼ cup shredded Swiss cheese, ¼ tsp chopped thyme and mushroom mixture; cover with 1 slice bread, toasted

1 cup frozen sliced peaches

Snack: 2 stalks celery and 2 tbsp hummus

Dinner: 1 serving *Balsamic Cherry Pork Tenderloin with Crispy Asparagus* (p. 98)

NUTRIENTS: Calories: 1,372, Fat: 55 g, Sat. Fat: 27.5 g, carbs: 149 g, Fiber: 28 g, Sugars: 62 g, Protein: 80 g, Sodium: 1,013 mg, Cholesterol: 252 mg

Tuesday

Breakfast: ¾ cup cooked hot cereal with 1 tsp honey, 2 tbsp raisins, ⅛ tsp cinnamon and ½ cup milk

Snack: 1 banana, mashed, with ½ cup ricotta and 1 tbsp almond butter

Lunch: *Thai Coconut Tofu:* 6 oz tofu, ½ cup each shredded carrot and zucchini, and 1½ cups cooked rice noodles topped with mixture of ½ cup coconut milk, 2 tbsp peanut butter, 2 tbsp chopped cilantro, juice of ½ lime, ½ cup water and 1 tbsp chopped peanuts (eat half; save leftovers)

Snack: 15 red grapes; 1 oz Swiss cheese

Dinner: 1 serving *Lamb Roast with Fava Bean Mash* (p. 105; save leftovers)

1 sliced and steamed zucchini

NUTRIENTS: Calories: 1,825, Fat: 76 g, Sat. Fat: 33.5 g, Carbs: 209 g, Fiber: 23 g, Sugars: 62.5 g, Protein: 87 g, Sodium: 918 mg, Cholesterol: 175 mg

Wednesday

Breakfast: 2 eggs, scrambled in 1 tsp olive oil, ½ cup beet greens cooked in ½ tsp oil, and 1 oz Swiss cheese on 1 toasted English muffin

Snack: 1 orange

1 granola bar

Lunch: 1 serving *Lamb Roast with Fava Bean Mash* (leftovers, p. 105)

Snack: 1 cup frozen sliced peaches, puréed, with ½ cup Greek yogurt

14 walnuts

Dinner: 1 serving *Red Curry Chicken Soup with Rice Noodles* (p. 107)

NUTRIENTS: Calories: 1,787, Fat: 90 g, Sat. Fat: 42.5 g, Carbs: 155 g, Fiber: 23 g, Sugars: 49 g, Protein: 98 g, Sodium: 1,484 mg, Cholesterol: 553 mg

Thursday

Breakfast: ¾ cup cold cereal with 1 cup milk and 1 sliced banana

Snack: 2 oz ground pork, cooked, and ½ cup cooked sliced cremini mushrooms on 2 slices bread

1 cup sliced apricots

Lunch: *Cod Salad:* 2 cups each raw spinach and chopped romaine lettuce, 4 oz cod fillet, broiled, 1 small white baked potato, diced, ½ cup cooked green beans with 1 tsp EVOO, 1 tsp apple cider vinegar and 1 tsp Dijon mustard

Snack: 1 cup raspberries

1 oz Swiss cheese

Dinner: *Thai Coconut Tofu* (leftovers)

1 cup cooked edamame with ½ tsp minced ginger and 1 tsp soy sauce

NUTRIENTS: Calories: 1,851, Fat: 65 g, Sat. Fat: 26 g, Carbs: 230 g, Fiber: 43 g, Sugars: 64 g, Protein: 99 g, Sodium: 1,050 mg, Cholesterol: 131 mg

Friday

Breakfast: *Cherry Chocolate Coconut Smoothie* (p. 314)

1 hard-boiled egg

Snack: Dice 1 cooked Yukon Gold potato, 1 cup cooked green beans and 1 cup tomato; add 1 tsp EVOO and 2 tsp apple cider vinegar

Lunch: 3 oz *Lamb Roast* (leftovers, p. 81), diced, with 1½ cup cooked quinoa, 3 tbsp raisins and 1 tsp each lemon zest and lemon juice 2 stalks celery and 6 carrot sticks with ¼ cup hummus

Snack: 15 red grapes

7 walnuts

Dinner: 1 serving *Mixed Mushroom Stew with Pork & Orzo* (p. 100; save leftovers)

2 cups steamed spinach

NUTRIENTS: Calories: 1,660, Fat: 55 g, Sat. Fat: 10.5 g, Carbs: 229 g, Fiber: 37 g, Sugars: 64 g, Protein: 86 g, Sodium: 906 mg, Cholesterol: 299 mg

Saturday

Breakfast: ¾ cup cooked hot cereal with 2 tsp maple syrup, 2 tbsp crushed walnuts and 1 cup raspberries

Snack: 1 orange

½ cup steamed edamame

Lunch: *Fava Bean Soup:* Cook 2 cups fava beans with 2 cups chicken broth, 1 minced clove garlic and 1 chopped small tomato for 20 minutes on medium; purée (eat 2 cups; save leftovers)

1 toasted English muffin

Snack: 1 banana and 1 tbsp almond butter

Dinner: 3 oz ground chicken breast, formed into 3 1-oz meatballs; cook with 2 cups chopped tomato, 1 tsp EVOO and 1 minced clove garlic; pour over 1 cup cooked orzo

1 cup steamed green beans

NUTRIENTS: Calories: 1,690, Fat: 42 g, Sat. Fat: 6 g, Carbs: 267 g, Fiber: 51 g, Sugars: 70 g, Protein: 85 g, Sodium: 623 mg, Cholesterol: 62 mg

Sunday

Breakfast: 1 granola bar, chopped, over ¾ cup Greek yogurt, 2 tbsp chopped peanuts and 1 tsp honey

Snack: *Cherry Chocolate Coconut Smoothie* (p. 314)

Lunch: 1 serving *Mixed Mushroom Stew with Pork & Orzo* (leftovers, p. 100)

1 cup steamed carrots

Snack: 1 cup *Fava Bean Soup* (leftovers) topped with ¼ cup chopped tomato and garnished with 1 apricot, chopped

Dinner: 4 oz tofu with 1 cooked large white potato, diced, 1 cup cooked edamame, ½ cup chopped cooked beet greens, ½ tsp each minced ginger and orange zest, 1 tsp maple syrup and 1 tsp soy sauce

NUTRIENTS: Calories: 1,690, Fat: 58 g, Sat. Fat: 19.5 g, Carbs: 227 g, Fiber: 41 g, Sugars: 64 g, Protein: 90 g, Sodium: 1,126 mg, Cholesterol: 57 mg

WEEK 1

Monday

Breakfast: *Peach Almond Cereal:* Top ¾ cup cereal with 1 peach, sliced, ¾ cup milk and 1 tbsp sliced almonds

Snack: 2 *Almond Biscotti Energy Balls* (p. 150; save leftovers)

Lunch: *Edamame & Quinoa Salad:* Toss together 1 cup cooked quinoa, ½ cup thawed shelled edamame, 1 cup chopped and sautéed yellow squash, 2 tbsp cilantro, 1 tbsp tamari, 1 tsp each sesame seeds and EVOO, and pinch cayenne

1 cup grapes

Snack: 1 cup sliced red bell pepper with 2 tbsp hummus

Dinner: 1 serving *Spicy Lentil Meatball Tacos with Lime Pepita Cream* (p. 190; save leftovers)

1 cup chopped pineapple

Tuesday

Breakfast: Tropical Smoothie: Blend 1 cup milk, ½ frozen banana, 5 strawberries, ½ cup chopped pineapple, 2 tbsp ground flaxseeds and ¼ cup protein powder with ice

Snack: 1 cup sliced strawberries

1 oz walnuts

Lunch: 1 serving *Spicy Lentil Meatball Tacos with Lime Pepita Cream* (leftovers, p. 190)

1 cup grapes

Snack: 1 oz crackers with 1½ tbsp almond butter

Dinner: *Summertime Salad:* Toss 3 cups mixed greens, ¼ cup dry-roasted edamame, ¼ cup each chopped cucumber, red bell pepper and tomato, 1 tbsp each chopped onion, goji berries and sliced almonds with 1½ tbsp balsamic vinegar mixed with ½ tsp tamari and 1 tsp EVOO

Wednesday

Breakfast: 2 *Almond Biscotti Energy Balls* (leftovers, p. 150)

1 cup sliced strawberries

Snack: 1 oz crackers with 2 tbsp hummus

Lunch: *Almond Butter & Strawberry Sandwich:* Spread 2 tbsp almond butter over 2 slices bread; top with 2 strawberries, thinly sliced, and 1 tsp maple syrup

1 peach

1 carrot, sliced

Snack: *Banana Smoothie:* Blend 1 cup milk, ½ frozen banana, 1 tbsp ground flaxseeds and ¼ cup protein powder with ice

Dinner: *Veggie Burger:* Place 1 cooked veggie burger, 1 slice tomato, 1 slice onion, 4 thin slices cucumber, 1 tbsp yeast seasoning and 1 tbsp cilantro between 2 slices bread, toasted

Cucumber & Onion Salad (p. 314)

1 cup chopped pineapple

NUTRIENTS: Calories: 1,833, Fat: 67 g, Sat. Fat: 10.5 g, Carbs: 256 g, Fiber: 47 g, Sugars: 94 g, Protein: 69 g, Sodium: 1,347 mg, Cholesterol: 71 mg

NUTRIENTS: Calories: 1,840, Fat: 83 g, Sat. Fat: 10.5 g, Carbs: 198 g, Fiber: 48 g, Sugars: 79 g, Protein: 84 g, Sodium: 1,257 mg, Cholesterol: 74 mg

NUTRIENTS: Calories: 1,657, Fat: 67 g, Sat. Fat: 7 g, Carbs: 210 g, Fiber: 40 g, Sugars: 71 g, Protein: 72 g, Sodium: 1,685 mg, Cholesterol: 0 mg

Thursday

Breakfast: *Grape Cereal:* Top ¾ cup cereal with ½ cup grapes, halved, ¾ cup milk and 1 tbsp sliced almonds

½ cup grapes

Snack: 1 oz crackers with 1½ tbsp nut butter

Lunch: *Summer Salad Plus Protein:* Toss 3 cups mixed greens with 1 cup chickpeas, ¼ cup each chopped cucumber, tomato and orange bell pepper, 1 tbsp each chopped onion and pepitas; dress with 1½ tbsp balsamic vinegar mixed with 1 tsp each EVOO and cilantro, ½ tsp maple syrup and pinch each salt and pepper; top with 1 hard-boiled egg, sliced

1 cup blackberries

Snack: *Simple Trail Mix:* ¾ oz walnuts and 1 tbsp goji berries

Dinner: *Lentil Meatball Bowl:* Combine ½ cup cooked farro and 3 *Lentil Meatballs*, halved; top with ¼ cup *Lime Pepita Cream* (leftovers, p. 190)

Cucumber & Onion Salad (p. 314)

Friday

Breakfast: *Berry Yogurt:* Top 6 oz Greek yogurt with ¾ cup blackberries and 1 tbsp sliced almonds

Snack: 2 *Almond Biscotti Energy Balls* (leftovers, p. 150)

Lunch: Smear 1 whole-grain bun with *Sweet Pea Ricotta Spread* (see recipe, p. 60; save leftovers); stuff with 1 slice eggplant, roasted and 2 hard-boiled eggs, sliced

Snack: ¼ cup dry-roasted edamame

1 nectarine

Dinner: *Grilled Portobellos and Squash:* Brush 2 portobello mushroom caps and ½ yellow squash, halved lengthwise, with mixture of 1 tbsp balsamic vinegar, 2 tsp EVOO and ⅛ tsp each garlic powder and dried rosemary; grill

1 cup cooked quinoa mixed with ¼ cup chickpeas and 3 tbsp chopped cilantro

1 cup chopped pineapple

Saturday

Breakfast: *Avocado Toast:* Mash 3 tbsp avocado with ¼ cup diced tomato and ½ tsp lime juice; spread over 2 slices bread; top with 2 tsp pepitas and 1 tsp cilantro

½ cup chopped pineapple

Snack: *Strawberry Smoothie:* Blend 1 cup milk, ½ cup strawberries and 2 tbsp protein powder with ice

Lunch: *Lentil Meatball Quinoa:* Combine ½ cup cooked quinoa, ½ cup chickpeas and 3 *Lentil Meatballs*, halved; top with ¼ cup *Lime Pepita Cream* (leftovers, p. 190)

1 cup grapes

Snack: 1 cup carrot sticks with 2 tbsp hummus

Dinner: *Rosemary Tempeh* (p. 314)

1 cup green beans, steamed; with 1 tbsp sliced almonds

1 sweet potato, cubed, baked; with 1 tbsp each balsamic vinegar, maple syrup and EVOO and pinch salt

Sunday

Breakfast: *Banana Cereal:* Top ¾ cup cereal with 1 banana, sliced, ¾ cup milk and 1 tbsp sliced almonds

Snack: *Berry Yogurt:* Top 6 oz Greek yogurt with ½ cup sliced strawberries

Lunch: *Tempeh Salad:* Toss 3 oz *Rosemary Tempeh* (leftovers) with ¾ cup cooked quinoa, ½ cup steamed green beans, chopped, and ¼ tsp sesame seeds

1 nectarine

Snack: 2 *Almond Biscotti Energy Balls* (leftovers, p. 150)

Dinner: 1 whole-grain bun with 1 cooked veggie burger, 1 slice eggplant, roasted, and *Sweet Pea Ricotta Spread* (leftovers, p. 315)

Toss 2 cups mixed greens with 1 cup chopped orange bell pepper; dress with 1 tbsp balsamic vinegar mixed with 1 tsp each EVOO and minced onion, and pinch each salt and pepper

NUTRIENTS: Calories: 1,960, Fat: 69 g, Sat. Fat: 9 g, Carbs: 274 g, Fiber: 54 g, Sugars: 69 g, Protein: 69 g, Sodium: 1,498 mg, Cholesterol: 274 mg

NUTRIENTS: Calories: 1,702, Fat: 73 g, Sat. Fat: 21.5 g, Carbs: 190 g, Fiber: 43 g, Sugars: 64 g, Protein: 74 g, Sodium: 1,253 mg, Cholesterol: 500 mg

NUTRIENTS: Calories: 1,849, Fat: 61 g, Sat. Fat: 10 g, Carbs: 259 g, Fiber: 53 g, Sugars: 82 g, Protein: 91 g, Sodium: 2,064 mg, Cholesterol: 62 mg

NUTRIENTS: Calories: 1,756, Fat: 69 g, Sat. Fat: 19 g, Carbs: 231 g, Fiber: 40 g, Sugars: 69 g, Protein: 67 g, Sodium: 1,835 mg, Cholesterol: 76 mg

EVOO = extra-virgin olive oil
ACV = apple cider vinegar

Monday

Breakfast: *Yogurt Oats:* Combine 6 oz Greek yogurt, 1 cup blueberries, ¼ cup uncooked oats and 1 tsp ground flaxseeds

Snack: 2 *Almond Biscotti Energy Balls* (leftovers, p. 150, thawed)

Lunch: *Quick Veggie Salad:* Toss 3 cups mixed greens, 1 cup kidney beans, ¼ cup each chopped cucumber and red bell pepper, 1 tbsp each chopped onion, pepitas and yeast seasoning; dress with 1½ tbsp balsamic vinegar mixed with 1 tsp EVOO and pinch each salt and pepper

2 plums

Snack: 1 cup snap peas with 2 tbsp hummus

¼ cup dry-roasted edamame

Dinner: 1 serving *Eggplant Hero* (see recipe, p. 175; save leftovers)

1 cup chopped watermelon

Tuesday

Breakfast: *Peach Cereal:* Top ¾ cup cereal with 1 peach, sliced, and ¾ cup milk

Snack: 2 *Almond Biscotti Energy Balls* (leftovers, p. 150, thawed)

Lunch: 1 serving *Eggplant Hero* (leftovers, p. 175)

2 plums

Snack: *Simple Trail Mix:* ¾ oz walnuts and 1 tbsp goji berries

Dinner: *Veggie Burger Bowl:* Toss 1 cooked veggie burger, chopped, with 1 cup cooked quinoa, ½ cup thawed shelled edamame and 2 tbsp each chopped carrot and cucumber; top with ¼ cup chopped avocado and 1 tbsp chopped scallions

1 cup chopped watermelon

Wednesday

Breakfast: 2 *Almond Biscotti Energy Balls* (leftovers, p. 150, thawed)

1 egg, hard-boiled

Snack: 1 cup blueberries

1 oz walnuts

Lunch: *Cucumber Kale Wraps with Zesty Peanut Sauce* (p. 166)

Snack: 1 oz crackers with 3 tbsp avocado, mashed

Dinner: *Stuffed Portobellos:* Brush 2 portobello mushroom caps with 1 tbsp balsamic vinegar mixed with 2 tsp EVOO and 1 clove garlic, minced; bake, then stuff with mixture of ¼ cup each cooked quinoa and diced tomato, 2 tsp each yeast seasoning, sliced almonds and chopped basil, and pinch each salt and pepper

1½ cups chopped watermelon

NUTRIENTS: Calories: 1,710, Fat: 63 g, Sat. Fat: 17 g, Carbs: 212 g, Fiber: 50 g, Sugars: 88 g, Protein: 73 g, Sodium: 1,360 mg, Cholesterol: 148 mg

NUTRIENTS: Calories: 1,834, Fat: 81 g, Sat. Fat: 11 g, Carbs: 249 g, Fiber: 49 g, Sugars: 87 g, Protein: 71 g, Sodium: 1,891 mg, Cholesterol: 111 mg

NUTRIENTS: Calories: 1,095, Fat: 62 g, Sat. Fat: 8 g, Carbs: 113 g, Fiber: 22 g, Sugars: 45 g, Protein: 33 g, Sodium: 316 mg, Cholesterol: 187 mg

Thursday

Breakfast: *Strawberry Cereal:* Top ¾ cup cereal with ½ cup sliced strawberries and ¾ cup milk

½ cup sliced strawberries

Snack: ¼ cup pepitas

1 tbsp goji berries

Lunch: *Almond Butter & Maple Sandwich:* Spread 2 tbsp almond butter on 2 slices bread; drizzle with 2 tsp maple syrup

1 cup carrot sticks

1 peach

Snack: ¼ cup dry-roasted edamame

2 plums

Dinner: 1 serving *Vegetable & Tempeh Coconut Curry* (p. 192; save leftovers)

Friday

Breakfast: *Watermelon Smoothie:* Blend 2 cups chopped watermelon, ½ cup milk, ½ cup coconut milk and ¼ cup protein powder with ice

Snack: 2 *Almond Biscotti Energy Balls* (leftovers, p. 150, thawed)

Lunch: 1 serving *Vegetable & Tempeh Coconut Curry* (leftovers, p. 192)

Snack: 1 cup sliced strawberries

Dinner: *Roasted Vegetable Medley:* Toss 1½ cups chopped sweet potato, 1 cup chopped zucchini, ½ cup each chopped carrot and sliced onion with 2 tsp EVOO, 2 tbsp yeast seasoning, 1 tsp rosemary and ⅛ tsp each salt and pepper; roast

Kidney Beans & Greens Salad (p. 314)

Saturday

Breakfast: Spread 2 tbsp almond butter on 2 slices bread, toasted; drizzle with 2 tsp maple syrup

Snack: 1 cup raspberries

Lunch: *Seed & Nut Salad:* Toss 1 cup cooked quinoa with ½ cup each chopped red bell pepper and thawed shelled edamame, 2 tbsp each pepitas and chopped walnuts, 1 tbsp each goji berries, yeast seasoning and chopped scallions and 1 tsp each tamari and sesame seeds

1 peach

Snack: ½ cup sliced zucchini

1 carrot, sliced, 3 tbsp hummus

Dinner: *Grilled Veggie Burger:* Place 1 grilled veggie burger, ¼ cup mixed greens, 1 slice each tomato and onion and 1 tbsp yeast seasoning on a bun

1 ear of corn, grilled, with 2 tsp olive oil spread

1 cup chopped watermelon

Sunday

Breakfast: *Raspberry Cereal:* Top ¾ cup cereal with 1 cup raspberries and ¾ cup milk

Snack: ½ oz walnuts

1 oz crackers

Lunch: 1 serving *Vegetable & Tempeh Coconut Curry* (leftovers, p. 192)

2 plums

Snack: 1 banana, sliced, with 1½ tbsp almond butter

Dinner: *Rainbow Salad with Beets, Kale & Avocado Dressing* (p. 184)

NUTRIENTS: Calories: 1,696, Fat: 68.5 g, Sat. Fat: 16 g, Carbs: 208 g, Fiber: 54 g, Sugars: 72 g, Protein: 72 g, Sodium: 1,112 mg Cholesterol: 0 mg

NUTRIENTS: Calories: 1,903, Fat: 80.5 g, Sat. Fat: 36 g, Carbs: 225 g, Fiber: 51 g, Sugars: 92 g, Protein: 89 g, Sodium: 1,484 mg, Cholesterol: 3 mg

NUTRIENTS: Calories: 1,753, Fat: 73 g, Sat. Fat: 9 g, Carbs: 235 g, Fiber: 50 g, Sugars: 70 g, Protein: 66 g, Sodium: 1,916 mg, Cholesterol: 0 mg

NUTRIENTS: Calories: 1,349, Fat: 57.5 g, Sat. Fat: 14 g, Carbs: 184 g, Fiber: 48 g, Sugars: 48 g, Protein: 47 g, Sodium: 701 mg, Cholesterol: 3 mg

WEEK 3

Monday

Breakfast: *Blueberry Ginger Smoothie:*
Blend 1 cup non-dairy milk, 1 cup spinach, 1 cup blueberries, 1 scoop protein power, 1 tbsp chia seeds and 1-inch piece ginger, peeled, with ice

2 hard-boiled eggs

Snack: 12 crackers and 1 carrot, sliced, with ¼ cup salsa

Lunch: *Asian Quinoa Salad:* Cook 1 cup quinoa and 1 cup frozen edamame separately; in a large bowl, whisk 3 tbsp soy sauce, ½ tbsp maple syrup and 1 tsp sesame oil; add quinoa, edamame, 1 cup grape tomatoes and ⅛ red onion, sliced; toss (eat one-third of salad; save leftovers)

Snack: 1 serving *Raspberry Lime Squares* (p. 150; save leftovers)

Dinner: 1 serving *Ginger Chicken Fajitas with Cashew Sour Cream* (see recipe, right; save leftovers)

1 peach

NUTRIENTS: Calories: 1,558, Fat: 67.5 g, Sat. Fat: 16 g, Carbs: 156 g, Fiber: 30 g, Sugars: 51 g, Protein: 95 g, Sodium: 1,941 mg, Cholesterol: 442 mg

Tuesday

Breakfast: ¾ cup muesli with 1 tbsp chia seeds and ½ cup non-dairy milk

Snack: 1 serving *Raspberry Lime Squares* (leftovers, p. 150)

Lunch: *Veggie Chop Salad* (p. 315)

Snack: 1 apple, ½ oz almonds

Dinner: *Maple Pecan Salmon:* Combine ¾ cup chopped pecans, ¼ cup maple syrup and ¼ tsp cayenne pepper; spread a thin layer of Dijon mustard over 3 salmon fillets, top with pecan mixture and bake, uncovered, at 425°F for 20 minutes (eat 1 fillet; save leftovers)

2 cups broccoli florets, steamed, with ¼ tsp salt

NUTRIENTS: Calories: 1,848, Fat: 104 g, Sat. Fat: 18 g, Carbs: 184 g, Fiber: 44 g, Sugars: 74 g, Protein: 64 g, Sodium: 1,096 mg, Cholesterol: 53 mg

Wednesday

Breakfast: *Blueberry Ginger Smoothie:*
Blend 1 cup non-dairy milk, 1 cup spinach, 1 cup blueberries, 1 scoop protein power, 1 tbsp chia seeds and 1-inch piece ginger, peeled, with ice

Snack: 1 serving *Raspberry Lime Squares* (leftovers, p. 150)

Lunch: 1 serving *Asian Quinoa Salad* (leftovers)

Snack: 2 hard-boiled eggs with 12 crackers

1 peach

Dinner: 1 serving *Ginger Chicken Fajitas with Cashew Sour Cream* (leftovers, p. 150)

1 carrot and 1 stalk celery, sliced, with 2 tbsp salsa

NUTRIENTS: Calories: 1,559, Fat: 68 g, Sat. Fat: 16 g, Carbs: 155 g, Fiber: 31 g, Sugars: 50 g, Protein: 95 g, Sodium: 1,893 mg, Cholesterol: 442 mg

Thursday

Breakfast: *Eggs Over Spinach:*
Sauté ¼ red onion, chopped, in 1 tbsp coconut oil; add 2 cups spinach and sauté until soft; move to side of pan and add 2 eggs; cook over easy; serve with dash hot sauce

Snack: 1 apple, ½ oz almonds

Lunch: 1 serving *Asian Quinoa Salad* (leftovers)

Snack: 1 stalk celery and 1 carrot, sliced, with ⅓ cup hummus

Dinner: 1 serving *Maple Pecan Salmon* (leftovers), reheated

2 cups broccoli florets, steamed

1 peach

NUTRIENTS: Calories: 1,463, Fat: 74 g, Sat. Fat: 21 g, Carbs: 144 g, Fiber: 32 g, Sugars: 59 g, Protein: 71 g, Sodium: 1,433 mg, Cholesterol: 422 mg

Friday

Breakfast: *Blueberry Ginger Smoothie:* Blend 1 cup non-dairy milk, 1 cup spinach, 1 cup blueberries, 1 scoop protein powder, 1 tbsp chia seeds and 1-inch piece ginger, peeled, with ice

Snack: 1 apple, ½ oz almonds

Lunch: 1 serving *Maple Pecan Salmon* (leftovers), reheated 2 cups broccoli florets, steamed

Snack: 1 serving *Raspberry Lime Squares* (leftovers, p. 150)

Dinner: *Deconstructed Fajitas:* In ½ tsp EVOO, sauté remaining Swiss chard, chopped, chicken and cashew cream (leftovers); stir in 2 tbsp salsa

NUTRIENTS: Calories: 1,517, Fat: 79 g, Sat. Fat: 15 g, Carbs: 124 g, Fiber: 30 g, Sugars: 65 g, Protein: 96 g, Sodium: 1,110 mg, Cholesterol: 122 mg

Saturday

Breakfast: ¾ cup muesli with 1 tbsp chia seeds and ½ cup non-dairy milk

Snack: 2 stalks celery with ⅓ cup hummus

Lunch: *Veggie Chop Salad* (p.315)

Snack: 1 hard-boiled egg with ⅛ tsp salt

Dinner: 1 serving *Herbed Skirt Steak Tacos with Beet & Fresno Chile Salsa* (p. 217)

NUTRIENTS: Calories: 1,608, Fat: 83 g, Sat. Fat: 14 g, Carbs: 160 g, Fiber: 39 g, Sugars: 40 g, Protein: 65 g, Sodium: 608 mg, Cholesterol: 256 mg

Sunday

Breakfast: *Eggs Over Spinach:*
Sauté ¼ red onion, chopped, in 1 tbsp coconut oil; add 2 cups spinach and sauté until soft; move to side of pan and add 2 eggs; cook over easy and serve with dash hot sauce

Snack: 2 stalks celery with ⅓ cup hummus

Lunch: 1 serving *Coconut Chicken Corn Chowder* (see recipe, p. 74)

Snack: 1 serving *Raspberry Lime Squares* (leftovers, p.150)

Dinner: *Veggie Chop Salad* (p. 315)

NUTRIENTS: Calories: 1,723, Fat: 115 g, Sat. Fat: 43.5 g, Carbs: 112 g, Fiber: 33 g, Sugars: 36 g, Protein: 75 g, Sodium: 1,271 mg, Cholesterol: 441 mg

EVOO = extra-virgin olive oil
ACV = apple cider vinegar

Monday

Breakfast: *Summer Omelette:* Sauté 2 chopped green onions, ¼ cup chopped fennel, 1 cup chopped Swiss chard, 1 tbsp chopped dill, pinch salt and pepper in 2 tsp EVOO; add 4 eggs, whisked with 1 tsp water, cook, flipping once (eat half; save leftovers); ½ cup cherries, 1 slice bread

Snack: 1 peach

½ oz walnuts

Lunch: *Halloumi Salad:* Toss 2 oz grilled halloumi, cubed, ½ cup chickpeas, ¼ cup each chopped cucumbers and sliced cherry tomatoes, 1 tbsp each chopped mint, parsley and dill, 1 cup arugula with 2 tsp each EVOO and lemon juice, pinch salt and pepper; serve with 3 oz tuna

Snack: 2 tbsp edamame hummus with ½ cucumber, cut into sticks

Dinner: 1 serving *Curried Apricot Pan-Roasted Chicken* (p. 191; save leftovers)

NUTRIENTS: Calories: 1,729, Fat: 87.5 g, Sat. Fat: 23 g, Carbs: 134 g, Fiber: 30.5 g, Sugars: 60.5 g, Protein: 112 g, Sodium: 1,941 mg, Cholesterol: 549 mg

Tuesday

Breakfast: *Strawberry Mint Smoothie:* Blend 1 cup kefir, 1 cup strawberries, 2 tbsp fresh mint, ½ cup ice, 1 tsp each honey and vanilla, 2 tbsp hemp seeds (eat half; freeze remaining half into a popsicle and reserve)

1 slice bread with 2 tsp peanut butter

Snack: 2 tbsp edamame hummus with ½ cucumber, cut into sticks

Lunch: *Summer Omelette* (leftovers)

½ cup cooked farro, 1 peach

Snack: 1 oz walnuts

½ cup cherries

Dinner: *Open-Faced Veggie Melts with Smoked Mozzarella* (p. 186)

NUTRIENTS: Calories: 1,372, Fat: 63 g, Sat. Fat: 13 g, Carbs: 151 g, Fiber: 30 g, Sugars: 48 g, Protein: 59 g, Sodium: 1,248 mg, Cholesterol: 412 mg

Wednesday

Breakfast: *Cherry Farro Parfait:* In a parfait glass, layer ⅔ cup cooked farro, 1 tbsp chopped toasted walnuts, ½ cup sliced pitted cherries, ½ cup kefir, 1 tsp hemp seeds, 2 tsp honey and dash cinnammon and nutmeg

Snack: 2 tbsp edamame hummus with ½ cup fennel slices

Lunch: 1 serving *Curried Apricot Pan-Roasted Chicken* (leftovers, p. 191)

Snack: 2 tsp peanut butter on ½ slice bread sprinkled with pinch each cinnamon and nutmeg, toasted

Dinner: *Barramundi with Herb Sauce* (p. 314) Trim asparagus bunch and brush with 3 tsp EVOO, pinch salt and pepper; grill; top with zest of 1 lemon (eat 4 spears; save leftovers)

1 cup cooked quinoa

NUTRIENTS: Calories: 1,731, Fat: 72 g, Sat. Fat: 13 g, Carbs: 182 g, Fiber: 31 g, Sugars: 59 g, Protein: 102 g, Sodium: 890 mg, Cholesterol: 195 mg

Thursday

Breakfast: *Green Egg Benny:* 4 asparagus spears (leftovers), plus 3 slices avocado topped with 1 over easy egg cooked in ½ tsp EVOO; drizzle with with one-quarter of *Herb Sauce* (leftovers)

Snack: Top ½ cup kefir with ½ cup sliced strawberries; drizzle with 1 tsp honey

Lunch: *Strawberry Kale Salad:* Toss 2 cups baby kale and ½ cup each sliced strawberries and cooked farro with 1 oz halloumi, grilled and diced, and 1 tbsp pistachios; whisk 2 tsp EVOO, 1 tsp balsamic vinegar, ½ tsp honey, pinch salt and pepper; drizzle over salad

1 slice bread

Snack: 2 tsp peanut butter on ½ peach, sliced

Dinner: 1 serving *Curried Apricot Pan-Roasted Chicken* (leftovers, p. 191)

NUTRIENTS: Calories: 1,687, Fat: 91 g, Sat. Fat: 22 g, Carbs: 151 g, Fiber: 33 g, Sugars: 59 g, Protein: 78 g, Sodium: 1,334 mg, Cholesterol: 339 mg

Friday

Breakfast: *Avocado Mash with Hemp Seed:* ¼ mashed avocado on 1 slice bread, sprinkle with 2 tbsp hemp seeds, ¼ tsp lemon zest and pinch each salt and pepper; 1 cup cherries

Snack: 2 tsp edamame hummus plus 4 asparagus spears (leftovers)

Lunch: *Halloumi Salad:* Toss 2 oz grilled halloumi, cubed, ½ cup chickpeas, ¼ cup each chopped cucumbers and sliced cherry tomatoes, 1 tbsp each chopped mint, parsley and dill, and 1 cup arugula with 2 tsp each EVOO and lemon juice, pinch salt and pepper; serve with 3 oz tuna

Strawberry Mint Smoothie Popsicle (leftovers)

Snack: ½ cup sliced fennel drizzled with one-quarter of *Herb Sauce* (leftovers)

Dinner: *Mediterranean Quinoa* (p. 197; save leftovers)

NUTRIENTS: Calories: 1,681, Fat: 96 g, Sat. Fat: 22 g, Carbs: 141 g, Fiber: 32 g, Sugars: 50 g, Protein: 77 g, Sodium: 1,881 mg, Cholesterol: 84 mg

Saturday

Breakfast: *Strawberry Farro Bowl:* 1 cup cooked farro with ½ cup kefir, ½ cup sliced strawberries, 2 tbsp chopped almonds, top with 1 tsp each honey and chopped fresh mint and dash each cinnammon and nutmeg

Snack: ½ slice bread with 2 tsp edamame hummus and ¼ cup sliced cherry tomatoes

Lunch: *Mediterranean Quinoa* (leftovers, p. 197)

Snack: 1 oz walnuts

1 orange

Dinner: *Grilled Steak & Romaine Hearts with Tangy Date Sauce* (p. 188)

NUTRIENTS: Calories: 1,503, Fat: 66 g, Sat. Fat: 12 g, Carbs: 180 g, Fiber: 32 g, Sugars: 57 g, Protein: 60 g, Sodium: 736 mg, Cholesterol: 83 mg

Sunday

Breakfast: *Clean Green Scramble:* Sauté 2 cups kale in 2 tsp EVOO; add 1 clove minced garlic, 2 tsp each chopped dill and parsley, 1 chopped green onion and pinch salt and pepper; transfer to a plate and scramble 2 eggs in same pan

½ peach

Snack: 1 cup kefir with 1 oz toasted almonds sprinkled with pinch each nutmeg and cinnamon and ¼ cup pitted fresh cherries

Lunch: *Sea & Pea Salad:* Combine 3 oz tuna with ½ cup chickpeas, 1 chopped green onion, ½ cup each chopped cucumber and sliced cherry tomatoes, 2 tsp EVOO, 1 tsp lemon juice and 1 tbsp each chopped dill and parsley

1 slice bread

Snack: ½ slice bread with 2 tsp edamame hummus and one-quarter of Herb Sauce (leftovers)

Dinner: *Mediterranean Quinoa* (leftovers, p. 197)

NUTRIENTS: Calories: 1,737, Fat: 102 g, Sat. Fat: 19 g, Carbs: 138 g, Fiber: 31 g, Sugars: 40 g, Protein: 80 g, Sodium: 1,401 mg, Cholesterol: 438 mg

Loaded Beef Gyro Bowl

(See recipe, p. 260)

Monday

Breakfast: *Avocado Egg Sandwich:* Between 2 slices toast, place 1 egg, scrambled in ¼ tsp EVOO, ¼ avocado, sliced, and 1 slice tomato

1 orange

Snack: 1 oz walnuts

Lunch: *Salmon Salad Sandwich:* Mix 6 oz canned salmon with remaining ¾ avocado, mashed, 1 tbsp diced red onion and ¼ tsp dill; spread two-thirds of salmon salad mixture between 2 slices bread and top with ¼ cup baby spinach (save remaining salmon salad for leftovers); 1 cup raspberries

Snack: 1 cup sliced cucumbers with 1 oz goat cheese

Dinner: 1 serving *Supercharged Chicken Parm* (p. 258; save leftovers)

½ cup canned chickpeas

NUTRIENTS: Calories: 1,668, Fat: 73 g, Sat. Fat: 13 g, Carbs: 154.5 g, Fiber: 51 g, Sugars: 41 g, Protein: 112 g, Sodium: 1,859 mg, Cholesterol: 441 mg:

Tuesday

Breakfast: *Salmon Toast:* On 2 slices toast, layer 8 thin cucumber slices and remaining one-third of salmon salad mixture (leftovers)

1 orange

Snack: *Nut & Seed Parfait:* Top ½ cup yogurt with 1 cup frozen berry blend, thawed, and 1 tbsp each walnuts and chia seeds; sprinkle with pinch maqui powder (optional)

Lunch: 1 serving *Supercharged Chicken Parm* (leftovers, p. 258)

½ cup canned chickpeas (leftovers)

Snack: *Mediterranean Power Snack:* 1 cup grape tomatoes, 5 olives and 1 oz goat cheese

Dinner: *Yacon, Spinach & Watercress Salad:* In a bowl, mix 1 cup each chopped spinach, watercress and sliced yacon, ¼ cup canned chickpeas (leftovers), 1 egg, hard-boiled and sliced, ½ oz goat cheese and ⅓ oz walnuts; top with 1½ tbsp lemon juice mixed with 2 tsp EVOO and pinch pepper; 1 slice bread, toasted, drizzled with ½ tsp EVOO

NUTRIENTS: Calories: 1,800, Fat: 78 g, Sat. Fat: 18 g, Carbs: 181 g, Fiber: 49 g, Sugars: 59.5 g, Protein: 106 g, Sodium: 2,336 mg, Cholesterol: 442 mg

Wednesday

Breakfast: *Blended Berry Oat Smoothie:* In a blender, combine ¼ cup oats, 1 cup kefir, ½ tsp maqui powder (optional) and 1 cup frozen berry blend; blend with ice

Snack: 1 apple with 1½ tbsp almond butter

Lunch: 1 serving *Mushroom Cashew Lettuce Wraps* (p. 242)

Snack: *Wild Sardine Toasts:* On 1 slice toast, spread ½ oz goat cheese; top with 1 oz shredded sardines (leftovers, see tip on p. 258) and ¼ tsp lemon zest

Dinner: 1 serving *Loaded Beef Gyro Bowl* (p. 260; save leftovers)

NUTRIENTS: Calories: 1,371, Fat: 62 g, Sat. Fat: 27 g, Carbs: 137 g, Fiber: 24 g, Sugars: 50 g, Protein: 74.5 g, Sodium: 1,966 mg, Cholesterol: 167 mg

Thursday

Breakfast: *Apple Cinnamon Oatmeal:* Cook ½ cup oats in 1 cup water with 1 apple, chopped; stir in 1 tbsp each chia seeds and chopped walnuts and ⅛ tsp cinnamon

1 cup kefir with ⅛ tsp cinnamon

Snack: 1 oz roasted chickpeas

Lunch: 1 serving *Loaded Beef Gyro Bowl* (leftovers, p. 260)

Snack: *Super Berries:* Toss 1 cup frozen berry blend, thawed, with ½ cup yogurt and 1 tbsp ground flaxseeds

Dinner: Pan-fry 4 oz pork in ½ tsp EVOO with 1 clove garlic, minced, and ½ tsp rosemary; 2 cups broccoli, sautéed in 1 tsp EVOO with 1 clove garlic, minced

1 sweet potato, baked and sprinkled with cinnamon

NUTRIENTS: Calories: 1,823, Fat: 75 g, Sat. Fat: 27 g, Carbs: 194 g, Fiber: 36 g, Sugars: 66 g, Protein: 99 g, Sodium: 1,654 mg, Cholesterol: 227 mg

Friday

Breakfast: *Almond Pear Smoothie:* In a blender, combine 1 cup kefir, 1 pear, chopped, 1 tbsp almond butter and ice, as desired

Snack: 1 cup red bell pepper strips with ¼ cup tzatziki (leftovers, p. 260)

Lunch: 1 serving *Supercharged Chicken Parm* (leftovers, p. 258), thawed and reheated with 1 cup cooked whole-wheat ziti; 2 cups chopped watercress with 1 tbsp lemon juice and 1 tsp EVOO

Snack: ¾ cup yogurt mixed with 1 frozen banana, thawed and mashed

Dinner: 4 oz mahi mahi; bake with 1 tbsp lemon juice, ½ tsp EVOO and pinch each garlic powder, salt and pepper; top with 2 tbsp tzatziki (leftovers, p. 260)

1 cup frozen corn, cooked and seasoned with salt and pepper

1 cup broccoli, steamed and seasoned with pepper

NUTRIENTS: Calories: 1,811, Fat: 74 g, Sat. Fat: 30 g, Carbs: 190.5 g, Fiber: 38 g, Sugars: 82 g, Protein: 115 g, Sodium: 2,126 mg, Cholesterol: 405 mg

Saturday

Breakfast: *Mushroom & Spinach Omelette:* Sauté 3 tbsp chopped mushroom stems and ½ cup baby spinach in ½ tsp EVOO; season with garlic powder and Italian seasoning; add 2 eggs, whisked with 1 tsp water; when eggs begin to set, add ½ oz goat cheese; cook until set and fold over

1 cup raspberries

Snack: 1 banana with 1½ tbsp almond butter

Lunch: *Red & Green Smoothie:* Blend 1 cup kefir, ½ cup yogurt, 2 cups spinach, 1 cup frozen berry blend, ½ cup seeded and chopped cucumber, ¼ cup oats and ½ tsp maqui powder (optional) with ice, as desired

Snack: 1½ oz roasted chickpeas

½ cup grape tomatoes

Dinner: 1 serving *Supercharged Chicken Parm* (leftovers, p. 258), thawed and reheated with 1 cup cooked whole-wheat ziti

NUTRIENTS: Calories: 1,619, Fat: 66 g, Sat. Fat: 20 g, Carbs: 166.5 g, Fiber: 44 g, Sugars: 62 g, Protein: 99 g, Sodium: 1,807 mg, Cholesterol: 598 mg

Sunday

Breakfast: *Monkey Toast:* 2 slices toast with 2 tbsp almond butter and ½ banana, sliced; remaining banana

Snack: ¾ cup yogurt with 1 orange, chopped, 1 tbsp chia seeds and pinch cinnamon

Lunch: 1 serving *Black Bean Tacos with Maqui Berry Salsa* (p. 238)

Snack: 1 egg, hard-boiled

Dinner: *Greek Burger:* Form 4 oz ground beef into a patty; season with salt and pepper; cook and place between 2 slices toast with 2 tbsp tzatziki and 1 slice each red onion and tomato

Chickpea Salad: Toss ½ cup each canned chickpeas (leftovers) and cucumber, ¼ cup each chopped tomato, watercress and frozen corn, thawed, and 1 tbsp each chopped basil, red onion and olives; season with 1½ tbsp vinegar and 1 tsp EVOO

NUTRIENTS: Calories: 1,839, Fat: 75.5 g, Sat. Fat: 23 g, Carbs: 216 g, Fiber: 41 g, Sugars: 61 g, Protein: 87 g, Sodium: 1,351 mg, Cholesterol: 356 mg

Monday

Breakfast: *Mango Smoothie:* Blend ½ frozen banana, ¼ cup mango, 1 cup spinach, 1 tbsp hemp seeds, 1 date and 1 cup almond milk

Snack: 2 tbsp hummus with 2 carrots, sliced, and 2 radishes, sliced

1 oz pepitas

Lunch: *Double-Protein Salad:* Top 2 cups spinach with 1 hard-boiled egg, sliced, ½ cup chickpeas, ¼ cup chopped cucumber, 1 tomato, sliced, and 1 tbsp chopped red onion; dress with 1 tsp avocado oil, 2 tsp ACV and pinch each salt and pepper

Snack: 2 *Almond Raspberry Thumbprint Cookies* (p. 235; save leftovers)

1 orange

Dinner: 1 serving *Pumpkin Turkey Lasagna with Spinach & Béchamel Sauce* (p. 255; save leftovers)

Tomato & Bread Salad (p.315)

NUTRIENTS: Calories: 1,778, Fat: 91 g, Sat. Fat: 30 g, Carbs: 174 g, Fiber: 41 g, Sugars: 73 g, Protein: 82 g, Sodium: 1,997 mg, Cholesterol: 283 Mg

Tuesday

Breakfast: *PB&J with Banana:* 2 slices bread, toasted, with 2 tbsp peanut butter, 2 tbsp raspberry jam and 1 banana, sliced

Snack: 2 tbsp hummus with 2 celery stalks and 2 radishes, sliced

1 oz pepitas

Lunch: 1 serving *Root Vegetable–Baked Quinoa with Kale & Goat Cheese* (p. 249; save leftovers)

Roast ½ cup sliced beets with ½ tbsp avocado oil and pinch each salt and pepper

Snack: 4 cups popcorn

Dinner: *Zucco Spaghetti with Walnut Ginger Pesto & Lemon Shrimp* (p. 259)

1 orange

NUTRIENTS: Calories: 1,722, Fat: 86.5 g, Sat. Fat: 14 g, Carbs: 185 g, Fiber: 38 g, Sugars: 62 g, Protein: 72 g, Sodium: 1,348 mg, Cholesterol: 179 mg

Wednesday

Breakfast: *Yogurt Parfait:* 1 cup yogurt topped with 1 banana, sliced, and 1 tbsp raspberry jam

Snack: 2 tbsp hummus with 2 celery stalks and 2 radishes, sliced

15 crackers

Lunch: *Tuna Salad:* Toss 2 cups mixed greens with 3 oz tuna, ¼ cup each chopped carrot and chopped celery; dress with 1 tbsp each avocado oil and ACV and pinch each salt and pepper

Snack: 2 *Almond Raspberry Thumbprint Cookies* (leftovers, p. 235, thawed)

1 orange

Dinner: 1 serving *Root Vegetable–Baked Quinoa with Kale & Goat Cheese* (leftovers, p. 249)

Garlicky Kale: Sauté 1 cup kale in 1 tbsp avocado oil with 1 clove garlic, minced, with pinch each salt and pepper

NUTRIENTS: Calories: 1,743, Fat: 106 g, Sat. Fat: 41 g, Carbs: 138 g, Fiber: 25 g, Sugars: 50 g, Protein: 69 g, Sodium: 1,445 mg, Cholesterol: 83 mg

Thursday

Breakfast: *Eggs 'n' Greens:* Toss 2 cups mixed greens with 1 tbsp each avocado oil and ACV and pinch each salt and pepper; top with 2 eggs, scrambled in 1 tsp avocado oil

Snack: *Green Mojito Juice* (p. 314; save leftovers)

Lunch: *Pumpkin Turkey Lasagna with Spinach & Béchamel Sauce* (leftovers, p. 255)

Cucumber Salad: ½ cup sliced cucumber with 1 tbsp each avocado oil and ACV and pinch each salt and pepper

Snack: 1 apple, sliced, with 2 tbsp peanut butter

Dinner: *Super-Stuffed Sweet Potato:* 1 sweet potato, baked and split, stuffed with ½ cup chopped yellow bell pepper, ½ cup black beans, ½ avocado, chopped, 2 tbsp chopped cilantro and pinch each salt and pepper

NUTRIENTS: Calories: 1,681, Fat: 92 g, Sat. Fat: 20 g, Carbs: 154 g, Fiber: 34.5 g, Sugars: 55 g, Protein: 70 g, Sodium: 1,110 mg, Cholesterol: 469 mg

Friday

Breakfast: *Cacao Cinnamon Smoothie:* Blend 1 frozen banana, 3 tbsp hemp seeds, 2 tbsp cacao powder, 1 tsp cinnamon, 1 date and 1 cup almond milk

Snack: 2 tbsp hummus and 2 celery stalks

15 crackers

Lunch: 2 hard-boiled eggs

Avocado Cucumber Salad: ½ avocado, sliced, and ½ cucumber, sliced; dress with 1 tbsp each avocado oil and ACV and pinch each salt and pepper

Snack: *Green Mojito Juice* (leftovers, p. 314)

Dinner: 1 serving *Root Vegetable–Baked Quinoa with Kale & Goat Cheese* (leftovers, p. 249)

Roast ½ cup sliced beets with ½ tbsp avocado oil and pinch each salt and pepper

NUTRIENTS: Calories: 1,534, Fat: 83 g, Sat. Fat: 18 g, Carbs: 154 g, Fiber: 30 g, Sugars: 53.5 g, Protein: 51 g, Sodium: 1,192 mg, Cholesterol: 394 mg

Saturday

Breakfast: *PB&J with Banana:* 2 slices bread, toasted, with 2 tbsp peanut butter, 2 tsp raspberry jam and ½ banana, sliced

Snack: *Green Mojito Juice* (leftovers, p. 314)

Lunch: *Pumpkin Turkey Lasagna with Spinach & Béchamel Sauce* (leftovers, p. 255, thawed)

Cucumber Salad: ½ cup sliced cucumber with 1 tsp avocado oil, 2 tsp ACV and pinch each salt and pepper

Snack: 2 tbsp hummus with 2 carrots, sliced

Dinner: *Veggie BLT with Coconut Bacon, Caramelized Leeks & Roasted Tomato* (p. 252)

NUTRIENTS: Calories: 1,591, Fat: 73 g, Sat. Fat: 22 g, Carbs: 182 g, Fiber: 32 g, Sugars: 63 g, Protein: 63 g, Sodium: 1,607 mg, Cholesterol: 97 mg

Sunday

Breakfast: *The Popeye:* Toss 2 cups spinach with 1 tsp avocado oil, 2 tsp ACV and pinch each salt and pepper; top with 2 eggs, scrambled in ½ tsp avocado oil

Snack: 2 *Almond Raspberry Thumbprint Cookies* (leftovers, thawed)

1 orange

Lunch: 1 serving *Root Vegetable–Baked Quinoa with Kale & Goat Cheese* (leftovers, p. 249, thawed)

Carrot Pepita Toss: Roast ½ cup chopped carrots with 1 tsp avocado oil and ⅛ tsp cumin; sprinkle with ½ oz pepitas and pinch each salt and pepper

Snack: 2 cups popcorn

Dinner: *Pumpkin Turkey Lasagna with Spinach & Béchamel Sauce* (leftovers, p. 255, thawed)

2 cups mixed greens topped with 1 oz feta; dress with 1 tsp avocado oil, 2 tsp ACV and pinch each salt and pepper

NUTRIENTS: Calories: 1,750, Fat: 100 g, Sat. Fat: 38 g, Carbs: 141 g, Fiber: 32 g, Sugars: 46 g, Protein: 84 g, Sodium: 2,133 mg, Cholesterol: 515 mg

EVOO = extra-virgin olive oil
ACV = apple cider vinegar

Monday

Breakfast: *Green Smoothie:* Blend 1 frozen banana, ½ cup mango, ½ cup spinach, 1 tbsp hemp seeds, 1 date and 1 cup almond milk

Snack: 2 tbsp hummus with 2 carrots, sliced

15 crackers

Lunch: *Chickpea Salad:* Toss together ½ cup each chickpeas, chopped cucumber and chopped tomato, 2 tbsp chopped red onion and 1 oz feta cheese; dress with 1 tsp avocado oil, 2 tsp ACV and pinch each salt and pepper

Snack: 2 *Almond Raspberry Thumbprint Cookies* (leftovers, p. 235, thawed)

1 orange

Dinner: 1 serving *Root Vegetable–Baked Quinoa with Kale & Goat Cheese* (leftovers, p. 79, thawed)

Roast ½ cup sliced beets with ½ tbsp avocado oil and pinch each salt and pepper

NUTRIENTS: Calories: 1,613, Fat: 74 g, Sat. Fat: 25 g, Carbs: 204 g, Fiber: 39 g, Sugars: 87 g, Protein: 48 g, Sodium: 1,650 mg, Cholesterol: 46 mg

Tuesday

Breakfast: *Eggs 'n' Greens:* Toss 2 cups mixed greens with 1 tbsp each avocado oil and ACV and pinch each salt and pepper; top with 2 eggs, scrambled in 1 tsp avocado oil

Snack: *Green Mojito Juice* (p. 314, save leftovers)

Lunch: *Tomato Avocado Sandwich:* 2 slices bread, toasted, with 2 tbsp hummus, 3 slices tomato, ½ avocado, sliced, and 8 slices cucumber, 2 tbsp hemp seeds and pinch each salt and pepper

Snack: 1 apple, sliced, with 2 tbsp peanut butter

Dinner: *Pumpkin Turkey Lasagna with Spinach & Béchamel Sauce* (leftovers, p. 255, thawed)

2 cups kale massaged with 1 tbsp each avocado oil and ACV and pinch each salt and pepper

NUTRIENTS: Calories: 1,758, Fat: 104.5 g, Sat. Fat: 21 g, Carbs: 138 g, Fiber: 29 g, Sugars: 52 g, Protein: 77 g, Sodium: 1,459 mg, Cholesterol: 469 mg

Wednesday

Breakfast: *Yogurt Parfait:* 1 cup yogurt topped with 1 banana, sliced, and 1 tbsp raspberry jam

Snack: 1 hard-boiled egg

½ cup radishes, sliced

½ avocado with pinch each salt and pepper

Lunch: 1 serving *Root Vegetable–Baked Quinoa with Kale & Goat Cheese* (leftovers, p. 249, thawed)

Carrot Pepita Toss: Roast ½ cup chopped carrots with 1 tbsp avocado oil and ⅛ tsp cumin; sprinkle with 1 oz pepitas and pinch each salt and pepper

Snack: *Green Mojito Juice* (leftovers, p. 314)

Dinner: *Almond-Crusted Cod with Green Olive Salsa* (p. 265)

1 orange

NUTRIENTS: Calories: 1,698, Fat: 100 g, Sat. Fat: 33 g, Carbs: 133 g, Fiber: 28 g, Sugars: 54 g, Protein: 79.5 g, Sodium: 1,315 mg, Cholesterol: 301 mg

Thursday

Breakfast: *PB&J with Banana:* 2 slices bread, toasted, with 2 tbsp peanut butter, 2 tbsp raspberry jam and 1 banana, sliced

Snack: *Green Mojito Juice* (leftovers)

Lunch: *Fried Egg 'n' Spinach Salad:* Toss 2 cups spinach, 1 tomato, sliced, 1 tbsp chopped red onion with 1 tbsp each avocado oil and ACV and pinch each salt and pepper; top with 1 egg, fried in 1 tsp avocado oil, and 1 oz of feta cheese

Snack: 2 tbsp hummus with 2 carrots, sliced, and 2 radishes, sliced

1 oz pepitas

Dinner: *Pumpkin Turkey Lasagna with Spinach & Béchamel Sauce* (leftovers, p. 255, thawed)

2 cups mixed greens; dress with 1 tbsp each avocado oil and ACV and pinch each salt and pepper

NUTRIENTS: Calories: 1,768, Fat: 97 g, Sat. Fat: 24 g, Carbs: 158 g, Fiber: 30 g, Sugars: 63 g, Protein: 77 g, Sodium: 1,768 mg, Cholesterol: 308 mg

Friday

Breakfast: *Cacao Cinnamon Smoothie:* Blend 1 frozen banana, 1 tbsp hemp seeds, 2 tbsp cacao powder, 1 tsp cinnamon, 1 date and 1 cup almond milk

Snack: 2 tbsp hummus with 2 celery stalks

15 crackers

Lunch: *Spinach Feta Omelette:* 2 egg omelette with 1 cup spinach, 1 oz feta and pinch each salt and pepper cooked in 1 tsp avocado oil

1 tomato, sliced

Snack: 2 *Almond Raspberry Thumbprint Cookies* (leftovers, p. 235, thawed)

1 orange

Dinner: 1 serving *Root Vegetable–Baked Quinoa with Kale & Goat Cheese* (leftovers, p. 249, thawed)

Roast ½ cup sliced beets with ½ tbsp avocado oil and pinch each salt and pepper

NUTRIENTS: Calories: 1,605, Fat: 85 g, Sat. Fat: 31 g, Carbs: 167 g, Fiber: 34 g, Sugars: 67 g, Protein: 55 g, Sodium: 1,791 mg, Cholesterol: 418 mg

Saturday

Breakfast: *Avocado Hummus Sandwich:* 2 slices bread, toasted, with 2 tbsp hummus, ½ avocado, sliced, 8 slices cucumber, 2 radishes, sliced, and pinch each salt and pepper

Snack: 2 *Almond Raspberry Thumbprint Cookies* (leftovers, p. 235, thawed)

1 orange

Lunch: *Pumpkin Turkey Lasagna with Spinach & Béchamel Sauce* (leftovers, p. 255, thawed)

2 cups kale massaged with 1 tsp avocado oil, 2 tsp ACV and pinch each salt and pepper

Snack: 2 cups popcorn

Dinner: *Kung Pao Chickpea Stir-Fry over Sesame-Fried Millet* (p. 257)

NUTRIENTS: Calories: 1,758, Fat: 89 g, Sat. Fat: 28 g, Carbs: 182 g, Fiber: 41.5 g, Sugars: 52 g, Protein: 73 g, Sodium: 1,966 mg, Cholesterol: 97 mg

Sunday

Breakfast: *Yogurt Parfait:* 1 cup yogurt topped with ½ banana, sliced, and 1 tbsp raspberry jam

Snack: 2 tbsp hummus with 2 carrots, sliced, and 2 celery stalks

1 oz pepitas

Lunch: *Pumpkin Turkey Lasagna with Spinach & Béchamel Sauce* (leftovers, p. 255, thawed)

2 cups mixed greens; dress with 1 tsp avocado oil, 2 tsp ACV and pinch each salt and pepper

Snack: 1 hard-boiled egg

1 orange

Dinner: 1 serving *Root Vegetable–Baked Quinoa with Kale & Goat Cheese* (leftovers, p. 249, thawed)

Tomato & Bread Salad: Toss 1 tomato, chopped, with 1 piece bread, lightly toasted and cubed, and 1 tbsp chopped basil; dress with 1 tsp avocado oil, 2 tsp ACV and pinch each salt and pepper

NUTRIENTS: Calories: 1,716, Fat: 87 g, Sat. Fat: 39 g, Carbs: 154 g, Fiber: 30 g, Sugars: 57.5 g, Protein: 88 g, Sodium: 1,718 mg, Cholesterol: 344 mg

ADDITIONAL WEEKLY MEAL PLAN RECIPES

Barramundi with Herb Sauce

Brush barramundi fillet with ½ tsp EVOO and sprinkle with salt and pepper and grill; in a blender, pulse 1 clove garlic, ¼ cup EVOO, 2 chopped green onions, juice of ½ lemon, ⅓ cup each dill, parsley and mint, and pinch each salt and pepper; drizzle one-quarter of sauce on fish (save leftover sauce)

Berry Salsa

Toss ¾ cup finely chopped strawberries, ¼ cup finely chopped cucumber with 1 tbsp each lime juice (or more to taste) and pinch salt; divide into 3 servings

Cherry Chocolate Coconut Smoothie

Blend ½ cup pitted cherries, ½ tbsp almond butter, 1/3 cup unsweetened non-dairy milk, ½ oz chocolate protein powder, ¾ cup coconut water and ice as desired

Chia Bowl

Whisk together 2 cups almond milk, 6 tbsp chia, 1 tsp each maple syrup and almond extract, or to taste. Set aside for 20 minutes and whisk again; divide to 2 bowls, refrigerate overnight

Chile-Roasted Walnuts

Whisk 2 egg whites until foamy. Stir in 2 tsp chile powder and 4 tsp raw honey. Add 2 cups raw unsalted walnuts and toss. With a slotted spoon, transfer to a parchment-lined baking sheet and bake at 350°F for 12 to 14 minutes. Let cool. (Makes 8 servings.)

Coco-Berry Shake

Blend ¾ cup plain unsweetened coconut milk beverage, ½ frozen banana, ½ cup halved strawberries, ¼ cup raspberries, 1 tsp chia seeds and 1 serving protein powder (optional) and handful ice. (You can also used BPA-free canned coconut milk mixed with water; if berries are tart, add ½ tsp honey.)

Cucumber & Onion Salad

Toss 1 cup chopped cucumber, 2 tbsp chopped onion, 1 tbsp pepitas, 1 tsp chopped cilantro and pinch garlic powder; dress with 1 tsp rice vinegar mixed with 1 tsp EVOO and ¼ tsp tamari

Dark Chocolate Bark

In a stainless steel bowl over a pot of simmering water, melt 5 oz dark chocolate (at least 70% cacao). Spread mixture evenly to about a 1-inch thickness on a baking sheet lined with parchment paper. Sprinkle ½ cup chopped pistachios and ⅓ cup unsweetened cherries or naturally sweetened cranberries evenly over top. Chill for 1 hour. Cut into 8 pieces. (*NOTE: If following our Meal Plan, you'll have 2 leftover pieces of bark. Freeze them for future use.*)

Editor's Special

Top 3 oz smoked salmon with ½ small avocado, sliced, ½ cup halved strawberries, 2 tbsp dill fronds and 2 tsp capers. (*TIP: Blackberries also work well in place of strawberries.*)

Green Goddess Smoothie

Blend 1 cup each almond milk and spinach, ½ cup pineapple, thawed, ¼ avocado, ¼ cup parsley, 1 tsp chia and ice as desired

Green Mojito Juice

Using a juicer, process all ingredients into juice: 3 limes (peel removed), 3 cucumbers (trimmed), 3 green apples (cut into chunks), 3-inch piece fresh ginger, 1 small bunch mint, 1 small bunch parsley.

Kidney Beans & Greens Salad

Toss 2 cups mixed greens with ½ cup kidney beans, ¼ cup each chopped cucumber and red bell pepper and 1 tbsp each chopped onion and pepitas; dress with 1 tbsp balsamic vinegar mixed with 1 tsp EVOO, ½ tsp maple syrup and pinch each salt and pepper

> Use Sunday for prep!
> Consider prepping ahead for the week for items such as the No-Cook Almond Cherry Bars, Dark Chocolate Bark and even the Orange Carrot Soup.

Kiwi Smoothie

Blend 1½ peeled and sliced kiwi puréed with ½ oz vanilla protein powder, ½ cup unsweetened non-dairy milk, ¼ banana, 1 tsp stevia and ice as desired (refrigerate remaining ½ kiwi and freeze ¼ of same banana for Sunday)

Middle Eastern Benny

Grill or sear 2 thick slices tomato, and poach 2 eggs; whisk 3 tbsp tahini with 1 tbsp lemon juice, 1 tbsp chopped parsley and water to thin; arrange each egg over 1 tomato slice, drizzle with tahini sauce and season with pinch each salt and pepper

Orange Carrot Soup

In a pot on medium, sauté ½ chopped onion in 1 tbsp EVOO until soft, about 8 minutes. Add 6 chopped carrots, ½ tsp coriander and 2 cups low-sodium vegetable broth. Bring to a boil, then simmer until carrots are tender, about 15 minutes. Let cool. Purée, then add juice and zest from ½ orange. Season to taste with salt and pepper. Divide between 2 servings (½ cups each serving).

Parmesan Popcorn

Combine 3 cups air-popped popcorn with spritz olive oil cooking spray and ½ tsp grated Parmesan cheese.

Pecan Cinnamon Apple

Halve and core 3 apples; sprinkle with cinnamon, to taste, and bake; top with 3 tbsp pecans, chopped, and 1 tbsp flaxseeds (eat 1; save leftovers)

Purple Power Smoothie

To a blender, add 1 cup frozen wild blueberries, 1 banana (frozen and cut into chunks), 1 cup soy milk, ½ cup pomegranate juice, 1 tsp matcha green tea powder and 2 tsp pumpkin seeds. Blend until smooth.

Rosemary Tempeh

Season 8 oz tempeh with 1 tbsp rosemary; cook in ½ cup broth and serve with 1 tbsp tamari (eat 5 oz; save leftovers)

EVOO = extra-virgin olive oil
ACV = apple cider vinegar

Thai Kabocha Squash Soup

(See recipe, p. 19)

Red Curry Chicken Soup with Zoodles

Secure 1 zucchini into a spiral maker and turn crank to create noodles. In a large saucepan on medium-high, heat 2 tsp coconut oil. Season 12 oz boneless chicken breast (or thigh) with ⅛ tsp salt and pepper and cook, stirring, until browned, about 5 minutes. Add 1 13½-oz can coconut milk and 2 cups water and bring to a boil. Stir in 3 to 4 tsp red curry paste and 1 tbsp fish sauce; simmer 2 to 3 minutes. Add 1 cup sliced red bell pepper and 1 cup zucchini noodles, or to taste, and return to boil, until pepper and zoodles are soft and heated through, 2 to 3 minutes. (Makes 4 servings.)

Spiced Walnuts

4 oz	walnut pieces
1 tbsp	raw honey
½ tsp	each ground cinnamon and cumin
¼ tsp	each ground cayenne pepper and sea salt

In a dry skillet on medium, add walnuts and toast, tossing frequently, until they begin to turn golden, about 4 minutes. Transfer to a small bowl. In same saucepan, reduce heat to low and combine remaining ingredients plus 1 tbsp water. Cook, stirring, until a glaze forms, about 1 minute. Add walnuts and toss until combined, about 1 minute. Transfer to a lined baking sheet to cool. Store in an airtight container.

Supercharged Winter Salad

Toss 2 cups mixed baby greens, ½ cup roasted butternut squash, ⅓ cup cooked quinoa, ½ oz Spiced Walnuts (leftovers, p. 81), 2 grated Brussels sprouts and 2 tsp pomegranate seeds with 2 tsp EVOO whisked with 1/2 tsp each mustard, balsamic and honey and pinch salt and pepper.

Sweet Green Smoothie

Blend 1 cup kale, ¾ cup each peeled and cubed honeydew and plain unsweetened almond milk, 2 to 3 tbsp fresh mint, 1 tbsp fresh lime juice, 1 tsp chia seeds and 1 serving protein powder (optional) and handful ice.

Sweet Pea Ricotta Spread

In a steamer basket set over a pot of boiling water, add 2 cloves garlic (pealed) and 1 cup fresh or frozen peas and steam, covered, for 6 minutes or until very tender. Meanwhile, to a medium bowl, add 1 cup ricotta cheese, 2 tbsp, finely chopped mint leaves, plus 2 tbsp lemon zest, ¼ each salt and pepper. Transfer peas and garlic to a strainer and rinse under cold water to cool; drain well. Add to a mini food processor with lemon juice and process until smooth. Stir pea mixture into cheese mixture and mix well.

Sweet Potato Toast–Two Ways

Toast two ½-inch-thick slices of sweet potato (slice lengthwise; save remaining sweet potato) in a toaster oven until soft and just turning golden.

For Avocado Toast: Smash ½ small avocado with 1 tbsp lime juice. Spread over sweet potato toasts. Sprinkle with pinch each salt and chile powder.

For Cashew Banana Toast: Spread 1 tbsp cashew butter over each sweet potato toast. Slice ½ banana thinly, divide over toasts. Sprinkle with ½ tsp hemp seeds or hearts and pinch cinnamon.

Tex-Mex Kale Chips:

Remove stems from 1 large bunch kale; toss leaves with 1 tsp EVOO, ½ tsp Mexican seasoning (leftovers, p. 26) and ¼ tsp salt and bake on a tray until crisp; divide into 3 servings (eat 1 serving; save leftovers) (*TIP: Store in a plastic bag or container, but don't seal completely as they can get soggy!*)

Tomato & Bread Salad

Toss 1 tomato, chopped, with 1 slice bread, lightly toasted and cubed, and 2 tbsp chopped basil; dress with 1 tsp avocado oil, 2 tsp ACV and pinch each salt and pepper

Veggie Chop Salad

Mix 3 cups romaine, ½ cup each grated carrot, diced red bell pepper, diced celery and chickpeas and ¼ cup almonds, chopped; top with mixture of 2 tbsp EVOO, 1 tbsp lemon juice, ½ tbsp maple syrup and pinch each salt and pepper

INDEX

(See also, Additional Meal Plan Recipes, p. 320)

CREDITS

RECIPES & MEAL PLANS

Tiffani Bachus
Heather Bainbridge
Sharon Booy
Elizabeth Brown
Dina Cheney
Loren Cordain
Cuisine at Home
Kate Geagan
Andrea Gourgy
Alison Kent
Jesse Lane Lee
Nathan Lyon
Cara Lyons
Erin Macdonald
Ivy Manning
Tara Mataraza Desmond
Liz Moody
Julie Morris
Alexis Nilsen
Julie O'Hara
Pamela Salzman
Jill Silverman Hough
Amy Symington
Liz Tarpy
Amie Valpone
Dorothy Vo
Laura Walsh
Gilean Watts
Abigail Wolfe
Laura Wright
Marianne Wren

PHOTOGRAPHY

Brandon Barré
Kelly Brisson
Aaron Colussi
Cuisine at Home
Gibson & Smith
Andrew Grinton
Darren Kemper
Dennis Kennedy
Beata Lubas
Ivy Manning
Ellen Charlotte Marie
Kris Obsorne
Natalie Perry
Jodi Pudge
Sukaina Rajabali
Ronald Tsang
Maya Visnyei
Laura Wright

FOOD STYLING

Bernadette Ammar
Kelly Brisson
Andrew Bullis
Ellen Charlotte Marie
Marylin Dunphy
Victoria Escalle
David Grenier
Matthew Kimura
John Kirkpatrick
Kate Kosaya
Beata Lubas
Nancy Midwicki
Terry Schacht
Beth Seuferer
Heather Shaw
Marianne Wren
Robin Zimmerman

PROP STYLING

Natalie Adamov
Catherine Doherty
Madeline Johari
Catherine Macfadyen
Erica McNeish
Sue Mitchell
Chantal Payette
Terry Schacht
The Food Group
The Props
Megan Wappel
Genevieve Wiseman

STORY CONTRIBUTORS

Sarah Tuff Dunn

ILLUSTRATIONS

Barb DiPietro

ABOUT THE AUTHOR

ALICIA TYLER, *Editorial Director*

Founding editor of *Clean Eating*, Alicia Tyler graduated print and broadcast journalism from Humber College and went on to lead the fitness department at *Oxygen* magazine as Fitness Editor before spearheading the launch of *Clean Eating* magazine in 2007. In addition to her role at the magazine, Tyler also oversees *Vegetarian Times*, an online magazine, is the author of three *Best of Clean Eating* cookbooks, is the co-creator of the Clean Eating Academy, the brand's online cooking school launched in 2015, and is a program adviser for Centennial College in Toronto, Canada. She lives in Toronto, Canada, where she eats her way through the city, one new restaurant at a time, visits farmers' markets spring through fall and experiments cooking all types of cuisines for her husband (and, occasionally, their two small dogs).